Praise for *Dr. Seuss & Mr. Geisel*

A *New York Times* Notable Book of the Year

"As entertainment, it's a lollapalooza!"   —*Baltimore Sun*

"The Morgans just may be very best reporter-writer team in journalism today, and here they capture with their trademark detail and vivid color not only the fascinating story of a unique literary figure but the history of an American era."   **—Walter Cronkite**

"[A] particularly intimate portrait. . . . Full of fascinating detail and personal insight about the good 'doctor.'"
—*San Francisco Chronicle*

"In selecting his biographers, Geisel's good fortune extends beyond the grave . . . [The authors] have mined every scrap of his surviving correspondence, sketch pads, notebooks and drafts to good effect."
—*Cleveland Plain Dealer*

"The Morgans reveal an intensely private man, his personal tragedies and public triumphs."   —*USA Today*

"Captivating."   —*Des Moines Sunday Register*

"[A] page turner."   —*Detroit Free Press*

"This biography makes you appreciate Dr. Seuss even more, if that is possible."   **—Art Buchwald**

"This witty and charming biography . . . maintains suspense as the authors unfold the facts of his life and art. It is full of wry Seussian limericks and interesting anecdotes."   —*Library Journal*

"*Dr. Seuss & Mr. Geisel* is warm, funny, affectionate, and yet unsparingly frank, painfully revelatory. . . . Seuss had style, and this meticulously researched biography, understated and yet rich in content, has style in abundance." —*San Diego Union-Tribune*

"This biography sheds dazzling light on a charmed life. . . . It treats his work with seriousness and weight. . . . In lighting up the corners of a creative life, the authors show us the 'hows' behind his creativity." —*Charlotte Observer*

"This book reveals the drudgery, as well as the delight, of being Dr. Seuss." —*Milwaukee Journal-Sentinel*

"A loving, funny, touching, and truly compelling biography that captures—to a degree that I wouldn't have imagined possible—the unique humor, warmth, insecurity, playfulness, complexity, mischievousness, almost maddening perfectionism, and sheer brilliance of Theodore S. Geisel. My father, Bennett Cerf, liked to say that of all the distinguished authors with whom he had the honor of working, Dr. Seuss alone was a true genius. Every page of [this book] confirms that insight." **—Christopher Cerf**

"One is carried along by an inexhaustible supply of anecdote and humor, describing the life and reflecting the thinking of [Dr. Seuss]. . . . His refreshing view of the world is the main source of enjoyment in this marvelous biography." —*Virginia Quarterly Review*

"[The authors] give an affecting picture of Geisel in his last years—struggling against cancer, yet producing sunny works to the end." —*Parade*

BY NEIL MORGAN

Know Your Doctor (with Leo Smollar)
It Began with a Roar
Westward Tilt
The California Syndrome
The Pacific States
San Diego: The Unconventional City
Above San Diego (with Robert Cameron)

BY JUDITH MORGAN

California (with Dewitt Jones)

DR. SEUSS & MR. GEISEL

DA CAPO PRESS • NEW YORK

DR. SEUSS
& MR. GEISEL

A BIOGRAPHY

JUDITH & NEIL MORGAN

Library of Congress Cataloging in Publication Data

Morgan, Judith.
    Dr. Seuss & Mr. Geisel: a biography / Judith & Neil Morgan.—1st Da
Capo Press ed.
        p.   cm.
    Includes index.
    ISBN 0-306-80736-X
    1. Seuss, Dr.—Biography. 2. Authors, American—20th century—
Biography. 3. Illustrators—United States—Biography. 4. Illustration of books
—United States. 5. Children's literature—Authorship. I. Morgan, Neil. II.
Title.
[PS3513.E2Z785   1996]
813′ .52—dc20
[B]   96-19313
                                                                                              CIP

Grateful acknowledgment is made to the following for
permission to reprint previously published material:

Audrey Geisel: The following Dr. Seuss figures: *Yertle the
Turtle*, TM and copyright © 1950, 1951, 1958 and renewed 1977,
1979, 1986 by Dr. Seuss Enterprises, LP; *The Cat in the Hat*,
TM and copyright © 1957 and renewed 1985 by Dr.
Seuss Enterprises, LP; *The Grinch Who Stole Christmas*, TM
and copyright © 1957 and renewed 1985 by Dr. Seuss
Enterprises, LP; *The Lorax*, TM and copyright © 1971 by Dr.
Seuss Enterprises, LP; *Horton*, TM and copyright ©
1940, 1954 and renewed 1968, 1982 by Dr. Seuss Enterprises,
LP; *Sneetches*, TM and copyright © 1961 and renewed
1989 by Dr. Seuss Enterprises, LP. Reprinted by the gracious
permission of Audrey Geisel.
PolyGram Music Publishing Group: Excerpt from "Little
Green Apples" by Robert Russell. Copyright © 1968
by PolyGram International Publishing, Inc. All Rights
Reserved. Reprinted by permission of PolyGram
International Publishing, Inc.

First Da Capo Press edition 1996
5 6 7 8 9 10   02 01 00

Published by Da Capo Press, Inc.
A member of the Perseus Books Group

Book design by Oksana Kushnir

FOR ADAM, MATTHEW AND BLAKELY

But on you will go
though the weather be foul.
On you will go
though your enemies prowl.
On you will go
though the Hakken-Kraks howl.

—Dr. Seuss,
   Oh, the Places You'll Go!

Acknowledgments

For their assistance with Seuss-Geisel papers we thank librarians
and archivists at the University of California, San Diego; the Uni-
versity of California, Los Angeles; Baker Library at Dartmouth
College; Butler Library at Columbia University, Lincoln College,
St. Anne's College and the Bodleian Library at Oxford University;
New York Public Library; San Diego Public Library; Springfield
(Mass.) Library; and the Connecticut Valley Historical Museum
in Springfield.

Vital clues to Ted Geisel's life came through hundreds of interviews and letters provided by friends and family members, notably
his niece, Peggy Dahmen Owens; his great-nephew Theodor Owens, and Helen Geisel's niece, Barbara Palmer Bayler. We are
grateful to Thomas Campbell and Dr. Donald Bartlett, Jr., sons of
Ted's closest friends at Dartmouth and Oxford, for sharing letters
between Ted and their fathers spanning many decades.

We thank the late E. J. Kahn, Jr., for access to his extensive
research for a profile of Ted Geisel in *The New Yorker* in 1960,
and Dean Edward Connery Latham of Dartmouth College for
interviews he conducted with Ted Geisel in the 1970s. We ac-
knowledge the generous assistance of editors and others who
worked with him in Hollywood, at Vanguard Press and Random
House in New York and at William Collins Sons & Co. in London.

The three women who served as secretarial aides at the Tower
in La Jolla have been as invaluable to us as they were to Ted; we

appreciate the memories and files shared by Julie Olfe, Joan Knight and especially Claudia Prescott, who worked with him from September 24, 1973, until his death precisely eighteen years later.

For her loving insights into the remarkably productive final twenty-three years of his life, and for countless hours of interviews and her forthright sharing of personal papers, we thank Audrey S. Geisel.

Above all, we thank Theodor Seuss Geisel for years of exhilarating friendship and for his confidence and candor during extensive interviews in the last year of his life. At sticky moments he would say, "You have to get it right. It's time to tell the truth!"

—Judith and Neil Morgan
September 26, 1994
La Jolla, California

Contents

Prologue

On a luminous Sunday afternoon in November of 1991, children thronged Balboa Park in San Diego, more than had ever been seen there before. They darted and danced across the wide lawns, hiding behind trunks of fragrant eucalyptus and shadowy pepper trees and in the alcoves and secret gardens of Spanish-style palaces. A mounted police officer sat captive above the horde, his horse hemmed in by children; he grinned and estimated the crowd at seventy thousand, "if you count their parents too."

The park was rippling with laughter and joyous screams in celebration of the magic of Dr. Seuss. Children glued together cockeyed versions of the Cat in the Hat's jaunty red-and-white stovepipe and careened through the park, visible only as phalanxes of jiggling hats. They lined up to crawl through a noisy Seussian contraption (". . . it bonked. And it jerked. And it berked. And it bopped them about . . ."), and when they emerged they wore stars like the Star-Bellied Sneetches. They gulped down green eggs and ham and then sprawled in the grass to hear costumed storytellers read Dr. Seuss books. Mimes and dancers and puppeteers paraded through the vast green park, where on that glistening afternoon the world seemed suddenly to have gone right. Above it all a towering Cat kept watch, peering over the stately façade of the San Diego Museum of Art.

On the next afternoon, inside that museum, about two hundred

mourners gathered for a quieter tribute to Ted Geisel, an exceed-
ingly private man who had lived in the nearby community of La
Jolla for the second half of his eighty-seven years and died there
eight weeks earlier. His real name would not have meant much
to the frolicking masses on the day before; to them, and to millions
around the world, he was known by his middle name of Seuss.
But now these adult friends took their seats as his bogus Latin
carol, written for the television version of *How the Grinch Stole
Christmas!,* boomed merrily out across a sculpture garden:

> Fah who for-aze!
> Dah who dor-aze!
> Welcome Christmas,
> Come this way!

Then Ted Geisel's widow, Audrey, tiny and intense, her blue
eyes shining, stepped forward to share some secrets about this shy
man who wrote for children but had none of his own and rarely
felt comfortable around them. Her Ted Geisel was a whimsical
and loving curmudgeon who emerged at the end of each day from
his mountaintop studio above the Pacific, where he lived curtained
in privacy. By sundown he was ready for a vodka martini and
adult laughter.

From her collection of bawdy Seuss, Audrey read her husband's
egalitarian outburst, written while he was scrimping through the
Great Depression in New York, about Mrs. Van Bleck "of the
Newport Van Blecks, [who] is so goddam rich she has gold-plated
sex." Then Audrey recited more recent nonsense that had erupted
when Ted retreated to his tower after a tedious afternoon as a
wedding guest:

> I took to bed some wedding cake
> To dream of lust and rapine.
> That fine old custom is a fake.
> I dreamed I was a capon.

Audrey Geisel had invited seven of Ted's friends to talk about
their memories, and a spellbinding admirer, actress Mercedes

McCambridge, to read his short tale of "Gertrude McFuzz." With each revelation laughter and surprise won over tears. These friends knew him in different ways, for while he loved them all he opened certain pavilions of his mind to each while keeping others locked. Among the several Ted Geisels recalled that afternoon, there ran the common strands of outrageous originality and a compulsive search for perfection in word, rhythm and drawing. His eccentric humor, often wicked but never mean, was pervasive.

One of these friends was Jed Mattes. When he became Ted's agent and friend he was twenty-four and Ted seventy-three. He was a member of one of the first generations who had learned to read not from the sterile primers of Dick and Jane but from the language of the reckless and impudent creatures in the books that followed *The Cat in the Hat*. He made the case that the age of children's rights had begun with Dr. Seuss. He talked of Ted's dignity and grace and of how, at the end of his visits to the Tower atop Mount Soledad in La Jolla, "Ted would walk me out to my car and thank me for my journey. He would stand at the gate, clasping his hands together, a salute that was unique to him, one which communicated a wonderful sense of warmth, of being included in his special world."

Next came Seuss lore from Robert Bernstein, the retired chairman of Random House, his publisher and the man whom Ted once saluted in verse for his "fine freckled flesh." Bernstein had persuaded Ted to make his first big autographing tour in the 1950s. As children lined up at Marshall Field in Chicago for Dr. Seuss autographs, a huckster in Indian regalia had stalked along the queue. He passed out cards for his nearby theater show and signed the name "Chief White Cloud" in Dr. Seuss books clutched by puzzled children. When Ted began to find those signatures, he called Bernstein over and said, "Tell him to write his own book." Chief White Cloud was hustled away. But days later in the basement of a Minneapolis department store, when Ted seemed to be tiring, Bernstein signed "Chief White Cloud" in a waiting child's book and stood back. In a moment Ted was yelling across the store, "Bob, that damned Indian's followed us all the way to Minneapolis!"

One of Ted's La Jolla friends rose, a writer who shared his outspoken aversion to pretense and for twenty-five years had chronicled his wit and nonsense. Sometimes she and Ted took refuge in secluded corners at noisy parties, trading satiric observations as they escaped the clatter. One evening a haughty hostess sailed over to inquire what they were talking about so intently. "Religion," Ted replied somberly. "We are both devout claustrophobics." This friend described Ted as a child at heart—rascally, optimistic, impulsive. "You might find Ted whiling away his time in the Neiman-Marcus shoe department during some charity gala, busily changing prices on the shoes, or in the hushed library of the Inn at Rancho Santa Fe, busily autographing books by Mary Baker Eddy."

The retired Marine Corps general Victor H. Krulak had espoused views about the Vietnam war that were anathema to the liberal Ted Geisel, but now he talked of the evening when Ted had hammered him with technical questions about nuclear arms and finally explained that he was "working on a little book that tries to show in humorous terms the utter futility of nuclear war." *The Butter Battle Book* appeared the next year, and in grateful remembrance of friendship and assistance, Ted added his father's chiming pocket watch to the general's watch collection.

Amid such anecdotes Ted Geisel took form also as a man driven to black depths of self-doubt. Yet he could be steely, uncompromising, demanding most of himself as he pursued his eccentric quest and defended his work against tampering, trivialization and exploitation. No one could testify to this more convincingly than his New York attorney, Herb Cheyette, who described the frustrations of representing "a genius and a gentleman." A television sponsor had offered "a vast sum of money" for rights to an unpublished verse that Ted had forgotten he had written. It was to be used on a Christmas billboard. Ted had protested that he didn't want to be linked with any single religious holiday or product. The incredulous sponsor increased his offer, and Cheyette, wide-eyed, went back to Ted. "This verse totals less than a hundred words," he said. "If you accept this deal, you will go into *The Guinness Book of Records* as the writer who received the most money ever per word." Ted was silent for a moment and then said, "I'd rather go into *The Guinness Book of Records* as the writer who refused the most money per word."

The pioneering film animator Chuck Jones offered a fraternal view of a fellow artist and friend. Like many artists, he said, he and Ted had communicated "through idiosyncrasies." Jones, who created Road Runner and Wile E. Coyote, had taught Major Ted Geisel of the Army Signal Corps the basics of animation during World War II in Colonel Frank Capra's film unit in Hollywood. Twenty-three years later he persuaded Ted to work with him to bring the Grinch and Horton to television. For Chuck Jones, Ted was "the one who stands out from all the rest." He thought the test of great children's writing was simple: "Can it be read with pleasure by adults? If it cannot, it is not a great children's book. Ted wrote great books."

The origin of Ted's exuberant creativity fascinated journalists, who seldom failed to ask where he got his ideas. Never wanting to disappoint, Ted would reply earnestly and graciously that it happened on his annual visit to Über Gletch, "a small town in the Austrian Alps," where he went each year to get his cuckoo clock repaired. Another La Jolla friend spoke about this, saying that during long interviews with Ted in the final year of his life he had pressed Ted to talk about creativity. Drawing was usually easy for him, Ted said, and writing always hard. "I stay with a line until the meter is right, and the rhyme is right, even if it takes five hours. Sometimes, I go counter to the clock." He fell silent for a long moment. "Hmmm . . . I don't understand what I just said, do you? Well, then. That's it! That's the creative process!"

His was a mind, his first wife, Helen, had said, that never grew up. For Ted it was not a calculated act to reach the heart of a child's imagination because he was amusing himself at the same time. At the core of his spirit was a child's sense of fun and curiosity. He took it to Dartmouth College, to Oxford and through the Great Depression as he struggled to learn who he might become, and it sustained him through those last days in 1991 when he looked up into Audrey's anxious face, smiled and asked, "Am I dead yet?"

CHAPTER 1

Springfield

1900–1915

By the arrival of the twentieth century in the western Massachusetts city of Springfield, there was a mood of such robust swagger that nothing seemed impossible. Her citizens considered themselves uniquely energetic, optimistic and self-reliant. They bragged about their Yankee ingenuity. Factories were pioneering in mass production, yielding a torrent of moving things: guns, watches, machine parts, bicycles, motorcycles, tires, toys, ice skates, roller skates, railroad and trolley cars, and both the Duryea and Knox gasoline-powered automobiles. Such a pace encouraged eccentrics and inventors and, as the population passed sixty-two thousand, tinkering was everyman's pastime, and patents a common dream.

When Bostonians, ninety-nine miles to the east, thought at all of Springfield it was not as a town that was proper New England but a rambunctious gateway to the American West. So the spheres of influence grew apart. For Springfield, astride the bountiful Connecticut River Valley, the outside world stretched north and south. Her bright sons and daughters often eschewed Harvard and Radcliffe and went north to school at Dartmouth, Smith and Mount Holyoke, or south to Yale. If they abandoned Springfield to seek fortunes and fame in the big city, they thought first of New York.

But European immigrants who had settled in Springfield had already made their grand moves and were building their New

World dreams. Beside the Boston Road at the eastern edge of town, on twelve acres of wooded land near Watershops Pond, stood the stolid red-brick compound of a prosperous brewery where two young German immigrants, Christian Kalmbach and Theodor Geisel, had begun business in 1876. Within fifteen years this brewery vied with Boston's best as the largest in New England, marketing seventy-five thousand barrels a year of lager, ale and the dark brown beer called porter. In its stables were twenty-five matched and groomed horses, the special pride of Geisel, who had served in the German army cavalry before coming to America at the age of twenty-seven. Four horses drew each of the heavy black-and-gold wagons clattering through the streets of Springfield, serving saloons, clubs and homes, and delivering hundreds of barrels each day to the railroad yards for customers throughout much of New England and eastern New York.

As they began suburban rounds, strong-armed crews wheeled kegs into the cellars of Springfield's Mulberry Street, a broad promenade that sloped down from the cemetery toward town, its expansive houses vying in the profusion of gables, dormers and curlicues. From Mulberry Street the wagons rattled off toward Sumner Avenue, a red-brick boulevard of Victorian homes, one of them a white mansion tiered like a wedding cake and owned by the brewer Geisel. Near the hilly greensward of Forest Park, a mile north of downtown, the horses turned into Fairfield Street and its snug arc of roomy middle-class homes. There, in 1906, the brewer's son, Theodor Robert Geisel, and his wife, the former Henrietta Seuss, settled with their four-year-old daughter, Margaretha Christine, and their two-year-old son, Theodor Seuss Geisel, whom they called Ted. Although the children had been born downtown at 22 Howard Street, just around the corner from Grandfather Seuss's bakery, it was the three-story frame house at 74 Fairfield Street that was the setting of Ted's earliest memories.

From the start this tall, skinny, dark-haired boy showed a love of the absurd and a penchant for exaggeration, elevating ordinary neighborhood happenings into events of excitement and intrigue. His parents came to consider his recall to be formidable and his ear for meter unrelenting—in both English and German, the language of the household.

Springfield characters with lollapalooza names like Wickersham, Terwilliger and McElligot never faded from his mind; the city's growing zoo, its ornate civic statues and rousing Main Street parades became sources for the children's tales he would begin to write thirty years later. Springfield, where he lived until he left for college, provided as vivid a catalog of impressions for Dr. Seuss as the Missouri town of Hannibal did for Mark Twain.

Nor were the steadfast faiths of the people lost on Ted. In his youth Springfield was one of those uncomplicated little cities that still clung to the notion that through hard work people could move up in the world and overcome adversity. Nineteenth-century virtues were revered. Horace Smith and Daniel B. Wesson had founded their revolver business here in 1852, lured by proud craftsmen who had made swords and guns since the American Revolution. The .30-caliber, magazine-fed Springfield rifle was produced in the local armory and adopted by the United States Army in 1903, the year before Ted's birth. As many as two hundred trains a day entered the city on three railroads—the New York, New Haven & Hartford, the Boston & Albany, and the Boston & Maine—to serve its prolific manufacturing. Barges and steamboats plied the Connecticut River and its tributary the Chicopee.

The aspirations of Springfield also encompassed the gentler arts. A downtown quadrangle of museums was taking form, soon to be anchored by a Carnegie library with a lofty marble rotunda. The Court Square Theatre had opened in the 1890s as a home to touring vaudeville companies and, increasingly, to the theatrical giants of the day. Springfield was the headquarters of G. and C. Merriam, the dictionary publishers who had bought out Noah Webster, and of the nimble minds of the Milton Bradley game company.

When Ted was born on March 2, 1904, the growing German American community numbered about a thousand, including Seuss and Geisel uncles, aunts and cousins, of whom the most influential and prosperous was the brewer Geisel. He was born in the Baden town of Mühlhausen in 1840, and at the age of fourteen had entered a six-year jeweler's apprenticeship at Pforzheim. With the cavalry, he fought in Germany's seven-week war with Austria, and later in battles between the south German states and Prussia. Mustered out in 1867, he sailed abruptly and gratefully for America to join family friends at Springfield, where he found work with a jeweler and was soon being sought out for his designs of brooches and pendants. Meanwhile his reputation for business acumen was also growing swiftly. Four years after arriving in Springfield, he married Christine Schmaelzle, who had migrated with her parents from the German state of Württemberg. The following year he became a United States citizen.

In 1876 Geisel and Christian Kalmbach, who had apprenticed in brewing, pooled their savings to take over a small brewery on the Boston Road. They renamed it Kalmbach and Geisel, which patrons soon dubbed "Come Back and Guzzle." Both men lived with their families in quarters beside the brewery, and Theodor Robert Geisel, Ted's father, was born there on June 28, 1879.

Henrietta Seuss, known as Nettie, was also a native of Springfield, the daughter of Bavarian immigrants, the baker George J. Seuss and his wife, Margaretha. (The family surname was pronounced, in the German fashion, as *Zoice*.) George Seuss was admired in the German community as the founding president of the Springfield Turnverein, a social and gymnastics club that was a focal point for the city's German Americans. But the popular baker lost customers in 1901 with his daughter's marriage to the brewer's son. The forces of Prohibition were gathering strength. "Seuss the baker puts the staff of life in people's mouths," one righteous neighbor declared. "Geisel the brewer takes it out and pours beer there instead, causing the children of drinkers to suffer the pangs of hunger."

Nettie was beautiful, an athletic woman of imposing scale, known for her fearlessness and grace as a high diver. She stood six feet tall and weighed nearly two hundred pounds. At the age of fifteen, when she had hoped to prepare for college, she had been needed behind the counter of her father's bakery. Now she was intent on securing for Ted and his sister, whom they called Marnie, the college education that would help them conquer the New World. She read bedtime stories to them, and often they fell asleep as she chanted softly, in the way she had learned as she sold pies,

"Apple, mince, lemon . . . peach, apricot, pineapple . . . blueberry, coconut, custard and SQUASH!" Ted later said that, more than anyone else, his mother was responsible "for the rhythms in which I write and the urgency with which I do it."

It was Ted's father, Theodor, who imposed discipline, although he rarely raised his voice or hand. When he grew angry, he turned away and ignored the offender, sometimes for the rest of his life; this was the fate of a cousin whom he saw almost daily on the Springfield trolley as he went to his office at the brewery. "You will never be sorry," he counseled his son, "for anything you never said." A tall, straight-backed man with black hair and a mustache, he dressed impeccably and looked especially dashing when he donned riding clothes and boots and took his horse for a canter. He drank beer and rye whiskey and smoked cigars, made in Springfield from tobacco grown in the Connecticut Valley. He was an expert marksman who, in 1902, held a world title at two hundred yards. Each morning, as calisthenic discipline, he held his favorite rifle extended at arm's length above his head for ten or twelve minutes. "My father had an all-consuming hobby," Ted recalled, "that I always thought was silly and unproductive. It was shooting holes in paper targets. But he was an inspiration. Whatever you do, he taught me, do it to perfection."

The pale-gray house on Fairfield Street was Ted's home for nearly a quarter of a century. It evoked the middle-class aspirations of Springfield: proud but unpretentious, spacious but taking its place dutifully among its neighbors. Its first floor bulged with three bay windows, its second was squared off, and the third steeply gabled beneath an ornamental parapet. From the front walk, flanked by bayberry bushes, three steps led to a trellis-shaded front porch, where Ted marched his toy soldiers. A carved Dutch door opened onto a small vestibule with an inner door for shelter against winter storms; after the harshest of these, when not even the brewery wagons could make their rounds, Ted and his father built snow tunnels and igloos in the backyard.

To the left of the entry hall was a dark oak-paneled living room with heavy wainscoting and a tall brick hearth and mantel. Family portraits hung here, and floor lamps were placed for reading beside high-backed rocking chairs. At the right of the entry hall was the music parlor with its upright piano, where his mother played and all four Geisels gathered to sing, his father leading in a strong baritone. In the dining room at the rear the family sat at six-thirty each evening around a massive oak table; on the walls were built-in china cupboards with leaded glass doors. The kitchen was in the adjacent corner, linked by a long pantry that overlooked a backyard brightened in spring with yellow forsythia.

Above the living room, and with a matching fireplace, was Ted's parents' bedroom; beside it, a tiny den held his father's trophies and rolltop desk. The children's bedrooms were at the rear, separated by a bathroom with a claw-foot tub. In his room, at the right corner of the house, Ted scattered books about and kept pencils near his pillow for doodling—and for idly gouging small holes in the wall. Out his wide windows, past elm trees, Ted saw empty fields and a distant ramshackle building that neighborhood children believed to be haunted; no one, they whispered, had ever been seen entering or leaving. For Ted and Marnie the mystery grew at night, intensified by the cries of animals at the Springfield Zoo in nearby Forest Park.

On the third floor a walk-in attic held wardrobe chests containing costumes that Ted treasured, odd furniture and cartons of Christmas decorations. Across the hall was the bedroom of the housekeeper, Anna. Ted, a lifelong claustrophobic, remembered her most clearly for the day when she despaired of his bad behavior and locked him in a coat closet.

At the rear of the house was an anomaly that fascinated youngsters from blocks around, a brick garage with space for two carriages or cars. In Ted's early years, Grandfather Geisel was regarded with awe for the two Packards he kept in his garage, and for the chauffeur who polished them; Ted remembered his "Grossvater" as a kind and magnificent personage who wore "boiled white shirts and diamond studs and sat in deep leather chairs with Persian rugs at his feet." The garage of the younger Geisels held bicycles, sleds and, eventually, a Hudson Six.

Ted's memories of Fairfield Street seemed mostly bathed in cheery colors, but one was dark. A third child, Henrietta, named for their mother, was born in 1906; she died of pneumonia eighteen months later, when Ted was not yet four. Marnie described the "terrible sounds of her cough that we heard all through that three-story house."

Ted's image of the child's tiny casket reposing in the music room was always mingled with that of the Pooley cabinet, a narrow New England–made chest in which his father kept Enrico Caruso records. The cabinet, Ted recalled, "was about the size, if you laid it on its side, of my sister's casket. No matter how thrilled I was later by my father's voice and my mother's accompaniment, I always saw Henrietta in her casket in the place where the Pooley cabinet was."

In his first memories there was an unremarkable stuffed dog, brown and fat, given to him by his mother. He called it Theophrastus, and kept it close to him throughout his life, often within sight from his drawing board, as a snug reminder of the tenderness and love he basked in during childhood. Such a need for reassurance remained part of him, though in his adult years some saw it simply as sensitivity or vulnerability. Because of it, he always found it easier to talk to women than to men about his misgivings, his insecurities and his agonizing fear of failure.

In the fall of 1908, when he was four and a half, Ted entered kindergarten at Forest Park School, walking back and forth with Marnie, a dark-eyed child of arresting presence and poise. He was under stern orders to hold his sister's hand as they neared the grand boulevard of Sumner Avenue. But sometimes he lagged behind to marvel at the commotion, the rattle of trolleys, ice wagons and grocers' delivery vans, the proud horse-drawn carriages, the horn-honking Hudson Sixes and the bicycles of all sizes chased by yapping dogs. He wondered where they all came from and where they were going.

No records are found of Ted's primary-school years and his memories told little of classroom hours, but his recall of extracurricular affairs came in exhilarated spurts. From kindergarten onward, he and his Fairfield Street chums referred to a wide part of their short dogleg street as the Soccer Field. They devised contests to determine who was best at chinning himself—Ted lost—or wiggling his ears—Ted won. His perspective was already askew, and he decided that it was because he viewed the world through "the wrong end of a telescope."

Eighty years later Ted was able to offer intimate details of Fairfield Street neighbors: the teetotaling Bumps and the Hayneses, against whom the brewer's family plotted practical jokes that were never carried out; his best friend, Bill King, who lived near the gas lamp at the bend of the street; the Bondis, an Italian couple whose daughters were named Venice, Florence and Roma; the Kleins (his uncle Will and aunt Bertha); the Mannings, whose daughter Evelyn wore glasses and was the first person Ted heard called Four Eyes; the Napiers, whose son Charles was a sometime ally; the newspaper editor Maurice Sherman, a Dartmouth man who lived directly across the street; the dentist Dr. Stebbins, who saw patients in his home; and Norval Bacon, whose given name Ted always relished and would employ in his books. The nearest neighbors included the ladies Bowen, a mother and daughter who lived across the driveway from Ted's bedroom window and were said to be hard of hearing, a condition deemed fortunate after Ted took up bugling for the Boy Scouts. On the other side lived a stern businessman, Horace Clark, who vetoed the stringing of a telegraph line across five backyards between Ted's and Bill King's bedrooms.

Years later Ted wrote: "All these people, who lived on a little street of a middle-class development of Springfield, Massachusetts, got me to do what I've done." Yet he did not recall them with equal magnanimity. Of the next-door Mr. Clark he wrote:

> No matter what anybody says to the contrary, I did not pee on Horace Clark's front porch on Halloween Eve, 1912. The culprit who perpetrated this ignoble act had the initials C.N. (Charles Napier). . . . I am afraid my father never believed me when for many years after I protested my innocence. Old Horace did collar me that night when I was rattling a "cricket" against his parlor window. (You make one of these things, as I remember, by notching the sides of a thread spool, winding a string around the spool, shoving a pencil through the hole in the spool, and yanking the string while holding the device against Horace Clark's parlor window.) The resulting racket makes nervous people like Horace jump out of their

pants and out the front door, where sometimes they catch you. Horace nabbed and blamed me for the nuisance that C.N. had committed at least half an hour before. He then dragged me to my house, rang the doorbell and told my father what I had not done to his porch, using, of course, the dignified sentence, "Theodor wetted my stoop."

Despite the false starts and prolonged silences common to most fathers and sons, Ted and his father became good friends. When he was six, his father read to him about the impending appearance of Halley's Comet, and on the night of April 20, 1910, they took up their positions in the field behind their home. The earth, his father explained, was passing through the tail of the comet, and this tail was hundreds of thousands of miles in length, farther than the distance around the world. But what really left Ted wide-eyed was the strange creature whose silhouette suddenly appeared in one of the elm trees. "I saw Halley's Comet and my first owl on the same night," he said.

His father's effort to stir Ted's interest in marksmanship disappointed them both. Buffalo Bill's Wild West Show came to Springfield, and Theodor Robert Geisel, the expert marksman, was intent on seeing it. He tried to excite Ted by calling it a circus, but at the end of a dispiriting outing—an aging Bill Cody and a rainy night did not help—they slogged home in silence. "All that shooting" left Ted unmoved. He preferred the costumes and music at the Episcopal church, which he attended with his mother. He liked to watch their druggist march down the aisle, swinging a metal pot that trailed smoke "and never hit anyone."

Nettie Geisel had already discovered that Ted responded to the magic of rhyme and repetition. He knew all the words to the hymn "Holy, Holy, Holy, Lord God Almighty!" and recited the books of the Old Testament in rhyme:

> The great Jehovah speaks to us
> In Genesis and Exodus;
> Leviticus and Numbers, three,
> Followed by Deuteronomy.

Ted later acknowledged that he tossed in the word "three" to make it rhyme, a portent of nonsense to come.

Father and son did find joyous common ground close by Fairfield Street after Theodor Geisel was appointed to the Springfield park board in 1909. The jewel of the park system was five-hundred-acre Forest Park, flanked by enormous Victorian homes painted in combinations of egg-yolk yellow, fire-truck red and pea-soup green. Here Springfield families fished, picnicked and swam in summer, and went sledding and ice-skating in winter. Its maze of dead-end trails delighted Ted, as did the bicycle paths. He remembered the first time he saw pink trees and heard their odd name, dogwood. His father's pride within Forest Park was the fledgling Springfield Zoo, and at the Geisel dinner table there were tales of an incorrigible bear, scraggly monkeys and the bearded Barbary sheep from North Africa called aoudads. On Sundays and holidays his father took him on behind-the-scene walks through the zoo, and Ted began to bring along a pencil and sketch pad. Marnie teased him, for his animals emerged with features that were mismatched and curiously exaggerated.

"Ted always had a pencil in hand," his father recalled. "I saw an ad in *The Youth's Companion* which asked that you send a drawing in, and the correspondence school would tell you if you had talent. I got him to send one of his drawings and staked him to the fifteen dollars. Yes, they said, he had talent, but, heck, they were after the fifteen bucks and they told that to everybody."

Ted's imagination was goaded by the comic strips of the day. His favorite was the outlandish Krazy Kat, drawn by George Herriman. In the evenings he ran to the corner to meet his father, who came home by trolley from the brewery, bringing a copy of the *Boston American* with its comic page.

Although Ted was never interested in being an athlete, he and his father managed successful outings as sports spectators. At the Springfield International YMCA Training School, young men were playing a game that an instructor named James Naismith had devised in 1891 for indoor exercise during the bitter winters. At first it was known as Naismithball, but its inventor preferred naming it for the peach baskets that he nailed to the gymnasium balcony as goals, so basketball it became. Ted's father wondered aloud, as they walked home, if their local sport would catch on across the country.

On one of their walks together, his father told him about his business trip that day to Northampton, where he had retained the young lawyer Calvin Coolidge to collect brewery debts from saloonkeepers. He and Coolidge had stopped in a saloon where the special was two martinis for twenty-five cents. After his first drink, the frugal Coolidge rose. "I'll be back tomorrow for the other one," he said.

It was in his father's workshop that Ted grew aware of the joy of invention, marveling at the elder Geisel's designs: a biceps-strengthening machine, a spring-clip top to keep flies off the spigots of beer barrels and a device that Ted called a Silk-Stocking-Back-Seam-Wrong-Detecting Mirror. Conversations around the Geisel table often focused on other breakthroughs by Springfield tinkerers. One company manufactured a coal stove that forced smoke to the flue through a labyrinth of chambers in order to extract more warmth, and Ted traced its bulbous drawings from a newspaper advertisement. The ice-skating enthusiast Everett Hosmer Barney had invented a metal clamp to fasten skates to shoes without cumbersome nails or straps. In death Barney willed more imagery to Ted; the winding stairways of his ornate mausoleum in Forest Park became a model for looping, gravity-defying Seussian stairs.

Each summer the Geisel family rented a cottage at Beach Park near Clinton, Connecticut, where Marnie and Ted built sand castles, learned to swim and mastered the intricacies of clamming, earning ten cents a quart. At night Ted cherished the hours of storytelling on the wide front porch, where he sprawled and counted stars and fireflies.

The sense of their German heritage was always close. "In 1905, while Albert Einstein was discovering relativity," Ted said later, "I, at the age of one, was going to German clambakes on Sunday afternoons in my diapers." Each Christmas Eve, when the German community opened gifts, Geisels and Seusses gathered beside the tree at Fairfield Street to sing "O Tannenbaum" and "Stille Nacht." Ted's father led in his jolly baritone and held a pointer to the lyrics of folk songs he had chalked on a slate. On birthdays, dozens of children arrived for Nettie's festive parties, replete with costumes and funny hats. A photograph of Ted at the age of eight shows him grinning, wielding a bat like a caveman and wearing a fur skirt, hat and single earring; another finds him in war paint and Indian headdress.

While his father encouraged Ted in his drawing, Nettie fostered his awareness of the pleasures of words. The books he cherished were fanciful tales that his mother found, particularly *The Hole Book*, by Peter Newell, with a hole punched through every page. He was six when he read this, and recalled it as the book that made him think writing could be fun. He remembered the rhyming verses of the *Goops* books, by Gelett Burgess, which his mother read aloud to teach her children manners: "Like little ships set out to sea, I push my spoon away from me. . . ."

Nettie Geisel learned that her son could be bribed with books. She enrolled him for piano lessons with their church organist at his studio above Court Square, and was seldom out of earshot during those lessons. If Ted did well she took him across the street to Johnson's Book Store and let him choose a book. By the time he was nine it was the *Rover Boys*. He read the entire series, about thirty of them, and declared his favorite to be *The Rover Boys at School*. What he liked best was the school cheer:

> Putnam Hall! Putnam Hall!
> What's the matter with Putnam Hall?
> Nothing, boys. Nothing, boys.
> She's all right, Right, RIGHT!

With its towering elms, Court Square was the focal point of parades staged at every opportunity. Main Street spilled over with oompah bands and shiny three-wheeled bicycles and horse-drawn floats wound in crepe paper. Independence Day festivities lasted until the evening fireworks at Forest Park, attended by as many as fifty thousand people. The Fourth of July float that haunted Ted's memory was from the summer of 1912, less than three months after the *Titanic* went down off Newfoundland, taking 1,513 passengers and crew to their death. Later he composed an epic rhyme:

> Dragged by two teams of sweating stallions
> Down Main Street the cardboard iceberg lurched.
> And on the top deck of the sinking Titanic
> A brave stringed quartette precariously was perched. . . .

As news of global events reached Ted, it tended to reinforce his notion that Springfield must be at the center of the world. The opening of the Panama Canal in 1914 convinced him that even California was not too far away. When Ted was eleven, his mother brought home a phonograph record that made a rousing pitch for the World's Fair in San Francisco. Together, as he recalled the lyrics, they would sing:

> "1915 San Francisco!
> . . . All the world will sure be there.
> Meet me, love, in San Francisco
> At the 1915 Fair!"

The song proved persuasive, and Ted's parents took the train West. Marnie and Ted each received a ten-dollar allowance for the month and remained in Springfield with Anna, the housekeeper. Ted later recalled, "Marnie spent hers in the first nine days. I had eight dollars left when my parents returned. Marnie called me a miser, but I wasn't. It's just that I didn't then want— and never would want—most of the stuff that money can buy."

The San Francisco trip brought local fame to Fairfield Street when Ted's father took advantage of an offer at a fair booth from which it was possible to telephone any city in the United States. Ted never forgot the newspaper headline in Springfield: GEISEL CALLS MAYOR! The story began: "The voice of T. R. Geisel came clearly over the wire from three thousand miles away."

But in this city of immigrants, dark headlines from Europe were turning attention back across the Atlantic. In 1915 there was outrage when the British liner *Lusitania* was torpedoed by the Germans and 128 Americans were among the 1,198 who died. Long before the United States entered World War I, German Americans were encountering hostile stares on the streets of Springfield. At first Ted was puzzled by insulting talk of "the Hun." Even his dog,

Rex, a Boston bull that tended to walk on only three of its four feet, came under fire. A schoolmate told Ted that he was being described as "the German brewer's kid with the three-legged dog." Feeling the first sting of the outsider, Ted tried to appear jovial and outgoing to prove that the gibes didn't hurt.

CHAPTER 2

Springfield

1915–1921

On Saturday nights at the Geisel dinner table Ted ate Boston baked beans with wursts of all kinds—leberwurst, bratwurst, schinkenwurst, cervelatwurst, blutwurst and "countless bolognas." There was beer from the family brewery for adults—and adulthood was assumed at fourteen. Thus the American assimilation continued, merging the habits of the Old World with those of the New. The Geisels talked of neighbors' eccentricities and of the prospects for legalizing Sunday baseball, for to them the restrictive blue laws smacked of America's Puritan heritage.

After supper they sang standing around the piano, and one evening Grandfather Geisel counseled Ted: "You really should try to see a Wagnerian opera sometime. That German music is not as bad as it sounds!" Ted, then eleven years old, searched his grandfather's benign, mustachioed face to see if he was joking, and was never sure.

By 1915 the German American community of Springfield had grown to twelve hundred adults, and about five thousand children had at least one German parent. Old-country traditions held strong at the Trinity Evangelical Lutheran Church, where services were conducted in German, at the Schützenverein riflery club, which Ted's grandfather had helped to found, and at the spacious Turnverein hall on downtown State Street. Gymnastic exhibitions by Turnverein members had grown so popular with the entire community that they were staged in the Court Square Theatre, accompanied by hearty German songs and food.

Ted's grandfather began spending more of his time in managing his considerable real estate holdings, and Ted's father succeeded him as general manager of their new Liberty Breweries, bringing home a salary that rose well above one hundred dollars a week and made him one of the more affluent men along Fairfield Street.

Like most immigrant families, the Geisels understood the social pecking order within their city, and by his earliest teens Ted began to think of himself as an incisive observer of class. At the top of his scale were families like the Wessons of Smith and Wesson, the revolver manufacturer, and the Barneys, who had grown wealthy by producing Barney and Berry ice skates with the popular quick clasp. Such families never ate sauerbraten, he was sure, but dined instead on "caviar and meringue glace." They had butlers and took Pullman sleepers to New York to attend the theater and opera. A notch or two below, Ted decided, were department store owners, several doctors and one dentist who had built a fortune, it was rumored, of a quarter of a million dollars. The most socially accepted member of Springfield's German community, in Ted's view, was Dietrich Sievers, who had bought the Highland Hotel from Ted's grandfather in 1910 and was thought to serve Springfield's finest food. Most immigrants were further down on Ted's scale, whether Germans, Italians or Poles.

"Our fathers did get into some clubs like the Elks," he recalled, "and they took us kids to Elks' clambakes where we ate lobsters and Quahog clams and corn-on-the-cob and our fathers drank beer until our mothers made them stop and we all came home on the trolley car singing and wildly happy."

But such outings grew rare as Germany became the common enemy and nativist prejudices arose; German Americans sought whatever anonymity they could. Ted and his sister, Marnie, grew even closer, sharing advice on how to cope with taunts on playgrounds and sidewalks.

Marnie was tall and pretty, two years older and more disciplined than her brother. She practiced the piano an hour or two each day and sometimes after school she challenged Ted to hard sets of tennis at the city courts in Forest Park. On weekends she curled up with books, oblivious to the rest of the family. Marnie's record at Central High School was a matter of family pride. She brought home the highest grades in English literature and in French, German and Latin. Despite periodic panic over math, she graduated magna cum laude in 1919 and went on to Smith College in Northampton, twenty miles up the Connecticut River Valley.

Ted had not shown such laudable interest in his studies, but the breadth of his curiosity led him to report insightful fragments of community lore, causing his parents to exchange amused or startled glances. He preferred the surprise of odd seasonal jobs to the routine of homework, and salted away scenes and characters. During the winter of 1916–17 he rose at dawn on weekends and drove with his father to the brewery pond, where a crew of French Canadians was harvesting ice. One blustery morning a worker fell through the ice and Ted joined in frantic efforts to rescue him. Dragged to safety and gasping for air, the shivering Frenchman realized that his hat was still in the pond. *"Mon chapeau! Mon chapeau!"* he cried and dived back in. Ted never forgot that he had witnessed a Frenchman "risk his life for his hat." During that winter Ted read in a movie magazine that "[his] hero, Douglas Fairbanks, shaved naked," and so, in an unheated bathroom on a snowy morning, he decided to emulate Fairbanks. "I almost froze to death," he recalled, "nicked myself with my father's razor and lost faith in Douglas Fairbanks, who was doing all his naked shaving in sunny California."

As Ted turned thirteen, two prospects clouded the Geisel household: their growing belief that America would enter the war against their ancestral homeland and that the momentum for banning alcohol would result in nationwide Prohibition. Sales from the Geisel brewery had grown to about three hundred thousand barrels a year, among the largest in New England, and economic ruin loomed with the proposed Eighteenth Amendment. Although there was friendly hat-tipping along the sidewalks, their neighbors the Bumps and the Hayneses were Prohibitionists, and the brewer Geisels became the enemy as the campaign for liquor regulation grew shrill. Ted sat at the top of the stairs late one evening as his father and his uncle Will Klein laughed and plotted over a bottle of Old Grand-Dad. They would sow seeds of suspicion between the Bumps and the Hayneses by sending a brewery wagon to pull up in front of each house and "misdeliver a keg of beer" to the other. It would be glorious revenge, Ted thought, but the prank did not survive morning light.

When German submarines began torpedoing American ships, all pretense of neutrality disappeared, and on April 6, 1917, the United States entered the war against Germany. There were reports of German Americans being stoned in some East Coast cities; books in German disappeared from Springfield libraries and book burnings were rumored. Congress established a Committee on Public Information, which declared that sauerkraut would be known as "liberty cabbage" and frankfurters would be "hot dogs." For Ted and his parents, loyalty had never been an issue, but like others of German heritage they recognized that the commonly hyphenated phrase German American was no longer acceptable. They were henceforth Americans. From the Springfield Turnverein, forty-seven young men, "the cream of the physical education classes," went into uniform to fight against the Fatherland. Marnie and her mother joined friends in the afternoons, knitting socks and afghans for American soldiers. English replaced German in the pulpit of the Lutheran church. As enemy-alien property was seized across America, federal agents came to Springfield and took over the thriving Bosch Magneto Company, which had been supplying the American military but was privately owned in Germany.

That autumn, while American troops dug trenches in France and starvation spread through Germany, Ted entered Central High School and sought escape in a frenzy of student activities. Across State Street from the new Carnegie Library, Central was an imposing four-story building of ocher brick with wide steps leading up to three neoclassical arches. In Springfield it was important to be a student at Central, the school for those who hoped to go on to college.

In his teenage years Ted grew tall, gawky and darkly handsome. He was developing strong likes and dislikes. He preferred to avoid athletics, but his father decreed that he take fencing lessons from the coach, Chris Neubauer, at the Turnverein, and he suffered through seventeen "hour-long agonies." Neubauer tried to teach him rope climbing and calisthenic leaps over the sawhorses in the gymnasium, but none of it suited Ted. He hated wearing the required pink jersey shirt. It was no better in Mr. McCarty's dancing class in the ballroom of the Hotel Kimball, to which he carried his dancing pumps in a green flannel bag. The "pink shirt and green flannel bag" came to symbolize Ted's scorn for compulsory activities that he felt added nothing to his life.

From the array of options at Central High, Ted signed on for his only formal art class, and it too was short-lived:

> Our model that day was a milk bottle containing a few scraggly late autumn daisies. I was having a real bad time trying to capture the beauty of this set-up and immortalize it with a hunk of charcoal and a sheet of paper. To add to my frustration, my teacher kept fluttering about and giving me hell for turning my drawing board around and working on my picture upside down. "No, Theodor," she said. "Not upside down! There are rules that every artist must abide by. You will never succeed if you break them."

At the end of the hour Ted transferred out of art class and soon signed on as manager of the high school soccer team. "We lost every game," he later said, "but I was free forever from art-by-the-rule books, so I considered it a highly successful season." He plunged into his role as team manager with his usual exuberance. For a game against nearby Worcester, he organized a cavalcade of Hudson Sixes, Maxwells and Hupmobiles, including one driven by his father. But he forgot to confirm the date of the game with the Worcester Academy team and his parade had to wait at the playing field while he rounded up the opponents.

During weekly assemblies at Central High the music teacher led students in the rousing songs of World War I. "Keep the home fires burning, while your hearts are yearning . . ." Ted sang in his grainy baritone. He collected tinfoil for the war effort and planted potatoes in a two-acre victory garden, but he forgot to harvest them.

Because of continuing hostility toward Germans, Ted was grateful when his Boy Scout troop, No. 13 of Faith Methodist Church, took part in a citywide competition to sell United States Liberty Bonds in support of the war. He made his spiel from door to door along Mulberry and Maple streets and throughout his own neighborhood. When Grandfather Geisel heard about the drive, that veteran of the Prussian cavalry demonstrated his loyalty to America once more by buying, through his grandson, bonds worth the princely sum of one thousand dollars; he had already bought and equipped a supply truck for a Springfield regiment. His support ensured that Ted ranked among the top ten Springfield Scouts in bond sales.

On May 2, 1918, at the age of fourteen, Ted stood with nine other Scouts on the stage of Springfield's Municipal Auditorium to receive an award from Colonel Theodore Roosevelt himself. Geisels and Seusses joined the thousands in the huge hall, and there was repeated applause as Roosevelt went down the line presenting medals. One by one each Scout saluted smartly and marched off-stage. Finally Ted was left alone onstage facing the former president, who was clearly out of medals.

"What's this little boy doing here?" Roosevelt bellowed at the scoutmaster, who frowned and scuttled Ted offstage.

In that pulverizing moment, Ted's wounded pride, his chagrin and, above all, his sense of injustice overwhelmed him. He had no memory of stage fright before that hour, but within a few years his fear of public platforms bordered on the neurotic and he began devising complex excuses to avoid them. Television, in its turn, became a nightmare for him. He always blamed this dread on a bungling scoutmaster who couldn't count and an embarrassed former president of the United States.

Ted was a sophomore in high school on November 11, 1918, when the Great War ended. Streetcars in Springfield were strung with flags, and boisterous parades celebrated the end of the "war to end all wars." German Americans, in the privacy of their homes across Springfield, offered toasts and fervently hoped that the suspicions that had overwhelmed them might finally fade.

Ted's teachers considered him a bright student but not a dedicated one. His high school transcript has disappeared, but Ted recalled a B average "without working," except for his nemesis, math. Instead of concentrating on Latin, which came hard to him, he avoided that class on any pretext, and more than once ducked it for a movie at the Bijou. His mother warned that people who went to movies in the afternoon would "never amount to anything." But theater became one of his lifelong joys. During high school he worked as an usher at the Court Square Theatre, finding a seat as soon as the houselights dimmed. He saw Helen Hayes in *Bab*, one of her first touring shows, and Alfred Lunt in the Broadway-bound company of Booth Tarkington's *Clarence*. Ted remembered that Otis Skinner also played Springfield, as did Al Jolson and the comedian Fred Stone.

For Ted's fifteenth birthday, his father, still intent on toughening his son, gave him a secondhand eighteen-foot canoe. It was the recommendation of the athletic director at the Turnverein, who insisted that Ted had "no pectoral muscles at all." Ted kept the canoe on Watershops Pond and rowed occasionally with school friends. He considered the pond prime territory for dates despite the summertime mosquitoes. But, he insisted, "nobody did much touching." His first love was Thelma, "whom I loved right down to the bottom of my boots." The Thelma of his memory was probably Thelma Lester, pictured in the yearbook as a member of the debate club and the cast of the senior-class play. But she was not the first girl he kissed. That was Libby Elsborg, and apparently it was not a pivotal moment for either of them. "I don't know why I kissed Libby," Ted admitted, "and neither did she."

He became increasingly absorbed in school life, even playing the mandolin and helping to organize the Mandolin Club. For the high school weekly newspaper, *The Recorder*, he wrote one-liners known as "grinds." He drew cartoons and wrote short paragraphs under the name of Pete the Pessimist—"It'll be just our luck to be in Latin class when they turn back the clocks." He reported on school debates and graduated to satires, poems and cartoons; he became so omnipresent in *The Recorder* that a future pseudonym made its debut. In a satire entitled "A Pupil's Nightmare," a student dreamed he had a butler who drove him to school in a Packard. It was signed by T. S. LeSieg, Geisel spelled backward. (Ted wasn't the first to use the pseudonym. When his father played the numbers games, his mother fussed that if he ever won, his name would be announced and it would ruin his reputation, so his father signed his tickets LeSieg.)

In January of 1919 the Eighteenth Amendment was ratified

by the states, and one year later Prohibition became law. Ted's grandfather had predicted it but did not live to endure it; he died on December 5, 1919. Ted's father rose, according to plan, from general manager to president of the merged Springfield Breweries, but it was a hollow tenure. The Volstead Act set the legal alcohol limit at one half of 1 percent and made it illegal to consume alcohol unless it had been bought prior to 1920. That meant the Geisel brewery was doomed.

After his grandfather's funeral and the Christmas school break, Ted plunged into the final flurry of senior activities. He was secretary of the student senate. He wrote and staged a minstrel show, in which he sang in blackface, to fund the traditional class trip to Washington—and a handshake with President Warren Harding in the Capitol rotunda. He took the role of the irascible Sir Andrew Aguecheek in the senior play, Shakespeare's *Twelfth Night*. He was "grind and joke editor" for the yearbook, *Pnalka*, and beneath his résumé in his graduating year were the words: "Next comedy appeared with great applause." His classmates voted him Class Artist and Class Wit, but in group pictures he stood in the back row, tall and unsmiling.

Ted was looking ahead to college with a sense of airy release. Under the energetic prodding of Edwin A. "Red" Smith, a twenty-three-year-old English teacher just two years out of Dartmouth College, he applied for admission to Dartmouth, and so did a score of his classmates. Smith had been the first teacher to stimulate Ted's academic interests and make him consider writing as a career. To Ted, Smith was fun and unpretentious; he talked to pupils about his father, who ran a candy factory in Vermont. Ted's younger cousin Ted Wallace, a Red Smith pupil eight years later, was more interested in science and math than literature, and he recalled: "Smith would say things like, 'Caesar! Come on! Hurry up, boy!' If you listened to the guy, you understood the original Shakespeare better."

Spurred by Smith, Ted made the happy discovery of a writer whom he adopted as soul mate, Hilaire Belloc. He admired the rhythm of Belloc's verses, and he read, over and over, *The Bad Child's Book of Beasts* and *Cautionary Tales*. As he walked home from school that spring he recited the Belloc lines, "As a friend to the children, commend me the Yak. / You will find it exactly the thing: / It will carry and fetch, you can ride on its back, / Or lead it about with a string." It was Belloc, Ted said years later, who introduced him to the hypnotic joys of rhyme.

A recommending letter to Dartmouth from the Central High principal, William C. Hill, was revealing. "Ted comes of a good family with high ideals for the success of their children, and I have sometimes thought that it was this influence which kept his head from being too much turned by the popularity which his natural gifts of good fellowship and humor brought him. . . . I remember him best as bringing down the house in comedy work in *The Mikado* and in *Twelfth Night*. . . . He has qualities of leadership which can be steadied and turned to serious purpose."

That "serious purpose" remained in doubt for years, despite sometimes exasperated efforts by those at Red Smith's alma mater on the Hanover plain of New Hampshire.

CHAPTER 3

•••••••••••••••••••••••••••

Dartmouth

1921–1925

For Ted and a dozen other young men from Springfield who entered Dartmouth College in September 1921 it was a four-hour trip by train and jitney up the Connecticut River Valley to Hanover. Gazing from his window along the placid, winding miles, Ted grew introspective. He saw Dartmouth as his initiation, but into what he had no idea.

From the start, Dartmouth's president Ernest Martin Hopkins, a champion of human rights, captured Ted's attention and his loyalty. "If Leon Trotsky were available," Hopkins said, "I most certainly would invite him to lecture at Dartmouth. Whatever he has to say, we should listen to it, and be able to answer it."

Hopkins was seeking a more diverse student body, and Ted fit the bill. Neither his father nor grandfather had gone to Dartmouth, or to any other college. He was untouched by great wealth or aristocracy and he had attended public school. Nothing in his transcript or in his letters of recommendation gave any intimation of a committed scholar. But he was a lively and handsome chap, well liked, sociable, entertaining, with decent grades and an enthusiastic letter from Red Smith at Central High in Springfield.

In registering at Dartmouth, Ted listed his father's occupation as "Temporarily retired—Brewer." Prohibition, in its second year as a law of the land, was good for a sly wink and a joke. But as for his father's livelihood, there was nothing funny. Prohibition had sent the Geisels' security tottering, and a family crisis was averted only by an inheritance from Grandfather Geisel and his Springfield real estate. By the time Ted moved into Room 416 at Topliff Hall, a red-brick dormitory down East Wheelock Street from the college green, his first-year tuition of $250 was safely in the hands of the Dartmouth bursar.

Planning to major in English, Ted looked forward to the compulsory course in composition and literature taught by Kenneth A. Robinson, a popular assistant professor known for his flashy dress and vivid language. Robinson was a disciple of H. L. Mencken, the Baltimore curmudgeon, and was already publishing pieces and poems in *Scribner's* and *The Saturday Evening Post*. His machine-gun delivery, it was said, made students "scrap their pencils and put their trust in God and memory." Robinson's enthusiasm intrigued Ted, who remained naïve but unawed. From childhood he had been adroit at sifting out and scorning the pretentious and the phony, a skill he exercised in Evolution, a course required for all Dartmouth freshmen, where such skepticism led to a grade of C.

Pledge Week came and went without even a postcard invitation to the earnest freshman from Springfield. Ted had made no overtures to any fraternity, but he was startled to be overlooked entirely. The rebuff helped him set his course. "With my black hair and long nose, I was supposed to be Jewish. It took a year and a half before word got around that I wasn't. I think my interest in editing the Dartmouth humor magazine [*Jack-O-Lantern*] began . . . that Pledge Week."

Long before the Christmas break, Ted made himself a fixture around the wacky office of *Jacko*, as students called their magazine. It was upstairs on Publications Row in Robinson Hall, the headquarters for most student organizations. While vying for printable witticisms, staff members could look across the campus green at a serene symbol of tradition: Dartmouth Hall, a classical three-story building of white brick with foundations laid in 1784. From its tower a bell tolled the hour and the start of class, sending many a *Jacko* staffer flying down the wide staircase. Ted found an invaluable friend in a craggy-faced sophomore, Norman Maclean, a Presbyterian preacher's son from Montana who became a professor of

English at the University of Chicago and later wrote *A River Runs Through It*. With Maclean as his sponsor, Ted began to get some lines published, and then some illustrations. One of his first cartoons, signed "Ted G.," showed a young woman's bulbous leg beneath the hem of a fashionably short skirt. His caption: "The Fatted Calf." Ted liked the laughter this evoked as the magazine was seen around campus; he thought briefly of sending a copy to his parents but concluded they might not be impressed.

Ted sat in sometimes at small-stakes poker with the staff of the student newspaper, *The Dartmouth*, as they marked each night's passage of another deadline. These upperclassmen took notice of the freshman's off-the-wall wit and appealing modesty. Older colleagues at *Jacko* began to mention his hard work and persistence; two of them, coming into the office after breakfast, found him with his head slumped on his typewriter, asleep in the glare of a gooseneck lamp. Ted liked late-night bull sessions at a hangout called Scotty's, where he usually ordered a "toast side," two pieces of toast on a plate with a mound of peanut butter on the side. He sat through football games wearing Dartmouth green, but preferred the camaraderie around the huge bonfires of pep rallies. He adopted bow ties as his trademark and wore them throughout his life.

"In person Ted could appear to be somewhat reserved," recalled Radford Tanzer, a classmate who became a pioneering plastic surgeon. "But he was always sunny . . . you never heard him grump." Friends agreed that Ted's humor was never mean. "He was a sweet man," said Frederick "Pete" Blodgett, who became a Boston banker. "He never had any money but he never spent much. He was always raising hell and laughing a lot and didn't study worth a damn."

Ted grew to respect the academic discipline he discovered at Dartmouth—not enough to pursue it, but to appreciate those who did. He reveled in Dartmouth's proud sense of isolation as the northern outpost of the Ivy League. While he admired the proper white brick buildings of Dartmouth Row, he felt more at home within the dark turret of Wilson Library, so overrun with books that they were piled on tables and under the circular stairwell. He had mounting affection for such landmarks as the granite watering trough on the green, where freshmen were dunked if caught sitting on the Senior Fence, and for Rollins Chapel, its rough pink granite walls and tower trimmed in red sandstone.

But at the center of his Dartmouth career, he decided, would be *Jacko*, for on a humor magazine, he felt, he would be most likely to ferret out his future. His decision was soon evidenced in his grades. In the first semester his only A was in German, a language he had brought from the family hearthside. Even that grade slipped to B in the second semester, and his 2.6 average fell to 2.4.

That summer Springfield seemed smaller and quieter. His father was looking for real estate deals and Ted took on odd jobs, although he preferred sitting at his desk and doodling. Marnie was home from Smith, trading letters with classmates, and Ted wrote to "Mac" Maclean and other *Jacko* friends. There were movies at the Bijou with Thelma, shows at the Court Square Theatre and a family week at the shore. By August Ted was eager for the conviviality of college. During a Sunday walk around the zoo, his father urged that he take better advantage of Dartmouth "as an educational facility." The family's economic future was clouded, his father said, but left it at that. In their separate styles, his parents loved Ted deeply and found unending pleasure in his unpredictable wit, his loyal concern and cheerfulness. They considered him a personality, and no Geisel wanted to crush that spirit.

In September, full of resolve, Ted stepped off the train at White River Junction, Vermont, found a classmate to share the cost of a red Cadillac taxi and returned to campus, where maple leaves already blazed among the pines. Again Ted exploited his heritage, signing up for German literature, and moved toward his major with an introductory course in English literature. At his father's urging, but with misgivings, he enrolled for two semesters of elementary economics, which the Dartmouth catalog noted was designed "to train for citizenship and for business life." Then came psychology of advertising (he never forgot that "red gets more attention than light blue"), and a semester each of botany and zoology. He intended to study but also to draw, and he carried his sketchbook to class. Pete Blodgett sat beside Ted and watched him pass the time sketching flowers or animals. Before exams Ted borrowed Pete's notes, but Blodgett wasn't a scholar either. Their salvation in botany was Professor Arthur H. Chivers, who, when he died at the age of one hundred and one, was Dartmouth's oldest alumnus and oldest emeritus faculty member. Chivers understood his two recalcitrants.

"If you will learn the Latin names of four trees we're studying," he told them near the end of the term, "I will give you a mark up from what I intended to give you."

So Ted and Blodgett, exploding with laughter, recited to each other the Latin: pinus, acer, quercus, homus americanus, and both got C's in botany. Their semester in zoology was a different challenge, and Blodgett recalled it more readily than his classmate. "Professor [Leland] Griggs loved the woods and hunting as much as I did. Ted didn't give a damn about hunting; he was at *Jacko* all the time. But I had a beagle named Spot, a rabbit dog I took to class with us, and Griggs had a mountain cabin. Ted and I and Spot went hunting with him for two days in the snow and had a hell of a time." That camaraderie squeezed out C's for the wily pair. But Ted's sketches from zoology were better than average, including a drawing of Spot with antlers.

To avoid studying, Ted relied on outrageous diversions like the care of Blodgett's bears. Pete kept two cubs named Whisky and Soda at the Phi Gamma Delta fraternity house because the cubs' mother had been shot by a hunter Blodgett knew in Maine, and he felt responsible for them. Ted drew pictures of the bears with wings and helped Blodgett fence off a wooded area for them behind the fraternity house. There the cubs slept the winter through, but in the spring they awoke to climb trees, stop traffic, terrorize neighbors and, worse, the fraternity housemother. Blodgett persuaded a zoo in Toledo, Ohio, to take the bears, and he and Ted put them in a large box and hauled them to White River Junction in Pete's Model T Ford. But within the hour police came looking for Blodgett. "When the train started the bears got scared and kicked out the sides of their box and the baggage man ran through the train shouting, 'The bears are loose!' They backed the train into White River Junction and called police. So Ted and I got a cage with iron bars and sent them off again."

By then Ted's work was appearing regularly in *Jacko*. His closest friend was Whitney Campbell, a classmate from Oak Park, Illinois, to whom he confided late one evening that he intended to become editor of *Jacko* in his senior year.

"Good," Campbell told him. "I intend to become editor of *The Dartmouth*."

Bonded by their aspirations through dogged days and nights along Publications Row, the two young men conspired with student allies, politicked among upperclassmen, and impressed faculty advisers with their dedication. Whit Campbell was smaller in stature than Ted, more studious and better read, but equally intense and determined. Although their calm faces masked their intentions, they were linked by a predilection for the mischievous. They played an occasional round of golf, mostly for the pleasure of the fresh New Hampshire outdoors and each other's conversation. Whit prodded Ted to read more of the classics and history, but Ted demurred: "I like to come and go in my reading." Later he acknowledged: "I am knocking off a bit of your old true God, Anatole France, and only now understand and appreciate your enthusiasm." When Ted dipped into Tolstoy and Flaubert, he wrote Whit: "I suppose I should say nothing, realizing . . . that these books are included in the first semester's work at the Oak Park kindergarten." They became trusting allies, their friendship exceptional throughout Ted's life for the intimacy of its confidences and for its durability.

By his sophomore year, Ted's drawings were a staple of *Jacko*. His influential friend Maclean caught Ted doodling in the margins of his hymnal during chapel and lauded his talent if not his timing. Ted was elected to the *Jacko* art staff in January 1923, and the following month he invited his sister, Marnie, an honors senior at Smith College, to the fabled Dartmouth Winter Carnival. With other girls from Smith and Wellesley and more distant campuses, she was met by horse-drawn sleigh at White River Junction. There was skiing on Balch Hill and ice-skating on Occom Pond, but the weekend focused on the mammoth snow sculptures that students created on the campus green and fraternity lawns. Although Ted was busy much of the time at *Jacko*, Marnie enjoyed a rush from Ted's brothers in the Sigma Phi Epsilon fraternity, which he had recently pledged; after he had become known through *Jacko*, some of the fraternities that had spurned him in his freshman year had sought him out. But his interest in fraternity life was minimal. "I wasn't a good brother," he recalled. "I didn't live in the frat house. [Being a member] didn't change the way I thought." Yet to his death he remembered the Sig Ep grip, and around a piano was prone to burst into song: "Have no fear that we will part," he would roar, "since you wear the Sig Ep heart."

To save money in his junior year, Ted gave up his dormitory room and joined Robert Sharp, another student from Springfield, at 14 South Massachusetts Hall. The move didn't bother Ted, since he expected to spend most of his waking hours at the *Jacko* office, where Norman Maclean had been installed as editor in chief.

Ted was intrigued by a writing course taught by W. Benfield "Ben" Pressey, aimed at the writing of marketable articles. Pressey held informal seminars with students at his home, and "in between sips of cocoa" served by his "very beautiful wife," students were encouraged to read their papers. These were the only creative-writing classes Ted ever attended. At one session he maintained that subject matter wasn't as important as method, and sought to prove his point by writing a book review of the Boston & Maine Railroad timetable. "Nobody . . . thought it was funny except Ben and me."

Ted also looked forward to two semesters in English and German thought, taught by Professor William K. Stewart, who studded his lectures with memories of Paris, Leipzig and Berlin, eyewitness portrayals of place and time that made Ted eager to see the world. "When I went to college," he recalled, "it was a campy thing to say, 'Oh, the places you'll go! The people you'll meet!' "

In December President Hopkins supported a student group's invitation to William Jennings Bryan to present his argument for the biblical interpretation of the divine creation of man. Less than two years later, leaving much of academic America agape, Bryan would oppose Clarence Darrow in a steamy Tennessee courtroom to prosecute John T. Scopes for teaching Darwinian evolution in the classroom. Ted was mesmerized by Bryan's oration at Dartmouth, but not persuaded. His eyes sparkling, he later recalled Bryan's argument: "My friends, there's milk in the milkweed, there's milk in the coconut, and there's milk in the cow, but who of us will go so far as to believe that the cow therefore is the descendant of the milkweed?" That winter day the captain of the Dartmouth track team agreed with Bryan so enthusiastically that Ted swore he could never again "look at any track event."

Ted was startled and pleased by the greetings that began to follow him from class to class. His reputation had grown as someone who was good company, and he was invited around for his wit and charm. Sometimes he joined friends on the mile-long hike down Hanover's steep hill, across the creaky covered bridge that spanned the Connecticut River and up the Vermont side to the Norwich Inn for "a feed," a family-style dinner of unlimited proportions. His signature is in an old register for a Sig Ep dinner, but he went rarely, since dining out was a splurge.

Even Ted's grades improved in his junior year, and in introductory sociology he managed his first A since freshman German. He discovered the excitement of blending words with pictures. "I began to get it through my skull that words and pictures were Yin and Yang . . . that married, might possibly produce a progeny more interesting than either parent. It took me almost a quarter of a century to find the proper way [to do it]. At Dartmouth I couldn't even get them engaged."

He kept trying. At *Jacko*, editor Maclean had discovered Ted's prodigious will to work, and they often wrote "practically the whole thing" themselves. Hunched behind his typewriter, Maclean would bang out a line or two. "Sometimes he'd tell me what he'd written, sometimes not. But then he'd always say, 'The next line's yours.' And, always, I'd supply it. This may have made for rough reading, but it was great sport writing." Sixty years later Ted called *Jacko* his education: "My big desire . . . was to run that magazine. If Mac hadn't picked me as his successor my whole life at college would have been a failure."

On May 15, 1924, the Jack-O-Lantern board elected Ted editor in chief of *Jacko*. Whit Campbell became editor in chief of *The Dartmouth*. A clue to how the two friends celebrated can be drawn from a wistful letter Ted wrote Whit from Paris two years later: "Tonight I'd like to chuck my tickets to *Tosca* and go body-snatching with you and Joe Murphy in the medical school. And sneak down-cellar at The Corner after some old green bottles to trade in for some full ones at Scotty's. Then some of Trueman's popped corn, and talk all night up in your room . . . When will we do all this again?"

The glory of this campus triumph receded in the hot summer at Springfield. Marnie was home with her master's degree from the University of Wisconsin, planning to settle in at Mrs. Phillips's boarding house in Cambridge in the fall to seek a doctorate at Radcliffe College. Ted's roommate, Sharp, was off to Maine with his family, and Ted was glad. "While Sharp was in town," he wrote Whit, "he would amuse himself nights by drinking innumerable quantities of Wawbeek ginger ale and stuffing the bottles with waste paper and cigarette butts." Sharp's conduct was especially offensive because Ted's job that month was washing ginger ale bottles at the Wawbeek plant.

Still, the two had made plans to room together for their senior year at the Randall Club, a two-story clapboard boardinghouse on West Wheelock where a dozen students and several faculty members lived.

During the summer Ted's father followed the example of shrewd Grandfather Geisel and turned a thirty-thousand-dollar profit on a Springfield property that he had held for only six months. His father attributed this coup to "clever business management," although his son was inclined to think that "luck entered into it somewhere." To Ted, as to his mother, it seemed his father had been out of "a real job" since Prohibition closed the brewery; most mornings, he went to his park-board office, but the work there was largely honorific. It was not until 1931 that he began a salaried job as park superintendent, a position he held for thirty years. Because of his father's real estate bonanza, however, Ted could focus on his coming year as editor. He wrote *Jacko* staffers to pass along "any wisecracks for the 'sheet' . . . the prospects are none too rosy just now."

Back at Dartmouth Ted loaded up on English courses: seminars in modern writing and criticism, English poetry with his old friend Robinson and twentieth-century prose with David Lambuth, the department chairman, who drove a cream-colored Packard and matched it with a "cream-colored dinner jacket . . . lined with scarlet." Lambuth's whiskers were generously Elizabethan, and his gestures too. Born of missionary parents in Shanghai, Lambuth spurred Ted's growing curiosity about the world. So did Robinson, who had lived in Europe and on a ranch in California, crewed on a Nile expedition and taken a freighter to Brazil.

At *Jacko* that fall, Ted warned his advertising salesmen "not to think like Babbitts"; Sinclair Lewis's satirical novel was the rage, and its protagonist, George Follansbee Babbitt, was about to surrender his surname to the language as a symbol for all that was trite, uncultured and blindly conformist in the American middle class. As editor, Ted sounded an egalitarian note: "This . . . differs from the standard first issue of college comics in that it does not put itself out to ridicule the incoming freshmen . . . The green lad, the boy with the *Popular Mechanics* trousers and red flannel insoles, is a relic of the past. *Jacko* is delighted to welcome the Man from the prep school this year. And the Man from the high school . . . He is glad that this delegation of Men learned to drink and pet while yet in the third grade . . ." Such noble sentiments aside, the new editor recalled rousing his staff in the middle of the night before that issue appeared. They sat and scissored out a dirty joke that had found its way mysteriously into "three thousand" copies, pasting "a new joke over the hole." No one ever confessed.

Whit Campbell celebrated his editorship by bringing a 1914 Ford back to Hanover, and he and Ted drove to Cambridge for the autumn football game with Harvard, cheering as their classmate Larry Leavitt scored the touchdown that led underdog Dartmouth to a 6–0 victory. They compared Leavitt with Cyril Gaffey Aschenbach, who had chummed with the editors and whom Ted called "a football-playing poet." The season before, Aschenbach had led a victory over Harvard so heroically that Ted's father had asked Ted to introduce him to the young man. That meeting eventually led to one of Ted's most tender links with his father.

Although the Sig Ep house was seldom part of Ted's campus rounds, he went often to an 1823 Federalist brick house at the corner of Main and Wheelock, the citadel of Casque and Gauntlet, the senior honorary society to which members were elected by their predecessors. In his senior year Ted was one of twenty members; fifteen lived in the house—known among them as the Corner—but Ted, still economizing, stayed at the Randall Club. Pete Blodgett lodged at Casque and Gauntlet, as did Whit Campbell and the football players Leavitt and Kenneth Montgomery, who was elected King Arthur to the knights of Casque and Gauntlet. The magic that Ted brought to their Round Table was never forgotten by Montgomery: "He was not gregarious in the sense of hail-fellow-well-met; there was no sense of self-importance about him. But when he walked into a room it was like a magician's act. Birds flew out of his hands, and endless bright scarves and fireworks. Everything became brighter, happier, funnier. And he didn't try. Everything Ted did seemed to be a surprise, even to him."

In a traditional final meeting Casque and Gauntlet members voted their predictions for one another. As chairman, Blodgett counted ballots and recalled that the vote on Ted was unanimous as "least likely to succeed." Blodgett said, "He never seemed serious about anything . . . and he turned out to be the greatest success of the whole delegation."

On a Saturday night in April 1925 Ted's reign as a big man on campus crashed. He and nine friends were sharing a pint of bootleg gin in his room at the Randall Club. President Hopkins, it was said, had made a pact with the upriver bootlegger who claimed Hanover as his territory: Hopkins would not interfere as long as the bootlegger didn't send down tainted booze. But the level of merriment that night in Ted's room offended "Pa" Randall, the proprietor. When Ted and Curtis Abel squirted seltzer water on the tin roof, Randall imagined the direst indignity and telephoned the police chief, who raided the party. In a hearing, Dean Craven Laycock placed Ted and his friends on probation "for defying the laws of Prohibition, and especially on the night before Easter." All were commanded to write letters to their parents relating their shame. Ted's probation terms were especially odious to him; although his name remained on the masthead, he was forbidden to continue serving as editor of *Jacko*. But the *Jacko* office was not off-limits and for the final issues Ted sought anonymity through pseudonyms. His telltale cartoons were signed with various names, including L. Burbank and Thomas Mott Osborne, the warden of Sing Sing Prison. Finally Ted turned to his own middle name and for the first time signed his cartoons as Seuss.

As graduation approached, Ted realized he was surrounded by classmates for whom the future was no secret. Whit Campbell had been accepted by Harvard Law School, and so had Ken Montgomery. Blodgett, despite his bears, was going to be a banker. Ted's roommate, Sharp, was pursuing graduate work and would become chairman of the English Department at Wheaton College. Others were going to work for their fathers in corporate posts, but, Ted thought wryly, there would be no vacancies for him at the Springfield Zoo. Just what, his father asked, were his son's plans for the fall? With his usual insouciance, Ted wrote that he would be attending Oxford University on a Campbell Fellowship from Dartmouth. Flushed with paternal pride, Ted's father crossed Fairfield Street to give the news to Maurice Sherman, the editor of *The Springfield Union*, who published it the next day.

But once again Ted had exaggerated. He had applied for a fellowship, but no decision had been made. Ted rallied his favorite professors to send letters to the selection committee. Ben Pressey wrote: "I have great admiration for his cleverness, the quickness and shrewdness of his mind. He is not profound, but he makes the fullest possible use of the abilities he has, which are not inconsiderable. . . . While he could not be described as scholarly, he is nevertheless interested in and responsive to the things of the mind." The worldly David Lambuth, who seemed to know as much about his dreams as Ted himself, wrote that Ted was not thinking of a teaching career but wanted "to fit" himself for writing of a "creative or editorial sort, perhaps in connection with the publishing business." But the previous year's winner of the Campbell Fellowship had applied for an extension to complete his Oxford studies, and in the end the committee approved his request.

On June 23, 1925, Ted graduated from Dartmouth College with a grade point average of 2.454 and a respectable ranking: 133rd in a class of 387. He confessed to his father that an Oxford fellowship would not be forthcoming. Theodor Robert Geisel stared hard at his son and shook his head, but soon agreed that since Ted's scholarship had been announced in the newspaper, the family must find a way to get him to England.

Ted looked back at his Dartmouth record philosophically: "English and writing was my major, but I think that's a mistake for anybody. That's teaching you the mechanics of getting water out of a well that may not exist."

For two weeks that summer, Ted filled in for a vacationing columnist on *The Springfield Union* and earned a few dollars toward Oxford by writing witty verses and responses to headlines. Answering a couplet from the Lowell (Mass.) *Courier-Citizen*, "In the name of our Republic, together with our love, / We extend felicitations to Alvin Fuller, Gov.," Ted escalated the game:

> We'll go you just one better
> (*The Springfield Union* says)
> And wish a happy birthday
> to Calvin Coolidge, Pres.

Happy-go-lucky as ever, Ted sailed from Boston on the steamship *Cedric* on August 24, 1925, with not a clue in the world as to what lay ahead.

CHAPTER 4

Oxford

1925–1926

The fog hung in silver wisps that October morning in 1925 as a black Morris-Cowley taxi pulled away from the train station in Oxford and rumbled off to the High Street. It turned at the half-timbered inn known as the Mitre and eased along Turl Street through a shadowy stream of bicycling students and black-robed dons walking two and two. Ted Geisel, its lone passenger, leaned forward for a better view of the spires and cupolas of this ancient university town and clasped his hands in unconscious applause. But when the taxi stopped beside a bleak stone wall, his smile faded and he looked warily about.

"Lincoln College, sir," the driver said, nodding toward a dark passage as he began to hand down the youth's luggage.

Drawing a woolen scarf around his neck and clutching the typewriter that had been his close companion at Dartmouth, the twenty-one-year-old American stepped to the street. He was an imposing young man, six feet tall and carelessly handsome in his woolen cap, plus fours and tweed jacket. His hair was black and unruly. As he smelled the coal smoke in the autumn air, his long nose quivered. Then he straightened his shoulders, loped through Lincoln's medieval oaken gate and announced himself at the porter's lodge.

Ted was enrolled at Oxford, he knew, through a blunder of bravado, one of many times in his life when his unleashed imagination and tendency to exaggerate would take him to surprising and wondrous places. Sometimes he questioned how he got into these jams, but more often he was plotting how to get out. This strange and distant citadel, he reminded himself, was where he must try to consider becoming a professor of English literature.

Such thoughts were interrupted by an aging scout who was assigned to show him to his quarters. They crossed the front quad, a gravel-and-flagstone courtyard that appeared to be a cul-de-sac, its sooty walls scarlet with ivy. Ducking through a low archway behind the fifteenth-century dining hall, they emerged on a shaded back lawn. The scout motioned up a stairwell, No. 11, and led Ted to a chill room overlooking a gnarled plane tree and a wall shared with Brasenose College. The room was large enough, about twenty feet square, with three deep windows and a small fireplace. Ted gazed through the cross-panes of his windows at a high stone wall studded with jagged glass and, in those first lonely moments, thought of a dungeon door clanging shut behind him. Yet for the rest of his extraordinary life, he would marvel at the unexpected events and influences of that Oxford year, none of them academic, that put his life in focus.

In 1925 Oxford was still recovering from the bloodbath of the World War, when so many of its students had marched off to the trenches of France. Lincoln College had added only two names to its rolls in 1916, and one in 1917, but now enrollment was approaching normalcy. As Ted arrived, Lincoln was about to mark its five hundredth year, and was little changed outwardly from its founding in 1427 by Richard Fleming, the bishop of Lincoln. The college, the eighth oldest at Oxford, had been established to combat heresy within the English Church or, as Bishop Fleming wrote so floridly, "to overcome those who with their swinish snouts imperil the pearls of true theology." It was smaller and poorer than most Oxford colleges. In some years its budget was as little as one tenth that of the far grander Magdalen College or Christ Church, whose members often came from titled English families and moved on to careers in government and business. At Lincoln, many students' fathers were in trade or the clergy. Its most acclaimed member was the sober founder of Methodism, John Wesley, who had lectured at Lincoln from 1726 to 1735 and whose murky, brooding portrait hung in the dining hall. All of this suited Ted, who had no use for pomposity, and he liked Lincoln's heart-of-Oxford setting on the narrow street called the Turl, just steps from Blackwell's cavernous bookshop and the fanciful dome of the Radcliffe Camera library.

In that "cold, dreary, dripping" autumn Ted and other outlanders donned their gowns and followed English colleagues through the rituals of morning chapel, lectures and tutorials. In the afternoons they gathered at Fuller's tea shop to swap tales "over tea and anchovy toast." Ted was beginning to feel "appallingly ignorant," preferring sketching to reading required books, and treasuring the eccentricities of Oxford above its academic life. These were readily in evidence at the Sunday-night student meetings in the Junior Common Room, once again caught up in such peacetime trivia as which brand of tobacco should be provided (Three Nuns was favored) or the impending election of one in their midst as the Guardian of the College Cat. The Junior Common Room purchased a group subscription to the saucy French magazine *La Vie Parisienne*, which was passed around, boosting attendance. When there was no quorum to debate such heady issues as "The poet is a more useful product of society than the scientist," students brought out a raveled rope and adjourned to the Chapel Quad to decide the issue in a tug-of-war. Ted found it easy to ignore most of these matters, saving his involvement for topics like the lack of hot water for showers in the communal bathroom, which was many cold steps from his lodging. By January, when heavy snow lay on the ground, hot baths were rationed, and during discussion in the Junior Common Room of an appropriate student gift to commemorate the college quincentenary, Ted enthusiastically supported a motion to contribute toward a larger boiler.

The Americans who came to Oxford as Rhodes scholars were welcomed socially and many made lifelong friends on the playing fields or in the crews. But in England, so soon after the war, Ted was sensitive about his German background, and since he was neither a serious intellectual nor an extrovert, and certainly not an athlete, he spent most of his free hours with "other outsiders."

"My big problem at Oxford," he recalled, "was whom to talk to." Then he met Joseph Sagmaster, a Rhodes man from Cincinnati who lived at Lincoln and shared Ted's interest in writing. Sagmaster befriended him, and as winter closed in, Ted made friends with a small group of "untitled foreigners" like chubby Fred Stokvis, a Hollander, and Cecil Stapleton, a Eurasian whose uncommon face, Ted confessed, reminded him of a white Oriental.

Even his few English friends were of the merrily rebellious sort, especially an undergraduate named Mirabel, whose father was "the twin brother of the Earl of Devonshire" and who had spent most of her life in "the India of the Raj, where Papa wore a pith helmet and shoulder straps." Her daring nature and affinity for pranks delighted the commoner from New England, who was put off by the celebrated Oxford reserve. When a friend acquired a movie camera, Ted and Mirabel played impromptu roles for a homemade epic. At the traditional spring boat races of Eights Week, with all Oxford beside the river in "silks and satins," the two amateur actors appeared in Turkish fezzes and, followed by the camera, "staged a love affair" before the rector, who was watching from the new Lincoln barge. The rector was the stiff and taciturn J.A.R. Munro, a scholar of classical archaeology and ancient history, who led Lincoln College from 1919 to 1944. Regarded with more respect than affection, the Munner, as he was known, announced that such high jinks were an American insult against English respectability, and he never acknowledged Ted again.

Not that they had ever been close. Early in the year, Ted had found a note in his box saying that the rector would be pleased to see him sometime. "Sort of elated," and never suspecting it was the customary gesture toward all new students, Ted slicked his hair the next afternoon and knocked on the rector's door at No. 15, the Turl. A butler gazed up at the lanky student, announcing that "Dr. and Mrs. Munro are at tea, sir," and closed the door. Days later, when Ted warily returned, the rector's only question was about team sports. Was Ted involved with rugby? Crew? All Ted could offer was that he played tennis regularly with an American named Donald Bartlett, a fellow Dartmouth graduate now at Exeter College, across Brasenose Lane from Lincoln. Munro was not impressed. But Bartlett, who saw Ted as "this extraordinarily clean and wholesome elf, not religious but humane," grew to be his lifelong friend.

Ted and Bartlett never forgot the afternoon when the dons of Lincoln College went into mourning over the ironic death of the Reverend Sir John Kingsmill, a Lincoln alumnus and the former canon of Zanzibar, who, it was said in a eulogy, "in his blameless life, had faced down hostile savages and marauding lions as he pursued the university mission in central Africa." The canon's long-anticipated return to Oxford ended abruptly when he was struck down by a motorcar on Banbury Road. That evening Ted went to his Dartmouth typewriter and set down the facts for his future story file.

The next morning his aged scout, Rawlins, brought him a message with breakfast. "There is a bit of talk, sir, about the clatter of your writing machine," he said. Suspecting that the comment came with the sanction of authority, Ted put away his typewriter. Rawlins bowed, smiled thinly and left with the chamber pot.

While others burrowed into the Bodleian Library, or cultivated the role of aesthete, Ted explored the crooked lanes of the medieval university and the even older town with which it was entwined. He began to figure out that the colleges differed in size and shape, odd pieces that fit together like a puzzle that had been dropped and then pressed back together so that it was almost right. Walls ran into higher walls; dead ends were common. He was intrigued by the sound of Great Tom, the Christ Church bell, which tolled its quirky curfew at 9:05 P.M. with 101 bells, one to call home each of the original members of the college that had been founded by Cardinal Wolsey and Henry VIII.

Only rarely did Ted and his colleagues muse over lofty concerns. They were part of what Kenneth Clark, who had been at Oxford's Trinity College three years earlier, described as the "socially irresponsible postwar generation." Clark himself remembered little from lectures or assigned books, and insisted that he, too, used "evasion and bluff" on written essays. Another Oxonian of that day, Evelyn Waugh, in *Brideshead Revisited*, portrayed the university of the 1920s as still a sanctuary of the aristocracy, but Ted saw little of that flamboyant scene. His brash and burgeoning sense of the absurd was beginning to shape his life; he hated pretense and wanted to laugh.

Ted dreaded slogging through the quad on dark winter mornings in dressing gown and slippers for roll calls. He disliked being consigned to the freshman table in the dining hall because, although he was a first-year Oxford man, he was a college graduate and three or four years older than most of his tablemates. He judged English food "tasteless" and scoffed at the dessert called trifle as "a soggy cake soaked in bad wine." Above all, he found strange the dining-hall ritual of sconcing, through which a student might challenge another over a presumed breach of manners (swearing was reason enough, but so was quoting Scripture, speaking in Latin or mentioning women). If the presiding scholar reckoned the deed sufficiently grave, the offender was challenged to down a two-quart tankard of ale in a single draft. If he failed, it was passed around the table. Sconcing, the new man from New England wrote his father, was silly.

Ted muffed his one known opportunity for social entrée in London when he cavalierly declined the invitation of Viscountess Astor for Monday, March 15, 1926, at No. 4 St. James's Square: "Dancing 10 p.m. Short coats and black ties." It was sent to Mr. T. S. Giesel. "Misspelled," he scribbled on the engraved card, "that's why I turned her down, the lout!" Yet he treasured the card enough to preserve it in the flap of his black loose-leaf Oxford notebook.

That notebook remains as the most enchanting of Ted's unpublished books, illustrated evidence of his wandering mind during lectures on Geoffrey Chaucer (whom he called Jeff), Shakespeare and Milton. Among its sixty-eight pages are a few with words only, but most are thronged with pen-and-ink Seussian cartoons. Sometimes a sketch erupted from the subject of the lecture, but any Oxford don confronted with the result would have felt ready to suggest to the young American (as one eventually did) that his future lay elsewhere. Beside his notes in Anglo-Saxon for Beginners stands a drooling milk cow burdened with a sagging udder, rams' horns and angel wings. A pair of baroque daggers decorates the margin, along with a coat of arms from which a trapped bird struggles to free itself. On the same page as desultory notes on Keats's odes, three dogs move in terror across high wires, a small chicken wears a windmill for a tail, and a despondent devil contemplates his failures. As Ted noted dutifully that the translation of the holy Bible was the greatest literary achievement in the reign of King James he was also deep at work creating a Chaplinesque clown, slumping beneath the weight of military epaulettes and a crown from which grew a soaring cross. In a lecture by Émile Legouis, an authority on William Wordsworth and Jonathan Swift, Ted sketched himself, sinking into deep water, with the caption "Mr. Legouis attempts once more to attract my attention in a lecture entitled . . . ?" Among his notes on Dryden, a black-faced Cupid appears with a quiver of arrows. So does the profile of a chic young woman wearing a snug cloche. "Yoo hoo," cries a male profile as he peers up the loose-leaf binder at the cloche.

An American girl shared this class and stared over his shoulder, astonished, as Ted busied himself in his own world through each lecture. She was Helen Marion Palmer, a slender Wellesley graduate, five feet three inches tall and five and a half years his senior. She had soft brown hair that brushed her shoulders; her eyes were pale blue. Helen had arrived at Oxford with her widowed mother a year earlier after teaching English at Girls High School in Brooklyn for three years. Most women at Oxford were the studious "horn-rimmed glasses, blue stocking" sort, but Helen had "a certain grace."

One day she watched Ted undertake to illustrate Milton's *Paradise Lost*; he drew the angel Uriel sliding down a sunbeam, oiling the beam as he went from a can that resembled a tuba.

"You're crazy to be a professor," she blurted after class. "What you really want to do is draw." She glanced at another page and smiled. "That's a very fine flying cow!"

Always hungry for encouragement and susceptible to praise from those he respected, Ted was intrigued by this strong-willed, good-natured girl. Sagmaster, who knew that both of them had been "down in the dumps," invited them to his rooms for a formal introduction. "You never saw a better case of love at first sight," he recalled. "They completely ignored the host, talked together for hours, left together, had dinner together and spent as much time together during term as the Oxford rules allowed." Helen became a lively addition to the outsiders' group while pursuing her own studies at the Society of Oxford Home Students (later to become St. Anne's College).

At the six-week Christmas break Helen sailed home while Ted toured the South of France with Bartlett, Sagmaster and Philip Blair Rice, who later served as professor of philosophy at Kenyon College. In Cannes, Ted illustrated every incident with drawings "of marvelous and wonderfully named birds and beasts," and Sagmaster urged him to pursue his gift for cartooning.

Back at Oxford for winter term, Ted and Helen, "less miserable" despite the worsening weather, explored the deer park behind Magdalen tower and dropped in at the Turf Tavern, an ancient pub hidden in an alley behind New College, with a ceiling so low that Ted had to stoop to enter. One evening, as they huddled near the pub hearth, Ted bemoaned the rule that prohibited a first-year student from owning a motor vehicle. Helen was in her second year, she reminded him, and over their pints they decided to pool funds. Soon they were putt-putting about on a two-horsepower motorcycle with a sidecar from the Raleigh bicycle shop on the High Street. Because another university rule prevented first-year students from driving vehicles, Ted bought "plucked ducks" and tied them into the basket. For the rest of the term he masqueraded, when necessary, as a poulterer's delivery boy, camouflaging himself from suspicious proctors.

With their new machine, Ted and Helen toured the country-side, visiting old market towns in the Cotswolds and enjoying spring picnics in the Lake District, where Ted sketched "fool's-parsley and daffodils." One weekend they went "Duke-ing" in Suffolk at a country house beside the North Sea owned by the parents of Mirabel, Ted's costar from Eights Week movies. "It seems that her father missed being the Earl of Devonshire by one minute," Ted said, charmed by the fact that their host was a twin. But two incidents marred the weekend and both involved Mirabel's father. "I played rotten golf and spoiled the old fellow's game, and then he caught me laughing in front of a portrait in the smoking room. 'That gentleman,' he said, adjusting his monocle, 'is my great-grandfather, the Duke of Wellington.' "

On the road back to Oxford, racing against the college curfew, Ted took a wide turn, the motorbike skidded, and he and Helen tumbled into a roadside ditch. "So we became engaged," Ted said, but for a time it was their secret.

The most reliable record of their courtship is preserved in the fifteenth-century stone tower above the Lincoln College gate. There, going back five hundred years, are dusty volumes of hand-written student accounts known as battel books. Ted's charges for meals and lodging for the first term ending a week before Christmas were similar to those of his classmates, but in the midwinter term his charges diminished sharply and did not resume. Years later, the Lincoln College historian pored over those penned entries, shook his head and frowned. "Geisel must have been off on his own somewhere else from the latter weeks of the second term through the spring."

For one thing, Ted was sharing off-campus lodging with Donald Bartlett. But student records in the archives of Helen Palmer's college offer further evidence. In her first year, she and her mother lived in a rooming house at 11 Polstead Road, and later on Wood-stock Road. After her mother returned to America in October 1925, Helen moved to rooms at Frewin Cottage, less than a block from Lincoln's wall. For the final spring term she lived at 14 Ship Street, an address of small residential flats two blocks away from the Lincoln College gate.

Toward the end of Trinity term in June, when examinations loomed for those who would return the next fall, the elderly and eccentric Dr. A. J. Carlyle, Ted's tutor, reached the same conclusion as Helen about his future. "He was the nephew of the great Thomas Carlyle and the oldest man I've ever seen riding a bicycle," Ted later said. "I was the only man he'd ever seen who never should have come to Oxford." Carlyle counseled Ted to take a year off to tour Europe, visit museums, read and improve his knowledge of history.

Yet Ted also claimed that what prompted him to leave Oxford was a dreary two-hour lecture on the punctuation of *King Lear*. "This don, Sir Oliver Onions, had dug up all the old Shakespearean folios and lamented that some had more semicolons than commas. And some had more commas than periods. . . . I listened for a while and then went to my room and packed."

In fact Ted had made some decisions about his future as early as April, during the four-week Easter break, which he and Helen spent in France, traveling on the motorcycle and staying each night, at Helen's insistence, in separate lodgings. He had had enough of university study, he would never teach school, and he would marry Helen Marion Palmer.

Ted, who rarely boasted, was proud of the "dazzling fashion" in which he and Helen broke the news to her mother, a social reformer and teetotaler who joined them during that spring break. On their first night together in Paris the three of them went to the theater, but Mrs. Palmer took little notice of Ted. At intermission, he and Helen excused themselves for "a stiff drink" and returned, determined to "explode the bomb." Ted wrote his Dartmouth friend Whit Campbell a dramatized version of what happened next:

> "Mother," Helen asked brightly, "what do you think of 'this' as a husband?"
>
> Mrs. Palmer's jaw dropped a bit and she fanned herself with the program. "You don't mean . . . ?" she asked.
>
> "Yes," Helen said very matter-of-factly, "we seem to be engaged."
>
> "But my dear girl," her mother stammered, "why, I don't even know his name!"
>
> Here was my opportunity. Out came my bill folder. I fumbled inside for a second and, with a magnificent sweep, tendered her a bit of pasteboard.
>
> "Madam," I bowed. "My card!"

Later they sat at a sidewalk table at the Café de la Paix and celebrated with Mrs. Palmer's favorite drink, lemonade. By the next day she had recovered her aplomb and proved herself willing to take a chance. Despite the threat of showers, the three roared out of Paris on the Oxford motorcycle, heading for Fontainebleau. Helen rode in the sidecar, and her mother bounced along in the rumble seat just behind. "Over cobblestone roads," Ted said. "Mother Palmer hasn't thought the same of me since."

For Ted, at twenty-two, Paris that spring seemed perfect. He delighted in the way the French laughed so openly, tied ribbons in their hair, walked arm in arm and kissed one another in public. He spent hours going to the theater and opera, taking "futile" French lessons and "trying to get some funny stories written." He fell in with a bunch of "very sophisticated White Russian taxi drivers," all of whom claimed to have been captains in the czar's guard. While plotting to recapture Russia, they taught Ted how to sip tea from a glass, eat blinis and sway to the old-country music of the balalaika. Yet Ted wrote Whit Campbell that he felt a twinge of homesickness, and enclosed a fuzzy snapshot of a Paris street corner showing "half our motorbike and three-fourths of Helen."

Although they did return to Oxford, where Helen completed her work for a master's degree, Ted spent even less time on studies. The final entry in the battels record of Theodor Seuss Geisel in the medieval strong room over the Lincoln College gate is dated June 10, 1926: "Name Removed."

In that carefree summer, a dizzy season when the American smart set thronged the French Riviera, with F. Scott Fitzgerald and Zelda in the fore and Dorothy Parker and Robert Benchley at Cap d'Antibes, Ted followed his heart back to the Continent, living and traveling on his "Grandfather's money," riding trains, drinking champagne and reading what he chose: Lytton Strachey's wicked, witty biography of Queen Victoria and *Bismarck*, by Grant Robertson. On longer rail journeys he translated "a page or two" from the German of Emile Ludwig's *Life Of Napoleon*—making only a small dent, he admitted, in its 660 pages.

Ted dismissed the suggestion by Helen's mother that he return to America and "go into business"; his latest scheme was to get a newspaper job abroad. Overwhelmed at Oxford by how much there was to learn, he reconciled himself to "man's limitations . . . I have said to hell with the whole of English literature and I am now reading for ideas, wherever they may be found."

In June Ted's parents and his sister, Marnie, had arrived in

England. They had not met Helen and they considered Ted's engagement impulsive. Ted hoped to smooth things over as they strolled around Oxford, but it was Helen who won them over with her quiet and gracious manner. Intent on getting her master's degree to upgrade her teaching credentials, Helen remained in Oxford while the Geisels had a sojourn on the Continent. For Ted and Marnie, a willowy beauty of twenty-four who was engaged to a Harvard law student, it was an especially happy trip, the last time they would be together before their marriages. One glittering day in Switzerland atop the Rigi, Ted persuaded Marnie to pose with a flower-bedecked cow for a snapshot. When they picked up the photograph at a Lucerne shop, a businessman sought to buy it for a chocolate-bar advertisement. She would be famous, he promised. Laughing, Marnie declined.

The Geisels traveled by train and hired car to Munich, Nuremberg, Dresden and Berlin, where Ted's father staged a scene at the "noisy" Adlon Hotel. "Before checking out," Ted recalled, "my dad went to the manager's office and said, 'Did you ever sleep in Room 309?' 'No, sir,' replied the manager. 'Neither has anyone else!' roared Theodor Robert Geisel." In July they made a pilgrimage to Mühlhausen, a village of four hundred inhabitants, the birthplace of Grandfather Geisel. Ted's memory of his grandfather as a wealthy man in America flooded back when he met a younger brother, Robert, gaunt and gray at seventy-five, still working eight hours a day at his forge and, like others in Germany after the war, living on "black bread and beer." Robert Geisel had also emigrated to America but returned to Germany because of a homesick wife. What haunted Ted was not only the poverty but the "lost opportunities."

On their final night in Mühlhausen, Ted's father entertained thirty relatives at the Gasthaus Zum Adler. They dined on black radishes and bratwursts, and the conversation was passionate, but Ted was saddened that these intense and bright cousins and uncles, some born in America and some crippled in the war, had had so little chance for an education. As the Geisels drove south into Bavaria to visit his mother's family, Ted puzzled about fate and luck. In the hamlet of Kleinschwarzenbach, the Geisels hosted a dinner for Seusses, and sixty-seven people came. They drank beer and danced to screeching fiddles, and again there were tears. "We gave my cousin Alvin, age twenty-four, his first automobile ride," Ted wrote. "Alvin thought it took a day and a night to get to Leipzig, which is just three hours distant. . . . He showed a tremendous desire to go to America, and, as we left, stood on the platform in silence, following the train with his eyes."

Ted, the young idealist, swore he would right this injustice by endowing two fellowships. One would take men from Klein-schwarzenbach and send them to world capitals for two years, and the other would bring world statesmen "who have proved their worth attending operas and prize fights" to Kleinschwarzenbach to live in thatched huts and "examine the war memorials, look through family albums and sit on a rock to watch the peasants dig turnips to pay the national debt."

In Paris, Ted's gloom evaporated. He was ensconced with his parents at the posh Hotel Continental, and Helen arrived from Brittany, where her mother had rented a summer cottage at Dinard. Ted and Helen invited the Geisels to see the dancer Mistinguett and the young boulevardier Maurice Chevalier at the Folies Ber-gère. That night the stage was full of "gorgeous girls and jiggling breasts" and suddenly Ted's father rose. "We're going back to the hotel," he said. "There's nothing here but tits and music."

"So you don't like music?" Ted shot back, brimming with sophistication.

No one spoke in the taxi as they sped through the dark streets and dropped Helen at her pension. In the Geisel suite, Ted's mother went to bed "in tears."

"Let's have a drink," Ted's father said, and then, "If you're going to make pronouncements like that, wait until we are man-to-man." The incident was never mentioned again.

After his family sailed for home, Ted settled in for some of his happiest days in Paris. With his parents no longer paying his bills, he moved to the Left Bank to escape "detested tourists" and save money, swearing to drink "café au laits instead of champagne." He stalked the Latin Quarter and Montparnasse, which was "thronged by the literati." On a breezy September evening, be-neath the green-and-white awnings of the Closerie des Lilas, Ted recognized Ernest Hemingway, a worldly man of twenty-seven, smoking a pipe and writing from time to time on a thick pad. "What he was writing I never knew," Ted admitted. "I was scared . . . to walk over and ask him, lest he ask me what *I* was writing. I was a twenty-two-year-old kid writing knock-kneed limericks about goats and geese and other stuff that I couldn't sell. He was probably writing *A Farewell to Arms.*"

Ted was joined that fall by Oxford friends, including Bartlett and Rice, and as they browsed in bookstalls along the Boulevard Saint-Michel, Ted recognized moving toward them the hulking form of Theodore Dreiser, whose *An American Tragedy* had been published the year before to acclaim. With him was Emma Goldman, the Russian-born anarchist, who had been deported by President Coolidge for her opposition to American involvement in the war.

Ted thought Dreiser "America's most ponderous-minded word slinger" but he and his friends doggedly trailed the pair to the Café Harcourt at the Place de la Sorbonne and sat near enough to eavesdrop on their "rapid fire" conversation:

> "What street is this?" asked Dreiser, who spoke no French and seemed to be on his first trip to Paris.
>
> "This is the Boulevard St. Michel," Emma said.
>
> "Oh!" said Mr. Dreiser, and thought it over for a long time. His next remarks were much more to the point. "I am half Jewish," he said. "The other half is German."
>
> "I am Jewish too," said Emma.

Suddenly one of Ted's friends, "a trifle intoxicated," bowed to Goldman and reminded her that they had had tea together at Oxford following her lecture the year before. Goldman responded politely, but Dreiser, "hat still on," ignored them. As the young Americans withdrew, talking of revenge for the slight, Ted dashed "like a chipmunk" to a hawker's barrow and bought "a lurid pair of galluses . . . which he gave to the *garçon* with a wad of francs, instructing him to [present] them to Dreiser with a speech: 'Monsieur, voilà! Un petit cadeau de l'Académie Française!'" Ted watched "from behind a pissoir." Dreiser kept repeating, "What?

What?" Emma laughed heartily as the boy walked away, leaving Dreiser holding the suspenders.

The Oxonians managed tickets at the Folies Bergère for a performance that was the talk of Paris—the American Josephine Baker dancing in the nude "except for a girdle of bananas which served to vivify rather than to conceal." Ted fretted about the "increasingly low opinion" of Americans in Paris, wondering whether it was brought on by the "crass success" of Josephine Baker or the flaunting of U.S. tourist dollars while the French were recovering from the war.

On a cool, overcast October morning, Ted hailed a taxi near his Left Bank hotel and crossed the Pont Neuf, heading for the Gare de l'Est and a train to Zurich. Looking back at the silvery ribbon of the Seine, he grew sentimental. "You must spend more time in Paris," he wrote Whit Campbell, "if only to see one of those gray morning Seines." He told Whit he was off to Vienna to join Helen, a "darn nice girl," supportive and encouraging, and "anxious to meet you." He bragged about her astuteness, and said that when Helen saw a photograph of the Casque and Gauntlet group at Dartmouth she looked at the picture and immediately "picked out the two of us for the well-read boys." Helen had just bobbed her hair and, as his own act of defiance, Ted was growing a mustache, although he vowed to shave it off if he couldn't "get the center to grow together."

In Vienna, Ted practiced his German in beer halls and coffee houses. His new favorite book was a thick red volume called *Europa, 1925*, which contained "all the European constitutions, the events of 1925, and a who's who of everyone who counted in Europe that year." Ted planned to begin a "complete study" of modern German drama, which, "if you include the Austrian, [is] the most fruitful in the world today." His grandiose scheme was "to correlate the German theater with the modern English and American literary movements, and later with the Russians, and see what kind of a thesis I can do." He pursued this program for three days.

Soon Ted was back in Paris, where, at the Sorbonne, he called on his former Oxford professor Émile Legouis, the authority on Wordsworth and Swift. Ted admired Swift's satire in *Gulliver's*

Travels, and Legouis tried to interest him in scholarly research. "He said that nobody had ever discovered anything that Jonathan Swift had written from the age of sixteen and a half to seventeen," Ted recalled. "If [he] had [written anything], I could analyze [it] as my D. Phil. thesis. Unfortunately, if he hadn't written anything, I wouldn't get my doctorate." He remembered leaving Legouis's "charming home," walking straight to American Express and booking passage on "a cattle boat to Corsica," where he proceeded "to paint donkeys for a month."

Ted was already honing his skill for exaggeration. In fact, that December, as snow fell lightly on Paris, he took a train to Italy, where Helen was touring with her mother. In Florence he prowled the Duomo and the Baptistery, whose bronze doors had been described by Michelangelo as "worthy of paradise"; Ted judged them "not too hot." He fumed over the bombastic speeches of Benito Mussolini, whose jutting jaw filled billboards and was "embroidered on silk sofa cushions." He and Helen stood in awe before Michelangelo's "David," and Ted wrote Whit Campbell that "Mrs. Palmer, whose retrograde tendencies you know, fainted dead away when she learned that Helen and I had seen [the statue] together." She would be happier, he speculated, if "all art, including Raphael's pre-puberty cherubs, wore jock straps."

At Christmas, with the pledge that they would not be apart for long, Helen returned to New Jersey to seek a teaching job. Alone, Ted "wasted the mornings," sleeping until noon, and then, with only a trace of a guilty conscience, wandered the streets of Florence in pursuit of terra-cottas, marbles, postal cards and "other manifestations of the glorious Renaissance." His evenings were enlivened with parties given by "wealthy widows in grand villas and attended by American girls and Italian men with titles, who click their heels and bow." One night, outraged as one of the guests, costumed as a toreador, "strutted . . . before the gilded mirrors," Ted donned horns, "gored" the man, and was "severely reprimanded for spilling a marquise."

At a pensione in Rome, Ted drew a series of biblical cartoons that included a particularly profane sketch he called "The Madonna of the Roller Skates." A vacationing artist from Santa Fe, New Mexico, glanced at it and informed Ted that he was in a stage of adolescent revolt that he "might someday overcome."

Not at all sure of this, Ted left Rome and sailed on February 13, 1927, from Palermo to New York. He posted a regretful last word to Campbell: "I who came to Europe to learn English literature am seriously considering buying a Hymarx crib for English I to cram up on as I travel homeward."

CHAPTER 5

Helen Palmer Geisel

1927–1928

When Helen Palmer returned from Europe in January of 1927, she made a single phone call from the dock in New York and accepted a job teaching at Miss Baird's, a private girls' school in Orange, New Jersey. A week later she was in the classroom as the new semester began. She was glad to be home; so much during her two years at Oxford had been marvelous, and so much baffling.

Nothing had gone the way she had planned. She did not yet have in hand her master's degree, since she had been in France when degrees were awarded, and she was crestfallen that her graduating record was marked Class III, which she considered no better than a C. "Quiet and intelligent," one tutor had noted. "Works quite well . . . steady . . . good enough brain. Cultured and able." But finally, "Missed classes . . . engaged to American." When she had received that final record in Brittany with her mother, she had written Christine M. Burrows, who presided over the Society of Oxford Home Students. "I should have done better, and I am sorry to disappoint [my tutors]. . . . It is as bad to disillusion others as to disillusion oneself."

Helen felt that New York had gone wild during her years in Europe and was hell-bent on making a mockery of Prohibition. Dandies lurched from speakeasy to speakeasy. Tall buildings with spires and recessed terraces were changing the skyline, turning streets into canyons that echoed with the clatter of newfangled drills called jackhammers. Broadway was host to an unprecedented number of shows; sixty theaters presented 268 productions in 1927, and grandiose cinema houses were opening along Seventh Avenue.

Born in New York, Helen had grown up in a large brownstone on Hancock Street in the quiet, prosperous Bedford-Stuyvesant neighborhood of Brooklyn. Her father, George Howard Palmer, an ophthalmologist, died of a heart attack in 1910, when she was eleven years old and her brother, Robert, thirteen. Her beloved grandfather, Adoniram Judson Palmer, who lived next door and was also a physician, died a year later. Both men held property, including a small yacht they owned jointly, but neither left a will. Helen's mother, Marie Estelle Clifton Palmer, known for her grit and sharp mind, moved with her children to a small apartment on Ocean Avenue while legal matters were untangled.

As a child Helen was spunky but never robust. Several years before her father's death, she was stricken with polio, but recovered completely except for what she called "a lopsided smile." In 1916 she entered Adelphi College on Long Island. Transferring to Wellesley College in her sophomore year, she graduated with honors in 1920. She had a flair for languages and for literature, but also showed a practical bent, receiving A's and B's in economics courses. Her dream of attending Oxford, where women had first been awarded degrees only four years earlier, was encouraged by her mother, who loved to travel and expected to go along.

Her two years at Oxford had widened Helen's teaching opportunities, but her fiancé sailed into Manhattan on a blustery Friday in late February 1927 with no degree, no job and no prospects. Helen met him for dinner, lavished encouraging words on him and saw him off as he left by train for Springfield and his childhood home on Fairfield Street.

Ted set up his drawing board and typewriter at his father's desk and began bombarding New York editors with humor pieces and cartoons, most of them inhabited by misshapen but strangely appealing animals and birds. He sent samples to Dartmouth classmates who were already established in New York, asking if they knew any editors who might look at his work. At Oxford Helen had nudged him away from academia toward a creative career, and now she was doing everything she could to keep his confidence high. She wrote often. Ted's animals, Helen told anyone who would listen, were "the sort you'd like to take home to meet the family."

In April, Ted brought his portfolio to Manhattan, checked in at the Hotel Woodstock near the frenetic new neon signs of Times Square, and began making the rounds. He had lunch at the Dartmouth Club with five classmates, and realized that all were ahead of him in launching their careers. On a midtown sidewalk he hailed another classmate, Brice P. Disque, who was disheartened and complained that while he and Ted—the "talented, intense, sympathetic" ones—were jobless, the "dubs" got the jobs. Ted talked breezily to the hangdog Disque about keeping his chin up and a stiff upper lip, but that night he wrote Whit Campbell at Harvard Law School: "I have tramped all over this bloody town and been tossed out of Boni and Liveright, Harcourt Brace, Paramount Pictures, Metro-Goldwyn, three advertising agencies, *Life*, *Judge*, and three public conveniences. My results are this: One picture 'taken' by *Life* to 'consider more carefully.' One order for half a dozen grocery store cartoons for *Al Brown's Journal*. One appointment with [Alexander] Laing, poet-author [and Dartmouth classmate] this afternoon. We are going to go in business together insofar as *The New Yorker* magazine is concerned. He has been accepted there and I am consciously cultivating him. Keyryst! What is this world coming to?"

Still, nothing sold and, after a week, he retreated to Springfield. At Dartmouth, Ted had admitted to days-long bouts of uncertainty, which he called "funks and depressions." But now he felt he could handle them better. "My policy," he wrote Whit, "is to laugh my god damned head off be the provocation ever so slight." He found such provocation in New York's playboy mayor, the wisecracking Jimmy Walker, whom he drew at the end of a long leash held by his estranged wife; in Bill Thompson, the mayor of Chicago; and in the philosopher Will Durant, who, for a New York tabloid, was covering the sensational trial "of the corset salesman who murdered [Al] Snyder." His sketches even spoofed "P. T. Barnum's White Elephant . . . and my mother-in-law-to-be."

While writing Whit that "what comes up *will* come up and will determine my future life," Ted told Helen that staff jobs seemed hard to find and he would probably be freelancing for a while. From Springfield he aimed another fusillade toward New York editors. Drawing on his European travels, he proposed to *Life*, a humor magazine founded in 1881, a series of cartoons and verses on "eminent Europeans . . . The Croupier, the Palace Guide, The Quack in the Baptistery in Pisa." For Laing at *The New Yorker*, a promising journal just two years old, he offered poems about the Hippocrass, and sent along sketches of a gangly two-legged animal with wings, horns and a smile. After hearing nothing, he wrote his classmate: "Not having received any checks, letters of praise or telegrams of disapproval, I take it that the Hippocrass has not been housebroken." In May he urged Laing: "Kindly write me your opinions post haste. I am sick and tired of being a Springfield Boy."

Ted saw New York as his mecca, the center of the publishing world and of wit, art and humor, the place where his life would happen. He read avidly about conversations at the Hotel Algonquin Round Table, and framed his own scathing witticisms in response. On June 13 New Yorkers in a frenzy of adulation honored Charles A. Lindbergh with a tickertape parade for his nonstop solo flight from New York to Paris. Lindbergh was just two years his senior; Ted read about the excitement and grimly went on with his drawing-board menagerie. Off motoring with her mother on a summer vacation, Helen wrote from the New Jersey coast. Springfield seemed awkwardly remote from Ted's overriding interests, both personal and professional.

Then, on a warm July morning, the mailman rang the bell at Fairfield Street and handed Ted a letter from *The Saturday Evening Post*. He ripped into it and found a check for twenty-five dollars for a cartoon of two American tourists riding on camels and blithely comparing their journey to that of Lawrence of Arabia. With a yelp, he raced upstairs to tell his parents that this sale augured a lifelong relationship with the *Post*. The cartoon appeared on July 16, 1927, bearing the signature "Seuss." *Post* editors indulged the young cartoonist in his pen name, but judging it inadequate identification, added in small type: "Drawn by Theodor Seuss

Geisel." Based on this sale and his unwavering belief in timing and luck, Ted packed his battered old European bags, bade his parents farewell and boarded a New York, New Haven & Hartford train for Manhattan. He took along one thousand dollars as his grubstake, the remainder of his share of the profits of *Jack-O-Lantern* during his tenure as editor.

Ted moved in with John C. Rose, who had worked on the *Jacko* art staff and was renting a one-room walk-up studio near Sheridan Square in Greenwich Village, the heartland for aspiring artists and writers. It was a hot and steamy August, and they propped the windows open in search of a breeze. By day the mellow sounds of the streets wafted in, radio music and a babble of conversations in English, Italian and Polish, but by night the noise level soared. Their studio was a floor above a raucous club, the Pirates Den.

"God, what a place!" Ted recalled. Noise was not the only problem. He and Rose bought canes to "play polo" with the rats in their room. "The last thing we used to do at night was to stand on chairs . . . and try to drive them out so they wouldn't nibble us while we slept."

Again stalking editors, Ted grew cannier. Rose knew someone who sold advertising for *Judge*, which called itself "the world's wittiest weekly"; Ted said, "I want to meet him." Founded in 1881 as a Republican rival of *Puck* in the field of political humor, *Judge* had become a magazine of social humor, outselling its equally venerable competitor *Life*; Harold Ross had been at *Judge* before leaving in 1925 to launch *The New Yorker*.

Soon Ted had an interview with Norman Anthony, the editor of *Judge* and a renowned talent hunter, who offered him a job as writer and artist and a desk at 18 East 48th Street. His salary was seventy-five dollars a week, and he was jubilant. This was the breakthrough about which he had fantasized since Dartmouth. To celebrate, Ted took Helen for a spaghetti dinner at a midtown speakeasy, and they agreed they had waited long enough. They would be married as soon as it could be arranged, in the Westfield, New Jersey, home of Helen's brother, Robert, and his wife, Gladys. Although some members of Helen's family believed that Ted and Helen had been secretly married in Europe, and that this ceremony would be a formality for the sake of Ted's parents, there is no record to support this. When asked about it years later, Ted merely smiled, his eyes twinkling.

The first wedding date was postponed when they realized that Ted's sister, Marnie, and her husband, Lloyd Dahmen, were expecting their first child at this time. Ted's mother did not intend to miss either event. His niece, Peggy, was born at Jamestown, New York, on November 1, and four weeks later, on the afternoon of November 29, about forty family members and friends gathered in the Palmer living room for a five o'clock ceremony. Ted, twenty-three and jittery, stood with his best man, Whit Campbell, in front of the parlor fireplace through an imponderable delay. In an upstairs bedroom, the emancipated bride, now twenty-nine, bristled in the final minutes at the idea of being given away in marriage by her brother or anyone else, so Helen's mother took her tightly by the arm, led her down the stairway and turned her over to Ted.

For the newlywed Geisels, the punch-and-cake reception that followed was an obeisance to conformity, one to be politely endured. Afterward, Ted's father hosted a small champagne supper in a neighborhood speakeasy, with the evening ending in laughter over a Lady Astor impersonation by Paul Jerman, a Casque and Gauntlet brother. The honeymoon at the luxurious Hotel Traymore in Atlantic City was paid with a *Judge* due bill, in barter for advertising.

In a sentimental letter of thanks to his best man, Ted wrote that Atlantic City wasn't the ideal honeymoon destination: "This will be a discordant note in my biography, a distinct departure from my usually highly inspired activities. But it is fun. We attend auctions and watch men with elks' teeth purchase $7,000 rugs that are alleged to have come from the Orient. We have not let any saltwater taffy pass the portals of our lips. But I have broken off three teeth trying to open pistachio nuts for my bride. . . . We are growing stout and catering to our predispositions toward laziness."

Ted was bursting with plans for *Judge*. He decided there were three major subjects for humor cartoons: Prohibition, booze and speakeasies. "As far as humor [in the 1920s] was concerned, sex had not been invented," he later wrote. "Dirty words were illegal as hell." Censorship abounded. Bookstore proprietors were in trouble with the law for selling the new D. H. Lawrence novel, *Lady Chatterley's Lover*. The ultimate underground title was Sylvia Beach's Paris edition of James Joyce's *Ulysses*, and book dealers were facing jail because of it.

Ted's debut in *Judge* on October 22, 1927, had depicted marital discord between two high-riding circus unicyclists. "And to think that today," she was saying, "I could have been the wife of a six-day bike racer—if I hadn't listened to your rot about Higher Art!" It was signed "Seuss," but within weeks Ted added "Dr." and used this pseudonym thereafter, explaining that the honorific compensated for the doctorate he never won at Oxford. ("I was saving the name of Geisel," he explained, "for the Great American Novel.") He expanded his pseudonym to Dr. Theophrastus Seuss for a recurring *Judge* feature called "Boids and Beasties, a Department for Indefatigable Naturalists." Ted had a backlog of these creatures from his Oxford notebook. He drew a teetering pileup of turtles with a spoof on novel ways to drink eggnog. He introduced an elephant as a heroic boozer in a satire called "Quaffing with the Pachyderms: Why I Prefer the West Side Speakeasies." That same month he launched a cartoon series, "being ye inside dope on King Arthur's Court translated from Merlin's Memoirs."

"From the sophisticated point of view," he wrote Whit, "I grant you they are terrible . . . but I am writing for *Judge*, and must dumb things up. Hence the assumed name [Seuss]." He asked for a frank opinion "because all I ever have handed me is a lot of applesauce from the numerous friends who drink my drinks and eat my provender." He said he was in it for the money and "playing it for all I am worth. At present I am the chief contributor in space . . . and the editor gets letters from every part of the country saying I should be hanged." He added, however, that a twelve-year-old boy "has written in asking for my autograph. If I can be of influence to one child in this great vice-ridden country, my life, I feel, has not been lived in vain." Among Ted's first fan letters at *Judge* was a curt note from a condemned murderer on death row in Huntsville, Texas, written on the eve of his electrocution. "If your stuff is the kind of thing they're publishing nowadays," the prisoner took the time to write, "I don't so much mind leaving." Ted was enraptured with the letter and kept it in his desk throughout his long life, always feigning fear of running into the felon, whose sentence had been commuted at the last minute.

Ted was in strong company at *Judge*. George Jean Nathan joined as dramatic editor, writing unflinchingly critical Broadway reviews. S. J. Perelman was a contemporary and friend who had already won a following for his humor in the Brown University magazine, *The Brown Jug*; Perelman was as prolific as Ted, both of them appearing almost every week with prose and cartoons. But *The New Yorker*, using one-line gags instead of the prevalent two-liners, was in hot pursuit of *Judge*'s advertisers and subscribers. Soon after Ted and Helen were married, salaries were cut from seventy-five dollars a week to fifty dollars; then for a time due bills from advertisers, like the one on which they had honeymooned, were distributed in lieu of paychecks. At least there was no income tax. "How can you pay income tax," Ted reasoned, "if all you get is a case of White Rock soda or 12 gross of Little Gem Nail Clippers? . . . I sort of loved trading my stuff for their stuff. I was happier in one way under the barter system than I've ever been since. When you get paid in money, it leads to accountants and lawyers."

Living from due bill to due bill, the newlyweds moved to their first home, a walk-up apartment at 319 West Eighteenth Street on the squalid Lower West Side in Chelsea, across from a livery stable. When horses died, attendants dragged the carcasses into the street to be picked up by city sanitation crews, and there were often delays of two or three malodorous days. It was a tense three-block walk to the subway and Ted carried a "loaded cane" with a spring blade. "Helen and I worked harder than ever to get out of that place," he recalled.

On March 2, 1928, Ted's twenty-fourth birthday, his parents came from Springfield for a party at the Chelsea apartment, and Helen's family came from New Jersey. But the well-rehearsed propriety of the evening was dashed by the unexpected arrival of Ted's Dartmouth friends Paul Jerman and Courtney Brown. They were "most horribly stewed . . . and gave [our families] the idea that all my time is spent in being ill with Jerman." On the next night Ted attended an alumni dinner of the Casque and Gauntlet, but found its "forced conviviality smacks a little too much of the Rotary. . . ." Jerman was in form again and redeemed the evening, Ted thought, when he repeated the Lady Astor impersonation he had done at Ted and Helen's wedding supper.

It was a giddy era in New York, a time of relentless optimism when even taxi drivers and housewives were speculating on the bull market and buying stocks on margin. The Broadway season was rich, and despite their lean budget the Geisels attended as many as three or four shows a month. To get the cheapest tickets, they joined the queue at Gray's drugstore near Times Square, where Joe Leblang sold cut-rate tickets and prices fell as curtain time neared. "We'd grab our 65-cent tickets," Ted recalled, "and run across Times Square and find our seats in the dark, squeezing past all those people in top hats and formal dresses and stepping on their patent leather shoes and collapsing into our own seats, front and center, just as the curtain rose."

Ted wrote Whit Campbell that he was still eking out an existence from *Judge*. "Perhaps it is bad for me to eke it out so easily. For it keeps me abed late of mornings, and it allows me to cavort in the evening." The Geisels had discovered a loft speakeasy called the Dizzy Club, and went there often with Al Perkins, a Dartmouth classmate whom Ted called "the funniest fellow I have ever met." Perkins devised a street pantomime based on the popular master-criminal character Fu Manchu. Along Fifth Avenue or in speak-easies, he would imagine himself poisoned, stabbed or throttled by the wily Oriental and go into a mimed frenzy. "Only Perkins could play a game like this," Ted said, "and not be murdered." He compared the Dizzy Club to a Klondike saloon. "They put you out at six [A.M.]. . . . One night I gravely endangered my life by locking a waiter into the ice chest. He had gone there after two dill pickles and a schooner of beer. Some ten minutes later I released the poor chap, thinking he would thank me for my kind-ness . . . he did not . . ."

But there were flickering signs of a career. Theodore Roose-velt, Jr., whose father had failed to produce a Boy Scout award for Ted in Springfield, wrote *Judge* to request an original Dr. Seuss drawing. The White Rock soda-water bottlers sent along forty-eight bottles of soda after he used their name in a cartoon, and Flit insecticide, which he mentioned in another cartoon, was dickering for a twelve-drawing advertising campaign, "and 100 berries the picture, God pray it go through."

In the days before air conditioning nearly every household faced the summer with bug-spray guns. The cartoon that attracted mighty Standard Oil of New Jersey, makers of Flit, showed a knight in armor, sprawled in his bed as a snarling dragon loomed over him. "Darn it all," the knight says, "another Dragon. And just after I'd sprayed the whole castle with Flit!" Ted attributed to luck the contractual bonanza that followed. Grace (Mrs. Lincoln) Cleaves, the wife of an H. K. McCann advertising executive who handled the Flit account, saw his cartoon at a hairdresser's and urged her husband to call the artist and sign him up.

"It wasn't even her regular hairdresser," Ted said. "He was booked that day, so she went someplace else. Her regular hairdresser was much ritzier and would never have had a copy of *Judge* in his salon."

Ted had flipped a coin between Flit and its rival bug-spray Fly-Tox before writing his caption. The cartoon led to a seventeen-year Dr. Seuss advertising campaign with the standing four-word cry for help: "Quick, Henry, the Flit!" In one panel a convict is besieged by mosquitoes in the midst of a prison break; in another a seance is interrupted by a genie emerging amid a swarm of bugs. The Flit phrase entered the American vernacular. A song was written around it, and Ted's cartoons spread from the pages of *Judge* and *Life* to newspapers, subway cards and billboards. Comedians Fred Allen and Jack Benny used the tag line over the radio networks for dependable boffs, and across America the folksy mention of a bug spray evoked laughter. Flit sales increased wildly. No advertising campaign remotely like it had succeeded before on such a grand scale. The series found its way into histories of advertising, and was compared with the Burma Shave series of ubiquitous roadside rhymes. The nearest thing to criticism was an agency warning that sometimes the bugs Ted drew were too lovable to kill.

Soon Ted was earning twelve thousand dollars a year from Flit, more income than most of his Dartmouth classmates who had entered family law firms or brokerage houses. When commencement and reunion time came on Hanover plain in the spring of 1928, he took Helen to Dartmouth to meet classmates and favorite professors. His celebrity, though not always understood, had been noted.

CHAPTER 6

New York

1928–1935

Because the Flit advertising campaign was geared to the summer bug season, Ted finished his work by the spring and took off with Helen on elaborate travels. In 1928 they toured Greece, posing at the Parthenon for a guide's snapshot: Ted, handsome and intent in Panama hat and white suit; Helen, smiling below a flapper's cloche. Sailing back to New York, they talked seriously about moving to a better neighborhood. Helen was administering her father's trust, and her share of the income from real estate holdings in Brooklyn gave the couple an added sense of security.

By September they managed to leave Chelsea, its stables and dead horses, and join the trendy exodus to large apartment houses uptown that were replacing old row houses. Their new home was on the fourteenth floor of 393 West End Avenue, across from the ornate limestone façade and iron gates of the Apthorp courtyard apartments, a West Side landmark that had been built with Astor family funding in 1908. This uptown migration even found its way nine years later into the Rodgers and Hart musical *Babes in Arms* and the song "Way Out West."

> Git along, little taxi, you can keep the change
> I'm ridin' home to my kitchen range,
> Way out west on West End Avenue. . . .

Ted felt flush. While shaving one morning, he pondered the swank party of the night before and composed what he called his first poem:

> Mrs. Van Bleck
> Of the Newport Van Blecks
> Is so goddam rich
> She has gold-plated sex
> Whereas Miggles and Mitzi
> And Bitzie and Sue
> Have the commonplace thing
> And it just has to do.

Ted worked into the night in his spacious new studio, his confidence soaring with recognition and success. He gave up trying to decide whether to be a writer or cartoonist and focused on ways to be both. He fired off cartoons and parodies to *Life* and *Liberty*, which paid an impressive three hundred dollars a page. He also collaborated with other humorists, such as Corey Ford, illustrating his popular satires in *Vanity Fair*.

To mark their first wedding anniversary, the Geisels boarded a train to Southern California, where they had hoped to go on their honeymoon until limited finances forced a delay. John Rose, who had been Ted's roommate in Greenwich Village, had invited them to his home in the coastal town of La Jolla. As the northernmost suburb of the city of San Diego, La Jolla nestled between sea and hills and maintained its village mood. It was a casual place, dotted by Spanish-style oceanfront estates and smaller summer cottages of "wealthy old people." The mild climate and crinkled coves reminded the Geisels of the Riviera, as did the town's new hotel, La Valencia. They were stunned by the contrasts in pace and style with their lives in New York. Ted began to sketch the exotic flora: luminous purple ice plant and orange nasturtiums strewn along the sea cliffs, twisted junipers, eucalyptus trees with artfully peeling bark, and agaves called century plants, which shot up like twenty-foot candles. Even in November there were bathers on the beaches. Walking along the shore at sunset, they agreed they must find a way to have a small home in La Jolla while they were young enough to enjoy it.

Returning to New York with prudent resolves, the Geisels cut out all-night partying and took up contract bridge, a new card game that was the rage, playing regularly with Helen's brother, Robert, and his wife, Gladys. Never wasting an idea, Ted satirized the game in *Judge*, tracing its origins to Aethelstan and Beowulf and cashing in on his brief brush with Old English at Oxford. According to Dr. Seuss, bridge had been played in ancient times with three players, not four, and with croquet mallets instead of cards.

None of the early Seuss wordplay delighted readers more than the fable in *Judge* entitled "The Tough Coughs as he Ploughs the Dough." It was a madcap series of anecdotes exploiting the multiple pronunciations of "ough" words:

> It was forty-five years ago, when I first came to America as a young Roumanian student of divinity, that I first met the evils of the "ough" words. Strolling one day in the country with my fellow students, I saw a tough, coughing as he ploughed a field which (being quite nearsighted) I mistook for pie dough.
>
> Assuming that all "ough" words were pronounced the same, I casually remarked, "The tuff cuffs as he pluffs the duff!"
>
> "Sacrilege!" shrieked my devout companions. "He is cursing in Roumanian! . . ."

Ted's fascination with sounds and invented words erupted in features like "The Idioms of Iceland at a Glance." Glnbokk, Dr. Seuss explained, was an old-fashioned tusking bee. Mnpf was one who went visiting on St. Swithin's Day, and ewth was a sweatshop snowball factory. A hoooah was a quintuple coincidence. In a helpful-hint series, the Seuss Travel Bureau offered alternatives to ocean passage across the Atlantic: "At ridiculously small charge we have recently sent a gentleman to France in his own dumbwaiter."

The cover of the March 23, 1929, issue of *Judge* was inhabited by ancestors of some of the most beloved Dr. Seuss animals. A cheerful elephant, beginning to look like Horton, practiced broad jumps over a dewy-eyed hippopotamus. A turtle, much like Yertle, perched in a treetop. At about the same time Ted's work was on the cover of *Life*. Any magazine cover gave an artist a boost, and this double triumph brought him a measure of fame.

On October 28 Ted was in his studio smoking his first cigarette of the day and drifting into his world of fantasy when stunning news came over his radio from Wall Street. The stock market was collapsing, taking with it billions of dollars. It was Black Friday; panic followed, and so did the Depression, with its widespread fear, hunger and unemployment. Across America there were lost savings, investments and homes. Helen's brother, a securities analyst, lost his job. Yet Helen and Ted, like much of the literary community, were insulated from the brunt of the blow. Those with the ability to entertain and distract—movie stars, comedians, cartoonists and newspaper columnists—remained in demand.

From their West End Avenue apartment the Geisels had a glimpse of the downtown skyline and the steel girders rising for the Empire State Building, which would be the world's tallest building. The new Waldorf-Astoria Hotel was under construction on Park Avenue, and New Yorkers saw both skyscrapers as symbols of hope. But as winter set in, and breadlines and soup kitchens proliferated, the joblessness and despair shook Ted. He had always believed in fair play and support for the underdog, and he brooded because there was nothing he could do about the tragedy of "all these people who have nowhere to go." For the first time he was seriously thinking about politics and politicians. The witty Mayor Jimmy Walker no longer seemed the man to run New York and, like others, Ted felt something had to be done about Washington. He and Helen were Democrats, a fact that was not discussed in either Palmer or Geisel family circles, both being vehemently Republican.

In Springfield, Ted's father sought the nomination for mayor on the Republican ticket but lost, and went back to work as superintendent of parks, including his beloved zoo. Ted's indomitable mother, Nettie, accompanied his sister to Reno for a divorce, and helped her move back to Fairfield Street with her daughter, Peggy, the first grandchild. Ted and Helen went to Springfield for the Christmas holidays of 1930, and were so charmed by their three-year-old niece that Ted inaugurated a holiday tradition. On Christmas Eve a rattling sound would begin in the attic, followed by stomping and snorting. In the parlor below, Peggy heard bells jingling, the hooves of reindeer and the shouts of Santa crying "Whoa!" She treasured the magic of this moment, and, even after she came to understand her uncle Ted's role, enjoyed it for several more years before telling him.

As a grandmother, Nettie Geisel rediscovered her magical play-fulness, a warmth that crossed the generational barrier and, Ted reminded her, had cast a glow over his childhood. She sang Peggy to sleep with the old pie chant she had begun at her father's bakery, the one that had lulled Ted on so many nights. But over the holidays Ted and Helen grew concerned about his mother's health. She seemed distracted and one night, just after dinner, she fell asleep in the midst of a bridge game. Ted believed she was masking apprehension with her unremitting sense of humor and her recent acceptance of the Christian Science faith. Nettie rejected pleas to see a doctor and resisted medical diagnosis until she was too weak to protest. In March 1931 Ted and Helen met his father at Peter Bent Brigham Hospital in Boston, where he had driven Nettie. The pioneering neurosurgeon Harvey Cushing found an inopera-ble brain tumor and closed the incision. Henrietta Seuss Geisel died on March 8 at the age of fifty-two. In Springfield, Ted, who had just turned twenty-seven, left Oak Grove cemetery in tears.

Ted's first break into books came as a "total surprise" that year when an editor at Viking Press telephoned, offering him a contract to illustrate a collection of children's sayings called *Boners*. It was a reprint of a British best-seller compiled from classrooms and examination papers by Alexander Abingdon and published there as *Schoolboy Howlers*. Brightened by Ted's pen-and-ink drawings, *Boners* sold famously in America at one dollar a copy, sweeping through four printings in two months to lead *The New York Times* nonfiction best-seller list. Before the year ended there was a sequel, *More Boners*. In *American News*, a reviewer wrote that "off-hand . . . we should have said this would be a flop. But the inimitable illustrations of the renowned Dr. Seuss, of *Judge*, *Life* and Flit fame, are not unlikely to put this over. They are simply swell." It was Ted's first review. The same publication later ran a letter to the editor that Ted clipped and tacked to his corkboard. "Seuss puts more naive satisfaction into the face of a cat, more passion into the face of a Cleopatra, more anticipation into the face of a Mark Antony, than many other cartoonists could do if brought together in the same speakeasy."

Encouraged by such praise, Ted undertook to write and illustrate an alphabet book, but his approach was less than practical. He recalled it as "an experiment . . . an ABC book of very strange animals. I had just discovered colored inks. . . . It had about seventeen different blues in it and three kinds of red. It would have cost about $150 a copy." He offered it to Bobbs Merrill, Viking Press, Simon and Schuster and other publishers before abandoning it.

Ted was worn down after months of dealing with lawyers following his mother's death, and in the late summer of 1931 the Geisels sailed to Europe on the Hamburg-Amerika line's motorship *St. Louis*, traveling for seven weeks in Yugoslavia "to clear the air and get new ideas."

Ted and Helen had moved to a larger apartment at 17 East Ninety-sixth Street, which they considered more convenient to publishing offices and friends, and they began to entertain at small dinner parties. Among their favorite guests was the notorious prankster Hugh Troy, a six-foot-five, barrel-chested artist who had graduated from Cornell. Troy and Ted formed a warm but competitive friendship that Hugh described as "a nutty feud" and Ted called "the one-upsmanship challenge of my lifetime." Troy had become a New York legend by ordering a park bench built to match those in Central Park, placing it there, and then hauling it away as police appeared. Brought before a judge, he produced his bill of sale and walked out of the precinct station carrying the bench that was to have been evidence against him.

On his first visit to the Geisel apartment, Troy arrived carrying a carpetbag. "I brought my maternal grandmother!" he said, dumping a bag of bones on the floor. Ted leaned over, examined the bones, picked up the smallest one and popped it in his mouth. "Delicious," he said, and from that moment mischief pervaded their relationship. One unborn scheme was to launch a private detective agency named Surely, Goodness, and Mercy. Its slogan was to be biblical: "Will follow you all the days of your life." The two men shared a love of language and a dislike of pomposity. With the cartoonist Abner Dean, Ted helped Troy work off his overdue apartment rent by slathering murals on the walls of his landlord's basement speakeasy, the Pilots' Club. But each man parodied the style of another—Dean by Seuss, Seuss by Troy, Troy by Dean—and the wild and wanton results brought such attention that the club's popularity soared and Troy's chits were torn up.

Through Troy, Ted and Helen met members of the wealthy Frank A. Vanderlip family and were soon included in parties at their town house at 115 East Fifty-fourth Street and their fifty-acre estate, Beechwood, in the Hudson Valley at Scarborough. As president of National City Bank, Vanderlip was one of New York's most powerful men. Although the Geisels were contemporaries of the six Vanderlip children and especially close to Kelvin and Virginia (known as Zinny), it was their mother who became the victim on a night when Troy and Ted came to dinner. The pranksters slipped into the kitchen and hid a large, dime-store pearl in an oyster. It was served to the head of a Wall Street firm, and after the pearl was discovered, there was serious discussion as to whether the finder or the hostess owned it. They politely pushed the pearl back and forth until Helen, increasingly embarrassed, intervened to explain that it was a joke. Years later Ted read an interview with John Cheever, "who told the story as if he had done it. He could have been there that night . . . he was a good friend of Zinny."

In the 1932 elections Helen and Ted voted for Franklin Delano Roosevelt, convinced that his leadership could undo the Depression, which they blamed on Herbert Hoover. During a visit to Springfield Ted had tried to persuade his Republican father to support Roosevelt, but their conversation had become so quickly explosive that he took an oath never again to undertake a political conversion. While disagreeing on Roosevelt and the New Deal, father and son were united in support of the repeal of Prohibition, which followed in 1933, soon bringing New York's speakeasy era to an end.

Ted was busy with another Standard Oil advertising campaign, this time for Essolube 5-Star motor oil. His commissions from Standard Oil supported the Geisels through the Depression. "It wasn't the greatest pay," he said, "but it covered my overhead so I could experiment with my drawings. . . ." A new Seuss menagerie appeared on signboards along America's highways, creatures that sat astride the hoods of automobiles, smirking rascals whose devilish destruction could be fended off with Essolube. Ted's headlines left no doubt that Essolube would FOIL THE KARBO-NOCKUS! or FOIL THE MOTO-RASPUS!

Prospering, the Geisels moved that fall to a spacious fourteenth-floor apartment at 1160 Park Avenue, on the northwest corner of Park and Ninety-second Street. "We moved," Ted said, "when we discovered we could live just as cheaply on Park Avenue." It pleased Ted to live on that grand boulevard because it sent a message to stuffy classmates and Oxford dons who had said he would never make a living with his doodlings. For the immigrant Geisel family of Springfield, it was a symbol of making it.

One Saturday morning an unwieldy crate arrived as a house-warming gift from Ted's father. Ted opened it warily and discovered a heavy stone slab; within it was embedded a dinosaur footprint eleven inches wide and sixteen inches long. The accompanying provenance placed its discovery at an excavation near Holyoke, Massachusetts, and the footprint had been adjudged by Yale anthropologists to be about one hundred fifty million years old. It bore a much more contemporary message: Ted's father had idolized Cy Aschenbach, whose heroics in Dartmouth football had helped to beat Harvard. Yet by the time they met, Ted recalled, "Cy had forgotten he had ever been a roughneck. He had become a collector of antiques. Instead of telling my father how he had beat Harvard, he took him around his Manhattan apartment and told him how old every piece was." Ted's father had promised, "I'm sending you an antique that will set that guy up forever." Ted and Helen shoved the stone under their bed, but it protruded and they stubbed their toes. Ted proposed hanging it on the building's exterior wall beneath his studio window and dangling guests outside to kiss it "like an ancient Blarney Stone," but Helen vetoed the idea. Yet Ted always kept it close, moving it with him wherever he lived for the rest of his life.

Barbara Palmer, Helen's niece from New Jersey, recalled the Park Avenue apartment vividly from childhood visits. "The entrance was on Ninety-second Street. There were only two apartments to each floor. You stepped into a foyer with a carpet in Helen's favorite French blue. They had two chairs from their Mexico travels, cockfight chairs, I think. . . . There was a large living room, and the dining room had a mural painted on the wall by one of their friends. There were two bedrooms, one of which Ted used as a studio. His desk had lots of charcoal, pencils and paint brushes which I was asked not to touch."

Their newfound elegance left the Geisels even more exposed to the practical jokes of Hugh Troy. Ted had initiated the latest round when Troy was away from New York one bitterly cold week in February. He bribed his way into Troy's apartment, carrying dozens of packages of Jell-O, a sack of sliced fruit and half a dozen goldfish. After filling Troy's bathtub, he threw open the window and built a tub-sized aspic of fish and fruit. Returning to this ghastly sight on a snowy night, Hugh plotted revenge. He learned that Helen and Ted had not met their fourteenth-floor neighbors, and, thereafter, each time he called on the Geisels he brought along some tasteless bit of decor and stealthily established it in the shared foyer. First it was a badly stained table teetering on uneven legs. Soon a ceramic lamp stood on it in the form of a belly dancer, and next a dime-store mirror appeared above it. It was not until a Niagara Falls pennant went up that the Geisels complained to the building superintendent about their neighbors' appalling taste.

"That's funny," the superintendent said. "They've already gone to the owner about you."

The apartment, its foyer by then cleared of kitsch, was the scene of a particularly festive party honoring the Broadway actress Peggy Conklin following her opening in January 1935 in Robert Sherwood's *The Petrified Forest* with Humphrey Bogart and Leslie Howard. As usual, the crowd ended up in Ted's studio. "That night was so lively," the actress recalled. "Hugh Troy and John Rose were there, and Helen and Ted were full of surprises. We stayed up until the *Times'* review came." Ted refilled glasses and read it aloud: " 'Miss Conklin gives her most perceptive performance to date as the gas station dryad.' "

Ted played the role of a riotously successful alumnus when a Dartmouth student journalist, Bob Warren, visited the apartment and reported in *The Dartmouth* that Ted answered the door at three in the afternoon with tousled hair, in his pajamas and bathrobe, looking as if he had just gotten out of bed. "He was tall, rather good-looking and had a noticeable air of congeniality about him. . . . There were models of some of the animals he has created lying around."

"Let's see," Ted had said. "You want an interview, a sort of life story, as it were."

The student nodded.

"Truth or fiction?"

Affecting an urbane and jaded pose, Ted held forth on his life and travels since Oxford. It is the first lengthy interview of Ted Geisel on record, and he approached it as though it were a blank canvas to be painted. From this time on, there was no way to guess what answer he might concoct to a reporter's question. His current travels, he explained that afternoon, were for animal research: "I just came back from Peru . . . [where I] looked into the llama situation. . . . They can spit at you and aim every shot they make. . . . The biggest disappointment I ever had . . . was when I went to Dalmatia to study the Dalmatian dog situation. I got there and found that all the Dalmatian dogs were in England. . . . I go all over looking for peculiar animals [and] I've discovered that God has turned out more ridiculous creatures than I have."

There was even a passing explanation for wearing pajamas in midafternoon: "I get to bed around three in the morning and about ten someone calls and says, 'We need that stuff right away. Can you hurry it up?' It's a bad life. . . . Don't even have time to get dressed."

Ted had turned thirty. As filtered through the Dartmouth reporter, his words suggest the world of F. Scott Fitzgerald; here was a Dartmouth man only a decade the reporter's senior who had lived the roaring twenties.

Whenever the Geisels traveled, Ted carried a sketch pad and, as it filled, resorted to hotel stationery. Returning from Turkey in 1934 to a steamy New York, they left impetuously for the second time in two years for Peru. It had become an exotic destination following Hiram Bingham's discovery of the ancient Incan stronghold of Machu Picchu, and on their first visit they had explored as far as Cuzco, above eleven thousand feet in the Andes, joining an archaeological dig. From then on Ted called himself an "amateur mummy digger," and listed it under "Hobbies" on his Dartmouth alumni form.

When they arrived at the harbor of Callao in 1934, a reporter from Lima's English-language newspaper expressed amazement that the Geisels had made the long journey to Peru two years in a row. Ted's imagination took over; on their first visit, he explained, he had suffered from altitude sickness at Cuzco, and since doctors had failed to find a way to control the "headaches and insomnia of anoxemia," he had undertaken his own research. Lining the walls of his Park Avenue studio with lead, he invented a device to pump air slowly out of the room until by the end of the winter he was "living at an altitude of 19,000 feet" and "enjoying superb health." His return to Peru was a field test of his research.

On the next day the front-page headline in Lima read YANK SOLVES MYSTERY OF THE ANDES. "Then my problem," Ted recalled, "was whether I should confess that it was a gag or go along with it. Everyone was curious, and I decided to go along. We got invitations to dinner at seven different embassies. One ambassador's wife almost did the dance of the seven veils to get the secret out of me. I didn't realize the whole economy of Peru was in the balance that year [and there was] trouble getting people to work in the mines because of altitude sickness."

At parties in Peru, Ted apparently left a blithe trail of invitations. Soon after the Geisels' return, Curtis Abel, a fellow victim of the Easter-gin-party purge at Dartmouth, came to dinner and found their apartment teeming with "polo players from Peru." Ted even developed a Sunday comic strip with an Andean theme. The Hearst newspapers signed him on in 1935 to draw "Hejji By Dr. Seuss."

It was set beyond awesome peaks in the Land of Baako, "shut off from our world by mountains so high that most birds cannot fly them, and the Baakinese eagle must taxi the more breathless creatures about on his back."

But after three weeks Ted's editor received a telegram from William Randolph Hearst ordering him to fire the last three people he had hired. "It was just as well," Ted said. "I didn't know where the story was going next."

....

CHAPTER 7

Mulberry Street

1936–1938

After nine years of marriage, Ted and Helen counted thirty nations to which they had traveled in Europe, the Middle East and Latin America, and they kept spinning the globe for more. Such trips were possible because they were free of the usual responsibilities of young married couples: they had no children, no pets, no ailing relatives who needed their care, and neither kept routine office hours. There was enough money, and long journeys were easy to rationalize because Ted felt they sparked his creativity.

In the summer of 1936 Ted and Helen boarded the new Swedish American luxury liner, the M.S. *Kungsholm*, to sail for Europe. The cloud of apprehension that had begun to hang over the Continent was apparent even before the *Kungsholm* cleared New York Harbor. Ted saw it in the eyes of homebound Europeans, and heard it over the dinner table. But growing Nazi power and rumors of war did not stop the gallivanting Geisels. At café tables in the Bavarian Alps they read about the Olympic Summer Games in Berlin, where Adolf Hitler accepted salutes from the crowds and the American track star Jesse Owens won four gold medals. From Interlaken at the base of the Swiss Jungfrau they ascended narrow, steep roads on toylike red postal buses that flirted with danger. Along trails white with edelweiss, Ted sketched sawtooth peaks and unlikely horned creatures hanging precariously from ledges.

He studied cuckoo clocks, and when he tried to learn yodeling, Helen persuaded him to restrict his practice to his shower.

They drifted through those holiday weeks, haunted by a sense of unreality. By the time they boarded the *Kungsholm* for their return Ted was in a somber mood. Hitler was threatening his ancestral homeland and all of Europe, and another war seemed likely. Ted was thirty-two years old, he reminded himself on the train to Bremerhaven, and it was time he got serious. Serious about work, Helen agreed, but not about serious themes; he had enjoyed illustrating someone else's words in *Boners*, so maybe it was time to try writing his own children's tale.

But once out into the North Atlantic, there was no thought of work. The sea frothed and a summer storm hammered the ship with gale-force winds. It was too rough to go out on deck and Helen took refuge in their cabin. Ted, finding it impossible to settle, strode from one to another of the *Kungsholm* bars, gripping the ship's rails. In an upper-deck lounge he ordered another vodka on the rocks, took two sheets of *Kungsholm* stationery and began scribbling a rambling plot:

> A stupid horse and wagon
> Horse and chariot
> Chariot pulled by flying cat
> Flying cat pulling Viking ship
> Viking ship sailing up a volcano
> Volcano blowing hearts, diamonds and clubs
>
> I saw a giant eight miles tall
> Who took the cards, 52 in all
> And played a game of solitaire . . .

As the ship plowed the sea for eight days, the chugging rhythm of its engines reverberated in Ted's head: *Da-da-DA-da-da-DUM-DUM, da-DA-da-da-DUM.*

To keep his mind off the choppy waters and the shuddering of the ship he began reciting words to the rhythm. " 'Twas the Night Before Christmas" fit well enough, but then he heard himself saying, "And that is a story that no one can beat, and to think that I saw it on Mulberry Street."

Days after the *Kungsholm* docked, the rhythm still rattled in his head, driving him "nuts." At Helen's urging, and as what he hoped would be therapy, he set out to develop a story around the rhythm, using the shipboard notes that began with "a stupid horse and wagon."

The adventures of *Mulberry Street* did not flow easily from the quirky brain of Dr. Seuss. Repeatedly he questioned every word of every verse, rewriting tediously, draft after draft. Although he lived for wit, his flights of fancy were subject to strict review. He insisted on momentum in his work and demanded excitement. Ted wanted to write a book whose young readers would "turn page after page" until there were no more. He drew illustrations that expanded in size and became more embellished as his young hero's imagination soared, describing the sights along Mulberry Street.

Ted printed the words in pencil on yellow sheets and asked Helen to read and discuss each page. It was six months before he was satisfied, and he began making the rounds in Manhattan, showing the book to publishers under the title *A Story That No One Can Beat*. He hit a wall of rejection. His humorous essays and cartoons found ready markets, but this reputation did not influence book editors. Their rebuffs were even more painful than those after his return from Oxford when he had stormed magazine offices with drawings. After being turned down a dozen times, Ted became gloomy, convinced that his style could never be adapted to books.

Twenty-seven publishing houses rejected *A Story That No One Can Beat* during the winter of 1936–37. The most frequent explanation was that it was "too different" from other children's books. Composition in verse was not in vogue, editors said, and fantasy wasn't salable. Ted argued that it wasn't fantasy, since Mulberry Street was real and its parade derived from his recollections of Springfield street life. But the editors' complaint that enraged him was that "no moral or message" could be found in his book, nothing aimed at "transforming children into good citizens." He roared across his studio at Helen: "What's wrong with kids having fun reading without being preached at?"

On the blustery day he learned of his twenty-seventh rejection, Ted fought back frustration and anger and decided to return to his apartment, stage a ceremonial burning of the now tattered manuscript, and get back to cartooning for adults. As he walked grimly along Madison Avenue, he was hailed by Mike McClintock, who had been a year behind him at Dartmouth.

"What's that under your arm?" McClintock asked.

"That's a book that no one will publish. I'm lugging it home to burn."

McClintock smiled. Three hours earlier he had become juvenile editor of Vanguard Press. "We're standing outside my new office," he said. "Come on up and let's look at it."

Half an hour later McClintock took Ted in to meet James Henle, president of Vanguard Press, and Evelyn Shrifte, an editor who later succeeded him. Henle agreed to publish the book. "But," he said, "you've got to give me a snappier title."

That morning's encounter did much to consolidate Ted's life-long fealty to luck. The *Judge* magazine cartoon that led to the lucrative Flit alliance had been discovered by the right advertising man's wife as she waited at the wrong hairdresser's salon. This time, Ted said later, "if I had been going down the other side of Madison Avenue, I'd be in the dry-cleaning business today."

No circumstances could have been luckier for him than the juxtaposition at Vanguard of a Dartmouth classmate to whisk him in off the street and a publisher to sign him up. Henle was building his reputation as a contrarian among book publishers by taking on new writers whom more prominent publishers had rejected. He had signed up the novelist James T. Farrell, who focused on proletarian themes, and published the first of his *Studs Lonigan* trilogy after the work had been turned down by more than a dozen houses. "Henle always let the author do what he wanted to do, however unusual it might seem," Evelyn Shrifte recalled. "He resisted the urge to give a lot of advice."

But one bit of advice was given and accepted. Booksellers concurred with Henle about Ted's title, so the author offered one that many considered unlikelier still: *And to Think that I Saw It on Mulberry Street*. As his grateful homage to luck, Ted gave the name of McClintock's son Marco to the storyteller of *Mulberry Street*, and dedicated this first book to McClintock's wife, Helene.

Shrifte, who loved *Mulberry Street* from the day she saw it, allowed Ted to work closely with her as she supervised production of the book. As he fussed obsessively over inks and color samples her patience with this first-time author proved astonishing. "This was before we used offset lithography," she said. "We printed by old four-color letter-press, and there was a great to-do with Ted about color samples. He knew what he wanted." She swung from initial alarm at his challenges to enchantment. In August Ted wrote to Evelyn, setting down his last-chance pleas before the book went to press. Then, exhausted, he and Helen boarded a train for Maine and a vacation at the Mountain Ash Inn near Blue Hill Bay. A telegram from Shrifte awaited him: "Thanks for most amusing letter everything okay don't worry."

In an act of faith, Vanguard printed fifteen thousand copies of the book, and Henle took a full-page advertisement in *Publishers Weekly* to herald "the good Dr. Seuss." It reproduced Ted's spirited drawing of a reindeer pulling a two-wheel cart along Mulberry Street, and urged. "Booksellers, hitch on! This is the start of a parade that will take you places!" Henle took great pleasure in guaranteeing the work of yet another unknown author who had been rejected by Henle's competitors. In the *Publishers Weekly Fall Children's Number*, Vanguard was reported as "considerably worked up" about the book, but the magazine did not review it.

When *Mulberry Street* appeared in September 1937, Springfield citizens queued outside Johnson's Book Store on Court Square to learn if it was an exposé of the residents of Mulberry Street. *The Springfield Union* reported their relief that it was a fantasy, and one citizen ventured that the book might make their street famous.

Ted considered his first book a breakthrough that might shape his career, and yet he remained edgy. The trade in children's books was modest in size, and this book, with its elaborate color artwork, cost a dollar, still a formidable price as the Depression waned. But to Ted's glee, good reviews came promptly. The shortest of them, just one sentence long, had a profound impact on the launching of Dr. Seuss as a successful children's author. It appeared as the final paragraph in Clifton Fadiman's book column in *The New Yorker* on November 6. Even for the distinguished Fadiman it was uncommonly prescient, anticipating the dual levels on which Dr. Seuss books came to captivate both parents and children. In the final year of his life, Theodor Seuss Geisel could still recite it word for word: "They say it's for children, but better get a copy for yourself and marvel at the good Dr. Seuss' impossible pictures and the moral tale of the little boy who exaggerated not wisely but too well."

A week later *The New York Times* chimed in: "Highly original and entertaining, Dr. Seuss' picture book partakes of the better qualities of those peculiarly American institutions, the funny papers and the tall tale. It is a masterly interpretation of the mind of a child in the act of creating one of those stories with which children often amuse themselves and bolster up their self-respect."

An indefatigable champion of the book from the start was Anne Carroll Moore, the legendary guardian of children's books at the New York Public Library from 1906 to 1941. She invited Ted to speak at the library and he agreed. At the appointed hour he got as far as the crouching stone lions at the entrance but was overwhelmed with stage fright and could not go inside. Nevertheless, she went on the record in the *Atlantic Monthly* with a review that must have swayed many librarians to risk adding this unconventional book to their shelves: "So completely spontaneous that the American child can take it to his heart on sight. . . . As original in conception, as spontaneous in the rendering as it is true to the imagination of a small boy."

The unqualified enthusiasm of these first recognitions of the world of Dr. Seuss was remarkable because in the constrained circle of children's literature Ted was a rowdy and, at first glance, an undisciplined revolutionary. He was among the first to link drawings as equal partners with text, risking comparisons to comic pages. He devoted his skills to drawing illustrations that carried the narrative so that children not yet able to read could follow the story. Beatrix Potter, the author of *Peter Rabbit*, received a copy of *Mulberry Street* that Christmas in England. Then seventy-two, she wrote a friend: "What an amusing picture book." And later, "I think it the cleverest book I have met with for many years. The swing and merriment of the pictures and the natural truthful simplicity of the untruthfulness . . . Too many story books for children are condescending, self-conscious inventions—and then some trivial oversight, some small incorrect detail gives the whole show away."

With the reviews in, Henle and Shrifte and their new juvenile editor, McClintock, congratulated one another. But they had warned Ted he would not get rich on children's books, and in that era they were right. It was about two years before *Mulberry Street* went into a second printing of 6,000 more copies. By 1943, six years after its publication, only 31,600 copies had been printed, and the author's royalties did not exceed $3,500.

When Ted's sister, Marnie, came down from Springfield that autumn for a visit, she reveled in her younger brother's acclaim as an author, but was startled by the Seussian creatures in the Park Avenue apartment: red turtles, purple elephants and green camels with bizarre beaks and horns. Ted had constructed a menagerie for mail-order sale that he called "The Seuss System of Unorthodox Taxidermy," and Marnie later told *The Springfield Union* that his animals all looked "like people you know . . . I am apt to have a nightmare whenever I visit them." With more enthusiasm, she talked of how Helen had been "a great help to him in his work." She was reassured about her brother's work habits: "He takes a short walk every few hours and indulges in handball and squash whenever he has a chance, so he hasn't put on surplus weight. He is as tall and slim as ever and his hair is still dark."

Like Marnie, the women who grew close to Ted throughout his life tended to watch over him in ways that roused their instincts as mother or lover, and sometimes both. With men he laughed, sang, drank and bantered, but with women he admired he always seemed to be on a first date. They considered him an unordinary mortal, a trusting and needful man who craved their understanding and approval. Some saw him as a gallant child-man full of wit and passion, and found themselves seeking to shelter and insulate him from the world he never entirely confronted. Helen, who knew him at all these levels, said that "his mind has never grown up."

On her New York visit Marnie was astonished to discover Ted's collection of several hundred hats, including a particularly ornate fireman's hat from Ecuador and a baroque helmet worn by some Czech functionary. They had become his favorite props in keeping dinner guests laughing, and served as models as he began work on his second book, *The 500 Hats of Bartholomew Cubbins*. There were admirals' hats of several nations, and Ted wore one like Lord

Nelson's when he donned an excessively braided dress uniform and presided over the riotous annual banquets of the Seuss Navy at the Biltmore Hotel in Manhattan. Abetted by the ingenious publicist Harry Bruno, who had escalated the fame of Charles Lindbergh and the Antarctic explorer Richard E. Byrd, he had launched this bogus navy in 1936, when he designed the Esso-marine booth for Standard Oil at the National Motorboat Show in Grand Central Palace. Visitors were signed on as admirals, handed diplomas and photographed with cardboard Dr. Seuss characters. As admiral in chief, Ted signed commissions that spread from boat owners to celebrities and newspaper columnists; by 1939 there were two thousand admirals. At banquets Ted stood on a nautical bridge and led an oath of allegiance to Mother Neptune. "A swarm of phoney Farraguts," *The New York Herald Tribune* reported, "were piped on board the good ship Nothing . . . creating admirals of the Seuss Navy almost as fast as Kentucky creates colonels." As a publicity prank, some prominent applicants were rejected, but several women became admirals, among them the aviator Jacqueline Cochran and Ted's friend Zinny Vanderlip.

Ted recalled that it was "cheaper [for Standard Oil] to give a party for a few thousand people, furnishing all the booze, than it was to advertise in full-page ads. We never mentioned the product at all. Reporters would cover the party, and then would write our commercials for us." When Vincent Astor and the bandleader Guy Lombardo hung diplomas on the walls of their yachts, the Seuss Navy burgee—the smiling skeleton of a herring in a red admiral's hat, swimming through a black sea—became a prized trophy.

Ted and Esso commissioned the entire fleet of Standard Oil tankers into the Seuss Navy. Then came ocean liners, even the *Queen Mary*, and Ted acclaimed it "the largest navy in the world." Journalists publicized Ted's gift for engaging nonsense and his reputation grew as a wit. At one Seuss Navy banquet, an oil-refinery band "played four notes and then walked off the stand just to attract press attention." Ted was showing a knack for it too.

For *The 500 Hats of Bartholomew Cubbins* Ted chose the genre of the fairy tale and moved from the verse style of *Mulberry Street* to prose. "I knew nothing about children's books . . . traditional fairy tales were still in order. I thought perhaps that was the thing to do."

Friends and journalists learned that it was folly to ask Ted where he got his ideas; his answers were charming but elusive, since he really didn't know. The incidents and characters that found their way into his books exploded from some odd grain of truth, some trenchant observation, some giddy insight. Yet they had all been passed through the Seussian filter, removing any semblance of ordinariness or predictability and intensifying the ridiculous.

It had been the engines of the *Kungsholm* that led to *Mulberry Street*, and now, Ted insisted, the stranger in the morning hat who had sat in front of him during a train journey from Springfield to New York was responsible for *The 500 Hats*. He had mused about what might happen if he reached forward and removed the hat. "I decided he was so stuffy that he'd probably grow another one." Bartholomew's problem was that hats kept growing out of his head. Repetition is a vital tool in the rhythm of the book, and on one occasion Ted traced this to Springfield. He told Marnie's daughter, his beloved niece, Peggy, who had grown up in the Fairfield Street house, that in writing *The 500 Hats* he remembered the fastidious housecleaning ritual of their next-door neighbor. Peggy recalled that "Mrs. Clark would clean her house and then come out on the back stoop and wash the mop in the pail. Then she would go down three more steps and wash the pail out. Then another step or so and wash out whatever she had washed the pail with. Uncle Ted and I both grew up laughing at this charade."

Ted believed that the work done with scissors and glue in dummying a children's picture book was pivotal, and in this book "meant just as much to the career of Bartholomew Cubbins" as the work he put in on the drawings and text. It is the most worked over of Ted's original dummies. Even the number of Cubbins's hats rose, from forty-eight to one hundred and thirty-five and finally to five hundred. Sometimes he phoned in corrections and insertions, and these were penned in by Evelyn Shrifte. Helen's handwriting also appears. On "the hottest day of July," McClintock met Ted at the Dartmouth Club to make the final fixes, and his hand, smearing with sweat, is there too.

Just as with *Mulberry Street*, *The 500 Hats* received enviable reviews. At forty-eight pages it was a thicker book, and Vanguard priced it at $1.50. *The New York Times* called it "a lovely bit of tomfoolery which keeps up the suspense and surprise until the last page." The reviewer for *Booklist* had grumbled a year earlier that *Mulberry Street* was "a gorgeous idea, but not more than enough for one thoroughly good comic strip." But the magazine called *The 500 Hats* a "brand-new idea, developed into a complete tale, not too long, not too short, just right. Somewhere between the Sunday supplements and the Brothers Grimm, Dr. Seuss has produced a picture-book combining features of both."

Ted's favorite review, because it echoed his hope and ambition, was written by his classmate Alexander Laing, who had served on his staff at *Jack-O-Lantern*. Laing wrote in the *Dartmouth Alumni Magazine*: "His several other occupations, madly fascinating as they are, may have been only preludes to a discovery of his proper vocation. That he is a rare and loopy genius has been common knowledge from an early epoch of his undergrad troubles. It now becomes plain that his is the self-consistent, happy madness beloved by children. I do not see what is to prevent him from becoming the Grimm of our times."

Laing, who became a member of the Dartmouth faculty and died at seventy-two in a bicycle accident at Hanover, had been a witness to the evolution of Ted's pronunciation of his pseudonym. Laing wrote a quatrain in *The Dartmouth*:

> You're wrong as the deuce
> And you shouldn't rejoice
> If you're calling him Seuss.
> He pronounces it Soice.

But by now the traditional German pronunciation had given way. Masters of ceremonies and readers, especially those who sought autographs, seemed less confused if Dr. Seuss rhymed with Mother Goose.

Dartmouth's Baker Library requested the manuscript of *The 500 Hats*. Ted wrote that the prospect of having a manuscript on file in the library at Hanover "comes as a thrill to a bloke who still can't make up his mind whether he is an author or just a lowly advertising man." But the manuscript was nowhere to be found. After weeks of confusion, someone at Vanguard thought to look in the G file for Geisel rather than the S file for Seuss, and there it was, a jumble of typescript, dummy pages and press sheets, which Ted mailed to Dartmouth, including "a very messy object which to my mind is more interesting than the manuscript. This is the dummy which Ernest Reichl, Mike McClintock and I pasted together for the printer."

This Geisel, the perfectionist, contrasted incongruously with the impractical dreamer over whom Helen watched as she handled their checkbook and calendar. As Robert Cahn later wrote in *The Saturday Evening Post*, "Even with the most serious intentions, the mind of Ted Geisel is so fanciful that he has never been able completely to subdue it. He depends at all times on the level-headedness of his wife, Helen, to pull him out of entanglements in which he has become errantly involved."

Soon after *Mulberry Street* appeared, Ted had agreed to speak at a women's college in Westchester, knowing that he had time to contrive an excuse. But the day of the speech arrived and he had done nothing to escape it. He told Helen he felt ill, but she insisted that he meet his responsibility and gently pushed him out the door to catch a train. Two hours later the program chairman telephoned to say his audience was waiting. Helen grew alarmed and called Vanguard and a few friends. Toward dusk Ted came home, confessing that he had spent the afternoon, white-knuckled, inspecting Grand Central Station.

CHAPTER 8

Horton Hatches the Egg

1938–1940

Helen and Ted toasted the success of the second Dr. Seuss book over dinner on November 29, 1938, their eleventh wedding anniversary. Ted was thirty-four and Helen forty. The dedication of *The 500 Hats* was the symbol of a turning point in their lives, meant to put at peace a private anguish. The words seemed mirthful, but they were bittersweet: "To Chrysanthemum-Pearl, age 89 months, going on 90."

Chrysanthemum-Pearl was the imaginary child that Ted had invented and discussed at every opportunity. When friends bragged about their children, Ted drew himself up and related with sober pride the most recent Olympian feat by Chrysanthemum-Pearl, ever clever and precocious. One evening with friends around their dinner table, he announced that she could "whip up the most delicious oyster stew with chocolate frosting and flaming Roman candles." She could "carry one thousand stitches on one needle while making long red underdrawers for her Uncle Terwilliger." For years the name of Chrysanthemum-Pearl had appeared on Geisel Christmas cards, but then so had Norval, Wally, Wickersham, Thnud and a dozen other fictional "kiddies."

The truth was not amusing. Early in their marriage, probably by the fourth year, Helen had been hospitalized in New York with worsening abdominal pain. The diagnosis is uncertain, but after hurried conferences doctors removed her ovaries. Her surgery was unknown to all but the closest members of their families, and at Helen's plea they were pledged to secrecy. Promising each other privacy on the matter, Helen and Ted developed the charade of Chrysanthemum-Pearl. Decades later Ted told his niece, Peggy, who had grown up with Chrysanthemum-Pearl almost as a contemporary, that "it was not that we didn't *want* to have children. That wasn't it."

In the summer of 1939 Helen and Ted invited Peggy, then eleven years old and living in the family home in Springfield, to visit during the New York World's Fair. Their visitor slept in Ted's studio after full days at Flushing Meadows, where the three of them trooped through the fairgrounds, visiting foreign pavilions but usually forgoing exotic foods to eat ham sandwiches, Peggy's favorite. "That week had to be a labor of love," she recalled. "An eleven-year-old sleeping in Ted's studio, and [his work] stopping so we could go off and ride Ferris wheels and things I now know he hated."

Ted very nearly had a commercial stake in that fair with what he came to regard as his most spectacular failure: the Infantograph. With Depression memories abounding, the impending arrival in New York of "all those suckers" set off a flurry of greed, and Ted was not exempt from it. The Infantograph was to have made him a fortune, and money was on his mind. His magazine income had trickled off to almost nothing, and he had learned from *Mulberry Street* that good reviews did not pay Park Avenue rents.

The Infantograph was born on a sleety day in the late winter of 1938 as Ted trudged home from the Eighty-sixth Street subway station. "It was a stroke of genius so brilliant," he recalled, "that I almost fell into a steaming Con-Edison manhole." It would provide history's first photographic answer to the question of young lovers: What will our baby look like?

Ted and a partner named Ralph Warren, a Wall Streeter who had been "unstreeted by the Depression," incorporated and patented a dual-lens camera intended to photograph a man and a woman simultaneously and superimpose their features on the outline of a baby's face. It is on the U.S. Patent Office record for March 14, 1939, as No. 2,150,853. Ted set the corporate goal by writing the copy for a sign on the midway at the World's Fair: IF YOU MARRIED THAT GAL YOU'RE WALKING WITH, WHAT WOULD YOUR CHILDREN LOOK LIKE? COME IN AND HAVE YOUR INFANTOGRAPH TAKEN!

Warren had some expertise with cameras, and they rented space in an unheated Bronx warehouse as they sought to perfect the process. With his eternal glee in the ridiculous, Ted later wrote, "It was a hair-raising experience to watch [Warren] disembowel a second-hand Graflex and recombine the parts with other odd objects such as alarm clock innards and perambulator axles. My job was to hand him the nuts and the bolts and the hammers and saws and the bourbons and sodas as needed."

Within six months, a rudimentary camera was ready and Ted's friends were enlisted to pose with their heads immobilized by wooden collars. But even the inventors agreed that the results were repulsive. A man's mustache kept intruding on the baby's face, or the spheres of the two cameras overlapped, creating baby pictures with crooked noses. All the pictures, Ted complained, "tended to look like William Randolph Hearst."

But they kept trying. Richard Condon, a fledgling novelist starting his career with the publicist Hal Horne, produced Infantograph Corporation letterheads and brought in lawyers who performed corporate chores in return for stock. Through Horne's office, and with the prospect of laudatory mentions in newspaper gossip columns, the architect Norman Bel Geddes volunteered to design an Infantograph pavilion at the World's Fair.

They had everything but a workable camera. Fearing the collapse of the pyramid he had helped to create, Horne sent for a well-known Hollywood camera technician, Herman Schultheiss, "to get it right." Schultheiss, setting out from California on the *Super Chief*, the crack train that the Sante Fe had launched two years earlier, considered himself too posh for the Bronx warehouse, and was installed in a Fifty-seventh Street studio leased by the Metropolitan Opera soprano Grace Moore. There, it was soon alleged, he employed her mahogany Steinway grand as a workbench. Things kept "going sour" and this Seussian fantasy never came true; the World's Fair opened and closed without an Infantograph. In 1944, still believing that it was a grand idea, Ted regretfully signed a certificate of dissolution of the Infantograph Corporation. The patent rights, its sole asset, were assigned to him and Warren. The publicist settled for a general release. The Los Angeles attorney who represented Ted billed him $1.16 for professional services and seventy-five cents as reimbursement for the county-clerk fee required for document copies. All that remained of the Infantograph was a serene photograph of Helen and Ted in the wooden collars designed for the prototype and several grotesque examples of its work.

Even before *The 500 Hats* was published, Ted received a summons from the ebullient young publisher Bennett Cerf of Random House, who with Donald Klopfer had won renown five years earlier by overturning the ban on United States publication of James Joyce's *Ulysses*. On a Saturday before Christmas in 1938 Cerf took Ted to lunch at "21" Club. Bennett was a canny gambler who acted on hunches. He had scant interest in or experience with children's books, but he wanted to steal Dr. Seuss away from Vanguard. He admired what he had seen of Ted's work and what he had heard about him as a person, and that day in the cozy downstairs dining room at "21" he liked Ted instantly.

"Have you got a book in mind?" Cerf asked as they finished hamburgers.

"Not especially," Ted said. "Maybe an adult book with naked ladies."

"Great!" Cerf replied. "I'll buy it! You come with me and I'll print anything you do."

That completed their negotiations. Bennett said he would draw up a contract, and then suddenly spotted the critic George Jean Nathan. "You ought to meet Nathan," he said, steering Ted across the room.

Ted was impressed by Cerf and was soon devoted to him. He felt twinges of guilt at leaving Vanguard, which had launched him, but he hoped that Random, a rapidly growing house, would promote his work more effectively. Bennett, who was a catalyst for prominent people from Hollywood, New York and London, believed Ted was on the verge of fame. Long before television, Cerf was ahead of the book trade in sensing that publishers and celebrities need each other.

Basking in the freedom granted by his new publisher, Ted reverted to the broader humor of his college days. Cerf was resigned to publishing a flop if that was the way to bring Dr. Seuss to Random House. Soon after their lunch he wrote Ted a straight-faced letter expressing his pleasure to be publishing a book to be called *The Seven Lady Godivas*. Encompassing one of Ted's rare attempts to draw the human figure, the book was a revisionist account of the eleventh-century ride of the Coventry gentlewoman who persuaded her husband to lower taxes; its subtitle was "The true facts concerning history's barest family." In a drawing on the endpapers, a small sap bucket, labeled "Bennett Cerf," hangs from a sawed-off limb high in the Godiva family tree. In the foreword Ted explained that not one but seven Lady Godivas existed, and their nakedness "actually was not a thing of shame." Peeping Tom never peeped: " 'Peeping' was merely the old family name, and Tom and his six brothers bore it with pride."

When the book appeared in 1939, Ted asked the imperturbable Cerf to mail teaser postcard drawings, and the publisher obediently did so. Then Random House mailed advance copies of the book, introducing its new author to a complimentary trade list that included such industry giants as Maxwell Perkins of Scribners and Cass Canfield of Harper & Bros., whose comments apparently remain unrecorded. The book failed not once but twice; Ted was still the rowdy schoolboy forty-eight years later when he persuaded Random House to reissue it in a "commemorative edition." This one carried the claim that it was "re-issued by multitudinous demand," which Ted admitted was "an outright lie, which I wrote myself."

There were no recriminations from Random House about the early *Godivas* failure, but Ted himself had a few. "The country was depressed [at the time]," he said, "and they were more depressed after they read the book! Nobody bought any of them, except when they were remaindered at Schulte's cigar stores for, I think, twenty cents." He told E. J. Kahn: "I tried to draw the sexiest-looking women I could, and they came out just ridiculous."

Eventually about twenty-five hundred copies of a first printing of ten thousand copies were sold, and Bennett took his bump as a badge of honor. In Cerf's memoirs can be found a copy of Ted's royalty statement for the book at the close of 1940. It reported that only twenty-three copies of *Godivas* had sold in the prior six months, for a credit of $2.55, leaving an unearned balance of $100.88 against his advance. At his drawing board Ted transformed the bottom lines of this statement into a pennant with the legend "Excelsior!" held aloft by one of the Ladies Godiva, and mailed it back to Cerf, matted for framing.

In a letter to Ted, Cerf got down to business. "I quite understand why you don't want to sign any definite contract now for future juveniles. . . . I do hope, though, that after your present commitments are fulfilled, we will be able to work out a contract whereby we will become the publishers of every book that you write, juvenile and adult." He then suggested a contract of 10 percent on the first five thousand copies of a book and 15 percent thereafter.

Louise Bonino, the juvenile editor at Random House, urged Ted to come right back with a juvenile, and he did. It was *The King's Stilts*, his spin on a conventional fairy tale, and his second book within his first year at Random. It affords insight into how Helen and Ted worked together, never on art but on words, from concept on through an awesome volume of notes about plot and character development to the final text. "Helen was an editor and a partner," Ted said. "Her words are in some of them." Through two or three drafts of *Stilts*, her small and precise handwriting appears at pivotal turns: inserting dialogue, expanding a theme, deftly turning the plot around, zeroing in on segments where Ted seemed to be having problems.

First Ted sketched illustrations in pencil, drawing them in pairs as they would appear on facing pages of the books. To establish conflict or menace immediately, he scrawled notes on yellow copy paper or on the sketches. As the king first mounts his stilts, Ted jotted: "High in the air, crown askew, ermines streaming behind him, the King . . . strutted, chuckling to himself, whistling . . . raced at breakneck speed. Black-spotted coach dogs romped along beside him and nipped at the heels of his flashing red stilts . . . townsfolk looked on and just loved it . . ."

Seussian characters rarely emerged full-blown; the process took months. Ted cast about for a description of Lord Droon, the villain of *Stilts*: "Even as a baby, [he] was a scowler . . . Had no use for a rattle . . . preferred to rub two pieces of slate together . . . He liked rasping noise . . . When they gave him blocks with the alphabet on them, he would only use three. He was always spelling BAH." Draft pages became a mangled mass of rewrite, Helen's words overwritten by Ted's heavier hand. In the typed draft the text was further edited with changes, his and hers.

Despite Ted's dogged search for perfection, *Stilts* was another disappointment. Its first-year sales were 4,648 copies; the following year, only 394 copies sold. Still, Random House arranged promotional appearances for Ted in Columbus, Ohio, Cleveland and Rochester, and sent along Pullman tickets "for your entire trip." From Columbus, Ted mailed an upbeat report to Lew Miller, the Random House sales manager, on a sheet of Deshler-Wallick Hotel stationery: "Sold a mess of books . . ." On the same page was "A Poem for Mr. Miller":

> Here I sit in the
> Hotel Wallick.
> You'll notice that
> The spire is Phallick.

The hard sell continued at a Random House sales conference when Cerf urged salesmen to take notes while he read aloud letters from fourth-graders in praise of *Stilts*.

That Thanksgiving Day in New Jersey, Ted dazzled Helen's nieces, Barbara Palmer and her younger sister, Virginia, who were practicing with stilts. He borrowed them and strode proudly up the front steps, into the dining room and around the table, narrowly avoiding the serving platters. The children were agape; he had learned stilt-walking, he told them, as research for his book.

On the day after New Year's in 1940 Ted was back at his drawing board overlooking Park Avenue, doodling in pencil on tracing paper in search of an idea. Among unrelated sketches on his desk was one of a gentle-faced elephant much like the blue pachyderm that had paraded down Mulberry Street and reprised as "the Elephant with a Mother Complex" in *Judge* in 1938. When Ted took a break for coffee and one of his frequent brisk strolls, he left the window open. Back in his swivel chair he saw that one transparent sketch had blown atop another so that the elephant appeared to be sitting in a tree. That started it. What is an elephant doing in a tree? he asked himself. Hmmm . . . Obviously hatching an egg. But how did the egg get there? Hmmm . . . a bird must have left it. Where did the bird go?

This moment launched *Horton Hatches the Egg* and provided Ted's most convenient answer to persistent questions about how a Dr. Seuss book was born. "I've left a window open by my desk ever since," he said, "but it never happened again."

The fortuitous juxtaposition of elephant and tree led to months of feverish work. "I keep losing my story line and Helen has to find it again," he said. But he was enjoying uncharacteristic euphoria. After a productive night of work and probably a hearty vodka nightcap, he wrote Louise Bonino:

> The new book is coming along with a rapidity that leaves me breathless. It is a beautiful thing. The funniest juvenile ever written. I mean, being written. Never before have I stood before myself and pointed so proudly, saying, "Genius, you are." I feel certain it will sell well over a million. . . . [Lew] Miller will hang himself with joy to every lamp post in town. . . . [Robert] Haas and Klopfer will buy Tahiti and Bali respectively. [Saxe] Commins will buy Russia. Cerf will buy Hollywood. Louise Bonino will buy a negligee covered with sequins and umlauts and fine nizzard Maribou. . . . P.S.: I like my new book.

Cerf shrewdly paired Ted with Saxe Commins, who was known and admired as Eugene O'Neill's editor. Saxe plied his skills subtly to guide Ted, hoping that no more *Godivas* would appear. He constantly pressed Ted to follow a logical progression of story line. When Louise shared Ted's euphoric note with Commins, he smiled and handed it back without a word.

Horton the elephant had many lives. In early drafts he was named Osmer, then Bosco, then Humphrey; finally Ted chose the name of a Dartmouth classmate, Horton Conrad. The lazy bird Mayzie was first Bessie, then Saidie. Both elephant and bird underwent total character reversals. In Ted's first draft, instead of the elephant being persuaded to sit on the egg by a shiftless bird, Horton volunteered and the bird was reluctant. Ted's first Mayzie was a model mother. "Who, you?" she asked Horton. "Why, of all silly things! / You haven't got feathers. You haven't got wings. / You on an egg? That doesn't make sense. / My egg is so small, sir, and you're so immense!"

That spring the Geisels took the train to Hanover and Ted's fifteenth class reunion at Dartmouth. Dorothy Leavitt, the wife of his classmate Larry Leavitt, sat with Helen at dinner. While Ted seemed carefree, Helen "never stopped stewing" about the impending book deadline. "At dinner Helen said, 'I'm very upset because Ted has that elephant up a tree and he doesn't know how he's going to get him down,'" Dorothy Leavitt recalled. "That's not the sort of conversation you forget!"

As Ted read newspaper accounts of the Nazi march on Paris his outrage pushed fantasy from his mind. By the time Paris was occupied on June 14, *Horton* was on hold and Ted was sketching, instead of a benign elephant, murderous images of Adolf Hitler. "I didn't know how to end the book anyway so I began drawing savage cartoons," he said. "I had no great causes or interest in social issues until Hitler." Soon it was clearly up to Helen to bring Horton down. Her pivotal contribution, Ted said, was the climactic lines that follow the hatching of the egg on which Horton has sat for fifty-one weeks:

> Then they cheered and they *cheered* and they CHEERED more and more.
> *They'd never seen anything like it before!* "My goodness! *My gracious!*" they shouted.
> "MY WORD! *It's something brand new!*
> "IT'S AN ELEPHANT-BIRD!!"

When the book came in, Cerf took one look and mailed Ted a contract with increased royalties, writing that "it is not the usual formal business document; it is a declaration of love." With it came an unscheduled advance of five hundred dollars that Ted had urgently requested, to go toward a vacation home in La Jolla.

Money in hand, Ted and Helen entrained in August 1940 for California. War had taken the allure out of their customary overseas travel and they intended to become bicoastal residents, summering in La Jolla, which had enchanted them since 1928. They had bought a two-acre hillside lot with a sweeping ocean view overlooking the La Jolla Beach and Tennis Club, and were about to build a small ranch house, set behind a farm gate and olive trees. The site remained rural; the house was costing eight thousand dollars. During their six-week stay, Bennett Cerf wrote to report an offer of two hundred dollars from Leon Schlesinger Productions for motion picture rights to *Horton*. Cerf had replied without enthusiasm that he would take up the proposal with Ted on his return to New York.

To Ted's delight *Horton Hatches the Egg*, published that fall, was an immediate success. Its rollicking rhythm and mesmerizing drawings marked it as an original. Forsaking his absorption with the rigidities of classic fairy tales, Ted had unleashed his imagination. Horton had human frailties and yearnings, but was placed in implausible and outrageous jeopardy. At the age of thirty-six, for the first time, Ted knew what he wanted to do in life. Not coincidentally, *Horton* was his first book with resonating morality:

> "I meant what I said, and I said what I meant . . .
> An elephant's faithful—one hundred per cent!"

"A moral is a new thing to find in a Dr. Seuss book," *The New York Times Book Review* noted, "but it doesn't interfere much with the hilarity with which he juggles an elephant up a tree. To an adult the tale seems a little forced in comparison to his first grand yarns, less inevitable in its nonsense, but neither young nor old are going to quibble with the fantastic comedy of his pictures."

A less guarded and more prophetic appraisal came in a letter to Cerf from Frances Chrystie, the juvenile buyer of F.A.O. Schwarz: "I've been sitting alone in my apartment reading *Horton* aloud to myself over and over again. . . . It's the funniest book I've ever seen. . . . [Our] merchandise manager thinks he can find an elephant in the store, and we can make a tree and lay an egg and have a very fine window for Book Week."

Cerf's hunch about Ted was paying off. Booksellers invited Ted for autographs, and Bennett suggested he tour several cities. In Cincinnati, Mary Stix of the James Book Store was "steamed up" about adult interest in his books, Bennett wrote Ted, "and she says you will have to divide [your time] between the adults and the infants." With *Horton*, Clifton Fadiman's early analysis of this dual appeal of Ted's work was being validated nationwide.

At a Random House party during the Philadelphia Booksellers' Association in November, Ted read an ode he called *Pentellic Bilge for Bennett Cerf's Thirty-ninth Birthday*.

> . . . Oh, Anguish of Age! Is there no one who cares? . . .
> I care, shouts a man with a face not unkind!
> I care, shouts a girl with a dancing behind!
> I care, shouts a youth with a nosegay of metal!
> We all hope that Cerf is in very fine fettle!

Neither the spirit of the verse nor the occasion was marred by the fact that Bennett had turned thirty-nine three years earlier.

Ted was haunted by the war in Europe, and one evening in Manhattan he showed an editorial cartoon he had drawn to his friend Zinny Vanderlip Schoales, the brilliant, hard-drinking intellectual he had admired since the days of the pearl-in-the-oyster prank at her parents' dinner table. She had joined the patrician liberal Ralph Ingersoll when he launched the tabloid newspaper *PM* in New York with the backing of Marshall Field III. Zinny took Ted's cartoon to Ingersoll and *PM* published it on January 30, 1941, with an editor's note identifying Ted as "a topflight advertising artist, famous for his Flit cartoons." In a short letter to the editor beneath his cartoon, Ted claimed rank as the world's outstanding writer of fantasy, but gave runner-up honors to the Italian Fascist party propagandist, Virginio Gayda, who was the target of his cartoon.

Ingersoll asked Ted for more. There would not be another Dr. Seuss book for seven years.

CHAPTER 9

World War II

1941–1946

One morning during breakfast, as the Geisels traded sections of *The New York Times*, their radio blared the voice of Senator Gerald P. Nye of North Dakota. Four months after the United States declared war against Japan, Germany and Italy, he was still urging Americans to stay out.

"That horse's ass!" Ted blurted.

"Ted, don't use language like that!" Helen said.

"But he *is* a horse's ass! I'll draw a picture of him as a horse's ass and put it in *PM*!"

"You can't," she said. "It's a vulgar idea."

But he did.

Ted went all-out as a cartoonist for *PM*, finding it a natural ally for his fervent if sometimes simplistic persuasions. "*PM* was against people who pushed other people around," he said. "I liked that." He admired its bluntness when the newspaper hammered the America First Committee, whose isolationism was permeated with racism. *PM* decried the rantings of the right-wing preacher Gerald L. K. Smith, and was hostile to the isolationist leaders Nye, Senator Burton K. Wheeler of Montana and the aviator Charles Lindbergh.

That morning Ted drew a circus horse, its parts labeled for various America Firsters, and the back end bore the name of Senator Nye.

"You're going to get in an awful lot of trouble," Helen said.

"It will get a lot of laughs," Ted said, "and nothing will happen."

PM printed the cartoon on April 26, 1942, but Ingersoll warned him, "You're going to get us in a million-dollar lawsuit, and you'll be sued yourself." Four days later, as Ted recalled it, a letter came from Nye. Ted's hands trembled as he opened it and read aloud to Helen: "Dear Dr. Seuss: Please, I would love to acquire that charming picture you made of me to put in my rumpus room." Ted's version was only slightly embellished. Nye's letter actually read: "[The] issue of Sunday, April 26th . . . carried a cartoon, the original of which I should very much like to possess. May I request its mailing to me?"

Rocking with laughter, Ted asked Helen if she thought they should send the cartoon to the senator. "And Helen, who never used any bad language, said, 'No, he's a horse's ass!'"

It was Ted's skewering of the hero Lindbergh that had first drawn astonished attention to the *PM* cartoonist and led Ingersoll to give him a job drawing three—and later, five—cartoons a week. Lindbergh had been decorated by the German government in 1938, which led to criticism at home, especially when he toured the United States making speeches urging neutrality. In April 1941 a Dr. Seuss cartoon introduced the Lindbergh quarter, a coin that depicted an ostrich with its head in a sand dune. Its imprint: "IN GOD WE TRUST (and how!)." President Roosevelt shared Ted's opinion, and went on the radio to criticize Lindbergh, who shortly thereafter resigned his Air Corps Reserve commission.

Calling Lindbergh "one of our nation's most irritating heroes," Ted wrote an unpublished verse and tacked it on his studio wall:

> The Lone Eagle had flown
> The Atlantic alone
> With fortitude and a ham sandwich.
> Great courage that took.
> But he shivered and shook
> At the sound of the gruff German landgwich.

But Ted's ultimate scorn was aimed at Adolf Hitler, whom he drew for *PM* as an arrogant, incorrigible infant in diapers. In a series entitled *Mein Early Kampf,* Hitler became an ungrateful child giving a hotfoot to the stork that delivered him, cutting a tooth on a statue of Bismarck and refusing his milk because it came from Holstein cows. Relatively few newspapers were excoriating Hitler and Mussolini at the time, and among some readers Ted was considered an extremist. Polls showed that more than two thirds of Americans were strongly opposed to involvement in Europe's war, and Congress was on the verge of junking the military draft. Ted opposed war too, but he believed "we were going to have no choice in the matter."

Ted had always worked alone, but he grew zealous in his loyalty to *PM*, stirred by the act of joining men and women he respected in an urgent common cause. He never forgot working beside Ingersoll, Kenneth Crawford and I. F. "Izzy" Stone, and marveled that despite losing millions *PM* refused advertising. *The New Yorker* crowd dismissed the exuberant *PM* staff as "a bunch of young fogeys," but Ted saw them as "a bunch of honest but slightly cockeyed crusaders." He enjoyed the newspaper because it gave him freedom of expression. "They were understaffed and didn't have the time and energy to monkey with everybody's stuff." Later he regarded his *PM* cartoons as "rather shoddy" art. "It was a short-order business," he said. "The one thing I *do* like about them . . . is their honesty and frantic fervor."

While *PM* was little known in Latin America, and Dr. Seuss even less so, Ted's cartoons grew notorious there through the efforts of Nelson Rockefeller, another Dartmouth alumnus, who coordinated inter-American affairs for the State Department. That office distributed Ted's cartoons and they were widely reprinted. Ted said, "Nelson found very few [other] cartoons . . . that cautioned the country that we were going to get into the war."

In June 1941 Helen and Ted went to California and moved into their new home for the summer. Ted airmailed his cartoons to *PM*, and La Jolla seemed more than a continent away from New York. He wrote Evelyn Shrifte, "All the enlightened members of this community know about my books . . . but nobody in Southern California seems to keep 'em in stock. . . . I gotta go out now and fight rattlesnakes, bees and man-eating rabbits in the patio, then go fight Lindbergh."

Ted was convinced that there would be war with Japan. In

September 1941 he drew Emperor Hirohito popping out of a box marked JAP WAR THREAT, with the caption: "Velly scary Jap-in-the-box, wasn't it?" In November Japan appeared as a shopper at Uncle Sam's country store: "Gimme some kerosene, some excelsior and a blow torch. Ma wants to bake a cake." But few Americans shared Ted's alarm.

His books were not forgotten. On the last Sunday of November the actor Sterling Holloway read *Mulberry Street* on CBS Radio's *Family Hour*, but Ted and Helen were on the *Super Chief*, headed home to New York, and missed it.

Settled back on Park Avenue for the winter, the Geisels were reading the Sunday *New York Times* on December 7, when WQXR radio interrupted its classical music program with the bulletin that United States warships had been attacked at Pearl Harbor in Hawaii. The death toll appeared to be immense. Keeping his radio on, Ted went to his drawing board in a fury. The United States Congress declared war on Japan the next day; Ted's cartoon in *PM* showed WAR as a bold black explosion, sending a gangly Seussian bird labeled ISOLATIONISM into the sky. The caption read: HE NEVER KNEW WHAT HIT HIM. Then Ted drew a battered Uncle Sam Cat trying to rise from its rocking chair. Its caption: "The End of the Nap!" Congress declared war on Germany and Italy on December 11, and the Dr. Seuss cartoon depicted a smug Hitler and a pig-faced Japanese emperor replacing the American presidents on Mount Rushmore: DON'T LET THEM CARVE THOSE FACES ON OUR MOUNTAINS! BUY UNITED STATES SAVINGS BONDS AND STAMPS!

Ted's cartoons grew savagely eloquent and often very funny, displaying his gift for derision. Set in a men's club, "The Battle of the Easy Chair" portrayed a member telling his valet, "Wake me, Judkins, when the Victory Parade comes by!" Australia became a boxing kangaroo, its tail being devoured by the Japanese. The French puppet Pierre Laval was a louse on Hitler's finger. Nazis were low-slung dachshunds—until American dachshund owners rose in protest. A favorite Seussian device of long, intertwining beards made Siamese twins of the Nazi party and the America First Committee.

In February 1942 *Newsweek* called Ted's satire "razor-keen" and noted that he was stirring "hornets' nests" with drawings so unflattering that even the United States had become "a scrawny

eagle with Uncle Sam whiskers and a star-spangled topper." Ted
had depicted John Haynes Holmes, a pacifist clergyman in New
York City, as being honored with a war monument for speaking
"the beautiful words 'The unhappy people of Japan are our brothers.'" Ted was stunned by the virulence of the backlash from
isolationists. He had spurred Americans into war, they argued,
because, at thirty-eight, he was too old for the draft; his battles
were only on paper. In July, when he and Helen loaded their
Oldsmobile and drove to California, he took along assignments
for drawings and posters for the Treasury Department and the War
Production Board, and the Dr. Seuss menagerie went to war.
"Starve the Squander Bug!" one of his posters urged. "This is in
no sense of the word a vacation," Helen wrote Evelyn Shrifte.
"Ted has endless government work to do besides his daily cartoon.
But the working conditions are so beautiful! He has . . . lunch
with sun and kittens every day, and sometimes even a swim."

Since their stay in the prior summer, the Geisels' seaside retreat
seemed to have become a battlefront. Japanese submarines were
reported off San Diego, camouflage nets hung over aircraft plants
and blackout curtains were in place. In a panicky response that
became one of the darker episodes of American human-rights
history, nearly 120,000 Japanese Americans were forcibly moved
from the West Coast to remote detention camps and their property
was seized.

Helen described California life to friends back East:

> There isn't a maid or gardener to be had. Literally everyone
> is working for Consolidated [Aircraft] unless he's in uniform.
> Our house is right up in no-man's land. Once a week the
> marines invade, and usually capture our hillside. We are dive-
> bombed at 5:30 A.M.—then we look out of the window to
> see hundreds of little boats, amphibious tanks, etc., rushing
> to shore. In a few minutes our house is in the midst of it all—
> tanks, jeeps, trucks, bayonets bared right on the driveway. The
> din of blank cartridges is so terrifying that I can't even conceive
> of what the real thing must be like!

By autumn Ted felt he could no longer justify or tolerate civilian
status and he applied for a commission with naval intelligence.

Weeks passed while his background was checked. An investigator asked a Standard Oil executive why Ted would work for a liberal newspaper like *PM*. "Oh, Geisel isn't a Communist," the executive replied. "He just does it for the money!" By the time a telegram finally confirmed Ted's fitness for the navy, he had been offered an army commission to join Frank Capra's Signal Corps unit in a leased Fox studio near Sunset Boulevard and Western Avenue in Hollywood. "I told the Navy, 'Thanks but I can't go,' and they said to me, 'You're AWOL.'"

While Ted prepared for "the Hollywood front," the New York Philharmonic gave the first performance at Carnegie Hall of a Deems Taylor piece based on *Mulberry Street*. Taylor called the work "Marco Takes a Walk: Variations for Orchestra Op. 25." "It resembles Beethoven's *Fifth Symphony* in that everything is evolved from a short, five-note 'motto' theme," the composer wrote in the program notes. "I can think of no other way in which it resembles Beethoven's *Fifth Symphony*." It was "a cute set-up for a series of variations," the critic Edward O'Gorman wrote in the *New York Post*, but Ted missed the event, and to his knowledge it was never performed again.

Suspecting that their New York years were ending, the Geisels decided to close out their Park Avenue apartment. On January 7, 1943, in New York, Captain Theodor Seuss Geisel, serial number 0921507, imposing and impeccable in a 40-long captain's uniform from Brooks Brothers, was inducted into the army, assigned to the Information and Education Division, and boarded a train for indoctrination in California. Within weeks he joined the Capra unit at the Hollywood studio known to its wartime occupants as Fort Fox.

As a director, Capra was already a Hollywood legend. Five years earlier, *You Can't Take It With You* had brought him an Academy Award, and just before the war he had formed his own production company to film *Meet John Doe* with Gary Cooper.

On Ted's first day, Major Capra took him on a tour. "Here are the Moviolas, Captain," he said, pointing to the film-editing machines.

"What is a Moviola?" Ted asked.

"Oh, my God!" Capra said. "We'll have to teach you how to become a producer."

With surprising patience, Capra managed to do so, while others tried less successfully to make a soldier of Ted. The historian and biographer Paul Horgan, a witness to these efforts, recalled that Ted "tried so earnestly in field drills that it was touching. He was warm and full of worthy convictions, and patriotic to the limit, but he was hopelessly uncoordinated. He was tall, skinny, his hair parted in the middle and falling like some of the birds he drew, and with that great beak of a nose." The Capra outfit was full of creative men at various stages of their careers. Horgan himself rose to lieutenant colonel, as did screenwriter Leonard Spigelgass. Composer Meredith Willson became a major, and screenwriter Otto Englander a lieutenant. The film producer Lehman (Lee) Katz, as a captain, was executive officer. Among enlisted men were novelist Irving Wallace (later Ted gleefully called him a "successful pornographer"), producer Carl Foreman, art teacher Eugene Fleury and illustrator P. D. Eastman. As civilian overseers, the animators Chuck Jones and Friz Freleng of Warner Brothers were joined by Bob Clampett and Frank Tashlin.

Members of Capra's unit wore army uniforms and endured drills, but the only shots fired were at a target range adjacent to the Santa Anita racetrack. There was infighting, though, carried over from show business. Wallace railed against Capra about the credits for a documentary called *Know Your Enemy: Japan*, which stalled in production for three years, largely because of shifting opinions in the War Department on its content and tone. Wallace later wrote that he had done most of the writing, but that Capra had omitted his name and given credit to better-known writers. He complained that all of the unit, including "such coworkers as Captain John Huston and Colonel Theodore Geisel . . . lived a schizoid existence, half the time playing soldier, and half the time playing Hollywood producer or director or screenplay writer." (Wallace was having problems with his own material: Ted never attained colonel's rank nor put a final "e" on Theodor.)

There were no barracks at Fort Fox; soldiers dispersed each evening to their own lodgings. For Ted this meant a three-bedroom white-stucco home that Helen found at 3595 Wonderview Drive on a peak high over Hollywood. The Los Angeles basin stretched sparkling clear below and they looked across miles of open Pacific to Catalina Island. From their back patio they saw the Warners studio and San Fernando Valley. Helen began to grow roses, fencing them in against wild deer. A neighbor bred Irish setters and a succession of them became a constant in the Geisels' life. "Uncle Ted would pick up a setter named Cluny," Peggy Dahmen recalled, "walk over to Helen and say, 'Here's your lap dog!' and put this huge dog in the lap of tiny Helen."

While Ted was at Fort Fox, Helen was writing her own children's books, always in prose, for Disney and Golden Books. The books were "successful but more or less conventional," with titles like *Tommy's Wonderful Rides, Johnny's Machines, Bobby and His Airplane* and *Donald Duck Sees South America*. Ted said later, "She supported us during the war." Only one of her books was rejected. Since visiting Rome with her family as a young girl, she had been intrigued by the Virgin Mary as "not just a shy, retiring mother, mentioned only a few times in the Bible, but really quite a woman." Her children's biography of the Virgin Mary was never published.

The Geisels did not seem to be "playing Hollywood"; they lived the way other military people did in Los Angeles. They went to hear a young pianist named Nat "King" Cole with his trio in a club on the Sunset Strip. They visited the Hollywood Canteen to gawk at the Saturday-night servicemen's dance scene. The level of theater they relished in New York was scarce in Los Angeles, but they attended a long-running revue called *Ken Murray's Blackouts*. On a hot Sunday afternoon they even took in a rodeo at the Coliseum, laughing about being "out West." Los Angeles seemed a jumble of palm trees, Spanish-style courts and bungalows, bizarre cult temples and hamburger joints, and they loved it. The city's population had nearly doubled in each recent decade, reaching 1.5 million. Aircraft plants had sprung up across the Los Angeles basin, attracting laborers from the South and Midwest as welders and riveters. Commuters traveled for miles on the big red Pacific Electric rail cars, and the new Arroyo Seco Parkway to Pasadena was heralded as the beginning of a fast automobile freeway network. *The Los Angeles Times* reported a rising "smoke nuisance" that was becoming known as "smog."

Unlike Irving Wallace, Ted considered Fort Fox a fortuitous learning experience. He worked diligently and built lifelong alliances with fellow soldiers. Often at lunch, if anyone had enough rationed gasoline, they drove to one of the Farmers Market restaurants near Beverly Hills; Lee Katz called it "our commissary."

Though Ted was occasionally a victim of Capra's crotchets, he revered the man as an editor. One day, particularly proud of his work on a training film script, Ted took it to his boss.

"The first thing you have to do in writing," Capra said, "is find out if you're saying anything."

With that he went through the script underlining in blue pencil each sentence in which Ted had managed to advance the plot line, and they were few. "The rest . . . he left unlined," Ted said. "He taught me conciseness, and I learned a lot about the juxtaposition of words and visual images."

The Capra unit produced biweekly newsreels for the armed services; they included animated cartoons with training messages and were part of the *Army-Navy Screen Magazine* shown to the American military from mid-1943 to 1945. Military people had been cast in conventional training films, but this tended to put recruits to sleep; when prominent actors were substituted, they elicited hoots of derision. But young trainees responded to animation; they wanted to laugh, and cartoons moved fast.

To exploit an acronym familiar in the services, the star of the new training series was named Private Snafu. In the introductory cartoon, after an arch pause the word "Snafu" was explained as "Situation Normal, All . . . FOULED . . . Up." The cartoons took aim at the incoming torrent of teenage recruits and taught them the importance of security awareness, concentration, health and discipline.

From Capra, but particularly from Chuck Jones, who at the age of twenty-six was already a master of animation at Warners, Ted received his indoctrination in that art. Jones's relationship with Ted, like only two or three others in Ted's life, was grounded in matters of art and bonded by shared lunacy and affection. Both men fancied bow ties, for instance, but got into elaborate arguments over how they should be looped.

Of the two dozen or so Snafu cartoons only a few were in rhyme, and these were all Ted's. His verse carried the cartoon called *Gripes*, in which Snafu rebelled against the dreaded kitchen duty, KP. The cartoon became a fantasy of how the army would be run if Snafu were in charge: discipline disappeared in an excess of girls and booze, and no troops remained on duty to rally against the predictable German attack. Collaborating on *Spies*, which dramatized the dangers of loose talk, Jones and Geisel won the Fort Fox version of an Academy Award, a statuette of the doltish Private Snafu.

In an episode that was a favorite with the troops, Snafu ignored warnings to take his antimalarial pills and was pursued by a slinky but deadly siren named Ann—for the Anopheles mosquito—who followed careless soldiers to war. Ted and Major W. Munro Leaf, who had created *Ferdinand the Bull*, adapted the script. As the voice of Ann, the aging stage actress Marjorie Rambeau delivered hearty double entendres, and the troops learned that malaria was as avoidable as syphillis.

Chuck Jones shared his expertise with Ted and also came to depend on him. Since the films were to be shown only to males, an occasional four-letter word was acceptable. Jones enjoyed the wordplay in a cartoon on survival in the Arctic, which opened with a camera panning across a whiteout. As the wind screamed the narrator said, "It was cold enough to freeze the nuts off a Jeep." Then, after a gleeful dare from Ted, the film cut to a drawing of a Jeep and its nuts dropped off.

Ted was too restless to spend the entire war with Snafu. His months as a *PM* cartoonist had developed his sense for the big picture. In March 1944 he was promoted to major, and Capra, convinced that he had taught his protégé something about story lines and film scripts, assigned him to a lengthier, more sensitive project. As the War Department made contingency plans for victory, Ted worked on a film for American troops who would occupy Germany. Called *Your Job in Germany* (coded Project 6010X), it took him to Washington for conferences at the War Department. He became a bicoastal commuter on military air transports—at first twin-engine DC3s and later four-engine DC4s. There were frequent stops for passengers and fuel, and sometimes the cross-country trip took him as long as three days. With a lower priority than many military commuters, he began to expect to be bounced at Big Springs, Texas, where he spent hours waiting in the lobby of the Hotel Rogers, reading and sketching.

After Paris was liberated on August 24, 1944, planning accelerated for the Allied occupation of Germany. In September Ted won Cabinet-level approval of his draft script for a live-action film, *Your Job in Germany*, subject to the approval of American generals in the field. The script was a tough-minded warning that the vanquished Germans must not be trusted, a theme of the hard-peace policy that emerged after Roosevelt and Churchill met that month in the second Quebec Conference. "The Nazi party may be gone," Ted wrote, "but Nazi thinking, Nazi training and Nazi trickery remains. The German lust for conquest is not dead. . . . You will not argue with them. You will not be friendly. . . . There must be no fraternization with any of the German people."

Ted, whose four grandparents had been born in Germany, wrote and produced the film, but had strong reservations:

> It was with this film . . . that the impossible and ill-advised non-fraternization policy was announced to the U.S. Army as it occupied Germany. I strongly believed in everything that I wrote in this film with the exception of the Non-Fraternization conclusion . . . which I wrote as an officer acting under orders . . . and later worked to get rescinded.

In fact Ted joked with colleagues about ending the film this way: "Just be a good soldier. Leave the bungling to the State Department!"

For a role as narrator, Ted interviewed a young army lieutenant named Ronald Reagan, who was attached to "Fort Roach," the Hal Roach studio not far from Fort Fox, but turned him down in favor of actor John Beal.

On November 11, the forty-year-old Major Geisel flew in a military C54 to Ireland, then England and on to Paris, his "top secret" film reels under his arm as ordered. Billeted at the Hotel Majestic near the Bois de Boulogne, he was issued a mess card for two months. Although bitter fighting and heavy casualties lay ahead, it was a time of euphoria for the Allied forces. Ted was astounded to find civilian VIPs seeking any credentials that would bring them to Paris, a battered city where Allied officers on leave sat in "unheated hotel rooms wearing overcoats as they played bridge."

While the Allied counteroffensive swept into Germany, Ted's mission was to seek out generals scattered with their troops in France, Belgium, Luxembourg and the Netherlands. His companions on these journeys out of Paris, ever closer to the front, were Robert Murphy of the State Department and Major John Boettiger, President Roosevelt's son-in-law. Murphy and Boettiger were there, Ted decided, to ensure that every appropriate American general took time to view the film and at least give tacit approval.

With a Michelin touring map as their guide, the three men set out by car from Paris on November 19 for Verdun and Luxembourg, which had been liberated just eight weeks earlier. Ted, who had failed to qualify with his .45 revolver after two weeks on a pistol range in Los Angeles, wore the weapon upside down in its holster, arguing that his "best bet in an enemy action" was to "grab it by the barrel and throw it." Rain was falling heavily as they neared the front, but they found Luxembourg City in a cheerful mood. Citizens had triumphantly rehung photographs of Grand Duchess Charlotte and Prince Felix in their windows, and crews were changing street signs back from German to French. Ted thought it eerie to be fifteen minutes from the fighting but to hear only "a few distant booms," and to be at the plush Luxembourg Theater that night as Marlene Dietrich entertained soldiers. As he walked back to his room in the blackout, a Red Cross nurse proposed that they swap rooms so that she could have a hot bath. He wrote in his spiral-notebook diary that she even offered to throw in a pack of Lucky Strikes.

The next morning was cold and wet as Ted and his companions drove north through the Ardennes Forest, over gray stone bridges and through gorges patched with snow, to meet General Omar Bradley with the First Army and General Frank McSherry at Supreme Headquarters of the Allied Expeditionary Force. They stopped to lunch on K-rations in the warmth of a small church where "American college football scores were posted over a crucifix" and a radio blared jazz from Armed Forces Radio. Bradley and McSherry approved the film and Ted set out to show it to other commanders.

Each night German buzz bombs whined overhead and artillery thudded at the front. Convoys of army trucks with dim yellow "cat's eye" headlights groaned past, and ambulances lumbered in with the wounded, "two pairs of bare feet in each back window." The three men abandoned the big car from Paris after it mired in mud for a second time, and moved on by jeep. In Verviers they were billeted in a "swank" château with "the latest canary-colored Crane bathrooms" and enjoyed bottles of Burgundy brought up from hidden cellars. The contrast of the bloody mop-up in the Rhineland and the mood of newly liberated towns confounded Ted, leaving him "elated in a depressed sort of way." On November 23, after a bountiful Thanksgiving dinner at Maastricht with American officers, he wandered through the old Dutch city, where most bridges lay in rubble and "residents were rummaging through garbage pails." He and his colleagues crossed into Germany and drove to the ancient town of Aachen, which had been liberated four weeks earlier, the first major German city to be occupied by the Allies. There they were served a second—and even more robust—Thanksgiving meal of "wienerschnitzel, wursts and wassail."

Robert Murphy took Ted along to a ceremony in an Aachen castle where a water main had broken and "water was cascading down a marble stairway into a ballroom." The room was lit only by torches, and shadows danced on the walls as Allied generals met Aachen city officials. Major Geisel arrived with his top-secret film under his arm as ordered. "My film said we should never shake hands with the Germans, but all the American generals ahead of me were shaking hands with them. I had to move the film from my right to my left arm so that I could shake hands with them too."

Of all the generals on his list, from Eisenhower down, only George Patton escaped Ted's screening. "Somebody else took the film and played it for Patton. . . . I was told he said, 'Bullshit!' and walked out of the room."

Back in Paris between forays, memories overwhelmed Ted. The Bois du Boulogne reminded him of his days after Oxford, though now the winter woods sheltered abandoned vehicles stripped of tires. He found the Left Bank shop where he had bought Helen's engagement ring and hotels where they had stayed.

At First Army headquarters in Luxembourg in December, Ted ran into Ralph Ingersoll, his old boss at *PM*, now a lieutenant colonel in army intelligence, who proposed to show Ted "some fighting." Ingersoll spread out a map and drew a ring around the town of Bastogne. "I'll send you to a quiet sector," he said. "There won't be much action because we've just done an intelligence sweep of the area."

With a military police escort, Ted was driven to Bastogne just hours before the outbreak of the Battle of the Bulge, when a carefully planned German counteroffensive took the Allies by surprise in the bloodiest fighting since D-Day. Later he recalled:

> The thing that probably saved my life was that I got there in the early morning and the Germans didn't arrive until that night. I found Bastogne pretty boring and . . . got on the other side of the line and got cut off. . . . With the aid of another MP who was also lost and hastening through a downpour in the opposite direction, we learned we were ten miles behind German lines. We were trapped three days before being rescued by the British. . . . The retreat we beat was accomplished with a speed that will never be beaten.

After the battle a horrified Ingersoll searched for Ted, even checking casualty lists. It was five years later at a party in New York before they met again and Ingersoll hugged him. "God, am I glad to see you!" he said. "I thought I'd killed you."

In Paris Ted lined up to buy a copy of the triumphant December 22 European edition of *The New York Herald Tribune*, the first published "in the freed capital of France" after a four-and-a-half-year silence. At an officers' Christmas party he ate "peanut butter and salami sandwiches and drank lemonade laced with gin" but was saddened by unlit Christmas trees and the lonely sound of "carols in the midst of war." Late on New Year's Eve he walked alone down the Champs-Élysées through the rain to stand at the Tomb of the Unknown Soldier, scrawling a verse that began:

> If he had lived, he'd probably have been 45 or so
> And he might have been standing there, saluting too

> At the grave of
> The Unknown Soldier . . .

His mission accomplished, Ted returned to California in the second week of January 1945. *Your Job in Germany* would be shown to American military forces when they occupied Germany following the surrender.

Ted's next assignment at Fort Fox was to write a film spurring postwar troops to help avoid a third world war. He found inspiration in a brief *New York Times* item: There was so much energy in a glass of water, scientists said, that if it could be harnessed it could blow up half the world. In the summer of 1945, with little further research, he drafted a film treatment that warned of the potential threat of devastating explosions. As he recalled it, an urgent call came two days later from a colonel in Washington asking the source of his information.

"*The New York Times*," Ted said.

"Burn it," he was ordered.

"Burn the *Times?*"

"Burn it, and report when you have carried out the order."

Ted sent a sergeant to find a copy of the *Times*—any copy. He put it in a wastebasket, burned it in front of witnesses and telephoned the colonel to report.

"Well done, Geisel," he was told.

Ted's recollection of this event was supported in certain particulars by Paul Horgan, who answered to the description of the Washington colonel who had telephoned Ted. Ted's "extraordinary projection of the most lethal weapons" had rung a warning bell with Horgan. He rushed Ted's script by messenger to Vannevar Bush, head of the wartime Office of Scientific Research and Development, who telephoned within the hour, ordering the immediate destruction of Ted's storyboards and scripts on grounds of national security.

"I called Ted," Horgan recalled, "and he was devastated, since he'd put three months in on the project. He told me he got the idea from the Buck Rogers comic strip. I left for Europe for six weeks, and while I was gone the first atom bomb was dropped on Japan. When I returned, my secretary said Major Geisel had been making daily calls from the West Coast. So I called back and before I could say anything but 'Hi, Ted,' he said, 'I understand everything now. All is forgiven.'"

Soon, like thousands of Americans, Ted began counting the accumulated service points that would govern the date of his return to civilian life, but that did not come until January 13, 1946, five months after the end of the war. He left active duty as a lieutenant colonel, receiving the Legion of Merit for "exceptionally meritorious service in planning and producing films, particularly those utilizing animated cartoons, for training, informing, and enhancing the morale of troops."

For Ted, the joyous relief at the Japanese surrender in August 1945 had been cut short. On September 14 he had been shattered by the sudden death in Springfield of his sister, Marnie, at the age of forty-three.

Marnie, the lively Smith College graduate who had abandoned her pursuit of a Ph.D. at Radcliffe to marry her Harvard Law School sweetheart, started her life beautifully. But the marriage ended in divorce, and Marnie returned to Springfield, where she worked as a tutor in German and French and as a part-time stenographer. After her mother's death in 1931, she gave up these jobs to maintain the home on Fairfield Street for her father and her daughter, Peggy. From then on little went right and she began to feel trapped in a spiral of failure; she drank heavily, and increasingly became a recluse.

"Mother was upset with me when I was about nine or ten," Peggy recalled, "and Grampie [Ted's father] went into the kitchen and said something to her to calm things . . . it was related to alcohol. . . . Then he walked out and did not speak to her again for four or five years, even though we kept living at the house. That's how he handled anger."

During this estrangement, Helen and Ted sent notes to Peggy but did not visit Springfield. Marnie grew bitter, feeling that they had taken sides against her. "I'm sure she had agoraphobia . . . in those days it was just a mental breakdown," Peggy said. In the summer of 1945, Peggy, then seventeen, was at home after her first year at Katharine Gibbs business college in Boston. Her mother called out one morning that her left arm was numb and she felt faint. "But she'd said that for years," Peggy recalled. "She wouldn't see a doctor. I started toward the kitchen and heard her fall to the floor. . . ."

Dead of a coronary thrombosis, Marnie was buried near her mother in the family plot at Oak Grove Cemetery. Her death was a subject so painful for Ted that he avoided talking about it for the rest of his life with a silent shake of his head. Helen wondered how soon he would be able to make people laugh again.

CHAPTER 10

Hollywood

1946–1950

Ted had gone to Hollywood in an army uniform, but now Hollywood came to him. The
flamboyant producer Jerry Wald telephoned from
Warner Brothers to say he had heard good things
about Ted's work on a wartime film that had helped Jack Warner
win the 1946 Academy Award for best documentary short subject.
Called *Hitler Lives?*, it was a remake of *Your Job in Germany*, Ted's
cautionary tale against troop fraternization, but gave him no credit.
Aware of deep American concerns about postwar Europe, Warner
had seen the film in 1945, negotiated for civilian rights and produced
an eighteen-minute film that warned of perpetual German mili-
tarism. On her Sunday-night radio show, the gossipy Louella Parsons
called it "the most startling factual film I have ever seen."

Ted signed a five-hundred-dollar-a-week contract with Warners
and went in to meet his new boss, who stood as Ted entered his
office and kept standing. "Joan Crawford has just lost her emerald
brooch in a toilet on Stage Seven," Wald said. "We'll talk on the
way."

In the furor that ensued as Wald helped to fish out the brooch,
he forgot about Ted, and several days later they tried again. Wald
showed him a row of file cabinets. "In these," he said, "are filed
. . . jokes for every occasion, indexed and ready to insert into your
script whenever the story needs to be brightened."

Then Wald began to talk about "a problem picture." Called

Rebel Without a Cause, it was based on Robert M. Lindner's case study of a criminal psychopath named Harold. Ted accepted Wald's challenge to write a screen treatment and began his research into hypnoanalysis. But the committee rule under which screenwriters worked was antithetical to the lonely, quirky creativity that was the only style Ted knew. During those first agonizing weeks at Warners, Wald scolded him for not including a girl named Amy in his draft. "She's the most fascinating character in the whole book!" he insisted.

Ted concluded that his boss had either not read Lindner's book or had distorted its contents. The only reference to Amy that Ted could find was "a few sentences in which Harold said, more or less, 'Then I went to the country and met a girl called Amy. Her I never screwed.'" Before the year was over, Ted "refused to be discovered by Jerry Wald any longer." The only words that survived from his screen treatment were those of the book title, which eventually was claimed for the classic James Dean film in 1955.

While Ted struggled at Warners, a call came from RKO proposing that he write a script for an adaptation of *Your Job in Japan*, another stern indoctrination film on which he had worked. The original had been twenty-two minutes long, bore no credits and ended with a hopeful crescendo from the "Ode to Joy" of Beethoven's Ninth Symphony. But the film's sympathetic attitude toward the Japanese people had helped to trigger a Cabinet-level debate. On August 28, 1945, a cable had gone from General Douglas MacArthur's Pacific headquarters to the Pentagon saying that Capra's *Know Your Enemy—Japan* would not be shown to troops "due to change in policy governing occupation of Japan. Also recommend no press releases or showing to public in United States." Ted blamed MacArthur for killing his film.

Ted accepted the RKO offer, bringing Helen in as collaborator. Drawing from wartime research, they wrote a script portraying the Japanese people as victims of seven centuries of class dictatorship and racketeering, reflecting Ted's concept of the Little Guy and the Big Shot: "the top men of these top families got together . . . and divided up the spoils." But significant changes made in their script discouraged the Geisels. A producer spliced Sherman tanks into the Geisels' lyrical sequence about sixteenth-century Japan.

"That wasn't so long ago," the producer insisted. "We can get away with it." Ever the perfectionist, Ted exploded to a friend: "We'd rather make our own mistakes than have squads of people make them."

RKO called the documentary *Design for Death*; it went through thirty-two major revisions, emerging as a forty-eight-minute film with forty-five hundred feet of confiscated Japanese battle footage. The narrator was Kent Smith, and Hans Conried spoke as the "voice of Japan." As writers, the Geisels shared equal billing with producers and narrators. To qualify for a 1947 Academy Award, the film was previewed in late December and, with strident studio ballyhoo, shown to the film trade on January 22, 1948. *Daily Variety* called it "a documentary of fabulous proportions . . . one of the most interesting screen presentations of the year." Helen and Ted attended the Academy Awards ceremony at Shrine Auditorium in Los Angeles and applauded as the film won the Oscar as best documentary feature. It was a significant career credit; the Geisels had had a hand in two Oscars in two years. Yet neither film would survive. As the years passed, prints disappeared—withdrawn, Ted was convinced, under government order.

Ted liked doing films but he knew he might spend his life as "a decent but forgotten filmmaker." He reveled in the freedom and relative permanency of books and, once out of the army, he re-newed his friendship with Bennett Cerf, who was enthusiastic about soaring postwar interest in children's books. Sales were rising; returning fathers vowed to stay closer to their children, and the baby boom promised a growing market. Ted was especially intrigued by breakthroughs in the cost and quality of lithography, which was overtaking letterpress printing with a spectrum of color never seen in children's picture books.

In the summer of 1946 the Geisels had a call from their New York friend Kelvin Vanderlip, offering them a tony summer retreat at his Villa Narcissa above the Pacific at Palos Verdes Estates southwest of Los Angeles. The Geisels accepted immediately, closed the Hollywood house and installed Ted's studio overlooking a formal Tuscan garden in a house furnished with tapestries and stately furniture from the Italian Renaissance. The estate had a celebrated history: Myrna Loy had lived there before the war with Arthur Hornblower, and Paulette Goddard and Burgess Meredith had honeymooned there. During the Geisels' summer by the sea, the social tempo reminded them of the lush life of Depression days at Beechwood, the Hudson River estate built by Vanderlip's banker father.

After a few golden mornings padding about the terrace, Ted declared that he wanted to live the rest of his life in a climate that allowed him "to walk around outside in my pajamas." The sunlight on the hillside and reflecting pools of the Villa Narcissa glowed with the bright, piercing colors of the Mediterranean, and Ted began painting in watercolor to illustrate *McElligot's Pool*, his first book in seven years. Elin Vanderlip, a handsome Norwegian who met and married Kelvin that season, recalled the shock of seeing Ted's still-damp paintings propped against antique chairs and tables throughout the high-ceilinged parlor and refectory. Even the Vanderlips' prized fifteenth-century credenza was submerged in swirls of blues and greens, inhabited by the oddest creatures Elin had ever seen. There was a fish that was part cow and another with a sawtooth snout so long it had to be towed by a gasping slave. Ted drew an Australian fish with a kangaroo's pouch and a fish from which flowers emerged in full bloom.

McElligot's Pool, published in 1947, became a Junior Literary Guild selection, and its art brought Ted his first Caldecott citation. In technique the book suggested the fantasy parade of *Mulberry Street*; Marco catches no fish in McElligot's pool, but dreams of the creatures that might exist there. *The New York Times* observed that it was characteristic of Dr. Seuss to have his worm "wrapping itself around a hook instead of being pierced by it." Ted dedicated the book to his father, "the World's Greatest Authority on Blackfish, Fiddler Crabs and Deegel Trout." (Deegel trout had been their private joke since a desultory fishing trip in his childhood when his father bought outsized trout from the Deegel hatchery and passed them off as their catch.)

For *McElligot's Pool* Ted chose to "exaggerate within a logical sequence" in creating an underwater world that would be plausible to a child. With a more formal style and beauty than previous Dr. Seuss books, it became treasured by artists. Such acclaim came even though the Random House budget dictated that only alternate pairs of facing pages be printed in color. It was his only book in watercolor because he decided that children prefer flat, bold colors and cartoon illustrations. Yet he had a "mortal fear" of his work looking "like a comic book."

For a time there was another Dr. Seuss book each year, and Ted's royalties, though small by movie standards, were growing. In 1948 *Thidwick the Big-Hearted Moose* appeared to splendid reviews and gave a name to the overly tolerant person for whom others' impositions become an insurmountable burden. It became another Junior Literary Guild selection and his editor, Saxe Commins, wrote Ted, "I shall never cease to wonder at these figments of your inexhaustible brain." In 1949, eleven years after *500 Hats*, Bartholomew Cubbins returned as a page in the court of a petulant king who growled in turn at the sun, rain, fog and snow, longing for anything different. *Bartholomew and the Oobleck* told of the gloppy green goo that spread over the Kingdom of Didd until the king spoke the difficult words: "I'm sorry. It's my fault." The book was dedicated to Elin and Kelvin Vanderlip's first child— and Ted's godson—Kelvin Jr.

Ted's explanation for *Oobleck* was uncommonly straightforward. "I didn't dream it up," he said. On a rainy night in Belgium in 1944, trapped behind the lines in the Battle of the Bulge, he had watched two American soldiers splash in out of the dark. "Rain, always rain!" one muttered. "Why can't we have something different for a change?"

As he worked on *Oobleck* Ted created advertising concepts for the Ford Motor Company, which was considering a television campaign involving animation. While he no longer solicited such work, he accepted it as prudent insurance for a children's book author. But the combined workloads led to eyestrain and the first of many visits to ophthalmologists.

Ted's savvy in production matters was becoming legendary at Random House, spurring extra effort to satisfy him. "About all we ever did to his words was cut back on his exclamation points," Louise Bonino said. When she expressed regret about a budgeted reduction in the publisher's use of color, Ted wrote: "Don't let it disturb you. I'll get you a strong cover and endpaper [without color]." The book appeared in black and a single color, the livid green of the Oobleck. Ted had chosen the green and mailed a sample to Bonino, writing, "Problem was to find something unusual . . . but something that wouldn't be weird or unpleasant. Pinks are out. They suggest flesh too much. Purples seem morbid. I sort of like this green . . . be sure the printer prints the Oobleck color first . . . there will be a light black tone in the Oobleck, and this would be muddied up and lost if the color went on top." Ted's persnickety approach could hardly be faulted after it led to a second Caldecott citation. Uncommonly, for a production manager, Ray Freiman became a total fan of his author. "He is his work, all the whimsy and zaniness of it is part of him, and his constant patter of wisecracks."

When an invitation came from Professor Brewster Ghiselin at the University of Utah to lecture at a ten-day writers' conference at Salt Lake City in July of 1949, Ted accepted with uncharacteristic alacrity. The company was lively: the Russian novelist Vladimir Nabokov, who had moved to America nine years earlier; a budding American novelist, the forty-year-old Wallace Stegner; and poets William Carlos Williams and John Crowe Ransom.

Ted had strong convictions about effective writing for children and spent weeks in research, making extensive lecture notes, for him an extraordinarily scholarly effort. Classical myths were lost on children, he believed, except for their vivid imagery: Hermes on winged sandals, Apollo pursuing Diana through the sky, Thor and his hammer, Pandora's box. He found Aesop's fables "too cold and abstract, too mathematical and intellectual" and Homer's *Iliad* "too complicated," but *The Odyssey* was "exciting" and *Robin Hood* rewarding for its "great roguish tricks." For Ted, *Robinson Crusoe* met "the seven needs" of children: love, security, belonging, to achieve and to know, and the needs for change and aesthetics. He particularly liked the books of wit and realism that had begun appearing in the Victorian era, tales by Hans Christian Andersen, Robert Louis Stevenson and Mark Twain with "characters of flesh and blood" where "warm tolerance replaced scoldings." In Utah Ted shyly allowed students to know where he placed himself: "In the realm of nonsense,

there are Mother Goose, (Edward) Lear, (Lewis) Carroll, P. L. Travers and Dr. Seuss."

He gave lectures and led six workshops. To fend off his habitual stage fright, Ted slipped into the lecture hall one night and filled forty feet of blackboard space with faint sketches to illustrate his points. When he arrived the next day the board was bare and a janitor proudly told him, "Some kids really messed up the blackboard last night and so I cleaned it for you." As Ted feared, he quickly ran out of space in his exuberance, and found himself "drawing in air." But he endeared himself by his charm and patience, and gave his students practical advice. "Write a verse a day, not to send to publishers, but to throw in waste baskets. It will help your prose. It will give you swing. Shorten paragraphs and sentences, then shorten words. . . . Use verbs. Let the kids fill in the adjectives. . . . Why write about the clouds over fairyland when you have better clouds over Utah that you know and understand?"

Ted had a marvelous time, sharing his philosophy more than ever before. "This is the crux," he said, writing in red chalk: "A man with two heads is not a story. It is a situation to be built upon logically. He must have two hats and two toothbrushes. Don't go wild with hair made of purple seaweed, or live fireflies for eyeballs. . . . Children analyze fantasy. They know you're kidding them. There's got to be logic in the *way* you kid them. Their fun is pretending . . . making believe they believe it."

The faculty lived in a sorority house, gathering in the afternoons around a swimming pool. Professor Ghiselin recalled Ted as being "in fine fettle, energetic, prolific, accommodating, adaptive, always in action—though never ostentatiously." He remembers Ted afloat at the deep end of the pool with Helen, calling her "Big Boy"— "evidently a pet name, not for the ears of the hoi polloi." Stegner found Ted "constantly gay and funny. I remember him [in the pool] playing seal, complete with barking. . . ."

One night the Stegners' thirteen-year-old son, Page, and the Nabokovs' son, Dmitri, fifteen, were late returning from a movie. Nabokov paced the front porch and finally called the police. The boys appeared after eleven, explaining that they had stayed for a second feature and had missed the last streetcar. Ted had tried to distract Nabokov by drawing a grotesque vacuum cup sucking up a wizened Page Stegner into a machine named the Stegner Junior Reducifier. Forty years later as a university professor, Page Stegner kept the drawing framed on his wall. "When Dmitri crashed in flames over a little California sexpot," Wallace Stegner recalled, "Ted was urged to make a Nabokov Junior Reducifier too, but refrained."

For Nabokov the lepidopterist, who more than once disappeared with his butterfly net, Ted wrote some verse that he called "To a Butterfly With Fallen Womb":

> No surgic band, no metal truss
> is on the market, little cuss,
> quite small enough to fit your groin,
> to gird your microscopic loin.
> You're destined til the day of doom
> to tote a badly fallen womb.
> But cheer up lass! Don't feel so low.
> The damned thing really doesn't show!

Coming forward to shake hands after Ted's first lecture, Libby Childs, a Salt Lake City teacher, and her husband, Orlo, a geology professor, introduced themselves and asked what they could do to make Ted's stay happier.

"I want to go swimming in the Great Salt Lake," Ted said. "I need to know what it feels like."

On Sunday morning, the Childses packed a picnic and picked up Helen and Ted. During a stop at their home, their son Brad, not yet three, recited all of *Thidwick*. "I don't write for kids that young," Ted said as they drove on. "How does he do it?"

They spent hours on the sandy shores of the lake, changing in beach huts that were numbered. Libby called out, "Ted, are you forty-eight?"

His voice boomed back. "I'm not *that* old!" Their playful day at the lake led to lifelong friendship.

Ted left Salt Lake City so exhilarated that he immediately mailed his bulky lecture notes to Louise Bonino and began outlining a textbook on children's book writing. But he heard nothing from

New York, and a month later he wrote again. "I've received invitations to give this same talk in half a dozen places from here to Chicago," he wrote. She did not respond. Six weeks later he telegraphed: COULD YOU PLEASE WIRE ... TODAY WHETHER YOU HAVE ANY INTEREST IN LECTURE NOTES SENT IN JULY. AM BEING CROWDED FOR DECISION ON THIS PROPERTY, BUT WILL STALL IF YOU WANT THIS AND OTHER CHILDREN'S WORKSHOP MATERIAL DEVELOPED FURTHER.

Louise telegraphed to say she was writing immediately. The notion of Ted as an expert on children's book writing had crashed at Random House. It had gone up the ranks to Bennett Cerf and stunned everyone along the route, and Louise wrote Ted:

> You enjoy the adulation not only of the general public but also of the children's librarians. . . . Some of them would feel an author-artist of picture books could hardly qualify as an expert in the entire field of juvenile writing. . . . [Saxe Commins's] concern is that it would interrupt you in the steady production of your marvelous children's books [and bring] down on your head all kinds of criticism for doing a semiformal book which tries to explain method, when there is so much inspired madness in your own work. . . . I am returning your notes under separate cover.

Ted was heartsick. He had endured many rejections, but never one that so unequivocally closed off an avenue he longed to explore. Subdued but respectful of market counsel, he wrote Bonino, "About the next book . . . (if you want a next book) . . . Would a story about the King's Magicians be a good thing to do? . . . Is it good to follow a *Bartholomew* story with another *Bartholomew*?" Bonino suggested he try another *Horton* instead, and four years later he did.

As the value of Helen's trust fund grew they had begun looking at sites for a permanent California home, and one evening in 1948 at La Jolla, by now a snug and upscale San Diego suburb of about twenty thousand people, they told the architect Tom Shepard they wanted to build "somewhere high up, overlooking everything."

"There's nothing higher than that old observation tower up on Mount Soledad where the kids go to park," Shepard said.

"Let's go look," Ted replied.

The air was dry and it was a starry night. All of Southern California seemed in their lap. The next morning they bought the tower and two acres around it, eight hundred feet above the center of La Jolla, launching the final step in the dream they had cherished since their first visit twenty years earlier.

Max Miller, who wrote *I Cover the Waterfront*, lived in La Jolla, and in his newspaper column he heralded the Geisels' hilltop acquisition as a joke on the locals, most of whom had thought the tower was city property. It had been built in the 1920s to show real estate customers the view they would have if they bought a lot. Soon it had become young La Jollans' favorite parking site, its walls carved with the initials of hundreds of lovers.

To the south, Helen and Ted could look across the city of San Diego to the ocher hills of Mexico's Baja California peninsula. Up the coastline toward Los Angeles, they saw an arc of sea and shore for sixty miles. Inland were buff foothills, citrus and avocado ranches, and, on clear winter days, the snowy heights of San Jacinto Peak above Palm Springs. They promptly sold their La Jolla Shores vacation house and put the Hollywood house up for sale.

Ted and Helen picnicked at the site as construction began on September 17, 1948, her fiftieth birthday. A year later they began settling into their new pink-stucco house with a red-tile roof, larger than either of their earlier houses. Two bedrooms and two baths clustered around the stairway to the two-story tower, and a large living room with wide windows looked down across the village to the sea. For shade they planted eucalyptus trees and oleanders.

Helen's stationery called their home "The Tower," and it became an instant landmark, silhouetted against the sky above the year-round green of the country-club golf course at the top of steep switchbacks on Encelia Drive. In this storybook citadel atop this fairy-tale mountain, the Geisels lived and worked for the rest of their lives.

At first Ted's studio was upstairs in the tower, but soon he moved to the ground-level room where he had a fireplace, wide bookshelves and running water. His concentration was so intense that the 360-degree panorama seemed less important to him. As he began sketching panels for *If I Ran the Zoo*, traceable to his Springfield childhood, he turned his five-foot-long desk so that he worked with his back to the view, a northerly light reflecting off the distant sea at his left.* *If I Ran the Zoo* was dedicated to other godchildren, Toni and Michael Gordon Tackaberry Thompson, the daughter and son of James "Bim" Thompson and Peggy Conklin, the Broadway actress who had been the Geisels' friend since the Depression. Ted loved what he called the "crazy iambic pentameter" of Michael's long, rolling name and gave him personalized stationery for his eighth birthday.

Ted's habits were rigid: he rose after nine, went to his desk by ten and stayed there throughout the day with only brief breaks. He worked seven days a week, secluded from the distraction even of radio or taped music. At the center of his desk was the stained wooden drawing board he had used since his cartooning days in New York. Every project began here as he doodled on a sketch pad for ideas. The board was surrounded by ceramic pots, mugs and trays crammed with hundreds of colored pencils, some down to two-inch stubs; paintbrushes permanently stained blue, lime-green or turquoise, and art gum erasers that seemed chewed to the nub. Ted was frugal, but he saved these pencil stubs and cracked mugs largely because they had become his companions and he abhorred unnecessary change. He kept a few travel mementos nearby: a wall hanging from the Peruvian Andes, a camel saddle from Turkey.

Ted sat in a high-backed swivel chair, often flinging his long legs on top of the desk as he stared into space. Every few minutes he would stride up and down the studio, leaning forward at full tilt as if "into a gale," his hands thrust in his rear trousers pockets. He lit one cigarette after another, pausing before the corkboard walls to scowl at his latest sketch, his glasses pushed up on his forehead, wondering if a new creature was about to emerge, who it might be and what it might say. He liked to approach a book "with a situation or a conflict and then write myself into an impossible position so there is no [apparent] way of ending [the book]. . . . People who think about the endings first come up with inferior products." When hit with a mental block, he threw himself on a mustard-colored sofa near the hearth to read mysteries. His "best stuff," he said, was written "on toward midnight" when he was looser, freer and "a bit tired." He preferred the late hours because the telephone was quiet and the stillness of the mountain-top enveloped him. "He has the endurance of forty buffaloes," Helen said, "and thinks he can work day and night." She served more regularly as Ted's voice, writing Louise Bonino to decline proposed promotional appearances for Ted in New York and Detroit. "Ted says he owes you a thousand letters, and will I please make peace."

As Dr. Seuss books became more popular few critics could refrain from trying to probe the simplicity and directness that so endeared them to children. Sometimes Ted read aloud from a pompous review, pausing to laugh and underscore its absurdities. Nine years after *Thidwick* appeared, David Dempsey asked in *The New York Times Book Review* if Thidwick's bigheartedness was "simply a form of moral pusillanimity." Yet Dempsey then wrote a passage that Ted found startling but credible:

> *Thidwick* is a masterpiece of economy, and a shrewd satire on the "easy mark" who lets the conventions of society get the better of him. The genius of the story, however, lies in its finale. A man of less consistency than Seuss would have let Thidwick be rescued by the creatures he is befriending (this is the customary Disney riposte in similar situations) but Seuss' logic is rooted in principle, rather than sentiment, and the sponging animals get what they deserve. Incidentally, this is also what the child expects.

Despite his success in the publishing world, Ted still remained fascinated with Hollywood and could not make a final break. His wartime colleague P. D. Eastman had joined a new animation studio called United Productions of America. "All the cartoons being made are obsolete," he told Ted over lunch. "Mice keep outsmarting cats, and rabbits are always wiser than foxes. UPA has a fresh outlook. You must have a story idea for us."

Ted did. He had recently sold a children's story to Capitol Records, a satire about people who ostracize those who are "different." "Just suppose," he said, "there was a little kid who didn't speak words but only weird sounds?"

CHAPTER 11

The 5,000 Fingers of Dr. T.

1951–1953

The story of *Gerald McBoing-Boing* brought a check for five hundred dollars from UPA, and Ted was so fascinated that he went to the studio each week to see how animation artists were bringing his character to life.

Gerald, who speaks no words, becomes a round-faced boy with a blond topknot; his parents are in despair, for all they hear from him is the sound of a horse's neigh, a creaking door or an airplane taking off. Everyone ridicules Gerald, so, sad and friendless, he runs away from home. A talent scout finds him shivering in the snow and offers him a job doing sound effects on radio.

"Don't make fun of him," Ted instructed in the margin of the script he wrote for UPA. "He's a success."

> . . . and ten minutes later
> throughout this great land,
> more than 10 million people heard Gerald let go
> with a (crash, crash, crash, crash) on a radio show.

Gerald's proud parents are guests in the studio audience. After his performance, the young celebrity is reunited with them and they depart in a chauffeured limousine.

Critics wrote that the cartoon raised the animators' art to a higher plateau, and Gerald brought UPA an Academy Award for the best cartoon of 1951. Now Ted had an interest in three Oscars.

Still, Ted's books rolled on. *If I Ran the Zoo*, written in the Tower at La Jolla, appeared in 1950. While its origins were often attributed to his father's role with the Springfield zoo, Ted linked it to his mother, who had been working on a zoo story when he returned from Oxford. "I did [it] in her memory," he said. Once again he relied on his cunning sense of a fantasy parade, promising action, novelty and surprise:

> "But if I ran the zoo,"
> Said young Gerald McGrew,
> "I'd make a few changes.
> That's just what I'd do . . ."

In this book, however, Ted invented words and creatures even less related than before to any known language or life. He was driving himself in a breathless search of Seussian sounds and rhythms.

> . . . And then, just to show them, I'll sail to Ka–Troo
> And
> Bring
> Back
> An It–Kutch, a Preep . . . and a Proo . . .
> A Nerkle . . . a Nerd, and a Seersucker too.

Random House sold out the first printing of *If I Ran the Zoo* more rapidly than expected, and it disappeared from stores weeks before Christmas. While Ted busied himself with a long-running series of monthly children's stories for *Redbook*, Helen was hoping for a time-out from work and looked forward to a leisurely trip; she was tired, and had developed painful ulcers.

But Ted had sent a story idea to Columbia Studios, and Hollywood again called. Lured like a moth to a flame by a $35,000 advance in February 1951, he was suddenly immersed with producer Stanley Kramer in a feature-length fantasy to be called *The 5,000 Fingers of Dr. T.* Ted saw it as his classic Hollywood break, a bold chance to do things his way. Helen smiled supportively, but to her niece, Barbara Palmer, she confessed, "We seem to be plunging right into a blitz . . . there'll be no book this year, no trips East, no trips anywhere."

Ted called his fantasy "a vicious satire." Like Ted as a child, Bart, the ten-year-old boy of the film (played by Tommy Rettig of the *Lassie* series), is bored by piano lessons. Falling asleep as he practices, he drifts in a Technicolor dream to a castle in which the evil Dr. Terwilliker (Hans Conried) presides over an endless keyboard two stories high. Confined like galley slaves and threatened with the dungeon, five hundred boys appear hypnotized into recital until the young hero, desperate to save his widowed mother from Dr. Terwilliker's spell, leads a rebellion and the villain is routed.

To be near the set, the Geisels took an apartment on North Kingsley Drive in Hollywood, driving back to La Jolla on weekends. "This picture is really such a long-time dream of Ted's," Helen wrote her niece, "that whatever we have to give up to do it is really of no importance. . . ." He was writing lyrics and the screenplay in collaboration with Allan Scott and drawing sketches for sets. By midsummer Helen, perhaps overstating her husband's naïve appraisal, described Ted as being "in charge of the entire production. He isn't officially the producer or director, but they have been instructed to work with him and plan everything in accordance with his ideas." Despite his years in Hollywood, Ted had no tolerance for infighting and was quickly overwhelmed by studio intrigue. When he was away from the studio, Helen said, "somebody always decides that some ridiculous thing should be done to the script."

When production was postponed from July to December, the Geisels visited Villa Narcissa and Ted talked incessantly with Kelvin and Elin Vanderlip about the movie. "He desperately wanted to be a success in films," Elin recalled. "He was so triumphant about the idea of *The 5,000 Fingers*." Helen reported that Roy Rowland, the director, had ulcers. "Ted . . . simply can't have one, for I already have too many for us both."

In late fall, production was postponed again. Several of Frederick Hollander's songs were ready, and Ted was elated at their use of his lyrics. "They're really so lovely that I feel quite optimistic about the whole thing being a success," Helen wrote. "Maybe we'll make a lot of money. In that case we'll go to Ireland, Japan, South Africa and Siam." Over Thanksgiving weekend the Geisels drove down the Baja California coast of Mexico with their La Jolla friends Marian and Edward Longstreth. They slept late, lounged in warm sunshine on the beach and dined on local lobsters. But their escape was short. "Alas, alas," Helen wrote, "we have no book this year, and if this film doesn't hurry up, we're likely not to have one next year either."

By New Year's Day of 1952 Ted was dejected, finally recognizing the chaos within the company. He felt that his script had been eviscerated and announced that he was withdrawing from the film. Stanley Kramer, astonished, told Ted he needed him to save the picture, and he listened quietly to Ted's complaints, promising to delete scenes that Ted considered vulgar. Ted relented. The recently wed Mary Healy and Peter Lind Hayes, cast as widowed mother and friendly plumber, flew from New York to rehearse the songs.

But as forty stage carpenters went on day-and-night shifts, production of *The 5,000 Fingers* was postponed once again, until late February. Although Ted saw little progress in resurrecting his concept, the sets were relatively faithful to his sketches— the monstrous piano, a subterranean castle with a dungeon and terrifying culs-de-sac, pirates' coves and ladders dead-ending in the sky. Helen compared them to Ted's drawings in *The 500 Hats*.

When shooting finally began in March, budget cuts abounded. Helen counted the "five hundred" boy pianists and found only one hundred and fifty. "There wasn't enough money to do what should really have been a musical extravaganza," Kramer said later. Helen termed the set a madhouse, "especially in one scene where [the boys] all have to kick and scream and jump on the piano and drag Dr. T. in his ermines . . . off to the dungeon."

One of Ted's few happy memories from those months was of the rainy day when the young pianists took a break to gulp down commissary hot dogs; one boy became ill and vomited on his keyboard. "This started a chain reaction," Ted recalled, "causing one after another of the boys to go queasy in the greatest mass upchuck in the history of Hollywood. . . . When the picture was finally released, the critics reacted in much the same manner."

With shooting over in mid-April the Geisels retreated once again to La Jolla. When he wasn't sleeping Ted was in his studio working, night and day, on the long-delayed *Scrambled Eggs Super!* On May 11 he drove alone up the Pacific Coast Highway to Kramer's home for a screening that left the producer depressed and Ted in despair. Ted felt that compromises had overwhelmed his spontaneity and the logic of his nonsense, and the picture had become more mime than fantasy. In a sad and bitter mood he joined Kramer and the company in frantic weeks of efforts to salvage the production. Helen was desperate. "Ted simply has to get his book done and get it to New York. It was due in January and if we don't get it there early in June, it will be too late for the Christmas trade."

Illness swept through the film company and tempers flared. Late one evening Ted drove back to La Jolla and paced the floor of his studio through the night. At daybreak Helen gave him two sleeping pills and telephoned Louise Bonino to say they wouldn't be coming to New York as planned and the book about scrambled eggs would not be delivered in time for Christmas sales. When Ted finally awoke, Helen was firm. "We have to get away. I've made reservations for a week at Lake Tahoe."

The first sneak preview of *The 5,000 Fingers* was in a suburban Los Angeles theater in January 1953. Ted had tried to forget the film by focusing on finishing his book, but both he and Helen yearned for a flicker of hope, and they drove up for the evening. It turned out to be a scene of acute professional embarrassment that haunted Ted for the rest of his life. Fifteen minutes into the movie the preview audience began filing out. Ted recalled, "At the end there were only five people left besides Kramer and our staff. It was a disaster. Careers were ruined." For him it was "the worst evening of my life." Helen agreed that it was "as bad as we had anticipated"; she desperately wanted to get Ted "to some foreign land" when the film was released so that he would not be dragged down by the wave of critical rejection that both expected.

"I wish Japan were a little nearer and a little cheaper and we could go there and collect our yen, take hot baths and begin life anew."

In the midst of disappointment, a phone call brought Japan "nearer and cheaper" for the Geisels when Ted was offered a contract with *Life* to go there and write about Japanese children. While packing for their departure, they received an advance copy of *Scrambled Eggs Super!* and Bennett Cerf telephoned from New York to bid them bon voyage and express his joy at being back in business with a new Dr. Seuss book.

Helen and Ted sailed from Los Angeles on March 24, 1953, on the *President Cleveland.* Aboard with them as far as Honolulu, they were charmed to discover, were the only surviving former presidents of the United States, Herbert Hoover and Harry Truman. With Truman were Bess and their daughter, Margaret, on their first vacation since his departure from the White House two months earlier. The Trumans seemed "extremely pleasant," and Helen observed that "even some of the most dour Republicans have been forced to break down and smile." During the ten-day voyage to Tokyo the Geisels pored over research materials on postwar Japan and marveled at how little they understood of Japanese culture despite their work on the military documentary.

It had been less than eight years since the first atom bombs were dropped on Hiroshima and Nagasaki. American civilian visitors remained a curiosity, and Japanese reporters and photographers crowded around the Geisels at the dock. Their Japanese publisher gave a banquet in a lavish geisha house, leaving Ted torn between awe and laughter. Helen, always an exuberant traveler, called their journey "the craziest operation we've ever embarked on. . . . Life couldn't be stranger if we were in Tibet. . . . We've been in Japan one week, and I've not met one wife, or even heard [one] mentioned!" But their three weeks in venerable Kyoto engrossed them. Its palaces and shrines, its temples and imperial gardens, had been spared by American bombers.

Ted's assignment was to learn how the years of American occupation had changed the aspirations of Japanese schoolchildren. His Dartmouth friend, Professor Donald Bartlett, with close diplomatic ties in Japan, had arranged with teachers in Kyoto, Osaka and Kobe to have their students draw pictures of what they hoped to be when they grew up. Almost fifteen thousand drawings were submitted and Ted saw that Westernization had indeed invaded their minds. Boys wanted to become aviators, but only one pictured himself firing a gun; another hoped to go to Mars to learn how to solve the rice shortage. Girls saw themselves as hostesses on interurban buses, in mimicry of Western airline hostesses. Ted considered their work superb, and, with his interpretive text, some of it appeared in *Life* as "Japan's Young Dreams." But his piece was rewritten, Ted grumbled, "almost entirely, substituting conclusions of their [own] not warranted by the facts. . . . Henry Luce was always anti-Japanese and pro-Chinese, and they raped the article." Ted offered intriguing evidence with his criticism: very few children drew themselves in Oriental clothing, but these few formed a high proportion of the ones published by *Life*.

When they docked at San Francisco aboard the *President Wilson* after a six-week absence, Helen and Ted brought ashore wicker trunkloads of children's drawings. "We only travel on ships named for Democrats," Helen told her niece, Barbara, at the dock. On the next day they traveled by train down the California coast to find the reviews for *The 5,000 Fingers* just appearing. Some of them were favorable, but not enough to encourage Ted to believe that his future lay in films. *Variety* called the dungeon scene worth the price of admission, and thought that "the mad humor of Dr. Seuss has been captured . . . in this odd flight into chimerical fiction." In *The New York Times*, Bosley Crowther conceded the "good intentions" of this "trickiest sort of entertainment—symbolic fantasy," but thought the film "abstruse in its symbols and in its vast elaboration of reveries [and] also dismally lacking in . . . humor or . . . enchantment." *The Christian Science Monitor* was aggrieved that "the makers of the film could not have scored their point about the rights of small fry without seeming utterly to condemn the study of the piano."

"It was one of my favorite properties," Kramer said later, "and one which I very much wanted to direct myself [but] Columbia Pictures wasn't ready for that yet. . . . Perhaps Rowland was not the right director. The picture required a tougher man."

Over the years *The 5,000 Fingers of Dr. T.* developed a cult of fans, and video rentals kept it in circulation. Its novelty remained its strong appeal; some fans treasured it as an arty feature-length cartoon with live actors and realized that nothing quite like it had been attempted by Hollywood. But for years Ted grew grim at any mention of the film, and declined to list it in his official Random House biography. He called the making of *The 5,000 Fingers* the greatest "down period" of his career. "As to who was most responsible for this debaculous fiasco, I will have nothing more to say until all the participants have passed away, including myself."

But he was resilient. The Japanese sojourn had been timely. "Fortunately," Helen wrote, "Japan cured Ted's wounds on the subject [of *5,000 Fingers*]. We consider it now only as serious as the fall of Rome."

In New York Ted had another long and rewarding afternoon of conversation with his editor, Saxe Commins, who had resisted Ted's impulse after his Utah lectures to become an authority on children's literature. Instead, Saxe rekindled his ambition to grow into a creative force.

Commins had imposing powers. Of slight stature, he was modest and reticent, but his intuitive strengths opened clear channels between him and his authors. Ted loved to relate how Commins had once moved quietly back and forth at Random House between three rooms where three of his authors struggled with last-minute revisions. The authors were Eugene O'Neill, William Faulkner and Ted Geisel.

"He was the kind of editor I loved," Ted said. "He never would tell you anything was wrong. He'd make you think, and you'd come around to your own conclusion. He'd spend an hour talking about three or four lines. He made me defend myself, telling me that what I'd said on page seven should have been on page three. We had almost abstract discussions of the logical order of a story. He helped me realize that a paragraph in a children's book is equal to a chapter in an adult book. He convinced me that I had as much responsibility to take as much time and work as hard as [adult writers] did."

Ted had written Saxe to compliment him on his recent piece in *Saturday Review* about the ideal relationship between editors and graphic-arts people, in which he pleaded for more publishing opportunities for young, offbeat talent. Ted called it "the clearest, brightest article I've ever read on a subject that most people, for some reason, seem to write inside of dark haggis bladders. . . . The important element, as you pointed out to me . . . is getting my soul out of the confines of a haggis bladder . . . and many things you said kept me from crawling back inside. . . . I'm really outside now. . . .

"What the hell *is* a haggis bladder?"

CHAPTER 12

La Jolla

1953–1955

On a wintry day in 1953, at lunch in New York with his agent, Phyllis Jackson, Ted was in his most entertaining and irresistible form. Even the ordeals of *The 5,000 Fingers of Dr. T.* sounded hilarious, and his proposal for an ad campaign for Ford was nothing less than a comic opera. There were stories about his hosts in Japan, but these were sympathetic; while Ted inveighed against stupidity in power, he always sided with the underdog.

Phyllis had brought him a lucrative proposal for an educational television series, but he shrugged it off. Knowing him well, she was not surprised when he leaned back, lit a cigarette and got to the point. "It's been seven years since I gave up being a soldier," he said. "Now I'd like to give up movies and advertising and anything else that means dueling with vice presidents and committees, hmmm?"

"So what will you do?" she asked.

"I want to stay in La Jolla and write children's books," he said. He drew hard on his cigarette, exhaled slowly and gave her a pleading stare. "If I dropped everything else, do you think I could count on royalties of five thousand dollars a year?"

Phyllis began to smile but thought better of it. "It's entirely possible," she said. "The children's market is building because of the baby boom, and you have a reputation."

His question had not been ingenuous. He had learned to expect no riches from children's books; *Mulberry Street* and *The 500 Hats* were yielding royalties of only a few hundred dollars a year. He had told his Hollywood friend Chuck Jones, "We can live on one hundred dollars a week. If I could get five thousand dollars a year in royalties, I'd be set up for life!"

Jones had cocked his head skeptically. "Don't forget," he said, "that good screenwriters are earning five times that much."

"If I'd wanted to live that way," Ted replied, "I'd never have left Warners."

In the flush of his new commitment to books, Ted settled more visibly into his community. He became a trustee of the San Diego Fine Arts Museum and of the La Jolla Town Council. The Geisels were prized as witty and urbane dinner guests, and Helen herself had begun giving small, elegant dinner parties, often to honor out-of-town visitors. Many of their friends were from the Scripps Institution of Oceanography, whose long ocean pier was part of Ted's studio view. They often saw the institution's tall director, Roger Revelle, and his wife, Ellen, a member of the Scripps newspaper family. With Gifford Ewing, another Scripps scientist, Ted flew to Mexico on expeditions. He and Helen shared Mexican meals with Francis Shepard, a soft-voiced ocean geologist, and his wife, Elizabeth, and sometimes went to Tijuana with them to bet on jai alai games. With Scripps friends they spent a boisterous winter holiday on the yacht of the wealthy and reclusive D. K. Ludwig, anchored in the Guerrero Negro lagoon on the Baja California coast where Ludwig owned a salt-processing plant. Here California gray whales mated, spawned and breached in such numbers and with such exuberance that Ted likened their underwater rumblings to the New York subway.

Ted spent quiet, happy evenings matching wits with the puckish Colonel Sawyer, an attorney for Consolidated Vultee Aircraft Company, introducing him to friends with elaborate explanations that "Colonel" was his given name, and that he had no rank at all. The Geisels often dined with their attorney, Frank Kockritz, and his wife, Susan. At holiday parties they invited hilltop neighbors, including journalist friends, the earnest psychiatrist Stanley Willis and Bert Hupp, who had retired as chairman of the Sunshine Biscuit Company in Kansas City.

One night they invited another local literary eminence, the mystery novelist Raymond Chandler, and his wife, Cissy, to dinner. The reclusive Chandlers had moved to La Jolla from Hollywood in 1946, just before the Geisels had built their home, driven by similar disillusionment with the film industry. Cissy had become an invalid, and Chandler, a shy and sensitive man when sober, came alone that evening, drank too much and alarmed Helen with his diatribes. "This town," he roared across the dinner table, "is inhabited by arthritic billionaires and barren old women!"

Helen was persuaded to join the board of directors of the La Jolla Museum of Art, a seaside gallery of contemporary works. It was housed in the former home of the community's most generous patron, Ellen Browning Scripps, a half-sister of E. W. Scripps, the founder of Scripps-Howard Newspapers. Helen was especially fond of Marian Longstreth, a Mississippi-born patron and cofounder of the La Jolla Playhouse, then in its infancy as a summer stock company led by three distinguished film actors, Gregory Peck, Dorothy McGuire and Mel Ferrer. After opening-night performances at the La Jolla High School auditorium, the Geisels gathered with the Longstreths and the theater company at the Whaling Bar in La Valencia Hotel, just above La Jolla Cove, where they had dined when they first visited La Jolla in 1928. Marian's husband, Edward, a jovial bumbler and religious dramatist who claimed to have edited an art magazine in Philadelphia, became one of Ted's favorite foils.

When Longstreth launched into a condescending lecture about modern art one evening, Ted decided to teach him a lesson. "Ed, I've never told you this," he interrupted, "but I have in my possession five Escarobuses."

Ed's eyes grew wide and his lips quivered.

"Of course you know his work," Ted went on, "the great Mexican modernist? Well, the authorities down there are after him for back taxes. It's the saddest case. I'm going to sell them and get the money to him."

"My God!" Ed said. "I'd give anything to have an Escarobus!"

"Someday I'll show them to you," Ted promised, and stayed up most of that night creating the world's first Escarobus. He peeled the wood off a soft pencil, scraped the lead lengthwise across art paper, dipped small hunks of bread in the vodka he was drinking, and dragged the soggy bread across the paper. Next he painted Godivas on the smudges, bisecting and trisecting them so that it was impossible to tell that they were naked ladies. Later that week, when the painting was dry, he took it to Ed's home and sold it to him for five hundred dollars. Ed stood in front of it at every angle, spoke with reverence of its technique, and offered to buy the rest.

But Helen killed the deal. "You can't take his money!" she said. "Marian is a very good friend of mine!"

Sometimes Helen was "too conservative," Ted lamented. "She spoils some of my best gags."

The Geisels had invited Ted's niece, Peggy, then twenty-four, to live with them for several weeks in 1951, when she moved West and began job-hunting in San Diego. She had grown up in Ted's childhood home in Springfield, and in La Jolla she slept in the tower studio he had vacated. At their request she dropped "Aunt" and "Uncle" and called them Helen and Ted, except during raucous canasta games when he became "Uncle Worm." For her the Tower, with the carved initials and hearts of lovers from years past, was a romantic place, and a year later in her wedding to a naval officer, Albert Owens, she walked down the winding tower staircase.

While living in the Tower, Peggy had a rare intimate view of the Geisels. When she went to bed, Ted would "still be in [his studio] drinking coffee and smoking his cigarettes, both of which drove Helen crazy, she worried so about them." Often he would still be at work at 2:00 A.M.; then he would sleep until nine or ten and begin again.

Peggy had been seventeen when her troubled mother, Ted's sister, Marnie, died, and Helen offered the gentle counsel Peggy had missed. She learned from studying their marriage, finding them "tremendously focused" in related ways. Ted could be difficult and "uptight," but Helen usually smoothed things over. "There was tenseness when he was finishing a book. There would be doom and gloom and 'I'm never going to write anything, I've lost it, I just can't do it.' Then suddenly when something would click he'd walk out of his studio and the world would be wonderful."

When no inspiration came, Ted retreated to his sofa and read.

More often he sat at his desk eight hours a day "whether [or not] anything happens," he said, "which is rough in a vacation community where everybody's down on the beach or out fishing or playing golf." Actually he was rarely tempted by such diversions. In most ways he was a loner; he went for long walks and he swam, which was all he ever listed on his Dartmouth alumni form under "Sports."

During afternoon breaks Ted and Peggy walked over the chaparral slopes of Mount Soledad. "He was forever pausing beside some little blossom to identify it for me," she said, "and . . . he always called it 'California Wildflower.' " On days when work had not gone well, he would change to old clothes and go straight to his rocks, which were scattered around their acreage. "It was his hobby and his therapy. He arranged them into paths and made borders around the succulents he planted." Helen said that her frugal husband had only two extravagances, "cigarettes and rocks." He shaped their desert garden with color blocks of luminous pink blooms, golds and purples, a Seussian "Ravenna mosaic," and placed the dinosaur footprint from his father beside a shady garden path.

Ted's passion for privacy impressed his niece and reminded her of her grandfather. One morning she watched him at the front door talking to a stranger who claimed to have known him in college. Ted was polite but skeptical. As the door closed he growled, "Never heard of him." Yet when a neighbor, the attorney David Casey, appeared at the door to ask the Geisels not to sign a complaint against a plumber who had stolen one of Helen's rings, Ted listened to his plea for an hour, finally promising leniency.

In the fall of 1953, recalling counsel that the juvenile editor Louise Bonino had given him four years earlier, Ted began work on another book about the elephant Horton, writing as usual in the meter called anapestic tetrameter—the rhythm of "'Twas the Night Before Christmas." His use of the beat was taut with excitement and momentum and, as the children's literature professor Francelia Butler wrote, "rollicking and easily remembered . . . so rhythmic it can be skipped to." The theme of the book—"a person's a person no matter how small"—had grown out of visits to Japanese schools, where the importance of the individual was considered an exciting new concept. Ted dedicated the book to his "great friend" Mitsugi Nakamura, a Kyoto university professor whom he had met through Donald Bartlett.

The original title in Ted's early typescript was "Horton Hears 'Em!" but he penciled that out and replaced it with "Horton Hears a Who." Helen was devoted to the theme, and her collaboration is apparent in its manuscript pages. She suggested that he take out " 'earsplitting' before 'hullabaloo' " and substitute a "Seuss onomatopoeic word." The result was "howling mad hullabaloo." For the opening line of the book she liked "On the fifteenth of June in the Jungle of Nool . . ." but he chose May instead. She reminded him to stick to the point: "The idea is that [Whos] are small but important." Ted rewrote himself for tempo and sound. In Horton's frantic search through a huge field of clover, the words "had plucked nineteen thousand four hundred and five" became "had piled up twelve thousand nine hundred and five," and finally "had picked, searched, and piled up, nine thousand and five."

Tardy in completing the book, the Geisels worked through Christmas, canceling plans to attend the ceremonial Bracebridge dinner at the Ahwahnee Hotel in Yosemite National Park, and in January 1954 they flew to New York with the manuscript. At the offices of Random House, in the imposing Italianate brownstone built on Madison Avenue in the 1880s for Henry Villard, who owned the *New York Post*, a Dr. Seuss tradition began: Louise Bonino asked Saxe Commins and Bennett Cerf to come to her office, and Ted read the new book aloud. The applause that greeted *Horton* was sincere and immediate, and Cerf knew it would be a success.

New York was in the midst of an ice storm that week. Helen and Ted, by now committed Southern Californians, winced as they made their rounds "through black ex-snow." They attended a meeting about adapting *The Seven Lady Godivas* as a Broadway musical, a project that Ted was convinced would someday succeed, and he had a reunion with Hans Conried of *The 5,000 Fingers of Dr. T.*, this time in a Rockefeller Center television studio. Ted had written a script about modern art for a half-hour Ford Foundation television workshop in the *Excursion* series, and it was broadcast live over NBC on Sunday afternoon, January 31. Helen said that by showtime "Ted will probably be five pounds thinner, as that is the amount he usually loses before facing the public!" But for a man obsessed with stage fright, he seemed remarkably at ease. Burgess Meredith was the host, and Conried was cast opposite Ted as an art connoisseur. Ted's theme was one that had nagged at him since long before he painted his fake Escarobus. "I know very little about modern art, and that's why I'm so interested in this experiment," he told viewers. "When a modern artist paints a picture of a horse, why doesn't the horse look like a horse?" With that, a white stallion was led onto the set and six art students from New York's Cooper Union set out to paint what they saw. No two paintings were similar, and to Ted none looked like a horse. It was a pleasant half hour of early public-service television, but it was slight, and despite the horse on the set not much happened.

Glad to be back in balmy La Jolla, Ted outlined a script for the *Godivas* musical and wrote lyrics for two or three songs before setting the project aside. Helen impulsively invited friends for three dinner parties in ten days, including one on March 2 for Ted's fiftieth birthday. "It's going to take me a week to recover," Helen wrote her niece Barbara, "and poor Cluny [their Irish setter] is having a complete and permanent hangover!" Another family wedding loomed when Barbara announced that she would marry in June, and Helen wrote, "Never never never have I heard a bit of news that made me more happy. Nothing else matters when you have someone to share things with." Helen gave motherly advice about choosing linens, silver and crystal, and promised eagerly to host a rehearsal dinner.

Even without the pressures of Hollywood, the Geisels were feeling besieged by work. Scores of manuscripts arrived from aspiring children's book authors in Japan, whom they had encouraged to try to break into the American market. Finally they asked Louise Bonino to write notes of regret.

Ted's forays into civic affairs weighed on him too. He had lobbied the La Jolla Town Council for a local billboard ban, and was writing and illustrating an eight-page pamphlet published by the council as *Signs of Civilization!* It was vintage Seuss. Two Stone Age competitors, Guss and Zaxx, hammer out signs for their businesses until their rocky wilderness is a litter of come-ons (GUSS-MA-TUSS IS STOOPENDOUS! 200 YARDS):

> And, thus between them, with impunity
> They loused up the entire community . . .
> And even the dinosaurs moved away
> From that messed-up spot in the U.S.A.
> Which is why
> our business men never shall
> Allow such to happen
> in La Jolla, Cal.

There followed a sign code that became part of a San Diego city ordinance, its first proviso being that there would be no commercial billboards in La Jolla. Soon thereafter, Holly Sugar canceled its contract with Ted for design of its billboards.

In sketches for a fable called *Whither California?* Ted widened his range to rail against the excesses of the postwar growth craze. During slaphappy evenings amid squawking peacocks at Villa Narcissa, he and Kelvin Vanderlip worked on this searing spoof of California's freeway society, its new towns, burger palaces and drive-in churches. Ted's favorite invention was the one-stop "Nata-Luba-Crema," which offered "a nice swim while we grease your car and finalize your loved ones." The book got no further; Helen called it "tasteless and not funny."

She too was deep into community responsibilities. She cared immensely about the Musical Arts Society, a group seeking to bring a resident chamber-music series to a new concert hall at the La Jolla Museum. Nicolai Sokoloff, a pianist and conductor who had retired in La Jolla, was often present at Geisel parties, and on a Friday evening in late May Sokoloff and his wife, Ruth, reciprocated with a dinner to launch the summer concert season. Ted and Helen were in high spirits but were keeping the reason secret: they would be going back to Dartmouth for commencement and Ted would be awarded an honorary doctorate degree. At dinner he received compliments on a mention in *Life* that week in which the author John Hersey bemoaned the general dreariness of children's school primers and suggested that some lively illustrator—perhaps Dr. Seuss—get involved and make reading fun. Ted was interested, and expounded on the deadly dullness of Dick-and-Jane readers.

As Helen stood to leave the party that evening she grimaced with sudden pain in her feet and ankles. Another guest, Dr. Francis M. Smith of the Scripps Metabolic Clinic, asked if he could help. She smiled and said a good night's sleep would cure her, but then took the unusual course of allowing Ted, always erratic at the wheel, to drive them home. Turning her heating pad up high, she tried to sleep, but the pain spread to her legs and lower back. Finally, two nights later, Ted drove her to the Scripps Clinic, and with his help she staggered inside. By the next morning a painful numbness had enveloped her arms, hands and face, and she could not swallow.

Their dinner companion Dr. Smith joined her case and tried to calm Ted, who seemed bewildered; he had always feared doctors and hospitals, and now the woman he leaned on was immobilized. Exhaustion could explain part of her plight, Smith said, but not all. Yet her bedside chart listed only the basics: age 55, height 66 inches, weight 105. Feverish, Helen tried to read, but was too weak to hold even a magazine. She became hysterical, and Ted grew frantic. Smith's preliminary diagnosis included a question mark: "Neuronitis acute, Landry type?, Guillain-Barré syndrome." He ordered a consultation with the neurologist Ralph Barris, and almost immediately the physicians announced that she must be placed in an iron lung. The nearest one was across the city at San Diego County Hospital, a facility best known for the treatment of indigents, and Helen was moved by ambulance to an isolation ward there. When she arrived, Barris noted the increasing weakness of her limbs and found her unable to speak or sit up unassisted. Paralyzed from the neck down, she was placed inside the massive metal respirator with only her head emerging, her eyes flickering wildly in the mirror above. Barris ordered a tracheotomy so that she could breathe, and intravenous feeding began. In the hallway, doctors conferred gravely and told Ted that it was "touch-and-go."

Barris confirmed Smith's diagnosis of Guillain-Barré syndrome, a rare but rapidly ascending paralysis that had often been fatal before the iron lung was developed for polio. Even with it, doctors told her husband, Helen's chances of survival were slight. His shoulders slumped, Ted sat in shock, his eyes intent on the mirror above her face.

For two weeks the paralysis deepened. Helen could not understand why she had been moved from La Jolla, and in her confused state believed it was because they had lost their money. She no longer seemed to recognize Ted. For a few hours each day he retreated to the Tower but talked to no one. During the long night hours at the hospital, he endeared himself to nurses by helping to carry trays and bedpans. Finally he thought to telephone Dartmouth and say he would not be present at commencement for his degree. To Ted, Helen seemed in an awful limbo, and each day's survival was "a miracle." Desperate to communicate with her, he strung up a Seussian relay of mirrors so that she could see their Irish setter, Cluny, waiting outside her window. If she knew they still had the dog, Ted told friends, she would realize they hadn't gone broke. There was nothing he could do but cling to wild invention.

Toward the end of June, doctors told Ted that Helen's condition had stabilized. There were signs that she was fighting back, and one day when Ted arrived he saw that the tracheotomy tube had been removed. Helen had to learn again how to swallow, and Ted began bringing Popsicles, holding one to her mouth to make a game of her attempts. That progress was medically significant; the paralysis had begun to recede and she was managing fragments of speech. On July 4 she was lifted from the iron lung into a Hubbard tank for a few minutes of passive water exercise. Barris recommended moving her to the California Rehabilitation Center up the coast in Santa Monica, and estimated that therapy there might require four months. Ted hastily wrote Louise Bonino "there is a very good chance she will walk again."

When Ted began to believe that Helen would recover, he telephoned Peggy in Falls Church, Virginia, and she flew out to help him close the Tower and prepare for the move. Peggy spent days dealing with the stacks of Geisel mail and bills, and on

July 9 drove their car, packed with suitcases and his drawing board, pencils and papers, as he sat in the ambulance with Helen on the slow drive up the Southern California coast. Helen had begun to regain some feeling, but had no use of her legs, and the pace of improvement was agonizingly slow. Over the weeks she began to control muscles in her face, then her neck, chest and abdomen. She began lessons on "how to dial telephones, unbutton buttons, brush teeth, comb hair." She was learning to speak again, to move her tongue to form words. She struggled to sit up in a wheelchair and feed herself.

Ted settled nearby at the Ocean Palms Hotel and tried to work. He felt helpless in unexpected ways. He had not kept a checkbook since early in their marriage when Helen had found him subtracting their deposits from the bank balance; he had not even made his own coffee. He drove to Villa Narcissa for dinner with Elin Vanderlip, who found him "frantic and frightened . . . Helen had always shielded him from the real world." Ted judged "the therapy is just about as painful as the disease was, but she's a terrific patient and wonderfully cheerful." Each day he brought her news of the world and messages from their friends. He read the mail aloud and talked about their work; she heard and understood and tried to respond. One August morning, as she and Ted stared out at the Santa Monica hillside, a small animal hopped by.

"R–r–r–r–aaa–bbit!" Helen said.

Ted hugged her and laughed for the first time in weeks. That night he wrote Louise Bonino: "Two months ago the doctors gave her up. Today, she can actually do a little bit of walking! Not much, but enough so we know that she's going to get out of here without any crutches."

When Ted received his first copies of *Horton Hears a Who* that August, he wrote Louise that he was anxious to know how the trade received it, "being in no position to see reviews out here." He suggested a minor change for the next edition and reported that the binding on the copies he received gave the text a downhill slant. "Not griping or complaining, mind you! Just still on my impossible hunt for ultimate ultimates."

The reviews reassured Ted and brought smiles to Helen's face.

The book was "wildly original," *The New York Herald Tribune* wrote. The *Des Moines Register* considered it "a rhymed lesson in protection of minorities and their rights." The New York Public Library requested the illustrations for a Book Week exhibition. Random House submitted the book unsuccessfully for the Jane Addams Children's Book Award, which often rewarded books meant to overcome racial prejudice and suspicion of minorities.

By late September Helen was speaking more normally and strong enough to return to La Jolla, but too weak to be left alone. She and Ted moved into a friend's guest house, where she would not have to climb steps, and Ted resumed work in his studio on Mount Soledad. Her therapy schedule was rigid, and her doctors marveled at the strength of her will. Exercises began at 7:00 A.M., followed by hot packs, pulleys, swimming and long walks in wet sand. Her friends formed a beach brigade, taking turns driving her to the wide, flat beach of La Jolla Shores, from which she could see their first La Jolla house. "She was so determined not to be an invalid," recalled Ellen Revelle. "She never wanted to be a burden."

Although she did not dwell on the terrors of her illness, Helen was never again out of pain. "From then on, walking was uncomfortable," Peggy remembered. "She told me she always felt that her shoes were two sizes too small." As the Geisels talked of moving back into the Tower, doctors told Ted that Helen should swim each day, so he contracted for a swimming pool. He called it "*The Woman's Home Companion* Memorial Pool"; a check for five-thousand-dollars from that magazine helped to pay for it.

Back home finally, Helen was able to resume some of her prodigious correspondence, although she admitted "it takes me so infernally long to do anything!" After lunch and a nap, there were more exercises and "a trip" on a stationary bicycle. Her flights of fancy brightened these tedious hours. "I'm en route from Gallup, New Mexico, to Shiprock, through the Navajo country, but am running into many detours and sheep." Within another six months, Ted wrote Evelyn Shrifte, he expected Helen to be "almost entirely recuperated from the whole nightmare." Helen added that "everything is going along just fine, thanks to my husband, who is really part man, part angel."

Buoyed by Helen's recovery, Ted's imagination soared as he

worked in his tower studio. For *Collier's* magazine he wrote and illustrated "A Prayer for a Child" with its much beloved opening lines, "From here on earth, / From my small place / I ask of You / Way out in space: . . ." For the book *On Beyond Zebra*, he concocted new Seussian words and invented a twenty-letter alphabet so that they could be spelled. He reached beyond Z to letters called Yuzz and Thnad and Vroo, drawing each fanciful letter with flourishes and peaks so that it resembled an elaborate monogram, "perhaps in Old Persian." He followed the morality tale of Horton with this book of ebullient nonsense, one that he dedicated to Helen. *The New York Times* wrote, "Nobody could possibly have ideas in any way resembling those that occur to this talented man."

In May of 1955, almost a year to the day after the onset of her paralysis, Helen and Ted flew to New Hampshire and Dartmouth, and a keenly anticipated reunion with his classmate Donald Bartlett and his wife, Henri. For Helen's prescribed daily swims Dartmouth cleared the students' pool. One morning students began pounding on the closed doors and Ted called out gleefully, "You can't come in! I've got a woman in here."

On the thirtieth anniversary of his graduation, in the company of the poet Robert Frost, Ted received a delayed doctorate from his alma mater. The citation noted of Dr. Seuss that "behind the fun there has been intelligence, kindness, and a feel for humankind." Ted and Frost had "several pleasant talks," but Ted "very carefully refrained from mentioning the kind of poetry I write." Years after his abortive attempt to earn a postgraduate degree at Oxford, the "Dr." in Ted's pseudonym became legitimate. But he remained characteristically unawed. He laughed at himself as "Dr. Dr. Seuss," and appeared on the Dartmouth platform in a cap and gown that he had bought secondhand in a backstreet shop in San Diego.

CHAPTER 13

The Cat in the Hat

1955–1960

Because Ted thought in scenes, he believed that *The Cat in the Hat* was born in the scarred brass cage of an ancient elevator at the Houghton Mifflin publishing house in Boston. This elevator rose and descended with shudders and whines, cajoled by a small, stooped woman wearing "a leather half-glove and a secret smile." Ted rode with her one day in the spring of 1955 and never forgot her, nor the noisy contraption that was her domain. On the elevator with them was William Spaulding, who directed Houghton Mifflin's education division. Ted had known him in Washington during the war, and it was at Spaulding's urgent entreaty that Ted had come to Boston.

The son of a Yale dean of education, Spaulding was zealous in his conviction that a lively new kind of primer could arrest growing illiteracy among children. A popular book by Rudolf Flesch, *Why Johnny Can't Read*, had helped to propel the issue into a national scandal. The newly arrived enemy was television, the sales of comic books were soaring, and pictures were overwhelming words. In a memorable outburst in *Life*, the novelist John Hersey, after serving on a citizens' school-study council in Connecticut, had attacked the typical school primer as an "antiseptic little sugar-book showing how Tom and Betty have fun at home and school . . . pallid primers [with] abnormally courteous, unnaturally clean boys and girls . . . uniform, bland, idealized and terribly literal. Why should they not have pictures that widen rather than narrow the associative richness the children give to the words they illustrate—drawings like those of the wonderfully imaginative geniuses among children's illustrators, Tenniel, Howard Pyle, 'Dr. Seuss,' Walt Disney?''

Over dinner Spaulding proposed that Ted write and illustrate such a book for six- and seven-year-olds who had already mastered the basic mechanics of reading. "Write me a story that first-graders can't put down!" he challenged. Though more polite than committed, Ted was intrigued with Spaulding's insistence that the book's vocabulary be limited to 225 words, and agreed to take Spaulding's word list home and "play with it."

Any serious work on the project would be contingent, Ted knew, on Spaulding's persuading Bennett Cerf to let Ted do the book for a rival publisher, and he doubted that Spaulding could pull this off. But Cerf realized that a long, loose leash was the only one that would hold his author, and he was also one of the book trade's canniest negotiators. Sure, Ted could write the reader, Cerf told Spaulding, but Random House must retain the rights to market the trade edition in bookstores. Houghton Mifflin would publish only the school edition.

Ted tossed Spaulding's word list in a tray on his desk and promptly forgot about it while he polished *If I Ran the Circus*, a book he had created in response to Cerf's plea for another with the winning formula of *If I Ran the Zoo*. But one afternoon he began pondering two of his favorite words from childhood and outlined a story about a Queen Zebra before discovering that neither "queen" nor "zebra" was on the list. He started over, tried a line or two, and then wailing to Helen, "There are no adjectives!" flung the sheet aside. But he dreaded disappointing a friend, and felt guilty. "I read [the list] forty times and got more and more discouraged. It was like trying to make a strudel without any strudels. I was desperate, so I decided to read it once more. The first two words that rhymed would be the title of my book and I'd go from there. I found 'cat' and then I found 'hat.' That's genius, you see!"

Ted described the ordeal as something like "being lost with a witch in a tunnel of love. . . . The only job I ever tackled that I found more difficult was when I wrote the Baedeker guide Eskimos use when they travel in Siam." Since *Bartholomew and the Oobleck*, he had been writing in verse, and intended to continue doing so. "In verse you can repeat," he said. "It becomes part of the pattern. To teach, you have to repeat and repeat and repeat." Yet the limited vocabulary posed excruciating complexities in rhyming.

"It took me a year of getting mad as blazes and throwing [the manuscript] across the room," he said. For much of that year he fought under this handicap to achieve a rollicking rhythm. The lines that finally appeared on page 21 of *The Cat in the Hat*, for instance, went from "He fell off of the ball" to "He came down from the ball" to "He came down with a bump / From up there on the ball."

As Ted struggled with the verse, he began doodling sketches of the Cat. He wanted a wily character but not a mean one, a suave troublemaker, a ringleader of uncontrolled enthusiasm who is surprised when he messes up. He had always liked sketching animals. His Oxford notebook was studded with hounds, monkeys and flying cows; he had drawn insects for the Flit campaign and elephants for *Mulberry Street*. Now, as he shaded in a tall feline in a jaunty red-and-white stovepipe hat, he was creating what would become the best-known member of the Dr. Seuss menagerie. This confident cat could stride on two legs, juggle and ski, and it wore white gloves and a red bow tie with three impossible loops. Finally the words began to click into place. Ted paced less often in the studio and spent longer hours at his drawing board. The Cat was taking charge.

The book appeared with relatively little fanfare in the spring of 1957, but reviews were swift and heady. It was an innovative coup: an enthralling book created outside the restrictive guidelines of the educational establishment. Even its use of intense 100 percent flat red and blue inks, at Ted's insistence, was technically unconventional. So was its tautly paced verse; Ted had mastered in print the cinematic knack of accelerating words as the plot quickened. The book jacket carried the claim that "many children . . . will discover for the first time that they don't need to be read to any more."

The critics agreed. Clifton Fadiman, the first prominent reviewer to have recognized Ted's fey talent in 1937, called it "probably the most influential first-grade reader since McGuffey." A grateful John Hersey described it as a "harum-scarum masterpiece . . . [a] gift to the art of reading." *Newsweek* declared that Ted was "the moppets' Milton." *The New York Herald Tribune* book reviewer confessed: "We were afraid that the limitations Dr. Seuss put upon himself might have shackled his marvelous inventiveness. Quite the contrary. Restricting his vocabulary . . . and shortening his verse story has given a certain riotous unity . . . that is pleasing."

As soon as the first cartons of *The Cat in the Hat* reached stores, Random House recognized the omens that publishers live for. At Bullock's in Los Angeles, the first 100-copy order disappeared in a day and a hurried call went out for a 250-copy reorder. The Random House trade edition quickly outran Houghton Mifflin's school edition, averaging sales at the start of about twelve thousand copies a month and rising rapidly. The book escalated into a sensation: spurred by playground word-of-mouth, children nagged their parents to buy it. "Parents," Ted said, "understood better than school people the necessity for this kind of reader." Within three years *Cat* sold nearly a million copies at $1.95 each, with editions in French, Chinese, Swedish and Braille.

Phyllis Cerf, Bennett's wife, saw the book and "went wild about it." She asked her husband if she might talk to his author about setting up a publishing house to specialize in such revolutionary supplementary readers. Though startled, Cerf soon agreed, with Random House to serve as the distributor. Except for Ted's books, he was rarely involved in juveniles. "Ted and Babar," one editor said, "were the only children's books that Bennett wasn't condescending about."

On Ted's next visit to New York, Phyllis Cerf invited him to lunch at Quo Vadis. Ted had known her only casually. She was Ginger Rogers's cousin, and Bennett liked telling friends that the dancing cousin might have the legs but that he had married the brains. Phyllis was twenty-three when *The New Yorker* editor Harold Ross introduced them; Bennett had impetuously kissed her and she had slapped him. Over lunch she set the stage with Ted for their historic but turbulent enterprise. *The Cat in the Hat* was stupendous, she said, but one book did not make a series and that was what was necessary for a big payoff. They would need four or five readers to launch simultaneously, and Ted was the only one who could make it happen. They would not interfere with his Dr. Seuss books, which he came to call, in contrast with the smaller readers, his "big books."

Ted and Phyllis had worked together before, she reminded him, when she was at McCann-Erickson while he was doing the Flit campaign. Since he had been working at home then, he had wanted only a drawer at the agency, and it had been in her desk. She was almost as glib and persuasive as her husband, and by the time she picked up the lunch check, she had asked Ted to be president of an enterprise to be called Beginner Books. Convinced that he could help other authors find the key he had discovered with *Cat*, Ted agreed. But always wary of losing control over his work, he drove a deal: Helen would be the third partner. Small amounts of stock would go to Bennett and later to others at Random House. At the end of lunch Phyllis and Ted shook hands.

Amid the flurry of added work, Helen's health deteriorated. In April 1957 she was back at Scripps Clinic; her sudden dizziness and confusion was diagnosed as a small stroke. She was dismissed three days later with weakness in her right hand and side, lacking her "usual talkativeness and spontaneity." As her speech cleared, she tended, Ted wrote Louise Bonino, to be "foggy, with lapses of memory . . . and very depressed." Yet through it all she remained Ted's best editor. In addition to his preliminary work with Beginner Books, he was writing a "big book" to protest the commercialization of Christmas, bringing back the creatures he called the Whos; his villain was an evil pink-eyed Grinch who scorned Christmas and became as vivid a character to Americans as Charles Dickens's Scrooge. Interviewing the Geisels for *The Saturday Evening Post* while Ted searched for an ending to *Grinch*, Robert Cahn wrote that Ted emerged from his studio shouting, "Helen, Helen, where are you? . . . How do you like this?" and dropped a page in her lap.

"No," she said, "this isn't it. Besides, you've got the Papa Who too big. Now he looks like a bug."

"Well, they *are* bugs," Ted said.

"They are *not* bugs," replied Helen. "Whos are just small people." So Ted retreated to his den to try again.

It was the easiest book of his career to write, except for its conclusion. Later he explained, "I got hung up getting the Grinch out of the mess. I got into a situation where I sounded like a second-rate preacher or some biblical truism. . . . Finally in desperation . . . without making any statement whatever, I showed the Grinch and the Whos together at the table, and made a pun of the Grinch carving the 'roast beast.' . . . I had gone through thousands of religious choices, and then after three months it came out like that."

In mid-May, Helen wrote Louise Bonino that the *Grinch* was in the mail, and that she expected it to be the second Dr. Seuss blockbuster of 1957. It was dedicated to Ted's one-year-old namesake, Theodor "Teddy" Owens, the only child of his niece, Peggy. Ted called it *How the Grinch Stole Christmas!*, and he sounded like a bashful schoolboy in his cover note to Bonino: "Hope you like it. I'm sorta happy about the drawings."

In June Ted took "my bride and weary self" to Honolulu and a cottage on Diamond Head for a month of vacation. Work went along with them; the galley proofs for *The Grinch* were checked and returned to New York from Hawaii. All the while Ted was scheming about Beginner Books, and both Geisels turned their full attention to the new venture when they returned.

Phyllis Cerf had been researching every primer in print, cross-matching word lists until she came up with 379 words from which their contract authors could choose 200, plus twenty easy-to-pronounce "emergency words" for each book. She attended educational conferences in various places, from New York to California, interviewing scholars and teachers and promoting the formal launching of Beginner Books with four titles in the fall of 1958.

The brave new enterprise was housed in the former servants' quarters under the eaves of the Random House mansion. Phyllis led the move to the walk-up sixth floor, overseeing its redesign into a fantasy attic with blue walls and stairwell. Doors and windows were particularly unpredictable; some doors closed over only half a doorway, and some windows disappeared within walls when raised. Ted loved it all. His name went up on an office door, and he walked around putting up signs; on one desk he placed the nameplate of DR. VIOLET VALERIE VOWEL, D.V., DIRECTOR OF CON-

SONANTS. The new quarters seemed just right for Dr. Seuss. Christopher Cerf, who joined his parents at Random House after graduating from Harvard, remembers Ted "bursting into the office . . . so sunny, so funny . . . He always made me feel great! His pranks, his pranks! He drew a picture for my mom called 'Woops, I swallowed my word list!' He and my dad created Dr. Outgo Schmierkase as the fall guy whose name would appear on letters of rejection to the friends who were always asking them to read manuscripts. . . . If Ted hadn't written *Cat in the Hat* I wouldn't be working on *Sesame Street*. In fact, *Sesame Street* wouldn't exist!"

The West Coast headquarters of Beginner Books was in Helen's office, formerly a garage, at the Tower. On the wall above her desk was a needlepoint of *The Cat in the Hat* stitched by Phyllis Cerf and inscribed: THIS CAT STARTED A PUBLISHING HOUSE. NO OTHER CAT CAN MAKE THIS CLAIM.

For Beginner Books, these were the honeymoon months. The new company borrowed about two hundred thousand dollars from Random House and began to sign contract authors and artists. Ted and Phyllis agreed to undertake printings of about sixty thousand copies of each Beginner Book. The management was cozy, absorbed and united in creating an innovative way of blending words and illustrations to teach reading. But everyone involved tended to explain the venture from a different perspective. For the instigator William Spaulding, who remained an outsider, it was an assault on illiteracy. From his office downstairs, Bennett Cerf looked with awe on the casual launching of this series of children's readers, soon calling it the "most profitable single publishing entity ever created." Phyllis talked of merging Ted's "happy genius" with the prosaic but precise science of vocabulary word lists. Helen remembered the astonishment of journeymen writers who discovered that they simply could not create a book using only two or three hundred words.

Still, from the start, there were hints of implosion; Phyllis and Ted shared deep respect for the books and their audiences, but each had dogmatic beliefs and their egos soon proved irreconcilable. Her son Christopher said later, "She is a woman who loves combat, and Ted was so much the other way."

As president, Ted laid down stringent quality-control codes for the books: there would be no more than one illustration on any page; the text should not describe anything that was not pictured, so that children could work out the story from the illustrations alone; and the design of each pair of facing pages would interlock as an artistic unit. He regarded these books as an art form that grew more complex and intricate as it reached toward younger and younger readers. He inveighed against contract authors and artists who could not simplify their styles, insisting that it was a test of their talents to reach for the irreducible basics of reading. Time after time he and Helen returned manuscripts and art to authors for major revision. A few rebelled, arguing that the Geisels wanted everybody to copy Ted. None could, nor did many live up to the Geisels' standards of intensity and perfection.

The Grinch appeared in the fall of 1957 and was acclaimed from the start. With *Cat* sales setting records, the first printing of *Grinch* was in excess of fifty thousand copies. That Christmas was memorable for sales of children's books. Along with Ted's *Grinch* were Ogden Nash and Phyllis McGinley with their own new children's Christmas books. Random House soon estimated that one third of its total sales volume was in juvenile books, and it had become the largest publisher of children's books in America. The postwar baby boom was cresting, and more than two hundred and fifty publishers had crowded into the children's book trade.

Two decades after his first children's book was published, Dr. Seuss suddenly became a top-tier celebrity. In November, California state librarians changed the date of their annual conference to coincide with his autographing party at a San Francisco store. The West Coast sales manager for Random House wrote Ted that his appearance before the librarians would be "significant," and promised that "all you have to do is get your suit pressed!" Ted did so, and charmed them with his reticence. He autographed *Cat* and *Grinch* in stores in San Francisco, Los Angeles, Santa Ana and Long Beach. A cozier arrangement was established in the author's hometown: Barbara Cole, a La Jolla bookseller, began accumulating autograph requests from around the nation, dropping off books at the Tower and picking them up when signed.

Robert L. Bernstein, boyish and freckle-faced, had moved from Simon & Schuster to join Random House as sales manager. He had formed a company with Kay Thompson to develop subsidiary rights for her *Eloise*, and had brought with him a vision of the riches that might be gleaned from marketing children's books. Bernstein received shares in Beginner Books and became a dedicated cheerleader, eager to spin off Dr. Seuss rights for clothing, toys, coloring books and greeting cards. "Once started," he wrote Donald Klopfer, "a property develops like a snowball rolling down a mountain. . . . I've worked myself into an absolute frenzy thinking about merchandising Dr. Seuss."

The irrepressible Bernstein was full of promotional ideas, including "Cat's pajamas" in all sizes, but Ted resisted. He was wary of anything—product franchising, most of all—that might cheapen the Dr. Seuss image.

To boost the newest Dr. Seuss books—*Yertle the Turtle* and *The Cat in the Hat Comes Back*—Bernstein persuaded Ted to make a ten-day autograph blitz before Christmas in 1958 and Helen joined them as they covered bookstores from Boston to Chicago. This tour was considered such an innovative approach to marketing children's books that it inspired a four-page account in *Publishers Weekly*. Random House provided tens of thousands of buttons of the Cat, librarians and teachers organized Dr. Seuss events, there were press luncheons, and Ted appeared on the Fran Allison television show. In Rochester, schoolteachers bargained for a visit from Ted by declaring a Dr. Seuss Day and busing pupils from outlying schools. In Washington, Woodward & Lothrop hosted officials from the Washington Zoo to inspect the animals of Dr. Seuss. At Marshall Field's in Chicago, five uniformed ushers patrolled a labyrinthine line of children (the one on which Chief White Cloud had intruded to sign his own name in Dr. Seuss books), and a thousand Dr. Seuss books were sold in ninety minutes, with another four hundred whisked away at a branch store. In Madison, Wisconsin, Ted spoke to teachers and received a Lewis Carroll award from the University of Wisconsin. Touring J. L. Hudson branches in Detroit, Ted stepped out of a helicopter, still a novel form of transport, to be surrounded by children "as if I were Santa Claus." In Cleveland at Higbee's, where the author had faced his first autograph party twenty years earlier, Yertlebergers and *Cat in the Hat* parfaits were served and two thousand books were sold.

Bennett Cerf was no less diligent than Bob Bernstein in promoting Ted, but a bit slyer. He reveled in other people's accomplishments and found joy in alerting his own column readers and television viewers to the wonders of Dr. Seuss. He made Ted Geisel stories a staple of his lecture tours and used his *Trade Winds* column in *Saturday Review* to write about Ted's campaign to ban billboards in La Jolla. Cerf relished his own role as panelist on the television show *What's My Line?*, and suggested Ted's appearance as a mystery guest in 1958 on a rival television game program, *To Tell the Truth*. Though Dr. Seuss was a household name, his face was not widely recognized, and the columnist Hy Gardner was alone among four panelists in guessing that Ted was Dr. Seuss. The others—Constance Bennett, Don Ameche and Polly Bergen—settled on pretenders like the Nobel laureate biochemist, Thomas Jukes, whose ten-year-old daughter, Mavis, "truly passionate about [Ted's] books," sat in a front studio row clutching her newly autographed Dr. Seuss book. Undoubtedly marked by that meeting with Ted, she went on to become an honored children's book author.

With persistent promotion and the spreading awareness across America of a fresh, funny and eccentric new talent, Ted was getting rich. "The money came in so fast from the start," Phyllis Cerf said. "It was instant, a flood of income." For the Beginner Books founders, these were heady moments. "Whoopee!" Helen wrote. "We're in the black after four months!"

Ted's relationship with his publishing house remained extraordinary. At his request, contracts were not drawn up until after he had delivered a book manuscript; he detested the pressure of a contractual deadline and was wary of receiving royalties before he had earned them. For him the fourth paragraph of each standard author's contract was crossed out: instead of "agrees to deliver," the phrase "has delivered" was typed in. On the advice of his tax specialist, each of Ted's book contracts called for deferral of royalty income in excess of five thousand dollars a year. Ted shook his head in wonder at this. It had been just four years since he asked his agent, Phyllis Jackson, if she thought he might come to count on five thousand dollars annually in royalties from all his books combined.

Still, writing the books grew no easier. As Ted wrestled with

Yertle in 1958, Helen wrote that he had "supposedly finished his new book but it's going backward. . . . I think writing is the worst job that anyone ever got into." Nevertheless, *The Cat in the Hat Comes Back*, a less successful reprise, also appeared that year, and by the fall of 1958 the Geisels and Phyllis had commissioned and published four other Beginner Books, including *A Fly Went By*, by Mike McClintock, the Dartmouth friend who had rescued Ted twenty years earlier when he had planned to burn the manuscript of *Mulberry Street*.

Awash in success, Ted reached out with earnest sentimentality to boost other old friends. His Oxford roommate, Donald Bartlett, hoped to take leave from his Dartmouth faculty post if he could win appointment as cultural attaché with the United States Embassy in Tokyo; Ted wrote a heartfelt recommendation and then mailed Bartlett a self-effacing confession:

> I stack you up on the top of my list as one of the greatest successes I have ever known. . . . You are tops among the few dedicated people who are doing the most important, most under-paid goddamn necessary job [teaching] in the world. You are doing what I didn't have guts enough to do, because I took the easier path. A much much easier path than you have taken.

As the first Beginner Books appeared the bicoastal infighting grew raw. "Ted and I don't think [the books] are awfully good," Helen wrote, "but they're as good as we can make them. And if they fail, WE don't have to take the loss!" When the Geisels opposed publication of P. D. Eastman's *Sam and the Firefly*, whose illustrations they considered were without merit, Phyllis went to Donald Klopfer, whom the Geisels adored. Klopfer wrote directly to Helen:

> . . . there is no question about whether we should publish [the book]. . . . Phyllis has worked like a dog and has made what even you consider a satisfactory script. . . . This has developed into a moral question. . . . [Beginner Books has] given our word and to me this is inviolable. . . . You use the words 'honest,' 'straightforward' and 'integrity' in your letter.

God knows that must apply to the people who are running
it or it won't percolate down to the books themselves. Helen,
I beg of you . . . agree—even though you hate the book.

This time the Geisels acquiesced. But Helen and Phyllis soon
clashed over *You Will Go to the Moon*, by Mae and Ira Freeman,
a physicist who had been a successful Random House author.
Helen, becoming proxy correspondent for Ted, wrote Phyllis,
"Before any illustrator can breathe any life into this story with
pictures, the authors have got to first breathe some life into it with
words. . . . It is infuriating to us to waste all this Moon rocket
space in sending up such a lunk-headed child. . . . As written now,
the boy gets to a dusty, rather disappointing locale where he
practically immediately goes to bed."

Eight days later Phyllis took the Nobel laureate Harold Urey
to lunch and, confirming that the Freemans' vision of the moon
was generally accurate, wrote Helen that she had been aware that
Helen loathed the book, but that Bennett was insisting the Freemans be allowed to write it in their own way. To avoid other
such impasses, Bennett asked that Beginner Books stay away from
Random House authors.

Helen was frayed by the transcontinental battling and the tensions
of watching over her husband, who "does have to be boosted up
every now and then." As she worked on her own new Beginner
Book, she wrote: "We have been living somewhat quietly as that
is what we always have to do when Ted is starting new things. It
is quite difficult for me . . . because the very time I make no plans
seems to be the time he wants to go out, and when I have a lot
of people coming, he wants to work."

Ted had been persuaded to sign with Revell Corporation to
produce Dr. Seuss animals. He set up a sculpting studio next to
the pool house in La Jolla and created the Cat, Horton and four
"Seuss multi-beasts"—one named Roscoe—to be marketed as
self-assembly polyethylene kits for the March toy show in 1959.
But no one else's version of a Dr. Seuss creature satisfied Ted.
Helen wrote Cerf that Ted was at the Revell factory in Venice,
near Los Angeles, "causing a hullabaloo over the animals not fitting.
But they have stopped production for ten hours, and Ted says
[that] now Roscoe's head balances."

Ted soon retreated from the alien quibbles of the toy world. After delivering *Happy Birthday to You!*, the Geisels spent four sunny autumn days at the Broadmoor Hotel in Colorado Springs. As California began to feel crowded the Rockies seemed idyllic. "One day we drove through a canyon for an hour and a half," Helen wrote, "without passing a single car." Back home Ted disappeared into his studio to create one of the most loved of Beginner Books, *One Fish Two Fish Red Fish Blue Fish*. Soon Helen was confiding again in Cerf, this time about Ted's progress with *One Fish:* "Now, if I can just keep Ted from fussing with it and telling me that it is no good. He gets me to the point where I don't know what is or what isn't, or was or wasn't, or could be or would be or should be."

Ted finally delivered *One Fish* to Random House, carrying "three grubby bits of crayon" as his color guide. In his production office, Ray Freiman noted that they were lemon yellow, carmine red and turquoise. Knowing Ted's demanding sense of color, no one laughed; only when he was certain that the book's colors matched those crayon stubs did the Geisels take a monthlong laze in Spain, lingering in Seville and Granada. In December they returned with gifts for Helen to wrap for her Christmas Eve dinner party, and she sounded like any other hostess: "Every year I think I will not do it again."

In his Sunday newspaper column, Cerf related the story of the Geisels' visit to a Mexico City restaurant where, on a bet, Ted was persuaded to try to catch a goldfish in a tank with his bare hands. He failed, splashed a party of strangers and paid for their dinners. Cerf used this anecdote on the imminent publication of *One Fish Two Fish Red Fish Blue Fish*.

But even the rigorous discipline of writing a book seemed more pleasant to Ted than battling with Phyllis. She called him unrealistic in choosing and dealing with other authors, and said she always had to pick up the pieces.

> First Ted would say to me that Truman Capote's manuscript [probably called *The Pig That Could Not Fly*] was his best [Beginner] book, and he and Truman would do all the books. But [later] he didn't like Truman's book and I had to tell Truman that Ted didn't feel it publishable. Then Nat Bench-

ley did a Beginner Book on a concept he came up with, and I [finally] had to tell Nat we were going to have someone else write it. But I was the one who had to find authors. The ones [Ted] found were . . . people who lived in California who weren't professional writers. . . . There was one book with a photographer at the San Diego Zoo who was a friend of theirs [and] we were all in despair. . . . It was [finally my idea] that [made] it a best-seller. . . . Ted didn't really have a lot of humor, you know.

As the hostility grew, Christopher Cerf showed Solomon-like detachment, moving delicately between his mother and his idol:

They'd spend three days talking about the placement of a word on the page. Both Ted and my mother and Helen were stubborn. . . . We [the Cerfs] were all as a family unbelievably involved. It came home from work with us. Helen sided with Ted much more than not, but she was an independent thinker and sometimes took my mother's side. Ted was incredibly rigorous about getting the books the way he wanted. [Mother] was incredibly brilliant about the discipline of vocabularies and the reading skills, stuff that became boring to Ted. . . . Neither one of them ever gave in. . . . My mother would sit on the phone for hours at home [with Ted in California] arguing over placement of a comma. My dad might want to talk to her and she was too worked up even when she got off the phone. It began to drive Dad crazy.

The Cerfs invited the Geisels for Thanksgiving in 1959, and at the dinner table Helen, Ted and Phyllis became embroiled in a Beginner Books discussion. Bennett, left to himself, finally pleaded, "Please at least eat your turkey!"

Though *The Cat in the Hat* occupied a triumphant niche in juvenile publishing, William Spaulding, the man who had suggested the venture, receded into the background. As Houghton Mifflin's Richard Gladstone, assigned to market *The Cat* to schools, recalled:

This reader was essentially a Houghton Mifflin project, but we never knew how many we sold. Thousands [of Random's trade edition] went into schools through jobbers. . . . Random was making much more money from this than we were . . . [and] very rarely in reports of Beginner Books was there any mention of Houghton Mifflin or of Bill Spaulding.

Bennett Cerf had lent his author to Houghton Mifflin and then run away with the book. The bizarre agreement between the two publishers to share Ted continued through *The Cat in the Hat Comes Back* and an educational edition of *Yertle the Turtle*, until finally Houghton Mifflin sold its rights to Random House. Then Cerf made an even bigger move. He had marveled at the spiraling profits of Beginner Books and finally could no longer endure being merely lender and distributor. He had begun to have dreams of empire; he was readying Random House for a merger with some major communications company, and he wanted Beginner Books and its bottom line tucked neatly inside. In the fiscal year ending April 30, 1960, Beginner Books had a sales volume far exceeding a million dollars. By the end of the year eighteen titles were in bookstores, including a new group of Beginning Beginner Books to supplement the earliest school readers. Eventually more than a hundred books were published.

Ted and Helen argued against the sale of Beginner Books because their La Jolla attorney Frank Kockritz saw it as an unneeded capital gain with unwelcome tax consequences, but Cerf proposed a way to offset this objection and prevailed. Random House would own Beginner Books, but it would still be run by Phyllis, Ted and Helen. As principal stockholders, the partners received twenty-five thousand shares of Random House stock, at that time worth about eight hundred thousand dollars. The Geisels owned 22 percent. But Ted and Helen were soon building up much larger sums in deferred royalties invested in mutual funds.

Though wealthy, Ted remained bored by money. He spent little and chose to spoof even his own financial advisers and attorneys. In the main he distrusted them. Back in their Oxford days, he and Helen had concocted an unlikely name for a stuffy law firm and used it as a code in their secret messages: Grimalkin, Drouberhannus, Knalbner and Fepp. He wouldn't be "anywhere in this world," Ted joked, without "Grimalkin, Drouberhannus, Knalbner and

Fepp." But now he wrote Louise Bonino, "our accountant and our attorney are still trying to figure out . . . how much should we defer according to this year's tax problem, next year's tax problem, and the cigar tax in Bulgaria in the year 55,202. If Bulgarians, according to my accountant, stop smoking cigars, the situation will be entirely different from what my attorney claims will happen if cigars suddenly start smoking Bulgarians."

When such whimsy flowed Ted was at peace, and marital accommodation and tenderness prevailed between the West Coast partners of Beginner Books. In a letter addressed to "Dear Spouse," he gave Helen formal permission to write a Beginner Book from "Gustave the Goldfish," which he had written in 1950 in his long-running series of children's stories for *Redbook*. "You have the right to use any of the situations or any of the words from the original story that your little heart desires. You must, however, comply with all necessary steps in protecting my original copyright. . . . Very truly yours, and I hope you will have dinner with me tonight, and many nights following."

And so they did, while Ted struggled with a challenge not unlike that of a blindfold chess player: Bennett Cerf had bet him fifty dollars that he could not write a Beginner Book using only fifty words.

CHAPTER 14

Green Eggs and Ham

1960–1963

Each of Ted's arrivals at Random House with a new Dr. Seuss book was cheerily anticipated through the often pedestrian days and occasionally abrasive explosions in a book publisher's world. "You would have no idea," Bob Bernstein said, "what to expect from him next." Thus a celebratory tone marked an inter-office memo in 1960 from Louise Bonino to the inner Random House family: "You are invited to stop in my office on April 19th at 11 o'clock when the great Dr. Seuss will give the first reading of his fall Beginner Book, *Green Eggs and Ham*."

But Bennett Cerf was chairing a Peabody Awards luncheon that day, and he rescheduled the reading for a small dinner party at which he would be sure to serve as master of ceremonies. Helen, ever apprehensive, wrote him a pleading warning: "Don't say 'the great Dr. Seuss, in person.' That makes him feel he has got to have something extra, like horns or three ears. . . ."

"If you do not like [the book]," Helen wrote Bonino, "we will return to our swimming pool on the [next] plane." But when Ted read *Green Eggs* aloud that evening the room erupted with huzzahs and demands that he read it again. For once Bennett seemed dazed, shaking his head over the clear triumph of *Green Eggs and Ham*, which had begun as their private joke. He made a ceremony of conceding Ted his fifty-dollar bet, but Ted's recollection was that Cerf never paid.

Upstairs in the old servants' quarters in the kingdom of Beginner Books, Phyllis Cerf was shocked to learn that Random House had already delivered advance sheets of *Green Eggs and Ham* to trade reviewers; she sent a clearly unsettled publicist back to request her major contacts—*Publishers Weekly*, *Library Journal* and *Kirkus Reviews*—to delay mention of the book because she intended to promote it as part of a package including P. D. Eastman's *Are You My Mother?* and Robert Lopshire's *Put Me in the Zoo*.

But Ted's books were beyond control; in the public mind Dr. Seuss had become a force that defied packaging. In May *The New York Times* listed the best-selling children's books of 1960. Five of the top sixteen were Ted's; booksellers could not remember when a single author had so dominated the market. The quirky *Green Eggs and Ham* was about to join the list and go on to sell tens of millions of copies, becoming the most popular of all Dr. Seuss books.

Ted had met Cerf's challenge by writing *Green Eggs and Ham* with a vocabulary of precisely fifty words. His work sheets were evidence of his marathon wordplay: charts, lists, number counts— mundane bookkeeping that was worlds removed from its result, the exquisite nonsense of Sam-I-am. The statistics of Ted's ordeal were ground into his memory. The words he had used most were "not" (eighty-two times) and "I" (eighty-one times). Each word was monosyllabic except "anywhere" (eight times). Ted made such obsessive demands on himself that they exceeded any quality controls ever demanded by an editor. But with the dare that led to *Green Eggs*, Cerf had again proved himself the ideal publisher for Ted. He was an unabashed, beguiled fan who revered his author and his work almost without reservation. Of Ted he said, "You don't tell Joe DiMaggio how to hit the ball." He liked to astonish audiences by naming distinguished authors of Random House—Eugene O'Neill, William Faulkner and John O'Hara—and to conclude that Ted, alone among them, was a genius.

The animator Chuck Jones, who had helped create Bugs Bunny, offered an insider's critique of *Green Eggs*. Oddity, he argued, is the key to such creativity; the most interesting thing is the unexpected. Ted took "the common phrase, *ham and eggs*, and commanded attention by reversing it." He compared it with phrasings found in Pennsylvania Dutch or Yiddish in which the subject comes last, as in "He doesn't like opera, my father." "Ted's stuff," Jones said, "has that quality of puzzlement. He uses Sam-I-am, not just Sam, and Sam-I-am not only rhymes with green-eggs-and-ham, but has the same metric emphasis."

Critics did not overlook the Seussian tone of defiance. Sam-I-am drives his victim crazy, pursuing him everywhere while he urges him to eat something disgusting. Literature had seldom afforded children an opportunity to ally themselves with such open antagonism. Ted was building on the breakthrough of *The Cat in the Hat*, whose boisterous rampage in the absence of adults went unpunished, alarming some of the school establishment who felt safer with Dick and Jane and considered the Cat "a trickster hero." Thereafter plates of green eggs pursued Ted at luncheons and banquets almost as relentlessly as the awful Dr. Seuss parodies composed by showboating critics and masters of ceremonies.

As his books swept the nation big media guns turned on Ted. In an essay in *Holiday*, Clifton Fadiman contrasted Ted with Kenneth Grahame, who had written *The Wind in the Willows* half a century earlier. Ted was providing ingenious and uniquely witty solutions to "the standing problem of the juvenile-fantasy writer: How to find, not another Alice, but another rabbithole." As his own illustrator, Ted could "make every page pull double weight." Fadiman found him an uncomplicated talent: "He may have a complete set of private despairs that he fondles lovingly in the dark . . . he may have a dandy buried life . . . [but] it is not reflected in any of the delightful children's books he has written. . . . He is not using his books for any purpose beyond entertaining himself and his readers. . . . I believe Dr. Seuss has not only added to the general store of happiness but . . . is himself a happy man." Ted offered no rebuttal; he seemed charmed and startled, like a man found out.

Soon a *Life* crew—writer Peter Bunzel and photographer John Bryson—came to the Tower. Ted was interviewed, Helen wrote, "until he was drained absolutely dry and absolutely flat." *Life* called Helen his "chief editor, chief critic, business manager and wife."

Cerf suggested to *The New Yorker* editor William Shawn that Ted had grown into a candidate for the magazine's profile series, and E. J. Kahn, Jr., won the assignment. Shortly before Christmas in 1959, Helen and Ted had settled down for a series of initial interviews that spanned four days. "I am so full of what I must tell [Kahn] and what I must not," Helen wrote, "that I will be really glad when he leaves." Kahn told a reporter that he always expected to interview his subject's enemies, but there seemed little chance in Ted's case "that any will show up."

Ted professed to dread interviews, but what he hated most were the exchanges of trivialities and trite misperceptions that so often ensued. "No matter what I say," he grumbled, "all these clippings keep repeating the same old lies from the library files, which unfortunately I usually started." Ted hoped that Kahn might provide the first "really definitive" treatment of him and his work. As the interviews continued in New York the men became guarded friends. Kahn later brought his wife and three young sons to the Tower during a California vacation, and the boys won Helen's rarest accolade: "the most well brought up I have ever met."

The New Yorker profile appeared on December 17, 1960, a year after the interviews began. Entitled "Children's Friend," it ran over twenty-three pages, opening this way:

> The face of Theodor Seuss Geisel—an arresting one, with soft eyes and a long, beaky nose—is not nearly as familiar as that of Santa Claus, yet its owner is an equally formidable contender for the adulation of many children. Santa Claus brings them presents. Geisel makes them laugh, and, what is more, he's real . . . a plain and gentle man who is now fifty-six. . . .

Kahn's was the most accurate and balanced account that had appeared about the complex man behind Dr. Seuss. Helen wrote Kahn that the profile led her to assess their lives and think about "what one has not achieved, and with so relatively few years left to do the right thing . . . !" Ted responded with a drawing that Kahn hung on his office wall; " 'No one,' the Cat said, 'has ever

Ted's grandfather, Theodor Geisel, German-born brewer and patriarch, in Springfield, Mass., c. 1905. (*Collection of Margaretha Owens and Ted Owens*)

Henrietta "Nettie" Seuss Geisel, with daughter, Marnie, and son, Ted, at Beach Park, near Clinton, Conn., c. 1907. (*Collection of Margaretha Owens and Ted Owens*)

Theodor Robert Geisel and his children, Marnie and Ted, at Beach Park. (*Collection of Margaretha Owens and Ted Owens*)

Ted dresses as an Indian, Springfield,
c. 1909. (*Collection of Margaretha
Owens and Ted Owens*)

Ted and his bulldog, Rex, in Springfield,
c. 1914. (*Collection of Margaretha
Owens and Ted Owens*)

Ted as a student at Central High School, Springfield, c. 1920. (*Collection of Margaretha Owens and Ted Owens*)

Commencement day at Dartmouth, June 1925; Whitney Campbell (left) and Ted with Ted's sister, Marnie. (*Collection of Margaretha Owens and Ted Owens*)

Ted at Oxford, 1926. (*Collection of Barbara Palmer Bayler*)

Two pages from Ted's Oxford notebook: Seussian drawings overshadow lecture notes, 1925-26. (*University of California, San Diego, Department of Special Collections*)

Ted's drawing of Romulus and Remus with the seven hills of Rome, on the letterhead of the Pensione Girardet, 1926. (*Collection of Barbara Palmer Bayler*)

Helen and Ted at the Acropolis
in Athens, 1928. (*Collection of
Margaretha Owens and Ted Owens*)

Helen and Ted on their first visit
to La Jolla, 1928. (*Collection of
Margaretha Owens and Ted Owens*)

The Dr. Seuss cover of *Judge*'s jungle number, March 23, 1929.

The Dr. Seuss cover of *Judge*, January 9, 1932.

Helen and Ted beside a Panagra airplane in Peru, c. 1933. (*Cine Foto Service; University of California, San Diego, Department of Special Collections*)

Ted at work on the *Hejji* comic strip, 1935. (*King Features photo; collection of Audrey Stone Geisel*)

Ted and the Seussian "taxidermy" menagerie, New York, c. 1937. (*University of California, San Diego, Department of Special Collections*)

Ted and Helen in wooden collars for the Infantograph, an invention for creating composite photos to show couples what their offspring would look like. Ted patented the device and dreamed of unveiling it at the New York World's Fair of 1939. (*University of California, San Diego, Department of Special Collections*)

Ted as *PM* political cartoonist, New York, c. 1940. (PM *photo by Mary Morris; collection of Audrey Stone Geisel*)

FLATTEN A FLEA!

CONSOLIDATED WORLD DAIRY
A. HITLER, Prop.

The head eats . . .
. . . the rest gets milked

YUGO SLAVIA ROMANIA GREECE AUSTRIA
BELGIUM
HOLLAND
DENMARK
NORWAY
POLAND
CZECHO SLOVAKIA
FRANCE

Dr. Seuss

Dr. SEUSS is the same
and only Dr. Seuss of
"Quick-Henry-the-Flit" fame

A *PM* cartoon for promoting the newspaper, referring to Dr. Seuss's successful "Quick, Henry, the Flit!" ad campaign for Standard Oil, c. 1940–41.

"Fort Fox," Hollywood, of the Army
Signal Corps, c. 1944. Ted is
second from right. Among the
group are Meredith Willson, seated,
and Lee Katz, far left.

Helen at the observation tower in
La Jolla, which became the
Geisel home and studio, c. 1948.
(*Collection of Margaretha Owens
and Ted Owens*)

On the Hollywood set of *The 5,000 Fingers of Dr. T.*: Ted Geisel, lower left, atop ladder; Hans Conried (Dr. T.) in drum major hat and cape; boy star Tommy Rettig in finger-cap at right. This 1953 Stanley Kramer film, which Ted considered a disaster, was his only attempt at a full-length feature. (*University of California, San Diego, Department of Special Collections; Collection of Audrey Stone Geisel*)

Ted and Helen in the Tower after publication of *Scrambled Eggs Super*, 1953. (*San Diego Union-Tribune*)

Neil Morgan, Ted, pilot Mayo and Bennett Cerf after a U.S. Navy
helicopter flight in San Diego, 1954. (*Fleet Air Photo Lab., NAS,
San Diego; collection of Judith and Neil Morgan*)

Ted at the drawing board in the Tower,
c. 1959. (*Gene Trindl photo; collection of
Audrey Stone Geisel*)

Ted during an interview with
E. J. Kahn, Jr., for *The New Yorker*,
1959. (*San Diego Union-Tribune*)

Ted at his desk in La Jolla with the Cat in the Hat, c. 1960. (Random House photo)

Ted in his studio with *Fox in Socks* storyboards, c. 1964. (*Ernest E. Reshovsky photo; collection of Audrey Stone Geisel*)

Ted, Jesse Kaye of MGM and animator Chuck Jones on the MGM-TV set of *How the Grinch Stole Christmas*, 1966. (*MGM-TV publicity; University of California San Diego, Department of Special Collections*)

Ted autographing in a London bookstore, c. 1969. (*Terry Hardy photo; University of California, San Diego, Department of Special Collections*)

Ted at the easel in his La Jolla studio, c. 1970. (*San Diego Union-Tribune*)

Ted and Audrey at the Jewel Ball in La Jolla, c. 1975. (*San Diego Union-Tribune*)

Ted and Audrey in raccoon coats on the Dr. Seuss float in the Thanksgiving Day parade in Detroit, 1979. (*Detroit News; University of California, San Diego, Department of Special Collections*)

Ted and Maurice Sendak lecturing at
the San Diego Museum of Art, 1982.
(*San Diego Union-Tribune*)

Ted's reunion with wartime colonel
Frank Capra at the Hotel del Coronado
in Coronado, California, in April 1983.
(*San Diego Union-Tribune*)

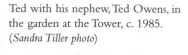

Ted with his nephew, Ted Owens, in
the garden at the Tower, c. 1985.
(*Sandra Tiller photo*)

Ted and Audrey at one of his last
formal parties, c. 1986.
(*San Diego Union-Tribune*)

In Springfield, Mass., in 1986, Ted and his young fans on Mulberry Street. (*Steve Miller, New York Times*)

Ted, at eighty-two, smiles as the twenty-two-foot Cat in the Hat rises above the roof of the San Diego Museum of Art for Ted's retrospective exhibition in 1986.(*San Diego-Union Tribune*)

Probably Ted's last photo. Standing outside La Valencia Hotel, La Jolla, in May 1990 are (from left) Judith Morgan, Art Buchwald, Ted and Audrey. (*Neil Morgan photo*) been nicer to my boss, the old Fritz, than E. J. Kahn, Jr.'" But Ted came to recall the profile with regrets. "I don't want you even to read that," he told friends years later. "It got butchered. It was going to be two parts instead of one and they cut it. They took out all the funny stuff."

It was an excessive reaction even for a man notoriously edgy about his press notices, and it revealed more about Ted than about the profile. Pranks and anecdotes that Ted regarded as hilarious were indeed absent from Kahn's piece, but some proved impossible to translate successfully to the written word. Kahn did manage to ferret out traits linked with this very private man's eccentricities. Kahn called him "staggered and a bit frightened by his opulence, for he has never learned to come to grips with money. . . . 'I wish people would stop talking to me about money,' he says. 'All I want to do is to *write* books, and everybody's forever nagging at me to *keep* them.'"

As Ted's fame grew and tourists began to throng La Jolla, it was harder for Helen to insulate him. "I have to screen all the crackpots, would-be authors, PTA's, and visting friends of sub-cousins, aunts-in-law," she wrote. "I will be glad when this 'white trash' [summer tourists] goes back from vacation." In August 1961 Cynthia Lindsay, visiting the Tower on assignment from *Good Housekeeping*, complimented Helen on how smoothly she ran the household. "But, oh, it's a struggle!" Helen said, guarding Ted's privacy as he began work on *The Sneetches*.

The four stories in *The Sneetches* explore morality themes that had always gripped Ted. The Sneetches of the title story discriminate against other Sneetches who have no stars on their bellies. Bob Bernstein visited the Tower while boards for the book hung in Ted's studio. "You've come the wrong week," Ted told him. "I've decided to abandon this book."

Although he had seen Ted before in the depths of despondency, Bernstein was taken aback and asked why.

"Someone I respect told me it was anti-Semitic," Ted said.

"How could anybody say that?" Bernstein said, scanning the corkboard wall again. "Why in the hell are you listening? How can a man of your tremendous accomplishments be so jarred by one stupid comment?"

"That's the way I am," Ted said.

Half an hour later, after a bracing lecture from Bernstein, he was back on course. Bernstein examined Ted's boards for the eerie final story of the book, "What Was I Scared Of?" which introduces Ted's most frightening character, the Empty Pants. The criticism of Ted's Sneetches had been like the Empty Pants, Bernstein decided, and his author had been briefly scared by a vision of authority that turned out to be empty: "Those spooky empty pants and I were standing face to face!" He left the Tower feeling that he understood his remarkable friend a little better.

The Geisels flew to New York to deliver *The Sneetches* and lived for six weeks at the Hotel Madison while Helen finished a Beginner Book, "the 9,373rd version" of *A Fish Out of Water*, published, like most of her books, under her maiden name of Helen Palmer. Their long escape to New York had another purpose, for the Tower was being remodeled. The old draperies and broken record player went off to Goodwill Industries, the rugs to the cleaners, the dining table to the refinisher. The living room windows that overlooked La Jolla were extended to the floor, the linen closet became a powder room and the coat closet a linen closet. A new dining room was added as the house grew outward toward the swimming pool. "We have given away the piano," Helen wrote, "the sideboard goes next, and, oh, dear, but life is full of changes."

By the time order was restored Ted's father had resigned, at eighty-two, as superintendent of parks at Springfield. After fifty-two years of city service, he felt adrift and flew to California, where the Geisels shared him with his granddaughter, Peggy, and her husband, Al Owens, who was working at the Hughes Aircraft Company in Los Angeles. Although Ted's father had remarried in 1946, his second wife did not accompany him West and Peggy and Ted joked about this handsome man's "bachelor days." "Grampie was popular with the ladies," Peggy said. "When he dropped one woman and started dating another, the first one sued him for breach of promise. It happened to be on the day that Edward VIII abdicated to be with Wallis Simpson. Uncle Ted always said the headline in the Springfield newspaper was 'T. R.

Geisel Sued for Breach of Promise' and the smaller headline was 'King of England Abdicates.' "

Early in October 1961 the Geisels boarded the new nonstop polar jet from Los Angeles to London to join the London publisher Billy Collins in launching Beginner Books in Britain. "I hope they won't schedule Ted for TV," Helen wrote, "for he will get right on a plane and disappear into the wilderness if he thinks he is going to be looked at."

But the British had not warmed up to Dr. Seuss. Ted was best known in Britain as the creator of *Gerald McBoing-Boing*. After *Horton Hatches the Egg* had been rejected by seven British publishers, Hamish Hamilton published it to modest success there in 1947. Later the London literary agent Elaine Greene sought doggedly to interest a British publisher in *The Cat in the Hat*. She recalled that "those genteel spinster ladies in their twin sweater sets and pearls who edited children's books thought Ted's *Cat* was too vulgar for words." By the time *The Cat* had sold a million copies in America, Greene managed to sell British rights in the book to Hutchinson, but they "got no place with it." While visiting America soon thereafter, Collins "encountered this phenomenon" and quickly bought the rights from Hutchinson.

The Collins ballyhoo was laid on, and Ted found London newspapers announcing his fan mail as forty thousand to fifty thousand letters a year and describing him as America's top-selling author. Amid some caviling, Collins launched six of his books. *The Observer* felt that Dr. Seuss's "rejection of Christian names gives him a misleadingly sinister sound," and suggested that "anyone who cares should thumb through the six titles carefully and choose the one with the fewest Americanisms, which have been kept in for rhythm's sake." School librarians took umbrage with Dr. Seuss as a teaching tool, declaring his books "too jokey."

Yet British parents bought the books because Dr. Seuss "made reading fun," and Collins pursued the mass market with bargain paperback editions. Four years later, as Beginner Books sales in the United States passed eight million copies, Collins reported sales in Britain of one million. "The English don't so much regard Ted's books as children's books," Collins's publicist Michael Hyde said.

"They're just bloody good fun and never condescending. They're often used for teaching adults to read; we sell a lot of them to prisons. An illiterate old convict would object to being handed a children's book, but he'll settle in with Dr. Seuss."

Back in New York the Geisels found Bennett exuberant over a Grolier Children's Book Club contract for the direct-mail sales of Beginner Book reprints; they would soon yield the Geisels "as much or even more" in royalties than Random House sales. Phyllis Cerf, who called herself "sort of the business person" of Beginner Books, had been in Jamaica with her husband when Donald Klopfer telephoned to say he had sold the rights to Grolier. "I asked what other children's book lines Grolier was going to offer," Phyllis recalled, "and he said, 'Harper's,' and I said 'No.' Donald said, 'You can't [say no].' I said, 'Yes, it belongs to Ted and to me and I don't want anyone else's children's books riding on ours.'" To Klopfer's astonishment Grolier quickly agreed, and by the time of Ted's death forty years later had paid more than forty million dollars in royalties to Beginner Books, a large portion of it for Ted's books. Grolier became the longest-standing children's book club of its kind and, by trade estimates, the most successful.

Still, during the 1961 Christmas season, Ted fretted over the business demands of success. He was happiest in his studio, and in the new year he intended to spend more time there. He made that clear to many of the forty-six guests who arrived for Christmas Eve dinner, and then led them to his studio to help set up his gift from Helen: an electric train.

Random House wanted a blockbuster "big book" for the fall of 1962 to mark the twenty-fifth anniversary of Ted's first book, *Mulberry Street*. It was to be *Dr. Seuss's Sleep Book*, but on New Year's Day Ted was mired in his third rewrite. As always when the pressure grew, he agonized. He had made notes for the *Sleep Book* for four months in the spring of 1961, but had failed to establish an idea. He went back to it in the summer and, rewriting spasmodically, "found something." He sequestered himself, leaving a record of his struggle in scores of pages of rough notes, mostly typed, that he called his "bonepile":

> One minute of sleep is worth 3,000—. . . Sleep's better than butter . . . I'd rather (be sleeping/have sleep) than—

... Longest sleep Shortest sleep ... They are snoring in throats, boats, goats, notes, thousands of throats ... The sweet sounding notes of goats snoring in boats. [Then, marked with an encouraging red margin rule] From all over the world, The great Snooze News comes pouring: Everywhere, more and more creatures are snoring.

With that he veered off to probe the language of snoring, sleep talking and sleep walking. Finally he began fashioning phrases that would become familiar to readers of the finished book. He took a draft to New York in April 1962 and continued to work on it there. The book went to the printer late that month, followed by changes in galley proofs; only then, as usual, did Ted sit down with Louise Bonino and sign a contract for the book.

The originals of his words and drawings, from rough notes to manuscript, page proofs and bulky cardboard-backed flats with his final art, were soon shipped, like those of most of Ted's books and other memorabilia through 1968, to the special collections library at the University of California at Los Angeles, which he considered a convenient locale for scholars of children's literature and films. The library's first exhibition of his work had opened with a sprinkling of movie people present on February 2, 1962, and it ran for a month. The first two Dr. Seuss books were represented at UCLA only by a few handwritten notes and illustrations; Ted had given the surviving press sheets of *Mulberry Street* to Baker Library at Dartmouth, as well as preliminary notes and a battered pasteup dummy of *The 500 Hats*.

After the *Sleep Book* was done, the Geisels sought diversion at a resort that never sleeps. Helen wrote, "I really don't think I ever saw anything as ugly as the city of Las Vegas, and I prefer to think of it as a completely foreign land." In June they met the Cerfs in Ottawa, where Ted gave a witty talk to librarians, after which the Geisels visited the Cerf country house in Mt. Kisco, New York, to work on the fall list of Beginner Books with P. D. Eastman and Roy McKie.

Ted was wary of success. He feared they were undertaking so many Beginner Books that a diminution of quality was inevitable. He complained whenever he detected flaws in paper, ink or binding. His next-door neighbor, Bert Hupp, spurred Ted on as they took the hilltop air together, tugging at rocks or watering camellia bushes. "Be tough," Hupp advised one day. "Keep your standards up. It's your product, and don't you let anybody talk you into letting it slip."

Dr. Seuss's Sleep Book, with superb illustrations that had caused Ted relatively little anguish, appeared in the autumn of 1962 with the usual effortless air of all Dr. Seuss books. Critics welcomed another opportunity to hail an author who made Americans smile, and even more children began falling asleep to Dr. Seuss. Ted returned to New York in October for twenty-fifth-anniversary interviews. A piece by Helen Renthal in the *Chicago Tribune* book section won praise from Helen as "the best thing that I have ever read about Ted [because] it doesn't seem too gushy." In London to help Collins launch *One Fish*, he and Helen visited a class of six-year-olds at a school in Kent. The *Daily Mail*'s Olga Franklin went along and awarded the pupils the best of the encounter:

> "Are they really only six?" asked Dr. Seuss. The coloured chalk broke in his nervous hands. The children laughed. "Now, children," said Mrs. Stripe, "what day is it today?" The children shouted back: "October 12th." Mrs. Stripe smiled and said: "Well, children, we all know what day that is, don't we? Don't we, Dr. Seuss?" Everyone waited. Dr. Seuss admitted he didn't know what day it was. "It's the day Christopher Columbus discovered America," the children chorused. Dr. Seuss said: "Oh, him, he's my uncle." "No," the children shouted back, "he did it in 1492." . . . Overwhelmed, Dr. Seuss asked to see the five-year-olds. . . .

For the next three years there was no "big book." Ted focused on Beginner Books, and for spring and fall release in 1963 he did *Hop on Pop* and *Dr. Seuss's ABC Book*. Ever playful, he liked to slip risqué words into his manuscript drafts as a trap to see "if Bennett is reading my stuff." *Hop on Pop* went off to New York with a page reading, "When I read I am smart / I always cut whole words apart." Thus Constantinople appeared as Con Stan Tin O Ple and Timbuktu as Tim Buk Too. For a Cerf check he sent a rhyming line: "Con Tra Cep Tive, Kan Ga Roo" and did not rest until a call came from Bennett, saying, "Hey, Geisel, you can't put words like contraceptive in a kid's reader!" Two years later Ted decided Cerf might be off guard again and provoked another call of mock outrage with a manuscript line in *Fox in Socks*:

> Moe blows Joe's nose
> Joe blows Moe's nose.

But in tedious day-to-day telephone conferences about Beginner Books, Ted was squandering his energy. He loathed his confrontations with Phyllis and grew tense and withdrawn. Helen persuaded him to stay off the phone, consider himself retired from Beginner Books and let her arbitrate. Wary that an absence might tip the scales in Phyllis's favor, the Geisels canceled a safari in East Africa. Ted's agent, Phyllis Jackson, warned Bob Bernstein, to whom Cerf had gradually turned over control of daily operations at Random House, that he had "better do something" or he would lose Geisel. Soon Bernstein himself clashed irreconcilably with Phyllis. Apprehensive, he went in to see Bennett and, as delicately as he knew how, outlined his predicament.

"Do whatever you have to," Bennett told Bernstein at such moments, "but don't talk to me about it."

Bernstein did just that.

The authors Stan and Jan Berenstain, who admired Phyllis, were in the offices of Beginner Books that day and recalled the scene. Cerf's old partner, Don Klopfer, "who never came up there, appeared under some ruse, pretending to want to show some cat pictures to Ted, and under his breath he was reassuring Ted that things were going to work out. After he left, P. D. Eastman took us aside to tell us Phyllis was out, and he thought it was because she had started trying to edit Ted's books."

Years later, reflecting on those days, Phyllis said, "Bob Bernstein was not supportive of me. His role was to keep Ted happy. He didn't need to keep me happy. . . . Since I could do what I wanted in another way, I went off and did it." She moved from Beginner Books back to Random House with Elma Otto as her assistant, and created other books. "Except for Ted I'd still be doing Beginner Books. . . . I think the best books were [those] we did together."

Ted calmed himself by beginning to paint each day, mostly in watercolors but sometimes in gouache, ink and casein. Midnight was his favorite painting hour. He said of his paintings, "I like them. Some people like them. Art critics say they aren't art. . . . I could be a good painter if I could devote myself to it, hmmm?" Some found Ted's titles more extraordinary than his paintings. There was "Cat in a Cradle Making a Cat's Cradle," and "Alley Cat for an Extra-Long Alley." Ted said that a painting called "Great Cat in the Uleaborg, Finland Subway" was as close as he came to serious painting. It is strong in its draftsmanship: a distant animal is moving into a tunnelized distortion of perspective. Helen encouraged him in such work, calling him "a man who isn't happy while he's working on a book and even less happy when he isn't." She found him "happier when he's drawing than when he's writing" but most content when he painted.

As a trustee of La Jolla Art Center, Helen persuaded Ted for the first time to offer a painting for sale at a benefit auction that August. He selected a recent canvas from what he called his "La Jolla Bird-Woman" series and was elated when it brought the evening's top price of $550—more than was paid for a Cézanne drawing. The title of his painting, he explained, was "Mrs. Schnee-lock Poured, Miss Nesselrode Sugared."

CHAPTER 15

Fox in Socks

1964–1967

At the Phoenix, a smoky pub close by the *Herald-Sun* newsroom in downtown Melbourne, Ted was sipping a pint and chatting with a reporter. It was May of 1964, a nippy late autumn Down Under.

"Yes," he was saying, "Helen and I went on digs in Peru. We're amateur mummy diggers. We get mixed up in these things on vacations. Last year we were giving electro-cardiograms to elephant seals off the west coast of Mexico. I wish we had time for a platypus hunt here."

Virtually true, every word of it. A year earlier, with Gifford Ewing of Scripps Institution, on a pitching, rolling oceanographic vessel off Guadalupe Island on the Baja California coast, Ted had endured the downwind stench of those enormous seals and helped some obsessed young man pursue his dissertation on their cardiovascular eccentricities. Now he would prefer to be in Australia's Outback gouging for opals, but this earnest Melbourne journalist was asking about Gerald McBoing-Boing.

"It was one of those lucky accidents that come out of nowhere," Ted answered. "I'd been making a sound track for a documentary, and that night I dreamed about noises coming out of people's heads."

Possibly true. He had not told it this way before, and might not again. But possibly.

In Sydney the next day, Helen told a reporter from *The Morning Herald* how she had first noticed Ted doodling in his Oxford notebook and suggested that he pursue drawing instead of teaching.

Almost forty years later she seemed amazed by her audacity: "Today I wouldn't dream of making a remark like that, a remark that could change the course of a person's whole life."

The Geisels worked hard—some friends said compulsively—but they had always known how to escape in travel. This journey Down Under brought Ted discovery and release. "Ted should be put on the Chamber of Commerce for Australia," Helen wrote. "He tells everyone he would go there in a minute to start life again if he were twenty years younger." For her the high point of their trip was braving a heavy New Zealand crosswind to land in a tiny ski plane beside "a bottomless crevasse" on Mount Cook's vast Tasman Glacier. Throughout the journey, shepherded by Collins's deputies, the Geisels marketed books so successfully that by per capita reckoning, New Zealand became the No. 1 Dr. Seuss market in the world.

Helen returned home happy but exceptionally weary. Although she pushed herself hard and without complaint, she had never recovered completely from her traumatic paralysis ten years earlier. She remained nerveless in travel while growing increasingly conservative in dress; at Random House she was known for "her perfect little pink suit and mink stole." The psychiatrist Stanley Willis, the Geisels' neighbor and frequent visitor, observed that Helen "was progressively more handicapped by the residuals of her polio, including one that particularly haunted her: she may have been going blind." Still, she was winning wide respect for her own juvenile books; *Do You Know What I'm Going to Do Next Saturday?*, with photographs by the artist Lynn Fayman, was listed by *The New York Times* as one of the best juveniles of 1963.

The Geisels' financial success, long assumed, became a matter of public record for the first time that summer when *Business Week* estimated Dr. Seuss's annual book royalties in excess of two hundred thousand dollars, a quite conservative figure. Ted's chronic fear of financial catastrophe had been calmed. At sixty, he estimated that he had twenty productive years ahead; he was trim, boisterous and in sturdy health, although from time to time when he tried to give up smoking, Helen called him "a bundle of nerves." They finally agreed that the time had come to hire a secretary or editorial assistant to help with the increasing volume of Beginner Book manuscripts and correspondence, and in August they shook hands with Julie Olfe, a spirited woman of twenty-five who had recently moved to La Jolla with her husband, a professor at the University of California's new San Diego campus.

The Geisels loved their mountaintop home and its work spaces, and fussed about the "bulldozing of La Jolla" for hotels and condominium buildings—"everything that we don't want," Helen said, "and where all the people are going to come from to [justify] these wild real estate ideas, I just don't know." On northerly cliffs seen from Ted's studio windows the University of California was ensuring more diverse growth for La Jolla, a suburb that had grown to about thirty thousand residents. The Geisels had cheered on their friend Roger Revelle, who had been pivotal in bringing the campus to La Jolla, when he warned civic and church audiences that they could not have a great university unless they forsook discrimination against Jews, specifically in home ownership. A chastened community had responded.

For the Geisels the university symbolized the transition of their community from the secluded resort village that had charmed them forty years earlier. Many of their closest friends came from UCSD. The historian John Semple Galbraith, its chancellor, and his wife, Laura, were frequent dinner companions. At a party given by Joan and Tom Braden, liberal expatriates from Washington who published a suburban newspaper in Oceanside, Ted fended off boredom by introducing Galbraith, a gaunt Scot, as Dr. Seuss, and himself as the university chancellor. The hostess did not seem amused as she set straight the confusion that ensued.

Faculty conversations made Helen's dinners livelier, and Ted said it was because finally there were some other Democrats in La Jolla. The Geisels worked hard seven days a week, but at their parties they drank, sang and told extravagant stories. Several media figures became close friends. They went to sea on day sails with John Kennedy, who had owned the *San Diego Daily Journal*, and his wife, Bruce. They enjoyed Jim Copley and his bride, Helen, who owned *The San Diego Union* and *Evening Tribune*; Ted learned not to talk politics with the conservative publisher, but Copley was a Yale graduate, and so they shared Ivy League stories and linked arms singing "Boola Boola." Jeanne and Clayton Brace were part of this group after coming to San Diego to run *Time-Life*'s television station, and Brace sang tenor in Ted's "barbershop trio," which included Percy H. "Duke" Johnston, a retired financier and an Oxford man who entertained after dinner with magic shows.

The faculty couples included Judith and Walter Munk, a Viennese-born oceanographer; the benign, round-faced chemist and Nobel laureate Harold Urey and his wife, Frieda; and Sybil and Herbert York, with whom Ted had long conversations about nuclear disarmament. The industrial designer Henry Dreyfuss was a regular, as were the *Los Angeles Times* cartoonist Paul Conrad and touring authors like Robert Ludlum, whose novels Ted favored during sleepless hours.

Marge and Fred Phleger were one faculty couple who became Beginner Books coauthors, and in the autumn of 1964 the Geisels traveled to Honolulu with them as the Phlegers began work on *You Will Live Under the Sea*. Fred was an expert on a form of plankton called foraminifera, a word Ted loved to roll on his tongue as he introduced Fred as author of a textbook called *Ecology and Distribution of Recent Foraminifera*. He had spent six years writing the book and expected it to sell three thousand copies in ten years. His first children's book, written with the Geisels' guidance, had been *The Whales Go By*, which sold almost one hundred thousand copies in one year.

The Tower became legendary with its out-of-town visitors for the Geisels' hospitality. Bennett Cerf told his column readers about a dinner there when Ted sang along while his army buddy Meredith Willson played songs from *The Music Man*; then Jonas Salk, who was building his research institute near the campus, expounded until after midnight on the evolution of mankind. The Geisels also arranged memorable daytime itineraries. Bennett had never flown in a helicopter, so pilots of the navy's first helicopter squadron, based in San Diego, took Bennett and Ted sightseeing. "If we had known then how undependable those early machines were," one pilot later recalled, "none of us would have gone up that day." Cerf, who thoroughly enjoyed the flight, framed and hung a photograph of himself and Ted in flight helmets.

Ted cherished his prankster pals. He and Helen became close to Audrey and Grey Dimond, a cardiologist who joined the staff of Scripps Clinic in 1960, and it was at their home that they first met Duke Johnston and his chic Bulgarian wife, Luba. Duke and Ted, partners in mischief, once disappeared from a long dinner party at the Inn at Rancho Santa Fe. By the time they were discovered in the hotel library, they had signed impertinent or salacious autographs in dozens of books in the names of their authors, most notably Robert Louis Stevenson and Mary Baker Eddy.

Audrey and Grey soon became social constants in the Geisels' lives, and the two couples often arrived together at parties, with the younger Dimonds driving. Ted enjoyed pointing out that Audrey had never read Dr. Seuss books to her children. Actually, she would add, her blue eyes twinkling, she had never heard of Dr. Seuss until she moved to La Jolla. During a party for the Scripps Clinic faculty at the home of Dr. Edward Hashinger she had been introduced to "a tall, distinguished man." Someone told her, "This is our very own Dr. Seuss." Assuming he was on the staff, she made a flip inquiry: "Do you have a particular specialty? Left nostril? Right nostril?" It was rare that Ted met anyone unfamiliar with the name of Dr. Seuss, and he seemed enchanted. He was working on the tongue-twisters for *Fox in Socks*, and Audrey, he said, was the only adult who could read them aloud. Petite and pretty, she joined the circle around the Geisel piano, whistling in a birdcall warble while others sang. She wore swirls of chiffon, and astonished strangers with her provocative questions at dinner parties. After Audrey's mother died of cancer at the Dimond home, Helen and Ted called; drained by grief, Audrey heard the doorbell but could not respond. Helen wrote a note of sympathy, closing with words that her young secretary, Julie Olfe, always remembered: "Even when a death is expected it leaves a hole in the heart."

As life changed in La Jolla, so did the Geisels' tight circle in New York. After Phyllis Cerf's departure from Beginner Books, new faces appeared in other offices. Louise Bonino was ailing, and Walter Retan replaced her as juvenile editor. The Geisels had grown too valuable to be dealt with only through normal channels, and Bob Bernstein's assistant, Anne Marcovecchio, became their New York gatekeeper. She was a warmhearted Dr. Seuss admirer, a Hunter College graduate, and Ted and Helen trusted her implicitly. Helen and Anne handled many Beginner Books decisions by mail. Anne set up conference calls, relayed Geisel decisions, arranged travel and settled disputes with unsatisfactory authors or artists. If Random House needed anything from the Geisels—an opinion, permission, publicity arrangements—the request went through Anne. An interruption or irrelevant inquiry from anyone else in New York could provoke an irritated outburst from one of the Geisels to Bernstein or Cerf. "If the news is bad," Helen wrote Anne, "I'd rather hear it from you than anybody."

At the production level, Ted began to lean on young Michael Frith, who had been Christopher Cerf's puckish colleague at Harvard on *The Lampoon* and soon became managing editor of Beginner Books. He and Ted sparked each other as they exchanged ideas about art in New York and La Jolla. Ted admired Frith's talents but found him disorganized. "It was a love-hate relationship," said Jerry Harrison, who became president of the juvenile division. "Mike was brilliant, but Ted believed in discipline and deadlines. In that sense Ted was a businessman."

Ted was still rewriting the phonic Beginner Book *Fox in Socks* in New York in April 1965 when he delivered his first "big book" in three years, *I Had Trouble in Getting to Solla Sollew*. "No theater tickets, Anne," Helen had written. "Ted has a book to put to bed." Helen described the tension: "About two weeks before the completion of every book, he seems to go into a tailspin, decides that nothing in the book is any good, that he can't possibly finish it, and . . . I have a great job to do in keeping everything from falling in the scrap basket." To Anne she confided: "I'm at my wit's end to try not to be rude."

Helen herself was planning the 1966 fall list for Beginner Books, including the French edition of *The Cat in the Hat Dictionary*. Ted's Dartmouth colleague Al Perkins was their current favorite at Beginner Books; Helen had him working "on verse, a dog detective story, a cowboy story. . . . I only wish that everyone was as energetic and talented."

Ted referred to *Solla Sollew* as "not one of my more successful books"; indeed its sales weren't remarkable, though many critics praised it. (As his own favorites at that time, Ted usually named the two *Hortons* and *The Grinch*.) *Solla Sollew* was a somber morality tale, a Seussian *Pilgrim's Progress* with the message that one can't run away from trouble. The hapless pilgrim has to find his way through thickets of harassments and burdens, and is conscripted into a cowardly army led by a bellowing bully in armor: "I'm General Genghis Kahn Schmitz!" ("The finest line I have ever written," Ted said in a fleeting moment of self-satisfaction.) He dedicated *Solla Sollew* to his niece, Peggy Owens. *Fox in Socks*, published that autumn, was dedicated to Audrey Dimond and Mitzi Long, another La Jollan, and their fictitious "Mt. Soledad Lingual Laboratories."

Grolier, busily selling Beginner Books by mail, added another unit to market the "big" Dr. Seuss books. Ted and Helen were astonished that retail booksellers didn't complain about being undersold by book clubs, but booksellers viewed their customers as a different market, and the Geisels prospered from each. "We have made the decision to do it," Helen wrote Bernstein, "but I must say when we are confronted with the price of $1.95 for three [of the 'big'] Dr. Seuss books, we are rather shattered." They had been similarly undone by the introductory prices that Grolier put on Beginner Books, and so had Billy Collins in London. "It's surely taking a high dive into cold water. . . ." Helen wrote. Bob Bernstein replied with his usual assurance that the high dive would be invigorating and highly profitable, and he was quickly proved correct. On July 19, 1965, he wrote, "I'm sending out this year's figures, which I regard as sensational."

Since Helen's frightening illness, when Ted had been touched by the kindness of friends and strangers, he had become less reclusive. In 1966 he approved a Dr. Seuss theme for the Charity Ball, an annual benefit for the San Diego Children's Hospital, and helped to create countless Cats as decor for the lofty old ballroom of Hotel del Coronado. The Cerfs flew in for the February weekend of the ball, and Bennett took the stage to remind his listeners how fortunate they were to have Dr. Seuss as a local. Then Bennett returned to New York to negotiate the sale of Random House to RCA on May 19, 1966. Random House sharcholders received $40 million in RCA stock, and Cerf attained his personal goal of becoming part of a major communications company listed on the New York Stock Exchange. Ted sat at his drawing board and, with a colored pencil, computed his own holdings in stock and deferred income, totaling many millions of dollars.

He still made time for neighborly good deeds. Though he invariably turned down requests to write book endorsements, he made an exception with a generous foreword for a newspaper friend's book about San Diego, confessing "I love this very wonderful . . . very complex place that is our home." Dapper in polished loafers and tweed sports jackets, he traveled to downtown San Diego for monthly meetings of Citizens United, a blue-ribbon panel aimed at civic betterment. Its members generally regarded him as a talented eccentric but one hardly acquainted with how things were done in the real world. When they voted to disband, professing to find little that needed fixing in San Diego, Ted became once again the angry *PM* activist, drawing a cartoon of protest that later provided a rallying cry. It revived a character from his *Sneetches* book, a pair of Empty Pants. In the cartoon Empty Pants teetered on the pediment of a park statue above the caustic challenge ONWARD TO WHERE?

Helen was "toiling busily away at Beginner Books" and "tiptoeing around the house so as not to disturb" Ted. She wrote, "We thought everything was under control, and then a couple of our artists really bogged down. . . . We're flying an author to New York from Madeira to work with us." But she too found time for the community. In 1966 she was elected president of the La Jolla Art Museum and Ted became a familiar figure at openings, promising to return to his painting so that the museum could mount his one-man show. Of Ted's exuberant approach to an easel, Helen wrote that "paint seems to land on everything from chairs to tables to sofa covers to his own hair."

Although Ted counseled young artists to "paint at least one picture a month that is just for fun," he could not justify his own painting, which he considered pleasure, when lively offers beckoned. The animator Chuck Jones, who had moved to MGM, telephoned Ted early in 1966, suggesting that they talk about adapting one of Ted's books for television. Ted declined. He remembered the terrors of *The 5,000 Fingers of Dr. T.* and suspected that television would induce similar anguish. "Everybody wanted to make a series—bat 'em out fast and use up my whole life's work in a year." But Helen urged him to listen, and Jones drove to La Jolla for their first visit since Helen's convalescence in Santa Monica twelve years earlier. Ted stood waiting for him at the side of the road, as he sometimes did for special friends who might lose their way in the maze leading to the Tower.

Jones loved Ted and recalled: "He was standing there alone in the bright sun looking not very different. He didn't change a lot. He'd always said he had two noses: a little one on top of a big one. We walked up the winding path and chatted, and I told him it was time to put Dr. Seuss on television. He was reluctant, but Helen was very interested and finally became enthusiastic. He had planned that we'd talk about old times and then I'd go home, but eventually he gave in. We didn't know which book to use, but it was early enough in the year that we could get it done for Christmas, so it had to be *The Grinch*."

Ted telephoned the news to Phyllis Jackson at International Creative Management and to Bob Bernstein, and thought both seemed wary. Jones briefed MGM, but met with no enthusiasm. Still, at Ted's request Phyllis negotiated a contract for a half-hour show. It was no windfall, yielding only an initial four-figure fee with no residuals, but it did allow for the reopening of contract negotiations. Jones created story boards and began searching for a sponsor. He made more than twenty presentations to firms like Kellogg and Nestlé that he considered dependable children's-program sponsors, but they saw nothing in *The Grinch* for them. Ted attended two presentations and was promptly disheartened. "I kept seeing his poor face," Jones recalled, "and told him to stay away." Finally the Foundation for Commercial Banks ("of all people," Jones said) became the sponsor.

The transformation of *The Grinch* to film became a strenuous series of revelations for Ted. Jones used the full-animation technique adopted by Disney; unlike most cartoons of the era, with about two thousand drawings per show, *The Grinch* required about twenty-five thousand. "The difference is you can turn the sound off and tell what's happening," Jones explained to Ted, "the same as if you're watching actors act." A primary challenge was to take a mean Grinch and make him even meaner. To achieve credibility in animation, the two men agreed on a three-dimensional Grinch—"how he thinks, how he moves, even the dimensions of his body displacement." Jones decided the Grinch was "a sloppy guy" who when he walked "would drag his toe."

Jones admired Ted's art but was a master of his own. "I had to change the Grinch's expression with a set discipline of moves . . . to hold onto that frown, for instance, right up to the time it changes. We brought the mouth clear down, so when he gets that horrible idea of making Santa Claus's rounds, it was like a rock thrown into a lava bed; it just kept spreading and spreading evil."

Ted and Jones battled. What color should the Grinch be? Just the way he had drawn him, Ted replied, in black-and-white with pink eyes. But for television, Jones convinced him, the Grinch's eyes should be a villainous green. He studied Ted's book and discovered that "lady Whos don't have high-heeled shoes—they have high-heeled feet." Little Cindy-Lou Who is "not a regular little girl; she has antennas." Ted was challenged to augment characters and situations over which he had already labored long in search of perfection. It took about twelve minutes to read *The Grinch* aloud; on television, it had to fill the major share of half an hour.

Back and forth their conferences went, in Los Angeles and at the Tower, with Ted as Jones's coproducer. As the Grinch grew more evil, it fell to the set designer Maurice Noble, another colleague from the wartime Capra unit, to cast a benevolent spell with his lavish opening scene of the village Whos, linking hands around their Christmas tree. "I was an admirer of Ted Geisel," Noble recalled, "but I loved Dr. Seuss." About two hundred and fifty backgrounds were drawn, another generous statistic for a cartoon. Ted worked on the lyrics with composer Albert Hague, and a thirty-four-piece orchestra and twelve-voice chorus recorded the music. By May of 1966 Boris Karloff, a master of horror roles, was recording the voice of the Grinch. Ted was fondest of his menacing Grinch Song, and so were American children:

> You're a mean one, Mister Grinch;
> You really are a heel.
> You're as cuddly as a cactus, you're as charming as an eel.
> Mister Grinch! You're a bad banana with a greasy black
>   peel. . . .

While writing the book Ted had agonized for months about how to keep the ending from seeming trite or religious, and the challenge arose again with the television version. But the filmed *Grinch* emerged as a rare Christmas special without religiosity. Noble recalled, "[Ted didn't want] a star coming down from the sky, so I had it come from the hearts of the people of Who-ville and float upward as the Whos sang Ted's beautiful song, 'Welcome Christmas,' with those wonderful lines 'Christmas Day will always be, / just as long as we have we!' "

CBS-TV bought *Grinch*, paying MGM $315,000 for the rights to two airings before Christmas in 1966 and 1967. In October, *Variety* headlined: "THE GRINCH"—IT NOT ONLY STOLE XMAS BUT PICKED CBS' POCKET FOR $315,000.

Variety speculated that it was the most expensive half-hour show ever made for television. Jones guessed it would be rerun "for at least the next ten years," with an initial cost to sponsors of one hundred thousand dollars for a commercial minute. The show was first seen on Sunday evening, December 18, 1966, in the 7:00 P.M. slot on CBS usually occupied by *Lassie*. In *The New York Times*, Jack Gould wrote that the Grinch might better have been left "undisturbed on the printed page, where the graceful simplicity of the language of Dr. Seuss weaves its own wonder. . . ." He thought the television version "fell a trifle short of expectation . . . the spell was not quite there." But this was a minority report; the Grinch was on its way to join Charles Dickens's Scrooge and Charles Schulz's Charlie Brown as television's most lasting Christmas entertainment traditions.

That holiday season at the La Jolla Museum, Ted threw a switch to light a Who-ville Christmas tree as the climax of a four-day children's jamboree. Helen agreed to continue as museum president "since nobody else seemed available." Then she turned to preparations for the Geisels' annual Christmas Eve dinner, this time for sixty-five friends, including Ted's father, still vigorous at eighty-seven and visiting for the holidays.

The Tower was a madhouse that Christmas. The senior Geisel, silver-haired and ramrod-straight, occupied Helen's office as a guest room, keeping his television turned high and favoring the soap opera *As the World Turns*. The telephone rang more often than usual, with congratulations on the televised *Grinch*. Guests called the Geisels' Christmas Eve party the best yet, and Helen gaily predicted that the guest list would "leap to eighty-five" by Christmas of 1967.

With acclaim for the television *Grinch* came increasing sales of the book. When Chuck Jones proposed that they next make a special of *Horton Hears a Who!*, Ted hesitated long enough to be assured of the success of *Grinch* and then joined in work on *Horton* for Thanksgiving release in 1967. Phyllis Jackson held out for a big payday from MGM, but Ted wanted to do the show for his own reasons. "It's the only way people will let me write song lyrics," he said, "and that's the only thing I want to do right now." Working with him on *Horton* was no easier than on *Grinch*, Jones recalled; it was "equally difficult and equally enjoyable."

The demands of the book business remained unyielding, and the West Coast office of Beginner Books still operated with one secretary and minimal equipment, not even an electric typewriter. After New Year's of 1967 the Geisels installed their first copying machine and tried to learn how to use a tape recorder. They took a break from their seven-day-a-week work schedule one Saturday in January and sailed with friends on Bruce and John Kennedy's boat to watch California gray whales on their migration from the Bering Sea to Baja California's calving lagoons.

Seeming distracted and even edgier than usual that winter, Ted disappeared on long walks and focused on *The Cat in the Hat Songbook*, a project he cherished. He had written lovely lyrics, but the tricky melodies by Eugene Poddany ("part Russian, part

Hollywood") made them difficult to sing. Yet Ted insisted that children would be able to sing them, and dedicated the *Songbook* "to Lark and Lea of Ludington Lane," a salute to the young daughters of Audrey and Grey Dimond.

In May the Geisels took the finished product to Random House, where Ted proudly showed it to the salesmen at their semiannual meeting. Although the sales force had learned not to bet against Dr. Seuss, their wariness was apparent. Late that summer at University House, the UCSD chancellor's residence, Ted led an august body of lay singers in attempting the Cat songs, provoking the university provost, John Stewart, to write a whimsical review that appeared in *The San Diego Union*. It may have been the *Songbook*'s best notice. The instincts of the Random House salesmen proved sound; sales were so sparse that the *Songbook* and the *Godivas* became the only Seuss books allowed to go out of print.

That summer the Geisels threw themselves into a frenzy of projects. Helen spent hours on the telephone with Beginner Books people in New York and Ted went back and forth to Hollywood for conferences on the television version of *Horton*. Bob Bernstein and his wife, Helen, came from New York for a visit; Bob found Ted "strangely down and jumpy," saying it was increasingly hard for him to work at the Tower and that he was "considering leasing a studio." The Bernsteins wondered for the first time if there "might be trouble" in the Geisel marriage. The juvenile editor Walter Retan, a quiet and intuitive man, visited the Tower and talked later of the tension he sensed there as Ted chafed at Helen's discipline: "They had so much in common, but they were driving each other crazy. Helen wasn't well, and she probably depressed Ted. She had been very, very good for him, but I could not say she was good for him at that time."

At Helen's request Ted visited the museum in August to spur on ninety schoolchildren turned loose to build a nonsensical "model city," and he told them he was busy inventing "a boomerang that won't return." In a review of the museum mayhem in *Time*, he said he was involved because "if you don't get imagination as a child you probably never will." He also told *Time* he had come to consider the word lists on which he had once based

Beginner Books to be "hogwash" because television had expanded children's vocabularies.

In September the Geisels' assistant, Julie Olfe, told them she was expecting her first child and would soon stop work. Helen asked her to concentrate her remaining time in helping to clean out files and throw things away. "Never in three years had we cleaned out files," Julie said. "She threw out letters and a lot of photographs."

Late that month, soon after Helen's sixty-ninth birthday, the Geisels took a vacation week in the Colorado Rockies, a setting Helen always found "serene." After three nights at the Garden of the Gods Club near Colorado Springs, they drove to Golden to visit Libby and Orlo Childs, the president of the Colorado School of Mines; these were the old friends who had taken them swimming in the Great Salt Lake in 1949. Their guests arrived "relaxed and refreshed," Libby Childs recalled, with Helen "in such high spirits." It was sunny and brisk, and the four of them took day trips into the mountains with the aspen "at their peak." Helen mailed post-cards and snapshots from Bear Lake in Rocky Mountain National Park. Back in La Jolla, she wrote an effusive thank-you note, telling Libby that Ted was busy at his easel "painting a Colorado ghost town."

On a warm Sunday in mid-October when the Pacific was unnaturally calm, Ted and Helen sailed off Point Loma with their psychiatrist neighbor Stanley Willis and his wife, Edith. Robert Tschirgi, the vice chancellor at the university, came along and brought his Polaroid camera. In his pictures the sails hang limp and windless. Helen wears a turquoise bandanna and dark glasses, a white sweater over a striped dress and pearls, and her broadest smile. Ted, deeply tanned and in open-collared shirt and slacks, sits with his arms around the two women, gazing up at the skipper at his tiller. "All seemed well to me that day," Tschirgi said.

On the following Saturday, at a dinner party at the Rancho Santa Fe estate of Luba and Duke Johnston, Helen seemed "strangely low." When the host hugged her, she looked up at him and said, "You don't know how I needed that!" Duke did know that because of her Beginner Books workload Helen had been troubled about whether she should accept another term as president of the Art Museum. He also knew that her close friend and confidante Marian Longstreth was in Europe for several months, and for the first time he wondered if Helen was lonely. At the end of the evening he hugged her again, wondering what to say, and said only good-night.

Two days later, just before 10:00 A.M. on Monday, October 23, 1967, Alberta Fouts, the Geisels' longtime housekeeper, arrived for work at the Tower. She was surprised that Helen was not bustling about as usual; Ted always slept late, but never Helen. Puzzled and soon concerned, she tapped on the bedroom door. When there was no answer, she entered and found Helen in bed in her nightgown. Realizing that she was dead, the housekeeper ran to awaken Ted, who later told Stanley Willis, "I didn't know whether to kill myself, burn the house down, or just go away and get lost." Helen had gone to bed shortly after 11:00 P.M., he said, and he had worked in his study until 2:00 A.M., when he had gone to his own bedroom.

The report of the San Diego County coroner noted "a large pharmacy-size stock bottle, at rest on the bed at the left side of the decedent's head. The label on the bottle indicated the contents were sodium pentobarbital capsules, one and a half grains. This bottle had originally contained 1,000 capsules; 706 capsules remained. . . . A despondent type note directed to the decedent's husband was also found. . . ."

The note was in Helen's precise hand on the stationery of the La Jolla Beach and Tennis Club. Her final writing became a sad fragment of the public records:

> Dear Ted,
> What has happened to us?
> I don't know.
> I feel myself in a spiral, going down down down, into a black hole from which there is no escape, no brightness. And loud in my ears from every side I hear, "failure, failure, failure. . . ."
> I love you so much. . . . I am too old and enmeshed in everything you do and are, that I cannot conceive of life without you. . . . My going will leave quite a rumor but you

can say I was overworked and overwrought. Your reputation with your friends and fans will not be harmed. . . . Sometimes, think of the fun we had all thru the years. . . .

She had signed with their old code words, the make-believe law firm with the Seussian rhythms: Grimalkin, Drouberhannus, Knalbner and Fepp.

CHAPTER 16

The Lorax

1967–1971

On that sunstruck October day, as Santa Ana winds swept off the Mojave Desert crisping everything in their path, Julie Olfe arrived at the Tower at her usual hour, just after lunch. She pushed open the wooden gate by the pool and saw the gardener watering a row of terra-cotta pots lush with white azaleas. He said "something about Mrs. Geisel," but she did not understand and strode on. Usually the living room was empty as she passed through to her office, but on this day Ted "stood grim-faced, with eight or ten friends in a loose circle around him." She saw the Phlegers and the Dimonds, but their voices seemed "tight and subdued." Both phones were ringing, and no one was answering. Audrey sat in the living room, looking out toward the sea; in front of her was an untouched grilled cheese sandwich, and Julie thought she looked pale and distracted.

Then Grey Dimond told Julie that Helen was dead. "Ted was standing across the room," she recalled, "and I looked over and said, 'I'm so sorry. I love you. . . . '"

Ted's attorney, Frank Kockritz, arrived with his wife, Susan. Marge Phleger returned calls to newspapers, wire services and television reporters. *The New York Times* had called, as had *The Washington Post* and *Time*. Bennett Cerf heard about Helen's death from a *San Diego Union* reporter and told her, "Helen was one of the most wonderful women I've met in my whole life. . . . We regarded Helen—as a worker, a creator—[as] the most unselfish person we've ever known." The next morning's *New York Times* obituary listed four children's books she had written, but noted that "her major activities . . . were centered on her husband, for whom she was chief critic, editor, business manager and wife for forty years."

A call had gone out to Ted's niece, Peggy, in Los Angeles, but she was not at home; when she returned the telephone was ringing and it was her husband's secretary. "Somebody named Helen has died," the woman said, "and Ted would like you to come." Within the hour Peggy, fighting back tears, was driving down the coast to La Jolla.

Friends were milling about as Peggy walked into the living room two hours later. She hugged Ted, who seemed "shocked into silence." No one mentioned the cause of death, and Peggy, trained to respect Geisel privacies, did not ask. As well as anyone, she knew of Helen's deteriorating health and the constant pain in her legs and feet since the paralysis. But Peggy was stunned when Marge Phleger told her the cause of death and the news was reported on television. It was days before Ted could talk to Peggy about it. "I guess you know it was suicide," he finally said. She nodded. They sat talking until 2:00 A.M. "He was in anguish," Peggy said. "I think he was trying to protect me. . . . Whatever Helen did, she did it out of absolute love for Ted."

Julie Olfe saw it in much the same way. Helen had "steadfast confidence in Ted," and her death "was her last and greatest gift to him." Helen's museum friend Eileen Vanderlaan, a physician's wife, could not escape a memory. Once when she chided Helen for not having told her that she was going into the clinic for surgery, Helen had smiled. "When I have a problem and something needs to be done," she had said, "I just prefer to go on and do it and not make a fuss."

Seven days after Helen's death, Ted arrived at dusk at the oceanfront cottage of two close friends. His eyes were flat from strain and grief, and he was dismayed by his sudden and painful public visibility. Yet over dinner his voice flashed defiance as he said he would go on with his work and stay in La Jolla.

· · ·

On the afternoon of November 9, as the first golden leaves of autumn swirled from liquidambar trees outside the La Jolla Museum, about one hundred and fifty friends gathered for a memorial service. Ted arrived with Peggy and, flanked by Audrey and Grey Dimond, leaned against a wall, staring straight ahead. Museum officers spoke briefly: the attorney Karl ZoBell, who had served as Helen's vice president, and photographer Lynn Fayman, a former museum president with whom Helen had written three books. The museum's art-reference library would be named the Helen Palmer Geisel Library.

Ted retreated into his studio that wet, blustery winter and lost himself in work. Only a few in the community reached out to him, or he to them. Julie Olfe agreed not to leave her job; she had her baby in March but returned to work soon after, bringing her son to the Tower in a basket. Ted looked in on them from time to time, staring into the baby's eyes and risking an occasional pat.

Between visits to La Jolla, Peggy asked Julie to keep her informed about Ted's spirits. "There's been a breakthrough," Julie wrote as Ted worked on *The Foot Book*, an experiment aimed at his youngest market ever. "But it's a struggle." Ted tried to take over Helen's role in Beginner Books, but it was difficult. "In his head, he had such definite ideas about books he wanted others to do," Julie said, "but they could not carry out ideas that he could not express."

There were other problems. Frank Kockritz talked to him about taxes; Helen's death had triggered a huge income-tax liability for gains realized through her half of their considerable community property, which she had willed to Dartmouth, establishing the Helen and Ted Geisel Third Century Professorship in the humanities. She had left her jewelry and silver to her nieces, Barbara and Virginia, and to Ted's niece, Peggy. Her nonbook properties involving Dr. Seuss—licenses, copyrights and franchises—went to the charitable Seuss Foundation, which had been set up in 1958. She and Ted had given the foundation all royalties from *Mulberry Street*, *The 500 Hats* and *Ten Apples Up on Top*, but by 1967 their community property involved an additional twenty-two books, including those continuing blockbusters *The Cat in the Hat* and *Green Eggs and Ham*.

A shuffle ensued in New York. Bob Bernstein's assistant, Anne—now married to Hugh Johnson and always "dear Annie" to Ted—became vice president of Beginner Books, the title Helen had held, to work with contract artists and writers. Mike Frith became editor, with Ted as his primary responsibility. "Ted always needed someone in New York to understand his artistic mind and playfulness," said Elma Otto, Phyllis Cerf's former assistant, who succeeded Frith as managing editor.

For the first time Ted avoided some of his two or three annual work trips to New York; instead Anne or Mike came to the Tower. Walter Retan, the juvenile editor handling Ted's "big books," also flew West, finding that he and Ted worked more efficiently in the quiet of La Jolla.

The Foot Book over which Ted busied himself was the first of the Bright & Early Books, designed as pre-readers. When it appeared early in 1968, friends were quick to reassure him that he still "had it"; the Seussian giddiness had not disappeared. From the first cadence ("Left foot/ Left foot/ Right foot/ Right/ Feet in the morning/ Feet at night"), it was a model of Ted's skill in linking illustration and text, and of his flawless ear for repetition and rhythm: "Slow feet / Quick feet / Trick feet / Sick feet . . . His feet / Her feet / Fuzzy / fur feet."

That spring Ted telephoned the architect Russell Forester to say that his earlier ideas for remodeling the Tower had changed. Beige and brown were out; it should be airier and brighter. When Forester arrived at the Tower for a conference, everything became clear. Audrey Dimond sat waiting with Ted, who, swearing Forester to secrecy, said that since she would be living there, her wishes should be respected.

Days before, Audrey had approached her husband, Grey, in the kitchen of their Ludington Lane house to say that she planned to marry Ted. She realized that "something was lacking" in their marriage; she considered Grey self-sufficient, she told him, "but Ted needs me." The cardiologist had stood silently for a moment as though he were thinking all this over.

"Who," he asked finally, "is going to do the driving?"

"Why, I guess I will," Audrey replied, astonished.

"Good," he said. "I don't want any wife of mine marrying a man who drives the way Ted does."

In late May, Ted wrote his Oxford roommate, Donald Bartlett, and his wife, Henri, what some La Jollans already suspected:

> . . . I've written you kids at least ten times about my future plans. And, everytime, torn the letters up. The letters get so involved, so unbelievable. So let me put it out, flat on the line, without any comment or begging for understanding.
>
> On the 21st of June, Audrey Dimond is going to Reno to divorce Grey Dimond. . . . Audrey and I are going to be married about the first week in August. I am acquiring two daughters, aged nine and fourteen. I am rebuilding the house to take care of the influx. I am 64 years old. I am marrying a woman eighteen years younger. . . . I have not flipped my lid. This is not a sudden nutty decision. . . . This is an inevitable, inescapable conclusion to five years of four people's frustration. All I can ask you is to try to believe in me.

Ted and Audrey trusted fate; theirs had changed, she said, during a winter day of whale-watching off San Diego on Bruce and John Kennedy's yacht. The seas had been heavy and Audrey remembered that "along came this big old heave of a wave and I was absolutely, honestly, inadvertently thrown at Ted. . . . He caught me and we looked at each other and the awareness was mutual. You look away and you talk about inane things, but it would never be the same."

With a determined show of bravado in June, Ted told a colleague, "My best friend is being divorced and I'm going to Reno to comfort his wife." On June 21, as Russell Forester's remodeling crew moved into the Tower, Audrey and Ted settled into Reno's Ponderosa Hotel for the legally required six-week wait. It was a somber time. Temperatures were in the high nineties, but neither the casinos nor the Sunday rodeo held any interest for the couple. Even Bobby Russell's hit tune "Little Green Apples," playing in every bar and elevator, brought only a flicker of a smile:

And if that's not lovin' me,
then all I've got to say,
God didn't make little green apples
and it don't rain in Indianapolis in the summertime.
There's no such things as Doctor Seuss,
Disneyland, and Mother Goose is no nursery rhyme

Frank Kockritz flew to Reno twice to arrange the legalities of divorce and marriage. Julie Olfe relayed letters and proofs from Beginner Books, and Ted wrote back long letters of instruction. He was encouraged by Al Perkins's latest draft of *The Hand Book*, but sent word that it must have more of a "story feeling . . . more exciting." For his magician friend Duke Johnston, he diagrammed a six-fingered juggling trick "using a grapefruit, an avocado and three small oranges. . . . Only trouble is, it calls for one more finger than I have."

Chuck Jones flew from Los Angeles and appeared at the Ponderosa, paying Audrey and Ted their first social call. Ted talked with him about a *Cat in the Hat* read-aloud anthology, a collection of forty-two of Ted's favorite tales for children by authors including A. A. Milne, Carl Sandburg, Lewis Carroll, William Shakespeare and Jesus Christ. But at a time of turmoil and a new start, Jones's visit meant more to Ted than a book conference. Unlike some of Ted's friends, Chuck assessed no blame in Helen's death. He felt that Ted had begun to rebel against her as his disciplinarian, and Chuck made an artist's appraisal: "Audrey came along and she was vital and pretty and young and had a wonderful charm about her. As one side went to the gray the other side came into the sunlight."

Ted and Audrey were married by a justice of the peace at the Washoe County Courthouse in Reno at 5:00 P.M. on August 5, 1968, a week before her forty-seventh birthday. No friends had been invited. After a two-day honeymoon at South Lake Tahoe, high in the Sierra Nevada, the Geisels returned to La Jolla, to a house still full of workmen and to a hostile community that, as the new Mrs. Geisel put it, was "full of broken glass."

The shift of her life patterns seemed to startle Audrey as much as anyone. She had planned to have one marriage and two daughters so they could be friends and share burdens, something she had missed as an only child. She had anticipated no emotional surprises when Grey joined the Scripps Clinic staff in 1960 and she and their daughters moved with him from Kansas City.

Looking back on her earlier life, she was not surprised that she had not read *The Cat in the Hat* to her daughters, nor ever heard of Dr. Seuss. "I was the kind of mother that I now regret," she said. "I did not spend sufficient time reading to them or playing with them. But I don't live with guilt, because what you see is what they got." Instead, she had focused her immense energy on clearing the Dimonds' ten acres along the Kansas–Missouri border, caring for their dogs and the Palomino horse, keeping house and serving as Grey's hostess when he became professor of medicine at the University of Kansas Medical Center in Kansas City.

Audrey Stone was born in Chicago in 1921 and moved as often as "an army brat." Her father, Norman Alfred Stone, was English. Audrey remembered him as dashing, charming and undependable, "the most exciting person in the world, almost a stand-up comedian . . . but he and my mother didn't do well as a couple." Her mother, Ruth Benson Stone, whose parents had come from Norway, went to work so that she and Audrey could survive whether or not the mail brought a check from Norman. When Audrey was five, her mother worked in New York as a vocational nurse at the Manhattan Eye, Ear, Nose and Throat Hospital; to save money she lived in the nurses' dormitory and Audrey went to live in Mount Vernon, New York, with a family friend she loved dearly and called "Grandma" Gottersen.

These were happier years than those when her parents made brief attempts at reconciliation. For a time the three of them lived at the Hotel Commodore in Manhattan, where her father, "always good at greeting people," was an assistant manager. Like Eloise at the Plaza, Audrey zipped up and down elevators and joked with the staff. When the Stones had supper in their room, her mother would whisper, "Save the rolls for breakfast!"

As a teenager, Audrey commuted by train from Long Island to the all-girl Julia Richmond School in Manhattan. She had always wanted to be a nurse "with a university degree" and finally chose Indiana University because of its "reputation and relatively small size." By then her parents had divorced and her mother was retired in Minneapolis, living at the Hotel Leamington, one of a group of Midwest hotels owned by Audrey's uncle Bill Benson.

At Indiana, Audrey met Grey Dimond, whose medical ambitions lay in cardiology. They graduated together in 1944 and married a year later. Her first position was as a surgeon's nurse, an experience she later related to scenes in the television series M*A*S*H—"so unbelievable, so funny, so ghastly!" But she seemed imperturbable and became night supervisor at the Coleman Obstetrical and Gynecological Hospital at the Indiana University Medical Center in Indianapolis, then at Cambridge General on Harvard Square. Grey's medical career was prospering. They spent a six-month sabbatical traveling around the world as he visited medical centers; in the Netherlands she took sculpture lessons while he taught as a Fulbright professor at the University of Utrecht. In 1948, after two years as an army doctor in Tokyo, he returned to study at Massachusetts General in Boston under the pioneering cardiologist Paul Dudley White.

The Dimonds waited eight years to have children. Audrey was thirty-two when Lark was born in 1953; Lea Grey came four and a half years later. The girls were opposites and were never close; Lark was tall, blond, rail-slim and artistic; Lea was shorter, dark-haired and feisty. In 1968, when they became Ted's stepdaughters, they were living with their father, who had moved to Washington, D.C., after the divorce.

Audrey and Ted were in La Jolla that August long enough to catch up on mail and make decisions on the remodeling; then they flew East to visit Ted's father in Springfield and oversee his move into a nursing home. The reunion was loving; it was the last time Ted saw his father, who died less than four months later, on December 9, 1968, at the age of eighty-nine.

Ted was anxious to get to New York. He looked forward to introducing Audrey at Random House, where her openness soon put everyone at ease; she was full of curiosity and appeared eager to become part of all of Ted's lives. Anne Johnson, Ted's "dear Annie," quickly became Audrey's champion, and the Johnsons and Geisels grew close as they attended annual meetings of the American Booksellers Association. In Anne's view, "Helen had become overly protective of Ted. She had held him back. I think of Helen as somehow frightened . . . of what? Of professional overexposure for Ted? But when Audrey appeared it was refreshing. She gave him new vitality and kept him alive longer."

Audrey had aptly described the hostility of many in the San Diego community, but Luba and Duke Johnston gave the first dinner party for the newlyweds and soon Jeanne and Clayton Brace gave another. Old friends found Ted wary, but enchanted with his bride. He would stop talking in midsentence to watch Audrey move about the room, working the crowd with aplomb. They acquired a miniature Yorkshire terrier of great charm and named her Sam—"as in Samantha, not Sam-I-am." Audrey learned to deal with both the despair that could overcome Ted in his studio and his occasional elation. "Sometimes he would bounce into the room in great excitement and say, 'Something's happening!' I learned never to ask what it was because his answer was always the same: 'I can't tell you until it's all together.' "

For Ted it was a winter of rough edges. In New York in December, he gave in to Phyllis Jackson, who proposed to boost sales of *The Cat in the Hat Songbook* by putting Ted on the television talk show of a popular newcomer, Dick Cavett. Ted agreed, with a proviso: he would write out ten questions for Cavett to ask and rehearse his responses, hoping that he might control his stage fright.

A storm struck New York on the night of the live telecast as Ted, Audrey and Phyllis Jackson waited in a small backstage room. Ted, who was the final guest, grew claustrophobic. Heavy rain and wind hammered the windows, the lights went out, and just as power was restored, Ted was called onstage. He was distracted, his voice was wispy, and when Cavett asked the last question first, he panicked. "I came out with a boffola gag and then everything went blank. I laid the most colossal bomb." Audrey recalled that Ted looked up "at some far distant corner and didn't say anything. He was *thinking* on live TV when he should have been *talking*." A desperate Cavett cut from the empty air to Mitch Miller's band and music from the *Cat Songbook* to close the show.

Another problem obsessed Ted that winter and intensified his distrust of lawyers and the judicial system. Outraged by the impending republication of his forty-year-old drawings and humor from *Liberty* magazine, and by plans to produce Dr. Seuss dolls without his approval, he filed a copyright suit against Liberty Library Corporation, which had bought the rights to the magazine's archives. He argued that the material he had sold *Liberty* was a professional embarrassment and a degradation of Dr. Seuss characters. But that December in New York, U.S. District Judge William B. Herland ruled against Ted, holding that by implication he had sold the complete rights to his work in 1932 for three hundred dollars a page.

Ted was angry and his attorney fees exceeded one hundred thousand dollars, but he went back to work, knowing that many were waiting to see how his books would fare without Helen. Mike Frith came to La Jolla in January to work with him on *My Book About Me*, a Beginner Book that would involve the child reader as coauthor. But Frith, a New Yorker and a football fan, had another interest that weekend, for he was avid about Super Bowl III. Joe Namath, the quarterback of the underdog New York Jets, had elevated the impending football game against the Baltimore Colts to a showdown of braggadocio that mesmerized sports fans. On Super Bowl Sunday Frith asked Ted to excuse him from their work at the Tower so he could watch the game in his hotel room. Ted was aghast, Frith realized, and then angry, and when they resumed work the next morning, "very put out, very cold. At bonus time, Bob Bernstein told me I wasn't getting a bonus that year and that I had really upset Ted."

Yet as their work went on by correspondence, Ted happily called himself the Walrus and addressed Frith as "Dear Carpenter." They worked artist to artist, page by page, on closing *My Book About Me*:

> Dear Mike: JEEEEEZUS! After a week of hell on this stupid problem, I think the enclosed might solve it. . . . Please phone me your reaction. This page has been destroying my life.

When Frith made his first trip to Europe, Ted urged him to write. "If I do not hear from you," Ted said, "I will contact you through the personals section of *The Times of London* . . . and use the pseudonym of 'David Eisenhower.'" Ted swung between surges of affection and dismay with his undisciplined young editor. Frith even forgot to answer urgent inquiries from Billy Collins in London. One day Ted called Bernstein and asked, "What am I going to do with this guy?"

Bernstein was sputtering. "What am I going to do with *you?*" he replied. Ted, who had periodically jarred Bennett Cerf by slipping some salacious outburst into Dr. Seuss manuscripts, had read a review of Philip Roth's *Portnoy's Complaint* and decided to test Bernstein with a five-page outline for a dirty Dr. Seuss book. It went no further.

Ted and Audrey flew to Honolulu in September 1969 on their first big journey together: seven weeks and around the world. Because he often hungered for travel, and used it to refurbish his creative imagery, Ted had talked for years about a Dr. Seuss travel guide. His unpublished notes from this journey were as close as he ever came to creating it. He wrote and drew on menus from Pan Am, BOAC, Air France and El Al, the jacket of a travel book and even on his expired Cambodian visa.

The Geisels paused for two nights at the Royal Hawaiian Hotel on Waikiki Beach, where Ted played in the surf; swimming had always been his favorite form of relaxation. Then they flew to Tokyo for book signings of *The Cat in the Hat* in a Japanese edition. There was a week in Hong Kong, during which the women's columnist for the *South China Morning Post* tracked Ted down at the Mandarin Hotel and reported that he was "stunningly handsome, tanned and charming . . . more like one's idea of a Hollywood film star than a world-famous author of children's books." Ted kept busy writing notes about "albino rickshaw men, motorized chopsticks and naked barbers." They stayed five days in Cambodia for repeated visits to Angkor Wat, the majestic Khmer temple. Ted had loved the ruins of Turkey, Peru and Yucatán, and in Cambodia he spent hours studying details in stone, his long fingers tracing the patterns. Mindful that travel guides must offer practical advice, he jotted down a menu tip: "To vary the rice diet of the Orient, travelers should try "rice-stuffed-rice . . . in the preparation of this subtle dish, each kernel of rice is hollowed out by expert rice-disembowelers, then stuffed with smaller kernels." In New Delhi they sat through a stirring sound-and-light performance at the Red Fort and went by car to Agra and the Taj Mahal, strolling hand in hand beside the great long pool. But lesser attractions were a flop. Writing on a ticket envelope, Ted urged all travelers to "by all means miss the floating gardens of Ibn Abba: The Chief Gardener . . . inadvertently pulled the plug in 1732, thereby causing the floating gardens to sink."

After a long flight to Teheran the Geisels tried to shake off jet lag by walking through the teeming streets. "All barber chairs in Sleefa," Ted wrote on a sheet of hotel stationery, "face in the direction of Sloofa, birthplace of Ali Hoofa, patron saint of the scissors." This led to another travelers' tip: "In certain enterprising Arab towns . . . when the wind dies down and the dust stops blowing, you can purchase packaged dust. . . ." At the King David Hotel in Jerusalem, he received a plaque for his contribution to "worldwide literacy" and was made an "Honorary Jew" by the ebullient mayor of Jerusalem, Teddy Kolleck.

By October they were at the Ritz in Paris. Ted tramped through Left Bank neighborhoods he had known during his Oxford days, and rose earlier than usual one morning to walk beside the Seine in the shimmering silver fog that he remembered and loved. His guidelines to tipping in Paris were written on Ritz notepaper:

> It is absolutely forbidden to give gratuities to kings . . . or to the first five chestnut trees to the left as you start walking up the Champs-Élysées.
> All other people, animals, or inanimate objects must be tipped, or else.
> Babies born in Paris hospitals must tip their attendant obstetrician. . . .

There followed a restful week at Brown's Hotel, that artifact of the Empire in London's Mayfair, and they ended their journey in New York to celebrate the publication of Ted's latest book, *I Can Lick 30 Tigers Today! and Other Stories*, which was dedicated to Audrey. If the new Bright & Early Books for prekindergarten children proved successful, Ted told *The New York Times* with a straight face, "we'll do prenatal books." He had sworn grimly he would never appear again before a television camera. "Television interviewers either are totally unprepared," he told a reporter, "or they ask unanswerable questions like 'Where do your ideas come from?' " The reporter promptly struck this question from his list.

Ted had never ranked higher as a celebrity. He and Audrey attended a vast cocktail party for the triumphant Joe Namath that was crowded with writers and sports heroes. Don Bell of the *Chicago Tribune*, who was trailing Ted for a profile, wrote, "After the party, I'm on the elevator with this girl writer from *The Wall Street Journal* . . . talking about all the people she'd met . . . Mailer, Plimpton, the lot, when the news is passed to her that Dr. Seuss was also there. Well, the girl almost passes out right there on the elevator. 'You mean I could have been standing next to him and not known it? Oh, my God, my God! I want to go back up.' Then she begins reciting by heart chunks of 'Green Eggs and Ham.' . . . In the lobby, she is still trying to persuade her husband to return."

Back at last in his studio in La Jolla, Ted resumed work on his next "big book," *I Can Draw It Myself*, which he called "a revolt against coloring books," and agreed to do another Bright & Early reader, *Mr. Brown Can Moo! Can You?* While he fussed with nonsense formulas for the very young, a powerful image captured his thoughts. He had come home eager to help the world and to fight greed and waste. He doodled and stared from his studio at the glittering north coast of San Diego, shores that had been empty when he first came and now teemed with condominiums and look-alike houses. He fumed about people's indifference to the environment and began to set down words, not pausing to agonize over rhyming and rhythm or even to sketch characters. He had read so many "dull things on conservation, full of statistics and preachy," that making such a subject amusing "was the hard part":

> It's one of the few things I ever set out to do that was straight propaganda. . . . It was also the hardest thing I have ever done, because the temptation was to fall into the same traps the others had fallen into. . . .

• • •

Soon Ted knew it wasn't working, and wanted to escape. He and Audrey had talked about going to East Africa, so in September 1970 they flew to Kenya. After three days of rambling through the Nairobi markets and sipping Sundowners at the old Stanley Hotel bar, they set out for the Mt. Kenya Safari Club. One afternoon Ted was sprawled reading, looking beyond the swimming pool, when "a lot of elephants" walked across the mountain. "I don't know what happened [but the logjam broke]. I had nothing but a laundry list with me, and I grabbed it . . . I wrote ninety percent of the book that afternoon. I got some kind of release watching those elephants."

Ted never traveled with a camera, but he brought home a Seussian image of the trees of the Serengeti, which inspired his silk-tufted Truffula trees. Still the main character of the book had not yet taken shape. Ted tried drawing him big, tried making him green; for a time he was mechanized, then shrunk to gopher size. Finally there appeared a stumpy creature with a walrus mustache:

> He was shortish. And oldish.
> And brownish. And mossy.
> And he spoke with a voice
> that was sharpish and bossy.

In Ted's mind it all became clear. His protagonist would be named Lorax ("I looked at the drawing and that's what he was!") and he would speak for conservation. On the other side would be the greedy old Once-ler, left alone in the graying remnant of a town he helped to blight—perhaps a California community, for he had come there by covered wagon. He tells a young stranger how the town declined after its Truffula trees were chopped down to yield the yarn to knit Thneeds ("a Fine-Something-That-All-People-Need!"). The Once-ler expanded factories that sullied the sky because: "Business is business! / And business must grow." In the final scene, with the air ruined, the animals gone and the last tree cut down, the Once-ler leans from his mysterious Lerkim and drops the last Truffula seed to the boy:

UNLESS someone like you
cares a whole awful lot,
nothing is going to get better.
It's not.

The Lorax was a polemic about pollution, impassioned and bristling with confrontation and name-calling. Ted unleashed some
of his most magical language, phrases that defied rational criticism
and enraptured a generation: the cruffulous croak and smogulous
smoke, the snergelly hose, rippulous pond, gruvvulous glove and
miff-muffered moof. His palette shifted from his usual primary
colors to mauve, plum, purple and sage-green. Audrey cheerfully
accepted credit for this change, and technical advances in high-
speed lithography made the colors possible; up on the walls of
Ted's studio were computer color charts offering him a huge array
of possibilities.

The book startled Dr. Seuss readers, and reviewers were divided.
Some called it a morality tale. Ted shrugged, saying, "It's impossible
to tell a story without a moral—either the good guys win or the
bad guys win." Others were disappointed that the book lacked his
usual zaniness. Sales were slower than Random House had come
to expect of a Dr. Seuss book; *The Lorax* was ahead of its time
and its popularity began to soar only a decade later when the
environmental movement exploded. Ted himself began to talk of
it as his favorite book.

Although *The Lorax* appeared in bookstores in the fall of 1971,
news of it had reached Americans the previous spring after Ted
was cornered at a brunch in San Diego by Liz Carpenter, Lady
Bird Johnson's press secretary. As they sipped Bloody Marys, Liz
questioned Ted about the theme of his book. It would serve Lady
Bird's environmental concerns well, she quickly said, if he donated
the book's art and manuscript to the Lyndon B. Johnson Presidential
Library in Austin, Texas, and attended its impending dedication.
Liz recalled:

I left the room and phoned LBJ at the ranch. He was on
the table getting a massage, but I told him about the book
and what I wanted to do and he bellowed, "Put him on!"

> So I got Ted and said the President wants to speak to you,
> and Ted kept saying, "From the massage table?"

When the Geisels landed at Austin they were met by groups of children waving campaign posters. "That had always been my job," Liz Carpenter said, "advancing the Johnsons' trips, organizing political rallies, so that's what I did for Dr. Seuss." News reports of the presidential library dedication focused on two gifts, a slice of moon rock sent by President Nixon and the original black-and-white drawings of *The Lorax*. President Johnson wrote Ted, "If anyone had been conducting a popularity poll in Austin the weekend of May 22, you would have won it hands down."

Ted sent a copy of LBJ's letter to Mike Frith in New York. Artist to artist, he confided, "Really makes me feel sort of good."

CHAPTER 17

Audrey Stone Geisel

1971–1974

During a meeting in Walter Retan's office at Random House, Ted, ever restless, began riffling through a sheaf of drawings on a side table. They were sketches for another children's picture encyclopedia by Richard Scarry.

"Does this sort of thing sell?" Ted asked.

"Oh, yes," Retan said, wishing he had put the drawings away before Ted arrived. "They sell very well." He failed to add that Scarry, recently coaxed away from Golden Books, had been selling books at an even faster rate than Dr. Seuss.

Ted had never heard of Scarry. He rarely prowled bookstores or read reviews of others' books, and he was bored by literary fashions and vogues. Much of the time he didn't think of himself as a children's book author. Ted simply did what he did: he drew and wrote rhymes. He honed his drawing style with his first books, and half a century later it was essentially unchanged. He had researched children's literature in a single brief spurt for his Utah lectures in 1949, but it was no longer on his mind. He was glad that millions of children and their parents liked his books, but he wrote and drew above all to amuse himself. Although his interests became more varied, there was an unshakable and comforting constancy about Dr. Seuss. He was a bit of a rowdy and an occasional critic made a case for labeling him a subversive, but he stood for solid virtues; he sincerely believed that "might never makes right, the meek inherit the earth, and pride frequently goeth before a fall."

Yet by 1971, as the Lorax appeared to help save the environment and expose corporate greed, Dr. Seuss was being hailed as one of the cornerstones of children's literature. Dr. Seuss as icon yielded theses, dissertations and book chapters, some so pretentious that Ted was appalled. The treatment he found most intriguing was in *Down the Rabbit Hole*, by Selma G. Lanes, a librarian and children's book critic who saw Dr. Seuss as a master of accelerating suspense that leaves the child reader "ready to settle for any resolution, however mundane, that will end his at once marvelous, exquisite and finally unbearable tension." Lanes went on doggedly: "If, as the British psychoanalyst Charles Ryecroft defined it, an orgastic experience consists of 'a subjective sense of excitation followed by a feeling of discharge,' then Dr. Seuss in his books . . . can be said to provide his young disciples with a literary release not so far removed from orgasm."

Ted promptly wrote Lanes, praising her for not allowing her "voluminous research to bog down the spirit of [her] writing." She cited Ted's books as the definitive example of the children's picture book that had evolved from the traditional illustrations of artists like Ernest Shepard in Kenneth Grahame's *The Wind in the Willows* and A. A. Milne's *Winnie-the-Pooh*, and Garth Williams in E. B. White's *Charlotte's Web*. These earlier illustrations were more decorative, but in the full-blown picture book, and particularly in Ted's, the illustrations enabled a child to follow the entire action of the story. They provided a "halfway house between the seductions of TV, film or the animated cartoon and the less blatant charms of a full page of text."

For his role as icon, Ted could hardly have overstated his debt to his publisher, Bennett Cerf, who, in retirement, was in failing health. Bennett had been uniquely supportive from the beginning. When Ted's career needed it Cerf had plugged him proudly in his columns, on television and through his network of celebrity friends. Beyond that, he loved Ted. His eyes crinkled whenever Ted peeked inside Cerf's office, where one of Ted's long-horned Seuss beasts smiled down on the comings and goings of the literati. No matter who was present at such moments or what was being interrupted, Cerf shouted greetings, jumped to his feet and slipped an arm around Ted's shoulders.

In 1971 Ted made long telephone calls to Cerf at his hospital bedside as they traded memories of heartier days. Cerf died on August 27, and the funeral, in the chapel of his alma mater, Columbia University, was one of New York's memorable convocations of the great and famous. Ted was unable to attend, but he called Anne Johnson the next day to hear her account.

As Bob Bernstein exerted his breezy leadership, Ted struggled to hold together the Beginner Books series. But his obsession with perfection made him a poor administrator and, in his eagerness to communicate his enthusiasm, he became a nag. He once lectured an illustrator: "I think you are taking this job too seriously. . . . Having sweat, rather than fun . . . you kind of lost your freedom and your joy in the job, and tied yourself up. I think the trap you have fallen into is the one that I fall into almost every day of my life. I continually forget that I am writing and drawing for kids, not critics. I get self-conscious about style and subtleties, when all I should be doing is knocking it out, and laughing while I'm doing it."

He tried but failed to redesign the straightforward, folksy style of the husband-and-wife Berenstain team, who wrote their first seventeen books as Beginner Books. He had shortened their names on the cover of their first Bears book, *The Big Honey Hunt*, from Stanley and Janice to Stan and Jan. "That's what you call each other," he said. "And that's what I call you. Besides, it fits on one line."

Talking with Ted about a second book, the Berenstains proposed a series about bears. "That's the worst thing you could do!" Ted said. "It would be like having a millstone around your neck. Do something as different as you can!"

The Berenstains worked for months on a book about a penguin and brought it in to Ted. "Terrific!" he said. "But you know something? The salesmen have your 'Bear' book out on the road, and it's being very well received. Did you ever think of doing a whole series on bears?"

So the Berenstains dropped the penguin and began work on

The Bike Lesson. Ted penned in the cover line "Another Adventure of the Berenstain Bears," launching it as a series that grew to more than one hundred books, with sales in the United States of more than 165 million copies. Yet with another Berenstain manuscript he sat up much of one night in his Plaza Hotel suite, trying without success to rewrite it. He continued as the Berenstains' editor, but it was not easy on either side. He lacked Helen's patience and tact.

"Ted was extremely centered on his own work," Stan recalled, "and it was a strain for him to be an editor. He was much tougher than any adult book editor I'd had. At our first meeting he said, 'These bears, who are they? What do they think about? What kind of pipe tobacco do they smoke? What is their motivation?' We learned a lot from him. He used his cinematic training to talk to us about 'moving the camera in or out' for an illustration."

Still, in 1973, eleven years after publishing their first book, Ted sent a sharp, hand-printed critique of the *He Bear, She Bear* story boards to its editor, Al Perkins: "It isn't a story because there is no conflict or competition. What exactly does this book do to interest a child reader? What's its message? Where are the laughs?"

"It helped," Stan said later, "that Ted had extraordinary charm. He didn't look like Cary Grant but he had that charm."

After Helen's death, Ted grew more open to editorial suggestions when he submitted his own books, and Retan became a trusted sounding board. "This doesn't sound quite right," Ted growled as he worked over a line of his verse. Retan offered a solution, "sort of holding my breath."

"I was afraid you'd say that," Ted said and made the change.

Retan became a familiar guest in La Jolla, his days beginning with a cheerful, singsong call from Audrey over the intercom. "Good morning, Walter! It's time for breakfast!" Once she even whistled reveille. During work breaks, Ted led Retan around his hilltop, pointing out his rock garden and collection of succulents. He bemoaned rising taxes and fretted about whether he could afford to keep the Tower. Having seen his royalty statements, Retan shrugged and grinned.

On his first stay in the new guest wing Walter found in Ted a kindred soul, as baffled as he by household mechanics. When he couldn't find the switch to turn off bathroom lights, Ted came to help, flipping several switches to no effect. "Let's ask Audrey," he said finally.

She came in, looked at the two men and shook her head. "Ted!" she said, staring up through a louvered skylight. "You're trying to turn off the sun!"

Ted thrived on such nonsense. He loved mischief and laughter, and his companionship with Mike Frith, about forty years his junior, was rejuvenative. Ted found a book about the obscure Navajo language and mailed Frith a fifty-word Beginner Book vocabulary in Navajo. Another time he attached to a note a newspaper picture of a toothless woman:

> Dere Micheal Frith:
> I have devoured every Book you rote! Will you pay to have my teeth fixed?
> Cassandra Fang,
> Upper Plate, Neb. 6753029674

Ted's concession to his trendy protégé from Harvard was to wear a monstrous butterfly bow tie as they worked, and Frith encouraged Ted's naughty streak. As they thumbed through the *Lady Godivas*, Ted named his editor the Eighth Peeping Tom. They began to talk to each other in the code numbers of their ink charts, and Ted scribbled a verse for Frith. Its title was "Love Song":

> Oh, to be under a Number 3 sky
> In the shade of a Number 12 tree!
> In the Number 9 grass
> I would gleefully lie
> With a Number 4 lass under me.

Working on one of Ted's "big books" with him was a "major labor of elaborate drawings and technical detail," Frith said. By contrast, doing a Beginner Book was "a romp." His favorite moments with Ted were collaborative, often late at night, the master at his big swivel chair in his La Jolla studio, Frith at a facing desk, both reaching into pots of colored pencils, working furiously, jotting words and pictures, grabbing a sketch, passing it back and forth, scribbling over each other's lines. They sat for hours "chewing on a word . . . asking each other 'How is this line going to carry over to the next page?'"

More than once, as they stared at each other long after midnight, blank and exhausted but never admitting it, Ted would announce: "Time for a thinking cap!" and stride to his studio closet with its hundreds of crazy hats. Grabbing a fez or sombrero or miner's helmet, they would sit on the floor of the living room, "two grown men in stupid hats trying to come up with the right word for a book that had only fifty words in it at most."

On one such night the author "Rosetta Stone" emerged. Ted and Mike had collaborated on a book to be published as *Because a Little Bug Went Ka-Choo*—their adaptation of the theme of "because of the nail the shoe was lost." Frith had a coauthor's pride in it, but Ted was not sure he wanted to grace it with his own name. As they debated, Audrey walked into the room.

"Name it for Audrey," Frith suggested.

"Her maiden name was Stone," Ted said.

"Rosetta Stone," Frith said, and it was done.

The pseudonym was ridiculed by some librarians who said that Beginner Books was not taking children's books seriously. Ted saw this criticism as evidence of a deeper problem—that some librarians had an arrested sense of humor.

Ted's health and spirits were buoyant. He lavished sentimental notes and *Cat in the Hat* drawings on Audrey, with more elaborate ones appearing on Valentine's Day and their anniversary. Audrey said, "He couldn't say 'I love you'—he was too private—but he could write it." They spent long hours alone and with close friends; they often were in Rancho Santa Fe with Duke and Luba Johnston for Thanksgiving, and the four went to Hawaii at Christmas. Audrey cooked with verve, abetted by a vivacious housekeeper, Ernestine Nolte, and entertained at Thursday-night dinners. She kept two hundred cookbooks and a file of party guests, noting what each had been served. Ted marveled over her place cards, penned in gold on glossy green camellia leaves from their garden.

But when she served candied violets, he pushed them away. "Audrey," he said, "I'm not eating flowers!" There were new faces around the Geisel dinner table: Jonas Salk with his bride, the artist Françoise Gilot, who had been Picasso's mistress; Betty and Pete Wilson, the San Diego mayor; and the recently wed architects Russell and Marie-Christine Forester.

When Julie Olfe moved with her husband to Chicago, Ted called a La Jolla employment agency to seek a part-time secretary. Only an hour earlier, Joan Knight, a slim and stylish newcomer to San Diego, had called on the agency to ask if they ever had a request for a part-time secretary. "Never," she had been told. She had left her name anyhow and got the job the next day.

Joan Knight found Ted to be a courtly and gallant employer, and regarded her tenure from 1971 to 1973 as a quiet time in his career, "more art than words." She spent most of her time answering fan mail—"readers treating him like a philosopher, trying to interpret what he wrote, trying to get him to say he was preaching some unsaid message, but he never would. All he wanted was for people to read."

On a flight home from Washington in 1972, after accepting an honor for *Lorax* from Keep America Beautiful Inc., Ted was captivated by some black-and-white photographs in a flight magazine, "about the strongest illustrations I've ever seen." They were primitive stone-cut silhouettes by the Inuits of northern Quebec—one a caribou hunter, another a beached whale. As his plane landed, Ted was experimenting with silhouettes of the Cat and the Grinch. He drew *The Shape of Me* in silhouette, and in 1973 it appeared as an engaging Bright & Early book.

He did not always write as Dr. Seuss. Because of the insatiable marketing needs at Beginner Books, he established lesser levels of involvement. In 1965 Beginner Books had published the first book by Theo. LeSieg, *I Wish That I Had Duck Feet*; its writing had a familiar lilt but the drawings were not Seussian. For several years LeSieg was as prolific as Dr. Seuss, with a new title each year, and in the book trade it became known that when Geisel was spelled backward it signified a book written but not illustrated by Ted. There were *I Can Write!: A Book by Me, Myself* (1971), *In a People*

House (1972), *The Many Mice of Mr. Brice* (1973), *Wacky Wednesday* (1974) and *Would You Rather Be a Bullfrog?* (1975). Roy McKie was often the LeSieg illustrator; he was fast and reliable and understood Ted. For the loyal McKie, Ted was "the center of my life for a long time. I believed in him completely. Whatever anybody might choose to say about his work, he was the one author who could make kids giggle."

Adults giggled too, especially over Ted's Bright & Early reader in 1972, a nonsense tale about a pest called *Marvin K. Mooney, Will You Please Go Now!* In the spring of 1974, as the Watergate scandal neared its climax, Ted met the satirist Art Buchwald at the San Diego Zoo, and they became mutually admiring friends. Buchwald mailed Ted an autographed copy of his latest book of columns, *I Never Danced at the White House*, and dared him to write a political book.

Ted's response was swift and Seussian. He grabbed a copy of *Marvin K. Mooney* and, with a few strokes of a pen, deleted each mention of that name and substituted the name of the president. Buchwald phoned Ted for permission to print it. Ted agreed but called back in an hour.

"Random House has gone through the ceiling," he said. "They won't let me do it."

"What do you think?" Buchwald prodded.

"Oh, go ahead," Ted said.

On July 30, 1974, Buchwald's syndicated column was a reprint of the altered book. The tale began:

> Richard M. Nixon, will you please go now!
> The time has come.
> The time is now.
> Just go.
> Go.
> Go!
> I don't care how.
> You can go by foot.
> You can go by cow.
> Richard M. Nixon, will you please go now!
> You can go on skates.

You can go on skis.
You can go in a hat.
But
Please go.
Please! . . .

Nine days later, on August 8, 1974, Nixon announced his resignation. Buchwald claimed full credit, Ted claimed full intent, and both were widely cheered. Ted wrote Art, "We sure got him, didn't we? We should have collaborated sooner."

Marvin K. Mooney had just appeared when Ted had a call from Peggy Owens, in Los Angeles. Her teenage son, Ted's great-nephew and namesake, was undergoing surgery for scoliosis, a lateral curvature of the spine. Much of his spine would be fused, leaving him in a body cast for nine months. Ted Owens was sixteen, tall and strong-featured, a dark-haired youth who had inherited the gentleness of his uncle Ted and was the sole member of his generation in the direct Geisel-Seuss bloodline. Ted wrote Peggy: "About all I've been able to do so far is to snarl, 'Son-of-a-bitch! Goddam it! This isn't fair!' " . . . But one thing . . . I can do . . . is the possible diversion that he might get out of coming down here much more often." Ted devised Seussian distractions for his nephew, inventing courses "especially prepared by the Geisel Correspondence School to keep Theodor B. Owens on his toes while on his back." He mailed foreign stamps, coins, postcards and newspaper clippings. He drew the Cat in a full body cast, with only its tail hanging out: "It is a bit confining, but all the best cats wear 'em."

Despite Ted's insistence that he was uncomfortable around children, his great-nephew proved a notable exception. Ted had always delighted in the youngster's company, and in 1957, when the boy was only a year old, Ted had dedicated *How the Grinch Stole Christmas!* to him. Later they romped in the swimming pool in La Jolla or escaped adult conversations to try on hats from Ted's closet. Young Ted recalled how his uncle "loved going in there and pulling them out. He had a crazy story to go with each hat—where it came from, who wore it—and you were never really sure where the facts ended and where his imagination took over."

Ted had acquired an early photocopier, and when his namesake visited the Tower "he would put his head on the Xerox and then put my head on the Xerox and make copies! Then we did our hands!" Ted demonstrated how to squirt acrylic paints on paper, stir them with a palette knife and crush them with another piece of paper to create abstract color blotches. "He knew how much fun it is for a kid to mess around with paint and not stay inside the lines."

Their bond grew stronger when the teenager attended the Art Center College of Design in Pasadena. "I was living and breathing painting and art because Uncle Ted said painting has to be full-time if you're going to be any good." Ted Owens was one of the very few ever welcomed in the studio when Ted painted. He remembered the worn, mottled pots and trays, paintbrushes and stubs of colored pencils. He watched Ted paint one of Ted's own favorite canvases, *A Plethora of Cats*, stepping back to stuff his hands in his hip pockets and scowl at his work. To young Ted some of the paintings seemed Cubist, and his uncle's crosshatching, such as the pen-and-ink tones that define the Grinch and Cat, was distinctive. Always there was the sense of playfulness. "He believed that life was a place to have fun. It was a game, and doing crazy things was part of it. We'd be sitting out beside the pool for breakfast and he'd make me laugh so hard that I could barely eat."

The teenager was sometimes joined at family gatherings by Audrey's daughters, Lark and Lea Grey, who were, respectively, two years older and two years younger than he. Audrey said of her daughters, "They are so different. Lark is six feet tall and nonflappable, and Lea is five feet three and flaps all the time. But they both loved Ted."

Soon after the marriage, while the twelve-year-old Lea was at boarding school, she asked Ted to sign his letters to her twice. When he confirmed his suspicion that she was selling Dr. Seuss autographs, he asked the price. Ten cents, she replied, and Ted, feigning indignation, suggested she might charge more.

In 1972, when Ted and Audrey attended Lark's graduation from the Judson School in Scottsdale, Arizona, he bragged that he would be carrying "the first seven daisies in Lark's graduation parade" and he gave her an oil painting of a Seussian bird with long blond hair, wearing a cap and gown and flying over the clouds. Lark went on to Stephens College in Missouri and became a sculptor.

Lea Grey, whom Ted called Lee Groo, was a rebellious fourteen when Lark went to college, and had been in and out of private and parochial schools. Ted often found her outrages amusing. "When she stayed with us, they would insult each other in the most graphic fashion," Audrey said. "I would shake my head and leave the table. The insults were terrible, but they loved trying to top each other."

Ted Owens remembered these exchanges and also the underlying affection. Lea had gone through a period where she was "anti-everything," he recalled, "and when you were supposed to follow rules she often broke them. Uncle Ted related to that because he preached that you should walk your own path in life."

When the television version of *The Lorax* appeared early in 1972, *Newsweek* called it "a hard-sell ecological allegory, stabbing mainly at big business through a deceptively gentle blend of gorgeous colors, superb animation, and a rippling imagery of words and pictures." With Eddie Albert narrating, its stern message about commercial greed had been softened for television, but Ted was especially fond of the last shot, in which the words "Maybe Not" were superimposed over "The End." That summer the Geisels traveled with the animator Friz Freleng and his wife, Lily, in Turkey and Greece before going to Zagreb to accept an award for *The Lorax* at the International Animated Cartoon Festival. Freleng regarded Ted as unique: "He worked absolutely alone, not influenced by anybody, doing only what he wanted." Ted added his Yugoslav award to the studio shelf that held the Peabody Awards he had received a year earlier for television adaptations of *Horton Hears a Who!* and *The Grinch*.

In London, at the Collins office on St. James's Place, Ted congratulated Billy Collins, recently knighted, and marveled with him at the long lines of children queued at Harrods for Dr. Seuss autographs. At Collins's country home in Kent, Ted spent hours in the swimming pool with the children of Collins directors. "He played the rascal," Michael Hyde recalled, "pulling them under, teaching them some of the dirty tricks of water polo."

Ted took Audrey to the London Silver Vaults in Chancery Lane, which he had first explored during his Oxford year, and they laughed over a smiling silver camel with candlesticks in its humps, a turtle that was a dinner bell, and a two-foot-long serving fork made from an impala horn that he likened to his sculpture of the rare "blue-green abelard."

Collins was much the most important link in overseas publication of Ted's books, but *The Cat in the Hat Dictionary* was selling in French and Spanish editions, and Dr. Seuss books had gone into about twenty languages, although a proper translation of his verse and rhythms could never be achieved. When *Yertle the Turtle* was about to enter the Scandinavian market, Ted sent a copy to his nephew with a note: "Do you know how to say 'Burp' in Swedish? RAAP!" His books were best received in English-speaking lands, where only minor editing was needed. For the British market, *Dr. Seuss's ABC Book* involved only one change: the British spelling of "pyjamas" was substituted. Collins's sales of Dr. Seuss and Beginner Books in New Zealand and Australia were especially strong, and the publishers negotiated an agreement with Grolier for a British children's-book club modeled on the profitable U.S. relationship between Random House and Grolier.

Back at the Tower, Ted was distressed by the increase in the number of low-flying private aircraft that droned overhead as instructors taught touch-and-go landings at a private airport nearby. He sputtered with annoyance to his new secretary, Claudia Prescott, a tall, gracious and accomplished woman who joined him in 1973. Soon a letter appeared in the weekly *La Jolla Light*, signed by Mrs. H. H. Thornton of Scottsdale, Arizona. She wrote that she and her husband had hoped to retire on Mount Soledad, but had changed their minds when they learned that "our Mt. Soledad friends can't even enjoy sitting out on their patio due to the incessant racket of airplanes coming over from Montgomery Field." The letter had been written by Ted, typed and signed by the obedient Claudia, and dispatched to Arizona to be mailed by a relative of hers. Soon, without explanation, the Tower was no longer used as a landmark pylon for student pilots.

Ted nicknamed his secretary Claudia the Prevaricator, and abetted her in creative alibis as he declined invitations to appear at schools and benefits throughout the land. Her tactful telephone calls and letters helped for the rest of his life to maintain his privacy and the good name of Dr. Seuss. They shared an interest in Irish setters, and Claudia even contributed a word to the Seuss lexicon. While learning to interpret Ted's scribbled printing, in which b's and p's were often reversed and V's and U's indistinguishable, she typed the manuscript of *There's a Wocket in My Pocket!*, putting a "Vug under the rug."

Ted said, "I wrote Uug, but I like your word better." It stayed.

In one stack of mail forwarded from Random House in 1973 was a letter challenging Dr. Seuss's grammar in a sentence from *Bartholomew and the Oobleck*: "The seat of his royal pants were stuck to his royal throne." Walter Retan asked Ted what he thought. "Grammatically speaking, the [letter-writer] was right," Ted responded. "The seat *was* stuck, rather than *were*. . . . If you feel it is worth the money to change this, go ahead. Inasmuch as it has taken since 1949 for someone to spot this, I don't think it makes too much difference."

Like "Vug," it stayed.

Ted's administrative frustrations as president of Beginner Books were becoming terminal. He looked back on his "two years of abrasive work to get *The Cat in the Hat Dictionary* published" and wrote that, in the process, "my love of writing for children was sort of trampled to death." In a final desperate effort to reorganize Beginner Books, he proposed a book project called *The Sea Encyclopedia*, with all the hard decisions to be made by friends who had neither crossed nor deserted him: Chuck Jones, Bob Bernstein, the Phlegers of La Jolla, Al Perkins and "any MGM writers and illustrators that Chuck wants. . . . Dr. Seuss doesn't want to write any more Beginner Books for other authors to sign."

This was Ted's vision of an editor's utopia, but *The Sea Encyclopedia* never got off the ground. When he finished his 1973 book, *Did I Ever Tell You How Lucky You Are?*, he passed more authority for Beginner Books to Walter Retan in New York. It was nearly too late. "Ted really should have allowed someone else to do more editing earlier," Retan said. "He didn't mean to, but he almost choked off that series."

On his seventieth birthday, Ted and Audrey flew with Luba and Duke Johnston for a weekend in Las Vegas. At the glitzy Caesar's

Palace they had a table beside the runway for the dinner show, during which twenty nude showgirls roared past on motorcycles.

"What do you think of those, Ted?" Duke asked.

"I haven't ridden a motorcycle for years," Ted said, "but I think they were Harley-Davidsons."

"I think your eyes are missing things," Audrey said, and she was right.

CHAPTER 18

I Can Read
with My Eyes Shut!

1975–1980

Late one morning in 1975 Ted burst from his studio, shouting for Audrey. "Am I going blind?" he asked in a voice thick with fright. "I can't focus! Everything is squiggly."

Audrey held him steady, trying to imagine the terror that loss of sight carries for an artist. Ted had known for a year that he was developing cataracts, and at his drawing board he had been choosing colors less from what he saw than from what he remembered or could feel: the knicks on a crayon, the heft of a familiar pencil, the number code from a color chart. But the squiggly lines were new, and Audrey immediately feared glaucoma.

In her calmest nurse's manner she talked him through his panic and telephoned David Worthen, who had just arrived as chief of ophthalmology at the University of California, San Diego, School of Medicine. So began a five-year series of cataract surgeries, lens implants and treatments for glaucoma, leaving Ted alternately hopeful and despondent. Worthen, one of the few doctors ever to win both Ted's respect and affection, operated on his left eye in 1976 with seeming success. The "dulling brownout" was gone and Ted saw colors "as bright as Picasso." But from his right eye, the world still looked "like Whistler's mother." On days when Ted lost his sight from glaucoma, Worthen came to the hilltop and sat patiently for an hour or two, adding eyedrops as Ted lay on the studio couch near his desk.

In disgust, Ted concluded that "with or without eyedrops, writing and drawing is an unpleasant experience which I find myself avoiding. I'm thinking of taking up paper-hanging or mushroom farming as a new profession." The final art he sent to Random House had always been drawn to book-page size with "magnificently clean black lines," but with his sight impaired he began sending larger drawings with thicker lines, which the art director Grace Clark reduced to page size. He was fuming at the humblings of age, and each day Audrey drew on the supportive skills for which she had been respected as a nurse. Ever since 1944 she had renewed her credentials, refusing to "hang up the whites." Now she also served Ted as eyes and driver, and he showered her with grateful verses and drawings. In one, a fuzzy swirl of eyes looked down on a creature reminiscent of his Lady Godivas. "My eyes," he wrote, "though unfocused, are still upon you on this Birthday." In another, a morose and droopy-eyed Cat rode the shoulders of a small person who staggered down a path marked CLINICK. He wrote: "Merry Christmas, much love and Great Gratitude to my Lovely Blond Ass't. Cat who patiently and selflessly lugs me to and fro."

Audrey had always thought the handsome Geisel profile would be enhanced by a beard, and now, since his failing eyesight made shaving hazardous, she persuaded Ted to let it grow. From then on she took over the trimming of his graying hair and beard, sparing them both from visits to a barber. His friend Duke Johnston feigned indignation over the beard: "I don't care if *you* look old but people know we were at Oxford together and I don't want them to think *I'm* old."

At his desk Ted did laborious exercises in lettering on pages labeled WITH EYE DROPS and WITHOUT EYE DROPS. "How small can you write? Can you cross t's? Make apostrophes? . . . There is more distortion. Lines seem to move as I draw them. The more I concentrate, the less control I seem to have."

But as his eyesight began to improve, Audrey conceded failure on another front: none of her wiles had persuaded him to abandon his lifelong addiction to cigarettes. He chain-smoked Camels. He pretended to quit, but he cheated, so she hid his cigarettes and doled them out. He instructed his secretary, Claudia Prescott, to pick up cigarettes on her way to work, but Audrey quickly stopped that. After dinner parties, he lingered near the table and, when he thought he was alone, scooped up loose cigarettes from table holders. He asked his restaurateur friend Dick Duffy to leave cigarettes for him under the seat of the Geisels' car. One evening he slipped money into Duke Johnston's hand and asked him to buy a pack, but Duke pushed it back.

"I thought you were my friend," Ted snapped.

"That's the point," Duke said. "I am."

As the fiftieth reunion of Ted's Dartmouth class approached in 1975, preparations began for a Dr. Seuss retrospective at Baker Library on the campus at Hanover. Edward Connery Lathem, the dean of Dartmouth's libraries, came to La Jolla in January to meet Ted and to propose recording his recollections for an exhibition catalog. The taping occurred on a visit in March, when, under Lathem's gentle probing, Ted began to offer glimpses of his long-guarded private life. As their friendship warmed Ted digressed, as he so often did, to regale the dean with outrageous stories. Lathem later acknowledged that their hours together would be better described as "playing together" rather than "working together." When the tapes were transcribed he interspersed Ted's words with narrative transitions, and although a catalog never developed, Lathem felt encouraged to press on, hoping eventually to spur Ted toward an autobiography.

The Geisels attended Ted's reunion that June, staying in a Hanover Inn room overlooking the college green. After Ted fell asleep one night, Audrey sat at the window watching students clamber up and down the flagpole and enjoying their songs. Charmed by the scene, she awakened Ted and drew him to the window; he stood silently in his pajamas, shook his head, and went back to bed; he'd seen it all before.

At breakfast his Oxford friend Donald Bartlett, now retired as a Dartmouth professor of English, was so excited by reminiscing with Ted that he ordered a martini with his scrambled eggs. The loyalties of Ted's college years were a matter of record. He had dedicated *Yertle the Turtle* to the Bartletts and the Joseph Sagmasters, and for *I Can Read with My Eyes Shut!* he drew a signpost to Salina,

Kansas, as "the birthplace of Curtis A. Abel." Bartlett joined Ted and Audrey at the Dr. Seuss exhibition, which filled seventeen exhibit cases at Baker Library. From the Mandolin Club at Central High to *The Lorax*, Ted's lifework was on display. At a reception in his honor he was charming as usual, but declined to give even the most informal of remarks. An appearance before the Los Angeles Library Association had strengthened his resolve. "I stammered around so badly," he told Lathem, "that I [swore] then and there that *that* was my swan song."

Though Dartmouth hailed Ted as its most influential author, the university's interests extended beyond pride. For many years Orton Hicks, a former MGM executive who served as Dartmouth vice president, had predicted that "the Geisel genius might turn out to be the greatest benefaction in Dartmouth's history," and now it had become true. Royalty income from the Helen Geisel bequest had endowed a professorship in the humanities, and continuing royalties from Dr. Seuss books were establishing a multimillion-dollar endowment that rose beyond any other gift to Dartmouth and kept on soaring.

Mike Frith visited Hanover in September and wrote a final interoffice memo before leaving Random House to work with Jim Henson and *Sesame Street*. "Ted is such a legendary part of our lives that it is . . . easy to forget just how fresh, funny, original and remarkable all these things still are. This exhibition is not just a matter of a college honoring an alumnus."

Lathem forwarded to Ted a letter from Priscilla Moulton, a librarian on the awards committees for the Newbery and Caldecott medals, in which she wrote that a Seuss-Geisel memoir would "give us some understanding of a major contributor to 20th Century American life."

Yet in the autobiography project Ted's old self-doubts proved overwhelming; in 1976 he began putting off further queries, pleading eye problems or gout or travel plans. Although pleased by Lathem's "nicely rounded short piece on a hunk of my life," which ran in the *Dartmouth Alumni Magazine* as "Words and Pictures Married: The Beginnings of Dr. Seuss," he wrote of his "uncomfortable feeling . . . that the antiphonal technique, while working effectively in a pamphlet-length segment, would become a source of irritation to the reader in a 200-page volume. I also feel . . . that the book, which started out to be a Catalogue with Notes, has become a Semi-Autobiography with Catalogue appended." Ted admired Lathem for what Audrey called his "Edwardian" elegance and language, and especially for the flourish of his correspondence, but he asked, "Who could possibly care about all these details?" He believed that his young readers would be disappointed to learn that Dr. Seuss did not have "a light-up nose or wear baggy clown pants," and that he more resembled a shy college professor. His argument began to sound like one of the incessant conflicts over a Beginner Book. Never comfortable in confrontation or in letting down a friend, Ted suggested turning the affair over to Phyllis Jackson, and Lathem wrote Ted: "I am quite content to have her resolve the . . . future or non-future of this . . . enterprise that has already embarrassingly, from my standpoint, caused you more bother and travail than I wish had been the case." That summer, the dean delivered a transcript of the material to Phyllis, who wrote him that "one of these days, there will be a biography of Ted but this is not, I'm afraid, it." Phyllis and Lathem agreed that a copy should go into the archives at Baker Library, embargoed until after Ted's death.

It was a period of increasing recognition for Ted, but one that was sparse in creativity. As he struggled to see well, he abandoned efforts on his "big books" but each year contributed one of the shorter, less complex Beginner Books. In 1975 it was *Oh, the Thinks You Can Think!,* and the following year a collection of nonsense questions, *The Cat's Quizzer.* He called *The Thinks* his "cabbages-and-kings job, in which I decided I would like to shock the child: lead him a certain way, get him into a plot, and then take it away from him on the next page and move him to another land or another completely different set of ideas." *The New York Times Book Review* acknowledged *Thinks* as "not exactly the master's Seusstine Ceiling," but said he already deserved the Nobel Prize. "Think of the influence he has had on the human race! And all of it good!" *The Southern Literary Journal* was less indulgent: "[This] is the latest of Dr. Seuss' mediocre nonsense rhymes which in no way measure up to his earlier stories."

Part of Audrey's therapy for Ted was to coax him away from their hilltop whenever she could, and she let Random House know that Ted might agree to some book tours. Book people at a Denver department store were dazzled by their good fortune when, in the midst of eye therapy, Ted flew in to sign books during a two-week Valentine festival billed as "Dr. Seuss We Love Yeuss." Ted had always felt at home in Australia and New Zealand, and in April 1976 Sir Billy Collins found it easy to persuade the Geisels to fly Down Under for a book tour. It was Audrey's first visit. In Auckland, Collins hired a band, leased a harbor ferry for a week, decorated it with *Cat in the Hat* posters, and filled it with children six times a day on free cruises. Ted went along twice and signed hundreds of books. Fans were everywhere; with a population of only three million, New Zealanders had bought more than a million and a half Dr. Seuss books. After fishing on Lake Taupo and signing books in Wellington, the Geisels flew to the South Island and Christchurch, a town that was reminiscent of 1930s England and set Ted off on an evening of Oxford reminiscences. Then they disappeared into the mountainous seclusion of Milford Sound for three days.

In Australia Collins laid on a leisurely, four-state tour. In high form, Ted gave interviews while Audrey stood by beaming. When he was away from his drawing board, his eyes troubled him less, and he was buoyed by the widespread respect for the craft of writing. A Sydney optometrist refused payment when he repaired his glasses, saying, "You're an *author*!" Ted drew strength from his welcome, and responded with warmth even on television, saying, "It's easier when I know none of my friends will see me."

But his unease was painfully apparent at a press conference the next December as a long-delayed seven-week exhibition of Dr. Seuss paintings opened at the La Jolla museum. "Do you associate yourself with any of your characters?" a television reporter asked. "Yes," he answered stiffly, "especially the devious ones." Too nervous to smile, he broke away to wander through the gallery. There were oils and watercolors, usually his favorite medium, and papier-mâché animals, mostly from the walls and closets of the Tower. Through that holiday season the emptied walls of the Geisel living room were dotted with cardboard Cats holding small signs that read, "A masterpiece is missing from this spot." Museum visitors stood in front of Ted's more outlandish paintings and laughed out loud at the titles. There were "Two in the Bush that the One in the Hand Is Worth More Of" and "Nude Blonde in White Kid Gloves Passing Southward over the Hotel Nanituck, Holyoke, Mass." A crayon drawing was called "Inferior Swiss Watch Main Spring Leaving His Native Land in Shame." An oil in which a cat preened in a gondola was "Venetian Cat (Singing 'Oh Solo Meow')." His neighbor Bert Hupp had lent a telling pen-and-ink self-portrait that Ted had done in 1960. A split face with the artist as comedy and tragedy, it was one of the few pieces he had ever been persuaded to sell. A friend paused with Ted in front of a group of watercolors he had painted in Peru in the 1930s. "You've always said you draw animals because you can't draw people," she told him, "but these are people." Ted leaned close and squinted. "It's easier when they wear fat clothes, hmmm?" One showed *campesinos* cheering at a cockfight while a priest stands disapprovingly in a mission doorway. "The name of that one," Ted said, "is 'The Power of the Church in Peru.'"

In March 1977, when Ted's agent, Phyllis Jackson, died suddenly of cardiac arrest, even Audrey was startled at the depth of his mourning. Months earlier Phyllis had visited La Jolla, a spry figure wielding her walking cane, and they had laughed about his decision almost twenty-five years earlier to make his living from children's books. She had counseled him and grown comfortably wealthy with him, always quick to anticipate his intent and opinion and to handle personal contacts that were difficult for him. For three days after her death Ted sat idle in his studio, brooding. Usually Audrey was able to cheer him up, but now she tiptoed. His friend Al Perkins had recently walked into the La Jolla surf and drowned. She recalled Ted's suffering five years earlier after the double suicide of his friends Doris and Henry Dreyfuss. But the death of Phyllis Jackson was even more wrenching for him. He sought to make his peace by writing a verse titled "How Long Is Long?" dedicated "with all my love" to Phyllis. When he emerged from his studio and handed Audrey the sheet of yellow paper, she knew the worst was over:

> "I'll be seein' ya," I said.
> And I said, "So long!"

When you say So Long
it's not usually too long . . .
But sometimes
So Long
is forever.
So . . .
So Long,
Pal,
I guess I won't be seein' ya.

For a commencement address that June Ted turned to verse. His
Dartmouth classmate Kenneth Montgomery, a trustee of Lake
Forest College outside Chicago, invited the Geisels for a Chicago
visit, promising Ted his third honorary degree as a filip. Montgomery delayed telling Ted that he would also be the commencement
speaker. Ted was still editing notes on the back of an envelope as
he and Audrey rode with Harle and Ken Montgomery to the
campus. He made his way to the lectern with his usual uncertainty,
fumbled beneath his robe in search of his notes, and read a seventy-
five-second address entitled "My Uncle Terwilliger on the Art of
Eating Popovers":

My uncle ordered popovers
from the restaurant's bill of fare.
And when they were served,
he regarded them
with a penetrating stare . . .
Then he spoke great Words of Wisdom
as he sat there on that chair:
"To eat these things,"
said my uncle,
"you must exercise great care.
You may swallow down what's solid . . .
BUT . . .
you *must* spit out the air!"

And . . .
as *you* partake of the world's bill of fare,
that's darned good advice to follow.

Do a lot of spitting out the hot air.
And be careful what you swallow.

As Ted sat down, there was bedlam. Students shouted, cheered and flung their caps into the air. He was startled, for it was his first experience with the fervor with which many young Americans had begun to canonize Dr. Seuss. These graduates were of the generation most critical of the Vietnam war, and from their earliest memories of Dr. Seuss books they had assumed that he too must be skeptical of the establishment. Now they'd heard evidence from the master's lips.

Pleased that he had found an acceptable device for speeches, Ted used verse again the following spring when Anne Johnson persuaded him to attend the annual convention of the American Booksellers Association at Atlanta. Bob Bernstein believed that sales of Ted's books would increase even more if he was not so reclusive. Anne stood beside him for hours as autograph seekers filed past, and later toured the stalls and receptions with him. In return for her fortitude Ted read the ABA a verse:

As everyone present undoubtedly knows . . .
Due to a prenatal defect in my nose . . .
(Which seems to get worse the longer it grows)
I am completely incapable of speaking in prose . . .
If I could speak prose . . .
You would be in a fix.
I'd harangue you poor people 'til quarter to six about
    Watergate memoirs and Richard the Nix. But I
    can't because Richard and poetry don't mix . . .
I've come to convey
In a most humble way
The thanks of all authors to the ABA.
Were it not for our friends in the old ABA,
Everyone of us authors, I vouch safe to say,
Would be engaged in the dry cleaning business today . . .

The booksellers cheered too, and Ted promised his "dear Annie" that he would attend the next convention in Los Angeles.

Audrey went on nudging him, and so Ted made more appearances, accepting more honors. He gave another rhyming commencement address, this time at Revelle College on the campus of the University of California at San Diego, where for five years he had served on the board of overseers: "I've been brought here to warn you / Of the stress and the strife / That you'll face as you bravely ride forth into Life." He was the man of the year at a San Diego Boys Club dinner. "When I get my other eye fixed up [by cataract surgery]," he wrote Anne Johnson, "I'm going after the Girls Club award." Cheered by an interval of improving vision, he decided "to stay alive a few years longer." He and Audrey boarded a Royal Viking cruise ship for a trip through the Panama Canal and shore tours of Mayan temples. They rode as grand marshals in the 1979 Thanksgiving Day parade in Detroit, their heavy raccoon coats soaked through by rain. He sat through a three-and-a-half-hour Emmy awards ceremony at Pasadena Civic Auditorium and was finally called forward to accept an Emmy for *Halloween Is Grinch Night.* But it seemed a wasted effort; the teenage presenter mispronounced Geisel and there was no mention of Dr. Seuss.

Enchanted by a friend's photographs of Morocco, the Geisels flew off in the fall of 1978 to tour Casablanca, Fez and Marrakech. When Audrey became ill, he wrote a verse on hotel stationery:

> In the grubby Hotel El Mansour
> my bride ate a stale petty four
> But I'm happy to say
> She got better next day
> with the help of the Marrakech Sewer.

Ted's fight for vision was not ended, but the ordeal had inspired him to write *I Can Read with My Eyes Shut!,* his thirty-ninth book. It was dedicated to his ophthalmologist, "David Worthen, E.G.★ (★Eye Guy)." On a platform in Cincinnati to promote the book, he pretended to read a verse with both eyes closed. There and in Chicago, with Bob Bernstein at his side, he gamely took on another round of autographing appearances. Over dinner they briefly discussed Beginner Books, but Bernstein did not urge Ted to resume his involvement, believing that any Dr. Seuss book that might come from the Tower was worth more to Random House than a string of Beginner Books by most other authors.

Ted was excited when Bernstein encouraged him to undertake "an autobiography-that-is-not-an-autobiography-according-to-the-Rules." He had abandoned a similar project with Dean Lathem, but now his interest was whetted. He wrote that the approach Bernstein had suggested "broke a log jam and opened up the use of hundreds of drawings and paintings and thousands of words that, for half a century, have been looking for a place to go." He went to work immediately on a draft in the form of questions and answers, but it seemed artificial and he abandoned it. Then he roughed out a preface confronting his tendency to blur fact and fiction.

> You'll discover a strange and disturbing thing when you start writing *your* autobiography . . . a lot of stuff that happened to you never really happened at all. . . . If you have a scar on your lower left leg, as I do, you might remember, as I do, how the police cars with wailing sirens drove up to the scene of the accident and kept back the crowds as they lifted you into the ambulance and rushed you to the hospital where teams of surgeons working around the clock finally rescued you from the Jaws of Death. The actual thing that happened to me on Sumner Avenue, Springfield, Mass., sixty-five years ago was that I was riding on the handlebars of my cousin Eric's bike, and fell off. Got a minor gash which my grandfather patched with a plaster after a wash in the kitchen sink."

Irrepressible as ever, Ted scrawled several drafts of a first chapter that began:

> I was Born
> one merry morn
> under the sign of Capricorn.
> (I wasn't really, but it rhymes.)

When Bennett Cerf proposed a biography in 1966, he had realized the challenge of keeping Ted's mind on the facts; half seriously, he had suggested a format in which Ted and Helen would address the same events on facing pages. Nothing came of this, but twelve years later Ted amassed many pages and scraps of pages of handwritten reminiscence and insight. Insofar as sources and records are available its major portions are verifiable. The most revealing pages are what he calls his credits: "There are hundreds of wonderful people who helped me, inspired me, encouraged me, bound up my wounds, and to the reader of the book they will mean nothing at all but I'd like to print them. To me they mean everything."

There followed this list, drawn up when he was seventy-five:

Helen Palmer Geisel, Donald Bartlett, Saxe Commins, Jonathan Swift, Benfield Pressey, Joseph Sagmaster, Bennett Cerf, Mr. and Mrs. Lincoln Cleaves, Bill Griffin, Alexander Laing, Peggy Owens, Sir Oliver Onions, Sir William Collins, Lady Pierre Collins, Donald Klopfer, Ernest Martin Hopkins, Hugh Troy, Henry and Doris Dreyfuss, "Red" Smith, Chuck Jones, Zinny Vanderlip, Frank Capra, General Omar Bradley, Mark Twain, Keats Speed, Robert Haas, Duke Johnston, Robert Louis Stevenson, Bob Stevenson, Lt. Col. Robert Lord, Friz Freleng, Meredith Willson, Judith and Neil Morgan, Ralph Ingersoll, Geoffrey Chaucer, Charlie Chaplin, Buster Keaton, Robert Lathrop Sharp, Ralph Boas, Norman Anthony, Dr. David Worthen, Bob Chandler, Sid Perelman, Ed Graham, Grace Clark, Bob Mosher, Robert Benchley, Dr. Solon Palmer, Russell Forester, Jack Rose, Joe Raposo, Hans Conried, Robert Bernstein, Bob Stewart, Elma Otto, Wm. Shakespeare, J. M. Barrie, A. E. Housman, R. Kipling, Phyllis Jackson, Nevil Shute, and, of course, Audrey S. Geisel.

In an unusual piercing of their privacy curtain, Ted and Audrey opened the Tower to a reporter and photographer for *Architectural Digest*. The published illustrations included photographs of Audrey's dinner table, set with crystal and silver, and chairs with Seussian creatures carved in their backs ("Heppelwhite Seuss," Ted said, done by a Dartmouth friend during the Depression); the living room and its ocean view; and the studio, with pencils scattered on his desk and sketches pinned to the corkboard walls. Ted considered the visit of the magazine team a concession to Audrey and an occasion for mischief. He never forgot how "to make copy" for journalists. "Where else," he asked the writer, "can you stand in one room and see the Pacific Ocean on one side and the Atlantic on the other?" The writer strove gamely to explain Ted's nonsense to magazine readers, though once again it was a mistake to try. "As always," he reported, "[Dr. Seuss] has seen what no one else can see."

Ted's seventy-fifth birthday party on March 2, 1979, was given by the Geisels' friend Jeanne Jones, a brisk, handsome divorcée, a cookbook writer whom Ted called simply "Jones" and once described as "someone I sometimes think I imagined." The party, in her home above the Windansea surfers' beach in La Jolla, was for twenty couples, and she asked each to contribute seventy-five dollars toward a pair of handmade gold Cat-in-the-Hat cuff links. Ted learned of the solicitation after the event and wrote chagrined thank-you notes to all guests, but thereafter wore the cuff links with pride.

Sometime later Jones's son Tom took up the Hindu faith, joined the Hare Krishna order and went to live in its San Diego temple. His quest fascinated Ted. Tom's indomitable mother visited him as often as permitted, and persuaded him to allow her to honor him on his twenty-third birthday with a home-cooked dinner. Audrey and Ted were guests that evening, along with the leader of the Hare Krishnas in London. Dignitaries came from the local temple, and two young women who had published a vegetarian Hare Krishna cookbook and regarded the hostess as a colleague. Often bored at dinner parties, Ted followed this one like a mystery drama. All but the Geisels and the hostess wore saffron robes, and Ted described the evening as being "like a simple Catholic family inviting the Pope to dinner."

Ted's seventy-fifth birthday set off a round of interviews by newspapers in Washington, Boston and Los Angeles. One reporter noted that Ted smoked as they chatted, but quickly put his cigarettes out of sight when photographs were taken because "children's book authors never smoke." For the *Los Angeles Times Book Review*, he gave a revealing reply to the question of why he wrote:

I tend basically to exaggerate in life, and in writing, it's fine to exaggerate. I really enjoy overstating for the purpose of getting a laugh. It's very flattering, that laugh, and at the same time it gives pleasure to the audience and accomplishes more than writing very serious things. For another thing, writing is easier than digging ditches. Well, actually *that's* an exaggeration. It isn't.

But Ted soon grew weary of talk about his seventy-fifth and told a *Washington Post* reporter, "It's getting awful, because I meet old, old people, who can scarcely walk, and they say, 'I was brought up on your books.'"

Ted's Beginner Book of tongue twisters, *Oh, Say Can You Say?*, appeared in the fall of 1979. He liked the title and wrote a book to go with it. It was dedicated to "Lee Groo, the Enunciator," Ted's nickname for his younger stepdaughter, who now spelled her name Leagrey and had inherited her mother's knack for tossing off tongue twisters.

Even with eye troubles Ted remained a perfectionist. When he scanned Random House color charts for inks that matched his pencil drawings of the book's green parrot, he found "sixty greens" but none seemed right, so he asked the art director, Grace Clark, to have the printer mix a "more parroty" sixty-first. "His color sense," she said, "is the most sophisticated I've ever run into."

As vision came and went, Ted felt he had to keep learning to draw; sometimes he "had trouble finding the paper with the pen." Often unable to work at all, he kept busy, even agreeing to have his hands cast in bronze for display at the medical school of the University of Iowa "between Harry Truman and Wilt Chamberlain." Audrey came home one day "and found him in the kitchen up to his elbows in goo with two doctors standing by." He worked with Roy McKie on *Hair Book* for Beginner Books, and oversaw an ABC television special about a dropout whom he called *Pontoffel Poc.* He continued to avoid television appearances; his young agent, Jed Mattes, who had worked with Phyllis Jackson and inherited Dr. Seuss at her death, screened hundreds of requests, but Ted rejected them all, including Johnny Carson and the *Today* show.

He began to spend more time with fan mail, which had surged after his seventy-fifth birthday. As usual, Random House sent form

responses to most of them—about 1,300 a week during 1979—
and selected about 150 more to send to Ted. His hand-lettered
replies on Cat in the Hat notepaper became collectibles. To explain
a delayed response, he adapted a *Judge* drawing of "an animal called
a Budget on which a Nudget rides, carrying mail. It is very hard
for anyone to stay on a Budget." The letters that Ted cherished
were from those who gave him credit for their love of reading,
"even if their spelling was abominable." At a time when children
were bristling with questions about nuclear-power plants, gay
rights, earthquakes and abortions, he considered it "unbelievable"
that his fantasies were selling better than ever.

On a July evening in 1980, at an American Library Association
awards banquet in New York, Ted, appearing zestful and fit, shared
a platform with much younger writers. He wore an oversized black
bow tie; his abundant silvery hair was combed with youthful
carelessness. He was receiving the Laura Ingalls Wilder Award for
his "lasting contributions to children's literature," and he had
worked particularly hard on his acceptance speech:

> . . . I ought to give due thanks, I think,
> to Mr. Higgins
> who furnishes my indispensable India Ink.
> And my thanks to Mr. Strathmore
> who furnishes the paper that I ink up.
> And to Mr. Smirnoff
> who furnishes the vodka
> that occasionally I drink up . . .

Ted had rocked the tight little world of children's librarians
twenty-three years earlier with his brash *Cat in the Hat,* and Bennett
Cerf had harangued them because they had not honored Ted's
work. Now Ted was onstage with winners of the coveted Randolph Caldecott Medal (the illustrator Barbara Cooney) and the
John Newbery Medal (writer Joan W. Blos). These were awards
he had never won, although three early books were runners-up
for the Caldecott.

As Audrey and Ted celebrated their twelfth wedding anniversary,
he wore a patch over his right eye following what he hoped was

his final surgery. He was beginning to see colors properly again. "For the next several weeks," he wrote, "I'll continue to have double vision, which causes me to burp and bite people and dogs." He and Audrey were "thoroughly therapized," for she was in a cast after breaking her ankle in a fall. But they flew to New York for a private tour of the Picasso retrospective at the Museum of Modern Art. "We ought to blend right in at a Picasso show," Ted wrote. "A one-eyed man and a one-legged lady." On their jet from San Diego, he drew a cartoon for her in which she appeared as "Mrs. Picatso," with her foot in a cubist cast, a cat leering at her with his one good eye. Then he drew the cartoon on her cast, and Audrey said that "it made me the toast of New York."

Ted was eager to meet with his new team at Random House. Bob Bernstein had promoted the marketing expert Jerry Harrison to head the juvenile books division, and from the start he understood the policy on Ted Geisel: "It had to be Ted's way. You worked and worked until he was happy." Janet Schulman moved from the library division to become editor in chief of juvenile books. The art director, occupying a pivotal role in Ted's life, was Cathy Goldsmith, who had graduated from Cornell as an anthropologist and decided it was invaluable training for the children's book world. Juvenile art directors came under the gun of Dr. Seuss at Random House, and his name was always on the door of the office above that of the incumbent resident.

Cathy Goldsmith turned thirty on the day that Ted, towering above her five feet one, strode into her office for the first time and she leaped up to take his extended hand. "He wasn't God to me but he was close," she recalled. "I had no idea what to call him. You couldn't call him Dr. Seuss, and I didn't hear anybody refer to him as Mr. Geisel. You didn't call your parents' friend by a first name, and certainly no one as important and famous as he was."

After two hours of working together, it became obvious to Ted that she had no idea what to call him. Suddenly he leaned down close to her face. "If you don't call me Ted," he said, "I'm going to call you Little You!" He left that meeting cheered at the prospect of doing more books. "Cathy is a fellow sewer worker," he said, paying her an artist's homage. "She finishes my sentences and I finish hers."

His eye patch came off a month later and his wondrous palette of colors was restored, as bright and sharp-edged as ever.

CHAPTER 19

The Butter Battle Book

1981–1984

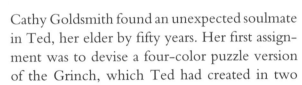

Cathy Goldsmith found an unexpected soulmate in Ted, her elder by fifty years. Her first assignment was to devise a four-color puzzle version of the Grinch, which Ted had created in two colors. When she sent him her sketch, he telephoned. "You know what's wrong?" he said. "You need some color in the snow."

"What do you mean?" she blurted. "Snow is white!"

"But here it's too white," he said. "You need a little color so it doesn't blind you."

From his chart he gave her a color number, a pale mint green. This guy's nuts, she thought. That's not snow color, that's green. But she learned quickly not to doubt him. Other colors overwhelmed the green and it became a soft snow-white. Just as some lucky people are born with perfect pitch, she believed, a few like Ted are blessed with perfect color sense.

Some critics wrote that Ted's words were the magic of his books, and put down his drawing as cartoonery. Others praised his imagery, his daring use of color and the economy of pen strokes he used in the revelation of characters like the loose-limbed Grinch and the Cat in the Hat. The animator Chuck Jones was awed by the maze-like intricacy of Ted's drawing and called him "the children's M. C. Escher."

"When Ted picked up a brush to paint," Mike Frith said, "magical things happened." Without telling him, Frith submitted

Ted's work to the Illustrators' Society, but it was never accepted for exhibition or award. Ted would hardly have been surprised. He once put down his painting as a "sort of psychosis deterrent . . . to keep from going batty." He tried to stay aloof from hurt by refusing to sell his paintings; since there was no market to consider, there were no jurors or patrons to become hostile critics. Painting served his soul. "Unless you break your pattern, you get awfully nervous. I have been working in the same style over forty years on children's books." But he continued to draw in a way that appealed to children: "Kids exaggerate the same way I do. They overlook things they can't draw, their pencils slip, and they get funny effects. I've learned to incorporate my pencil slips into my style." A child's idea of art, he contended, was "pen-and-ink outlines filled in with flat color, with no modulation and no subtlety. . . . That's the way kids see things." Ted once happily quoted the poet and critic Karla Kuskin, who wrote that his creatures all have "slightly batty, oval eyes and a smile you might find on the Mona Lisa after her first martini."

His energy and spirits restored by the summer of 1981, Ted began work on *Hunches in Bunches*, his first "big book" in nine years. But in September his body interrupted. Always pleading with Ted to give up cigarettes, Audrey conspired with Jeanne Jones before a dinner party to post a NO SMOKING warning on a card at each table. Ted called a waiter, set his card on fire and sent it flambé on a tray to his hostess.

The next day he asked Audrey to bring him something for indigestion. She did so, and checked his blood pressure; it was normal. He complained again the following morning. "I'm not waiting for your third 'indigestion,'" Audrey said. "I'd rather have everybody laugh at me than be sorry. I'm calling 911." An hour later he was in intensive care at Scripps Clinic with a minor heart attack, which damaged about one tenth of the muscle. Ted had always been a slim six-footer; he had a horror of being fat. His cardiologist asked for no sweeping reform in lifestyle, only the one that so far had proved elusive: no more cigarettes.

Ted's approach to abstinence was Seussian. Twenty years earlier, when he had last tried to quit smoking, he had chewed for days on a corncob pipe and diverted himself by planting strawberry seeds in it. He found his old pipe, filled it with peat moss and planted radish seeds. Audrey brought a medicine dropper to his bedside and another to his studio. Each time he wanted a cigarette, he watered his pipe and clenched it between his teeth. The toughest part, he admitted, was not being able to light up when answering the telephone "to ease the embarrassment of talking to someone." As he regained his strength he sat for a portrait by E. Raymond Kinstler, who had worked on Beginner Books; it was commissioned by Dartmouth to hang in Baker Library close by that of another Dartmouth man, Daniel Webster.

Rested and restless, Ted returned to his old tilt-top drawing board and completed *Hunches in Bunches*, a book of nonsense that emerged from the frustrations of his disabled years. It begins, "Do you ever sit and fidget / when you don't know what to do?" It is a curious book that poses mature adult perplexities and childhood solutions, as in its final lines:

> . . . the best hunch of the bunch!
> I followed him into the kitchen
> and had six hot dogs for lunch."

Its illustrations conveyed Ted's elation in getting back to work, and include one of the most haunting images in any Seuss book: a lonely ocean pier ("some dead-end road in West Gee-Hossa-Flat!") held aloft by the upraised arms of stark cut-out human figures.

The Geisels flew to New York and introduced *Hunches in Bunches* with a Random House reading. This was new to Cathy Goldsmith, who sensed his joy in sharing what he had done. "He had one of us read so he could watch what everybody saw and heard and felt. We asked him to read it next . . . in that booming voice he gave such grand readings." Afterward his friends teased Ted about a recent Seussian uproar at City Hall, when Carol Bellamy, president of the New York City Council, had compared Mayor Ed Koch to the power-mad Yertle the Turtle and herself to poor Mack at the bottom of the heap. Ted was "delighted to be caught in the middle of such a mess."

Soon after *Hunches* appeared, in the autumn of 1982, Ted joined the children's author Maurice Sendak onstage at the San Diego Museum of Art during an exhibition of Sendak illustrations. Fans filled the hall. Sendak's new book was *Outside Over There*, and critics were berating him for his exploration of dark sibling jealousies. Professor Glenn Edward Sadler introduced the two men as "the foremost children's authors of the era," and for more than an hour they took questions amiably, deferring to and bolstered by each other. Though Ted was oblivious to the work of most children's authors, he admired Sendak's and said that if he were a kid, he'd be reading Sendak. Both made it clear that they considered children's books to be demanding adult work. Ted said he might write two hundred lines to salvage four. His key to productivity? "Meticulosity," Ted answered. "Is that a word?"

When asked if they liked their characters, both writers responded with hostility. "If my characters gave me a dinner party, I wouldn't show up," Ted answered. "If we lived with them," Sendak said, "we'd be in the madhouse . . . Writing is a way to exorcise them." His appraisal of Ted's work suggested the bond between them; he called Dr. Seuss "revolutionary—vital, wild, disorderly and personable in the most intense way." Little such work is published, Sendak argued, because publishers aren't appealing to children but "to the sweet grandmas who buy for them. They tend to have a totally false illusion about their own childhood and that's what they want for their grandchildren." That night he invited Ted to write a text for him to illustrate, but nothing came of it.

Like most of the people with whom Ted was working, Sendak was many years younger. The next week Ted flew to New York for a dinner honoring Bob Bernstein, almost twenty years his junior, for his twenty-five years with Random House. In verse he toasted the chairman:

> Like Gandhi he brought to our souls new-born hope
> Like Einstein he broadened our breadth and our scope
> To our restrooms he brought better paper and soap
> He brightened our darkness, he gave us more rope . . .

Ted's associations with the young were instinctive; critics pointed out that he always took the side of children. In interviews with Jonathan Cott for a book on children's literature, Ted agreed: "I'm subversive as hell! I've always had a mistrust of adults. And one reason I dropped out of Oxford and the Sorbonne was that I thought they were taking life too damn seriously."

On a winter's day early in 1983, a limousine made its way up the hillside bringing deal makers to the Tower. Jed Mattes and Herb Cheyette of International Creative Management had negotiated a $10 million contract with Coleco, the toy manufacturer whose Cabbage Patch Dolls had made it a wunderkind of Wall Street, and it called for the marketing of Dr. Seuss characters as toys and video games over ten years. With Cheyette and Jed Mattes were two Coleco executives. Soft-spoken and intuitive, Mattes had been just twenty-four when he assumed the role of Ted's day-to-day agent after the death of Phyllis Jackson, and he quickly came to respect Ted as the ultimate and unerring authority on what was best for Dr. Seuss. He and Cheyette had warned Coleco negotiators that Ted would insist on absolute product approval, and they had agreed.

Ted's eyes sparkled as he pored over the contract, but he pushed it aside. "I don't know that I want to spend the last several years of my life doing this," he told Mattes. But he telephoned the attorney Karl ZoBell, who came quickly to the Tower and scanned the contract, and by noon, amid camera flashes, Ted had agreed to sign. As the visitors departed, Mattes said he would call within a week to set a date for another signing that Coleco would use as its public launching of the Dr. Seuss line.

But a routine dental appointment the next day brought Ted frightening news; the dentist detected a small lesion on the floor of his mouth at the base of the tongue. A biopsy confirmed that it was malignant, a cancer typically linked to smoking and drinking. Doctors recommended surgery to remove a portion of the tongue, which would certainly affect his speech. Ted was appalled and sought another opinion.

Audrey telephoned her friend Ruth Grobstein, an oncologist with the University of California Medical Center at San Francisco, and the Geisels flew there. Grobstein confirmed the diagnosis of one abnormal node and presented Ted's case to a tumor board, which recommended radiation and an iridium implant into the tongue area. Radiation would mean temporary loss of facial hair, including his beard, and his voice might be affected. Although Grobstein warned him that the implant alone might not be sufficient, Ted decided against radiation.

When Jed Mattes called with a date for the Coleco press conference, Ted said, "That won't work. I have to go up to San Francisco for a couple of days." He did not mention the cancer.

The implant was installed on Valentine's Day, with plastic catheters placed from under his chin through the tongue. For five harrowing days Ted was hospitalized, and "resembled a porcupine." But within two weeks he was home and strong enough to escort Audrey on a stormy evening to the opening of a La Jolla boutique and then to San Diego Harbor to board the British royal yacht *Britannia* for a reception hosted by Queen Elizabeth II and Prince Philip, who were cruising northward along the California coast on a state visit. Well briefed, Her Majesty told Ted she found his books charming, and they chatted about the impending royal visit to Yosemite National Park.

Seeming as durable as ever that April, Ted reveled in a reunion at Hotel del Coronado with Frank Capra, who was being honored by the San Diego Museum of Photographic Arts. The two men spent hours trading memories of Fort Fox and the Hollywood of the 1940s, and attended a benefit showing of Capra's *Mr. Smith Goes to Washington*.

Angry at his body for wasting his time, Ted returned to his drawing board. It had been twelve years since the environmental plea of *The Lorax*, and another message was on his mind. He was brooding over the mounting cold war with the Soviet Union and believed that under Ronald Reagan the nuclear arms race was beyond control. Over dinner at La Valencia, he wondered out loud how a democratic government could impose "such deadly stupidity" on people like him who were so opposed to nuclear proliferation. "I'm not antimilitary," he said. "I'm just anticrazy. We did the same thing in World War I and World War II. Why can't we learn?"

Ted recalled his Oxford studies of the conflict between the thirteenth-century Guelphs and Ghibellines of northern Italy, a deadly quarrel between those loyal to the Pope and those pledged to the Holy Roman emperor, setting cities like Florence and Siena at each other's throat. As Ted chose to remember history, they had fought because the Guelphs cut their apples vertically while the Ghibellines cut theirs horizontally. Such nonsense became his metaphor for mounting cold war tension, and he plunged into the nuclear-war theme with a vigor that he had not felt for years. He posed technical questions to retired military friends in San Diego, especially Victor H. Krulak, a Marine Corps lieutenant general who had been prominent in the Vietnam war. With this book Ted saw himself as an old *PM* reporter telling the truth about the world.

He wrote his nephew that he was working eight to ten hours a day on "the best book I've ever written." With *The Butter Battle Book* the words came first. When he had finished the sketches, he invited Jed Mattes from New York and watched his young friend closely as he walked from panel to panel tacked to his studio walls. Jed was startled by the subject but not alarmed. He regarded Dr. Seuss as Ted's voice in dealing with a world that distressed him. He told Ted that the book's inconclusive ending—would there be nuclear war?—would trouble some readers, but he agreed that it was the only honest one. With a smile, Ted replied, "I've always wanted to write a "Lady or the Tiger" ending."

An in-house memo to Random House salespeople described *The Butter Battle Book* as "probably the most important book Dr. Seuss has ever created." But when Ted brought it to New York in October no one liked the cover, a simple image of the Yooks' cheerleader holding a pennant aloft. Ted listened quietly and said, "I have no idea if this is an adult book for children or a children's book for adults. What exactly do you have in mind?" Cathy Goldsmith suggested that the cover be "more confrontational, maybe using a drawing of the two characters on the wall, each holding a bomb."

Their discussions grew intense as the morning passed. Jerry Harrison planned to take Ted and Cathy to lunch at Lutèce, and Cathy, who had never been there, looked forward to it. But Ted was flying to San Diego that evening and didn't want to leave the matter unsettled. Harrison suggested that Cathy stay at the office and work up ideas for their inspection after lunch. Ted returned with paté and a split of champagne for Cathy, stared at her cover proposal and said he would call after he got home. She read the signs immediately. "If you were his friend, he couldn't look you in the eye and say he didn't like something. Next day he probably called Anne Johnson, who called Bob [Bernstein], who called us and said to use his original cover."

But soon the title came under attack; the sales staff argued that it was a handicap, and Bernstein persuaded Ted to change its name to something less enigmatic and more Seussian: *The Yooks and the Zooks*, the names of his warring tribes. A press release announced this title, but Audrey watched Ted brood and grumble about it and broke her own rule about intruding on his professional life. "As I dialed New York I said to myself this is the worst thing I could possibly do! I'm meddling in what is his prerogative. Ted was so wonderfully agreeable, too much so sometimes . . . he never knew his strength or used his clout. I spoke with Anne and Bob in strictest confidence and tried to explain how much Ted wanted that title [*Butter Battle Book*]." The title was restored, and when Ted later learned of Audrey's end run he was grateful.

But challenges to *The Butter Battle Book* continued. For the first time in memory, editors questioned a Dr. Seuss text. An unawed copyreader observed that Ted's devices reminded her of Jonathan Swift's in *Gulliver's Travels*, in which the Lilliputians make war over which end of an egg should be broken. She deemed the story "a bit too terrifying" and urged a new ending to reassure children that the Yooks and Zooks would not destroy each other—"an illusion that I think children are entitled to have."

As the book reached the page-proof stage, the editor in chief, Janet Schulman, attempted to deal with a confusion of tenses. From the start, the grandfather, as the narrator, relates the arms escalation between the Yooks and Zooks as a flashback ("In those days, of course . . ."). But five pages from the end the action is suddenly in the present as a boy races toward a Berlin-like wall to see if his grandfather will drop the Bitsy Big-Boy Boomeroo on the Zooks. Janet called Ted to suggest a clarifying change.

"I see what you're saying," he said slowly, "but I'm not going to change it. The grandfather is just a device."

After the book was published, a reviewer called Janet. "You know," she said, "something about this book doesn't make sense."

"I know."

"Well, how could you publish it like that?"

"When you're dealing with a genius and he won't change, you don't change," Janet replied.

But she was hugely excited about the book and shrugged off early critics who called it bleak, for she considered arms escalation a monumental theme for Ted. She sent proofs to Maurice Sendak, who wrote an endorsement that she hoped to use on the book's back cover, and read his blurb at the sales meeting:

> Surprisingly, wonderfully, the case for total disarmament has been brilliantly made by our acknowledged master of nonsense, Dr. Seuss. . . . Only a genius of the ridiculous could possibly deal with the cosmic and lethal madness of the nuclear arms race. . . . He has done the world a service.

For a long moment the salespeople sat silent; then they rose and applauded. "If there are any hawks on the sales force, they were being very quiet," Schulman wrote Sendak. But by that evening some argued that Sendak's "message" on the cover would turn away parents. Bernstein telephoned Ted, who reluctantly agreed that Sendak's words be withheld from the cover. Schulman was disappointed. "After all," she wrote, "it is just a book about the end of the world!" But the presses began rolling, and when, two days later, she learned that Ted was about to have major surgery, she knew that he had other problems on his mind.

Cancer had spread to a lymph node in Ted's neck, and on December 16, 1983, he underwent a radical neck dissection and a deep biopsy of the implanted area. Audrey had already mailed invitations for a Christmas party at the Tower, and though he would not appear, Ted insisted that she go through with it. The surgery left him with a neck deformity, which was usually hidden by clothing but was "a problem for him . . . such a handsome man," his physician Ruth Grobstein observed. She was nearer at hand after moving to San Diego to join Scripps Clinic. For two months after the biopsy Ted suffered severe pain from soft-tissue necrosis and was on heavy medication. The wound might have healed sooner with treatment in a hyperbaric oxygen chamber, with hours in a small room commonly used by divers to counteract bends. But Ted was claustrophobic, and despite Audrey's entreaties, he found this impossible. It was March before he was out of pain, apparently free of cancer, and hopeful.

After going through two titles and many cover designs, *The Butter Battle Book* was published on Ted's eightieth birthday, March 2, 1984, and heralded with full-page newspaper advertisements headlined FOR HIS 80TH BIRTHDAY DR. SEUSS HAS GIVEN US ALL A MOMENTOUS PRESENT. Critics were divided. Some thought the arms race was an inappropriate issue for a children's book, but others welcomed it as a way to help children deal with a matter vital to their future. *The New York Times Book Review* rated it a game try: "Thank you, Dr. Seuss, for attempting this cautionary tale," but called it his "bleakest book." Art Buchwald proposed Dr. Seuss for a Nobel Prize. But the *Kirkus* trade reviewer was unmoved: ". . . in the aftermath of wide exposure to 'The Day After' [on television] and other 1980s arousals, all this seems, however well-intended, a little simplistic, a little out-of-date, even a little out-of-keeping."

Random House gave a sumptuous birthday party at the New York Public Library for about two hundred guests. The inner guard at the publishing firm knew of Ted's cancer surgery and looked at him in wonder as he made his way through a swirl of notables, looking trim and energetic. While popping champagne corks echoed through the lofty hall, Vartan Gregorian, the library president, observed that Dr. Seuss "helps us always to remember that we are young, and never to forget that we are responsible." A greeting from Mayor Ed Koch yielded the pun that the new work was "a far, far butter thing you've done" than any book before.

From the library, Audrey and Ted went by limousine to "21," where Bennett Cerf had taken Ted to lunch almost fifty years before and stolen him away from Vanguard Press. This time there was a formal birthday dinner in an upstairs dining room for fifty-nine guests, hosted by Donald and Samuel I. Newhouse, Jr., whose Advance Publications had acquired Random House from RCA.

Around the tables, each decorated with a Dr. Seuss toy from Coleco, were Maurice Sendak, E. L. Doctorow, Stan and Jan Berenstain, and a few friends from La Jolla and Dartmouth. The pianist doing the birthday songs was the songwriter Joe Raposo of *Sesame Street*, with whom Ted had won an Emmy for the children's television special *The Grinch Grinches the Cat in the Hat*. Always wary of being the center of attention, Ted seemed uncomfortable as the evening began; but after a vodka martini on the rocks he was soon smiling. The tributes tended to be bad Seuss parodies, but Ted, honoring the sources, listened raptly. One was from Art Buchwald and another was a review that Charles Osgood had read on CBS News, "The *Butter Battle* of Dr. Seuss / Is much too much like the Evening Neuss. . . ."

In response Ted stood and read a birthday verse of his own:

> If my Daddy hadn't met up with my mommy,
> I'd have missed this fine party tonight . . .
> If my daddy had shacked up with somebody else,
> just supposing, for instance, Miss Abigail Schmelz, or
>   Patricia McFish or Louella McGee,
> I wouldn't have resulted, I wouldn't be me . . .

Toasts continued around the United States, even on the floor of the Senate, where Daniel Patrick Moynihan read his own mock-Seuss birthday greeting, "Mr. President, Mr. President, / I rise to set a precedent. . . ." Seuss characters took over the cover of the mass-circulation *Parade* magazine in a euphoric birthday salute.

The Butter Battle Book aroused public opinion and controversy, giving the Random House juvenile department an unaccustomed challenge. Congressman Edward J. Markey of Massachusetts, who had sponsored a successful nuclear-freeze resolution in the House, wrote the publisher offering to speak on behalf of the book. "A concerned Christian mother" in Texas wrote of her effort to ban the book and halt future editions. "How dare a well-respected publishing firm . . . the most blatant form of brainwashing I have ever encountered . . . I had long respected the Dr. Seuss books as light, whimsical and enjoyable. . . ."

Janet Schulman replied calmly to all, writing the Texas mother that "children are going to have to start thinking and using the brain that God gave them. *The Butter Battle Book* takes no sides. It simply presents the arms build-up as it is right now. You call this brainwashing. We call your response fear of ideas."

A California woman was one of many who protested the inconclusive ending, and Schulman wrote her, "If there were a happy ending in reality, then there would have been no need to write this book. . . . The book tells the truth and the truth is our only hope. . . . [It] is the most important contribution Dr. Seuss has made in his many years of giving children something to think about."

Amid such passion, *Butter Battle* soon led juvenile best-seller lists and also *The New York Times Book Review* fiction list. It sold heavily in Britain, and the first of many foreign translations appeared in Japan; Israel soon followed. While some thought the book risky, Ted said he would have been greatly upset if it had failed; instead, he was "pleased and proud." In subsequent printings, at Ted's urging, Sendak's endorsement was displayed on the back cover, and on New Year's Day of 1990 *Butter Battle* was televised in the Soviet Union. "Right after that," Ted bragged, "the U.S.S.R. began falling apart."

Momentum swept Dr. Seuss through the spring of 1984. As Ted sat in his studio one April morning wondering, as he often did, if he could manage another book, an Associated Press reporter telephoned to say that he had won a Pulitzer Prize, a special citation "for his contribution over nearly half a century to the education and enjoyment of America's children and their parents." Ted was flabbergasted: "It comes right out of left field, particularly after all these years." The Pulitzer was "usually given to adults. I'm a writer who has to eat with the children before the adults eat." But one judge said the proposal to award a Pulitzer to Dr. Seuss, initiated by San Diego newspaper editors, had met with "as close to immediate unanimity" as any he recalled.

After that first phone call, Ted said, "all hell broke loose." Although he refused to allow television "to set up all that gear here in my studio," the prize brought him a flurry of exposure on network television, a medium he had avoided ever since the Dick Cavett fiasco sixteen years earlier. For the first time, Ted's benign and bearded face and his shy half-smile became almost as familiar across America as the lilting verse of Dr. Seuss. Like less reclusive celebrities, he encountered the intruding stares and fatuous remarks of strangers, but he scoffed at his fame. "When you get to be eighty," he said, "people will recognize you on the streets too."

The Geisels celebrated the Pulitzer at a dinner with friends, and on the way home, with Dick Duffy at the wheel, a red light flashed behind them. A towering police officer suggested that Duffy had been weaving. Duffy explained that he had turned briefly toward the backseat to hear a story, and when he mentioned the name of the storyteller the officer asked to meet him. Not entirely sober, Ted stepped out of the car and gravely the two men shook hands. Then the officer gave Duffy a lecture: "Go straight home. Drive very carefully. You have precious cargo."

In May, Ted's new celebrity brought an invitation to the White House for a state dinner honoring Miguel de la Madrid, the president of Mexico. The guest list amused Audrey; they were in the company of Ricardo Montalban, Vicki Carr and Rock Hudson. As they were about to shake hands with Nancy and Ronald Reagan, Ted whispered to Audrey, "Now seven presidents have met me." Moments later he was recalling with the president and television anchorman Tom Brokaw how he had rejected Lieutenant Ronald Reagan forty years earlier as narrator for the wartime film *Your Job in Germany*. Reagan had not forgotten. "But you were right," the president said with an engaging smile. "John Beal did have a better voice."

At eighty, Ted forced himself to ponder his financial affairs, never his favorite use of time. It had been decades since he had written checks or kept financial records, and he seldom carried a wallet. Jed Mattes and the lawyers and accountants of ICM oversaw his income flow from royalties. For years an accountant had come to the Tower to handle home and office bookkeeping and to pay bills, a duty later assumed by Claudia Prescott. Beyond the role of money as a reassurance of the worth of his work, Ted was remarkably oblivious to his wealth and abnormally uninterested in material goods.

Although he scorned lawyers, he began discussing financial and trust affairs with Karl ZoBell. On August 27 they signed a trust agreement as an umbrella over the Geisel millions, with ZoBell, Ted and Audrey as trustees. Into the trust went over $5 million in deferred income from Random House that had been accumulating in mutual funds since the start of Beginner Books in 1958. Along with it came other millions in royalties. Ted had become a classic beneficiary of the pyramiding nature of royalties from successful children's books, which often have longer sales lives than adult ones. His share of book sales was as much as 15 percent of the retail price, and with more than forty books in print, many of them selling in numbers higher than when initially published, there was a logarithmic rate of increase. Those to whom Seuss books had been read when they were children, going back as far as 1937, grew up to read those same Seuss books and newer ones to their own children, and on to the next generation and the next. By 1984 there were trade estimates that the author's royalties from Dr. Seuss books yielded an annual average of $750,000 or more from Random House and that much or more from Grolier book club sales. All Seuss book copyrights were now held jointly in the names of Audrey and Ted, and this income began to be channeled into the new trust.

Still, little changed in the way they lived. She drove their one car, a silver-colored Cadillac with license plates that read GRINCH. Their one assistant, Claudia Prescott, was a Random House employee, and there was a part-time housekeeper and part-time gardener. Ted resisted Audrey's proposals to remodel their home because he dreaded the upheaval. He refused to "complicate" his life by having a word processor or fax machine and was not interested in an electric typewriter, calling it "too sophisticated." He still answered his own telephone, and would have nothing to do with answering machines. Occasionally Audrey chose a new suit for him, but he never shopped; when they flew to New York, it was on American Airlines, not—as some of their La Jolla friends did—on a private jet.

But Ted did spend money in pursuit of privacy. When any adjacent acreage became available, he was ready to invest a few hundred thousand dollars to add to the open space surrounding their mountaintop home; this land was the investment he trusted most. He enlarged the homesite to about ten acres. He knew he was paying top dollar, but it was worth it to prevent adjacent homebuilding.

The Geisels were known increasingly as philanthropists, but they declined to lend their name to any building or wing. The Seuss Foundation, sustained by a portion of book royalties invested in securities, was growing in capital and range. The largest recipient was the Scripps Clinic and Research Foundation in La Jolla, but other grants reflected their catholic interests. Among them each year were Tougaloo, a small Mississippi college in which Bob Bernstein had interested Ted, and SOFA (Strongly Organized For Action), a nonprofit group that operated a child-care center for La Jolla's ethnic community.

The passage of time had calmed most of the furor that followed Helen's death. Ted was, after all, a community icon, and Audrey was devoted to seeing him through a series of ailments that might otherwise have crushed his spirit. Jerry Harrison watched Audrey in awe at Random House parties. "She can work a room of strangers better than anyone I ever knew," he said, "and she schlepped Ted off to Africa and Europe and kept him alive."

When Jed Mattes was at the Geisel home, he found them so loving that he sometimes felt he was intruding. "I thought of her almost as a geisha," he said, "unobtrusively anticipating his needs so he never had to be aware of them. It wasn't subservience or chauvinism, but she made his life as stress-free as possible." Once when Audrey served lunch, Ted suggested the two men trade plates because his portion seemed larger. Audrey intervened. "Jed's casserole had a little more salt than yours," she told Ted.

Audrey took pleasure in food and in overseeing menus for benefits and galas, and sometimes her husband went along, poking fun. After their trip to Morocco, she had experimented with cous-cous and the big pigeon pies called bastilla, which were eaten with the fingers, but Ted quickly pleaded for a meal he could attack with a knife and fork. When Jeanne Jones became one of the first women members of the San Diego chapter of the Confrérie de la Chaîne des Rôtisseurs, Audrey urged Ted to join. "I don't want those guys pretending to be French and kissing me on both cheeks," he said, feigning horror. He abhorred pretense, but he did attend once as Jones's guest and decorated his menu with the face of a scowling Cat saying, "I hate food and all the fol-der-ol that goes with it." As guests filled out course-by-course scorecards, he turned over his menu and sketched a capon. "The dish I liked best was the capon-stuffed lentil," he wrote. "And did you know that it takes only one capon to stuff 30,000 lentils?"

Ted had grown tired of big parties and was ready to leave them long before Audrey was; he preferred quiet corners with a close friend or two. Often Dick Duffy joined him near the exit as Audrey and Jones said their long good-byes, sweeping happily from table to table. "Why do we have to stand here and watch them do the Stations of the Cross?" Ted muttered. Toward the end of a strenuous La Jolla summer, he drew a cartoon and mailed it to a fellow artist whom he had seen at parties four nights in a row. His Cat, of course, did the talking:

> Said an artist with minutes to live:
> "I have very few minutes to give
> to the Smarties and Farties
> at long local parties,"
> And he ended his life with a shiv.

Jed Mattes, who revered his client's integrity, soon bore million-dollar scars as evidence. Ted began to have grave doubts about the Coleco franchising contract soon after he saw the products. The most intractable problem was the Cat. "The facial expression of the Cat just drove Ted nuts," Mattes said. On the Coleco toys it looked to Jed like a smirk "or Edward Everett Horton pursing his lips, and of course the Cat is a little of both." Even Ted conceded that the Coleco problem with the Cat was his own fault, and he thumbed through *The Cat in the Hat* to show Mattes why. On one page the Cat's back is long, on another it is short; when the Cat stands, it is long; when he sits it isn't. "When you go to three dimensions," Ted explained, "there will always be something wrong with the Cat."

The Coleco people came to La Jolla to discuss changes, but the meetings bored Ted and drained his patience and energy. His priorities never had much to do with money, and Coleco was coming on hard times. After a meeting early in 1987 Cheyette arranged a buyout of Ted's contract. "He was very happy to say good-bye to the last few million," Mattes recalled, "so he wouldn't have to endure this artistic problem for one more day." Ted always hated the face of the Coleco cat; it wasn't his Cat in the Hat.

CHAPTER 20

You're Only Old Once!

1985–1986

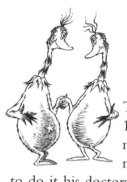

The members of Princeton University's Class of 1985 had no reason to know that Ted had spent many months in pain, in and out of clinics and medical offices, determined to live but refusing to do it his doctors' way. It might have surprised them to know how craftily his wife had encouraged him to go to New Jersey to accept one more honorary degree. When he stood and moved toward the lectern they sprang to their feet and thundered in unison, "I am Sam! Sam I am!" and then proceeded to chant the full text of *Green Eggs and Ham*.

Nothing that medicine could do for him gave Ted such a lift as that welcome at Princeton. Warmed by its memory, he returned to his studio and completed a Dr. Seuss book based on his recent illnesses, which had included "a series of everything." For months it had been "a matter of sitting in waiting rooms being bored. I began sketching what I thought was going to happen to me for the next hour and a half. I had no idea of doing a book. I just began drawing hospital machinery. . . . In the interest of commerce, I wrote a happy ending. The other ending is unacceptable." In *You're Only Old Once!* Ted was less a storyteller or narrator than a memoirist. The book was his unexpected lamentation about the infirmities of age and the indignities of the health-care system, written when he was "fed up with a social life consisting entirely of doctors."

In waiting rooms at the University of California Medical Center in San Francisco and at Scripps Clinic, Ted had been not only bored but frightened. In San Francisco he sat beside a sad-eyed fish he called Norval, who swam in his bubbling tank in dirge time as patients padded by. After the book appeared and Norval had become notorious, Ted took a friend to meet him, conceding that "other hospitals have a better display of fish by far." He considered his book a protest against medical procedures that were unnecessary or overpriced: "I had a pinhead-sized cancer on the back of my tongue and they removed it, for which I was very grateful. They inserted some radium material to keep it clean and that impaired circulation in my jaw, and my teeth began to come loose, but they wouldn't pull them because they were concerned the gums wouldn't heal. If I would go into an oxygen cylinder for several hours a day they would heal. But I couldn't. For this I received a bill of $75,000."

Ruth Grobstein, the gentle physician who saw him through those months, had a clearer frame of reference, and after she saw the book she astonished Ted. "Do you realize," she asked, "what you've done in that drawing where the patient is lying on a bed of nails? Those were the needles going from below your jaw through your tongue. And the person watching through the glass? We had to take you into a simulator to determine the dosage of iridium, and the doctors stood behind leaded glass. In your head you were lying on a bed of nails while the doctors stared!"

Everyone around Random House agreed that *You're Only Old Once!* was not a children's book and should be handled by the adult division. Ted argued that his cartoon style and verse made it a Dr. Seuss book, whatever its subject. He pointed out that his story moves, however fleetingly, from the Golden Years Clinic to the mythical land of Fotta-fa-Zee, inhabited by Seussian creatures. Because of his proven expertise in Seussian affairs, Ted exercised powers at Random House that are rare in publishing. He wrote and drew, designed, laid out, chose colors and papers, approved or rejected cover designs, and could veto advertising and promotion copy. This time he used his clout to hold out for his juvenile team, particularly the art director Cathy Goldsmith and editor Janet

Schulman. Only then did he compromise to allow the adult trade book department to market his book.

Random House was in a quandary about the book's audience. Many factors blurred the matter, and there had even been a brief challenge about the title: Jed Mattes recalled that a newly arrived executive thought it was "a turn-off" and said, "No one wants to think about being old." Mattes mused, "Well, that's the beginning and end of a relationship." The title stood. The subtitle called it *A Book for Obsolete Children*. The Book-of-the-Month Club announced it as a book for "ages 95 and down." It was dedicated to Ted's Dartmouth mates in the Class of 1925, about two hundred of whom were living. In the margins of an early draft, Ted subtracted 1937 from 1986 to confirm that it had been forty-nine years since *Mulberry Street* had been published. He was seeking to rationalize an adult Dr. Seuss audience for a book about aging: "The kids I first wrote for . . . are not old poops yet but they have their feet in the door." He guessed that by this point in his career one fourth of his readers were adults. Ted managed to make the book funny, partly because Audrey persuaded him to delete sequences about health matters that, as Ted conceded, "are not funny, no matter how much you disguise it."

The writing was a classic example of Ted's fill-in-the-blanks technique in constructing verse. On his studio wall he tacked up drawings in nearly random order and sought to connect them, seeing how they might fit. He explained that he was "not a consecutive writer." Among work sheets for *You're Only Old Once!* is this uncompleted opening stanza:

> I remember hearing my grandfather speak of a (blank)
>   that is old at the end of one week
> And a Nutchworm that's old at the end of an hour
> And after three minutes a (something) feels sour
> (BLANK BLANK something) . . . reckoned
> There were germs who get ancient in only one second.

The book, Ted's forty-fifth, was to be published on his eighty-second birthday, March 2, 1986, and he attended a launch party at the New York Public Library. On the next day he went to a shopping mall in Yonkers to sign books. "I don't mind autograph parties," he admitted. "A person who wants an autograph is obviously an enthusiast. . . . You get very few insults. It bucks one up." This time he was bucked up by his old friend Elma Otto, now retired from Beginner Books, who saw an advertisement welcoming Dr. Seuss to Caldor department store, and drove over. But when she arrived, she saw that the waiting lines for Dr. Seuss snaked out into the parking area. "I thought if I tried to break through I'd get belted," she recalled. "I just wanted to wave, so I stood on the outskirts, but he got up from the table and called, 'I think I see an Elma!' and . . . ushered [me] in."

In the often rigid world of book publishing, *You're Only Old Once!* defied the most basic categorization. It baffled critics; most notices were either cautiously polite or reticent, and some reviewed the author rather than his book. *The New York Times Book Review* inquired about his health at eighty-two: "I still climb Mount Everest just as often as I used to. I play polo just as often as I used to. But to walk down to the hardware store I find a little bit more difficult." For other critics the book was a "charming guide through a daunting maze of geriatric medicine which Geisel knows well" or "it has forced him to remain healthy after a decade of ailments because, he says with a twinkle, 'I can't go back to doctors after what I did to them in the book.' " With trepidation, Ted autographed one of his ten advance copies to Ruth Grobstein; he had promised her there would be no women doctors in it, and there weren't. He signed another for Dr. Charles Edwards, the president of Scripps Clinic, and was relieved when Edwards responded that the book "may even result in heightened sensitivity."

It quickly became clear that parents and grandparents across America were reading this newest Dr. Seuss book to children at bedtime, but who was enjoying it more? The book became a popular gift for older Americans. The novelist Irving Wallace, an alumnus of Ted's World War II film unit, mailed the copy he received for his seventieth birthday to "my superior officer" for autographing. *The New York Times* placed its review by cartoonist Edward Sorel under the category entitled "Mind / Body / Health." Sorel found "something amiss in the blithe assumption that the sort of rhymes which delight a 4-year-old (or an adult reading to

a 4-year-old) will still entertain when read alone through bifo-
cals. . . . Is [this book] really suitable to place in the hands of a
sensitive adult?"

But the Dr. Seuss bandwagon rolled on, and the first printing
of two hundred thousand copies sold out promptly. *The New York
Times* reported it on its adult nonfiction list, where it climbed to
first place. In some publications it appeared on fiction lists. After
five months and six hundred thousand copies, it was in its ninth
printing, and within a year a million copies had sold.

Satisfied that he had skewered the medical profession, Ted began
to work on a book about lawyers. As he wrote and drew, he grew
"angrier and angrier" and finally abandoned the book. "I hate
lawyers," he said. "I found I was being mean. I knew that wouldn't
work." No trace of that book remains, but there are fragments of
another abortive undertaking, a Dr. Seuss book about religion in
which the unheroic central figure was one Archbishop Katz, a
relative of the Cat in the Hat.

When the Geisels' closest neighbor, Bert Hupp, died in 1980, his
eucalyptus-shaded Spanish house across their driveway had been
acquired by Ingrid and Joe Hibben. He was a tall, sandy-haired
investment banker from Chicago; like Audrey, Ingrid was a
younger, later wife. The son of an artist and art teacher, Joe was
intrigued with his new neighbor. He and Ted began to chat beside
their mailboxes, to share tips on pruning camellias and to debate,
each pickup day, who had the more interesting trash.

As a trustee of the La Jolla Museum of Contemporary Art,
Hibben asked Ted's permission to propose a retrospective Dr. Seuss
exhibition. Ted protested that there was not enough material, but
by then Joe knew what was on the Tower walls, in his studio files
and in the archives at the University of California at Los Angeles.
When Hibben failed to rouse interest in a Dr. Seuss show at the
La Jolla gallery at that time, he talked to the director of the San
Diego Museum of Art, Steven Brezzo, who had grown up with
Ted's books and had previously mounted an exhibition of Muppets
art. Brezzo was eager. In November 1985 Hibben, who now was
treasurer of the San Diego Museum, phoned Brezzo to say, "It's
time." He feared that Ted's health was failing rapidly, and he

knew that his friend was still hungry for recognition as an artist of significance.

The museum staff adopted an accelerated schedule for a Dr. Seuss exhibition to open in just over six months. An executive memo warned, "He is ill. . . . So all guns ahead." But the short lead time worked against placing the exhibition at favored galleries in other cities. Mary Stofflet, the curator, inventoried the collection at UCLA and manuscripts and drawings from Dr. Seuss books of the past eighteen years at the Tower.

Ted remained on guard. He wanted the show to trace a single Dr. Seuss book through all its phases, but he was also eager to include his paintings. Brezzo proposed a maximum of three paintings and Ted asked for more; the final count was three watercolors, three oils and two ink-and-crayon drawings. Editing the text for the catalog, Ted deleted references to his early design of children's furniture for Sears Roebuck and his franchise collaborations with Revell and Coleco. He struck out mention of his abortive negotiations for a Broadway musical based on *The Seven Lady Godivas*, and of a fund-raising evening when he had "taken the stage with Barbara Walters, Walter Cronkite and the Rockettes" at Radio City Music Hall for an Actors' Fund benefit. (He had announced that he was not the senior honoree; Linus Pauling was three years older.) During planning sessions, Brezzo saw Ted as "either Peck's bad boy or demandingly serious. He was concerned [the show] would become a Disneyesque celebration of fluff and frivolity. You could see his jaw set when we started making selections. He knew this would be his retrospective, and like any artist, he dreaded what it might say about his life."

On the morning before the exhibition opened on May 17, 1986, Ted spent an hour walking slowly through the gallery with Mary Stofflet, who recalled, "It seemed overwhelming for him. Seeing your own retrospective can be a shock. I've been involved in several when the artists died within months. Both of us were finally in tears, [but] he was very pleased."

A twenty-two-foot plywood Cat beckoned from above the roofline of the gallery in Balboa Park. "They'd tried everything for years to keep pigeons off their roof," Ted exulted. "Rubber snakes, owls, spikes, chemicals . . . The first thing that worked was the Cat in the Hat!" It was so prominent a sight on the Lindbergh Field landing approach that airline pilots pointed it out that summer to their passengers.

Inside the gallery viewers were led along by engaging graphics, banners and Seussian arches. There were two hundred and fifty-two drawings, illustrations, manuscript pages, paintings and proofs, ranging from *Jack-O-Lantern* to *You're Only Old Once!* and representing most of his books and animations. There were Flit ads and *PM* cartoons; even Ted's double failure, the twice-published and twice-remaindered *Godivas*, was included with a watercolor of Lulu Godiva.

But the exhibition did not achieve what Ted had hoped for: a critical consensus that he was an artist. In *The San Diego Union* the critic Robert Pincus lambasted the museum: "This is simply not an art exhibition; it is a survey of a figure who achieved great things in illustration and children's verse. . . . The chief function of an art museum is to show art." On the morning the review appeared, Brezzo called Ted, and there was silence on the phone, "a pause that if you were writing a film script, you'd play to it. This was his hometown. He was hurt."

But the public loved the show; almost a quarter of a million visitors saw it during its ten-week stay in San Diego, setting gallery records. A hardbound 96-page catalog, its text by Mary Stofflet, sold well, but not nearly so well as the Dr. Seuss books that were stacked anew each day in the museum shop. For Ted that catalog— *Dr. Seuss from Then to Now*—was blessedly free of the cuteness prevalent in much that had been written about him; it was thorough and took him seriously as an artist. Brezzo, who called Ted "the poet laureate of baby boomers," found him "starved for somebody . . . who understood what he was trying to do [as an artist] and did not see him solely as a children's author, a Disney or a Jim Henson, the children's entrepreneurs with whom he was being compared."

The producers of CBS's *60 Minutes* regarded the exhibition as a timely peg and proposed a fifteen-minute interview with Dr. Seuss. Morley Safer stood by with cameramen. Then a producer sent word that they would question him about hard times as well as good ones. "But life has not always been kind to you, has it?"

the question might go, and Helen's death was mentioned. Ted refused to make this a topic of a television chat and broke off negotiations.

The exhibition had been scheduled to move to the Carnegie Museum of Art in Pittsburgh and then to the New York Public Library, Baltimore Museum of Art and New Orleans Museum of Art. The New York showing was the one that Ted wanted most. But when he learned that an exhibition of medieval manuscripts was scheduled for the main library gallery, and that he would be relegated to the third-floor corridor, Ted, bitterly disappointed, canceled. (The show eventually reached New York, opening at Queens Museum on November 20, 1988.) Still, the exhibition traveled, and the Geisels along with it. Helen Copley, the San Diego newspaper publisher and one of the exhibition patrons, persuaded Ted and Brezzo to arrange a showing in the Carnegie Library in the town of her birth, Cedar Rapids, Iowa. They flew from San Diego in a private jet, and as the pilot maneuvered to evade a thunderstorm over Iowa, he told passengers he had decided against landing at Cedar Rapids.

Clearly perturbed, Ted asked, "Where will we land?"

"Waterloo," the pilot said, and Ted filed that exchange away for dinner-table banter with other nervous flyers.

A smaller Dr. Seuss exhibition had been assembled in Springfield, Massachusetts, as the city approached its three hundred fiftieth anniversary. It opened at the George Walter Vincent Smith Art Museum with sketches and drawings from fourteen books, including *Mulberry Street*, a namesake favorite with the locals. Springfield schools conducted a three-month program in reading and creative writing called "Seussamania," and Ted promised to appear. In May, after a large tented dinner launching his exhibition at the San Diego Museum of Art, Audrey and Ted flew to Connecticut, and at the University of Hartford, along with actress Julie Harris, he received another honorary degree. He delivered the ninety-seconds-long "popover" speech he had first given at Lake Forest College, and received the standing ovation that had become a recurring collegiate salute. Then the Geisels went on to Springfield for the first time since his father's death almost twenty years earlier. He and Audrey walked along Mulberry Street and at twilight Mayor Richard E. Neal led a tour through Ted's father's park.

The mayor presented a memento: a weathered iron sign, GEISEL GROVE, which children had found high in a tree near the Forest Park picnic grove frequented by the family in Ted's youth and named in his father's honor.

At Ted's insistence, there were no scheduled interviews or autographing during the Springfield tribute. They toured in a half-century-old bus as the mayor described changes in the city. On Mulberry Street, two hundred school pupils, gathered with teachers and parents, roared their welcome as he stepped from the bus: "We love you, Doctor Seuss!" AND TO THINK, their banner read, THAT I SAW HIM ON MULBERRY STREET! Ted walked among the children, squeezing small hands that clutched at him. As he stepped back aboard the bus, they chanted lines from *Green Eggs and Ham*. His voice breaking, Ted wiped away tears.

As a sudden rainstorm ended, the procession paused outside Sumner Avenue School, which Ted had attended; hundreds of children, wearing Cat and Cubbins hats, seemed to regard him, a reporter wrote, as a "trusted friend and fellow playmate." Welcome signs lined the dogleg street where he had lived for twenty-two years, and at 74 Fairfield Street, the current owner, Ronald Senez, an Army National Guard officer, led a tour. "Behind that wallpaper," Ted told Audrey in his old bedroom, "you will find holes I gouged in the plaster with a pencil." In his sister's room he showed five-year-old Arnold Senez where he had drawn a mural of "crazy animals" on the wall between wallpaperings. Nancy Senez, the boys' mother, returned home from jury duty to find reporters from Boston and New York following the Geisels through her home. "Dr. Seuss is in my house," she called out to an inquiring neighbor. "I'm glad I made the beds!"

Ted paused in New York for dinner with Bennett Cerf's old partner, Donald Klopfer, flew to New Orleans to promote *You're Only Old Once!* at the ABA convention and returned to La Jolla exhausted. Once again he was at the top of best-seller lists. He spent hours each day reading fan letters forwarded from Random House; they reassured and amused him. They reached out with sentiment or sometimes unintentional humor, and he scrawled replies on his Cat in the Hat notepaper. Sometimes he printed longer replies for Claudia Prescott to type.

A Nevada woman wrote about reading *You're Only Old Once!*

as she sat beside her husband's hospital bed waiting for him to awake after chemotherapy. When he did, she read the book aloud, "acted it out and showed him the pictures, and he chuckled and I knew I owed you a debt." It was "one of the most beautiful letters" Ted had ever received, he wrote her, and promised to drink to her each March second, a birth date they shared.

His favorite letters whetted his sense of the ridiculous. He had once been so delighted by a sixty-foot-long scroll of fan letters from pupils in the Ninety-third Street School in Niagara Falls, New York, that he took it to the lobby of La Valencia Hotel to unfurl it. He was amused by adults who sent along photographs of themselves. In Ohio, two Dr. Seuss fans, engaged to be married, asked him to write their wedding vows with the promise that if he did they would name their firstborn for him. He declined but could not resist a scrawled effort for his own amusement: "I vow, you vow, he vows, she vows, WOW!"

Autograph seekers were common, and thousands sought permission to use his words or characters in everything from school yearbooks to national campaigns against abortion and disarmament. Most were rejected for reasons of copyright or common sense. Those who asked for nothing were more likely to hear from Ted. When eight-year-old Gregg Lewis sent along a copy of his published review of *You're Only Old Once!*, Ted replied, "Of all the reviews my books have received . . . from the *N.Y. Times* to the *Tokyo Shimbun* . . . your review in *Kidsday* was the one my cat and I liked best."

As he grew older the age span of Ted's fans grew too, and their letters were often introspective and familial. They talked of being members of "the Seuss generation" and usually noted that they had never written a fan letter before. He saved the letter from Susanna Styron, who wrote seeking an autograph for her baby daughter. "The most memorable event of my life, perhaps, was the night when I was five years old that you came to my house. Bennett Cerf brought you to have dinner with my parents, Rose and Bill Styron. I sat on your lap and you signed my tattered copy of *One Fish/ Two Fish/ Red Fish/ Blue Fish* and drew a fish with an extra eyelash. I thought I had died and gone to heaven."

Thousands of classroom projects included letters to Dr. Seuss, especially around his birthday. The children of Creative Ways Day School in Collinsville, Connecticut, mailed a list of questions about the Cat, reporting that after their classroom reading of *The Cat in the Hat Comes Back,* they found "mysterious pink spots all over our play yard." Ted replied:

> The Cat in the Hat sometimes lives in Agawam, Massachusetts. But not very often. He eats Brie Cheese whenever he can get it. He buys his shoes at a Florist Shop in West Hartford, Ct. He does have a very fine brain. But he keeps it home in his next-to-top left Bureau Drawer. He did NOT leave the Pink Spots all over your playground. The Grinch did THAT.

There were sophisticates among his fans. Dr. William O. Baker, a retired chairman of Bell Laboratories, sought out Ted to say that his books had been computer-tested with other print media and proved uniquely effective in conveying information. "This confirms Shannon's Law," Baker told Ted, "which holds that we absorb information in inverse ratio to its credibility."

At summer's end in 1986 the Geisels attended a charity gala at a new Neiman-Marcus store in San Diego. Bobby Short was at the piano, and a scavenger hunt for merchandise prizes sent guests stampeding throughout the store. Audrey was among the canny few who wore tennis shoes to the party, intending to move quickly and win prizes. Ted was not in a party mood and soon disappeared. Friends finally found him in the women's shoe department, happily changing prices on every box of Ferragamos and Bruno Maglis in sight. On the ride home, he made a pact with himself: it was the last big party he would attend. In his studio he composed "A Poem of Protest" entitled "Ah, Social Whirl!":

> Oh, to live in San Diego
> and be happy evermore
> and attend the nightly opening
> of some brand-new Dry Goods Store!

In November Ted made an exception and flew to New York, where Dr. Seuss was among twenty-one writers saluted at the New York Public Library's sixth Literary Lions dinner. Because of the cachet of its honorees, including Alistair Cooke, Joyce Carol Oates and Nora Ephron, the evening yielded the library a quarter of a million dollars. Ted was jaunty in black tie, wearing his Cat in the Hat cuff links, the account in *W* noted, quoting him as assuring Dick Salomon of Salomon Brothers that "nobody's older than me."

Jackie Onassis stood nearby, and on a nudge from Audrey, Ted turned and introduced himself.

"Oh, Dr. Seuss," Jackie said in her hushed voice. "There's a question I've always wanted to ask you."

Ted looked at her in dismay, for he had heard what was to follow far too many times.

"Tell me," Jackie said, "where do you get your ideas?"

"Über Gletch," Ted replied.

CHAPTER 21

Oh, the Places You'll Go!

1987–1991

Ted had not been seen in public for months. He had sworn off social life but insisted that Audrey keep hers, and when a new La Jolla restaurant opened one wintry night, with yet another charitable gala, she attended with friends. Jed Mattes had flown in from New York and persuaded Ted to go down the mountain for dinner at La Valencia.

"I'm happy I can give you an excuse not to go to a big bash," Jed said.

"I don't need excuses anymore," Ted said. "As far as this town is concerned, I'm already dead." With a malevolent smile he handed Mattes a scrawled verse he had entitled "I Am Prepared."

> When I cross the Bar of the Great Blue Beyonder
> I know that my Maker, without pause or ponder,
> Will welcome my soul. For my record is scar-less
> I've eaten no oysters in months that are R-less.

When Mattes chided him for its morbid theme, Ted chortled; he had written it half a century earlier.

Ted had known La Valencia through all of those years, and enjoyed thinking that it was unchanged. From curbside to dinner table was only a few level strides; this was important because, while Ruth Grobstein and her doctors held his cancer at bay, his latest malady was gout. His hearing was failing too, but once among the hotel's cushioned booths he could understand normal conversation and turn off the hearing aid that so annoyed him. His Christmas card to Audrey that year had been a cartoon in which the Cat wore a hearing aid. "Damn it all, Audrey!" the Cat says, "of course I heard you! You said, 'Nerry Jistmas.' And so do I."

Despite his virtual seclusion, the world still pursued Dr. Seuss. Early in the 1986 Christmas season he had declined when his newspaper friend Herb Klein asked him to serve as honorary chairman of that season's Holiday Bowl football game in San Diego, but half an hour later he called back. "Audrey tells me I should do this," he said. He wore a red jacket, smiled through the parade and sat in the official box for the game. At a reception, Klein observed that the players, who usually gathered around other players and coaches, thronged around Dr. Seuss.

Ted's mood of retrospection had much to feed on. In April a *Publishers Weekly* headline read "Look Who Just Turned 30!" and there, all by himself on the cover, was the Cat in the Hat. After Ted's retrospective closed in Pittsburgh that month, the Geisels flew to Dallas for its opening at the Ling Temco Vought Center Pavilion. They were met by Ted's old friend Cecil Green, who stayed busy in his eighties by parceling out the fortune he had acquired as a founder of Texas Instruments. Ted had serious conversations with him about philanthropy, for Green and his wife, Ida, were endowing educational institutions in Australia and Canada and at Oxford, where a science-oriented college bore their name. "I've never met anyone who gives his money away more wisely," Ted said. Together they visited the exhibition, which was drawing large crowds in each city it toured and receiving more respectful press notices than it had in his hometown.

At Brown University in May, Ted received his eighth honorary degree and talked intently with two other honorees: producer Joan Ganz Cooney from *Sesame Street* and an entertainer whose name was new to him, Stevie Wonder, who stood on a campus porch and sang "I Just Called to Say I Love You." Ted liked his sound and talked about him on the flight home.

But for Ted it was a summer of agony. He rarely spoke of it, t Audrey and Ruth Grobstein saw that he was in pain. He was acutely embarrassed by his slurring speech. The ulcer under his tongue had healed, but after root canal surgery he developed mandibular osteonecrosis, leading to multiple infections and the erosion of his right jawbone. He resisted further surgery and doctors agreed on a "conservative approach." He had seen more doctors than he wanted and gained a reputation as a difficult patient. When he sought to see a senior cardiologist at Scripps Clinic, a nurse insisted that the doctor was away. Audrey was skeptical; nosing about, she intercepted the unfortunate man as he was slipping out the rear door of his office. It was a scene Ted might have included in *You're Only Old Once!*, and thereafter Dr. Grobstein assumed oversight of Ted's medical care, choosing his doctors and consulting on procedures.

Ted's earliest book, *Mulberry Street*, turned fifty in September, and Random House was negotiating with Vanguard Press to buy the rights to both this book and *The 500 Hats*. These early titles were selling faster than ever before, and Ted and Bob Bernstein were eager to unify the Dr. Seuss library. Ted was elated when Random House acquired the books in 1988 by buying out Vanguard entirely. He could finally get the "funereal black" off the cover of *The 500 Hats*, which Vanguard had put there fifty years earlier when its editors considered it "a mystery book." Soon both books appeared under the Random imprint, along with *I Am Not Going to Get Up Today!*, Ted's first Beginner Book in eight years. He had the time but not the energy to do the drawings, so the artist James Stevenson shared cover credits with Dr. Seuss.

In all the years since *Mulberry Street* Ted had made remarkably few revisions in ongoing editions of his books. Sometimes his stubbornness was involved. Janet Schulman told him that the time had come to delete the reference to Spam in *The Tooth Book*: "No teeth at all, / says Pam the clam. / "I cannot eat / roast leg of lamb. / Or peanuts! Pizzas! / Popcorn! SPAM! . . ."" "It's such a World War II word," Janet argued, "that kids today don't have a clue!"

Ted conceded the point, but after working on the rhyme for several days he called her and said, "Nothing else works."

"I knew you were going to say that," Janet said, and the presses rolled again with Spam intact.

The revisions that Ted considered most significant involved *Mulberry Street*. "I had a gentleman with a pigtail," he said. "I colored him yellow and called him a Chinaman. That's the way things were fifty years ago. In later editions I refer to him as a Chinese man. I have taken the color out of the gentleman and removed the pigtail and now he looks like an Irishman." Despite protests from feminists, Ted refused to change the line in *Mulberry Street*: "Even Jane could think of *that*." "It remains in my book," he explained, "because that's what the boy said."

His only other text change was in *The Lorax*. It had appeared in 1971 with a line about pollution that read, "I hear things are just as bad up in Lake Erie." Two research associates from the Ohio Sea Grant Program wrote him fourteen years later about the cleanup of Lake Erie: "Improved conditions exist [in water quality] . . . we wonder if you would consider changing that line to past tense in future editions."

Ted agreed, but replied, "Unfortunately, the purification of texts, like that of lakes, cannot be accomplished overnight. . . . the objectionable line will be removed from future editions." Normally that would have involved tedious revamping of rhythm and rhyme, but this time the change involved only the final line of a four-line rhyme (dreary, weary, smeary, and Erie) and he simply deleted it.

He had accumulated a small file of other requested changes, mostly trivial. After *The Grinch* appeared on television, two brothers, David and Bob Grinch, wrote from Ridgewood, New Jersey, to say they were tired of being the bad guys and wanted him to change the name of the Grinch. "I disagree with your friends who 'harass' you," Ted wrote. "Can't they understand that the Grinch in my story is the Hero of Christmas? Sure . . . he starts out as a villain, but it's not how you start out that counts. It's what you are at the finish." Ted sent the brothers' letter to Chuck Jones, who had produced *The Grinch* for television, writing that he could "visualize these poor kids being chased home from school, being clobbered . . . with brickbats in the same way I was when I was a kid with a German father. When they clobbered me, they yelled, 'Kill the Kaiser!' "

Such correspondence brightened his days. A San Francisco plastic surgeon who spelled his name Suess wrote Ted that he frequently received calls from children complimenting him on his books; in response Ted sent the doctor a rhyme: "Poems are made at Seuss's place / But only Suess can make a face!" When Christopher Sickels, a hilltop neighbor and book collector, was suffering real estate reversals, Ted presented him with a cartoon of a curved tool with a drooping blade he called the Hammered Sickels.

Wondering about his literary legacy, Ted began poring through his books. He had withdrawn the only book he disliked, *I Can Write!*, signed by Theo. LeSieg. Although *Mulberry Street* had been dissected by critics for decades, Ted was amazed at an interviewer's inquiry if Goethe's poem of father and son, "The Erl-King" (also written in anapestic tetrameter), had influenced the dialogue of Marco and his father. Ted mumbled Goethe's opening lines in German (he had memorized them in high school) and said, "It could tie up, though I never thought of it before."

Too ill in December to travel, Ted canceled a planned appearance as his retrospective opened in Baltimore, but two months later he was fit enough to go to the New Orleans opening as the plywood Cat from San Diego towered over Canal Street during Mardi Gras. Ted read and rested by day in his suite at the Windsor Court Hotel and appeared at dusk, regal in dress shirt and black tie, for parties at which he was widely celebrated. On the evening he enjoyed most, a driver took the Geisels to a buffet dinner at the wrong pillared mansion, and they were welcomed amid such conviviality that it was long into the evening before anyone discovered the mistake.

As his books became more topical, unaccustomed controversies swirled around Dr. Seuss. Despite his gentle tone, his concerns had moved him beyond the popular fabulist who created *Green Eggs and Ham*. His words were being adapted, and often misappropriated, by board chairmen, ministers, presidents and propagandists. Calculated distortions of his meanings were not new, but he was outraged when antiabortionists adopted as a battle cry the plaintive assertion of his elephant Horton: "A person's a person, no matter how small." This usage was abruptly ended with the threat of legal action.

After the Vietnam war the energy of the antiwar movement

gravitated to ecology, and sales of *The Lorax* surged. The book was invoked without apology on behalf of the Brazilian rain forests, the spotted owl, population limits, smog control and countless commercial ventures. In 1989 it became the center of a book-banning controversy in California redwood country at the logging town of Laytonville, 150 miles north of San Francisco. An eight-year-old Dr. Seuss fan came home from school and said to his mother, "Papa doesn't love trees anymore, does he?" Papa sold logging equipment, and a campaign began to remove *The Lorax* from the second-grade reading list. This stirred a national media frenzy and ended in cheers after the school-board president closed a public debate with the cry "We are insulting our children. Who do we think we are kidding?" *The Lorax* remained on the shelves.

"*The Lorax* doesn't say lumbering is immoral," Ted insisted. "I live in a house made of wood and write books printed on paper. It's a book about going easy on what we've got. It's antipollution and antigreed."

Although he declined most requests from academicians for interviews, copies of theses on Ted's works accumulated in a deep desk drawer. Like George Bernard Shaw, he had lived long enough to make sport of critics and scholars who probed his words for hidden meaning. But one who won his admiration was Terry Cronan, a young psychology professor at San Diego State University, who wrote him about her Project Primer, a literacy program in which student tutors, most of them black or Hispanic, visited low-income families to read books to preschool children. When Ted telephoned her, he learned that she was using thirty-three of his books, which she favored "for their rhythms and repetitions and because the characters are asexual and free of ethnicity." In each home the tutors fashioned a bookcase from a cardboard carton, leaving Dr. Seuss books behind, sometimes as the family's only books. Project Primer went to the roots of Ted's fervor for literacy. "Teaching a child to read is a family matter," he said. "Books should be stacked around. Pretty soon most kids will get curious and want to read them." He felt that "hippies helped alert the world" about environmental decay, but "they won't bail us out of illiteracy.

is turning into a third-rate nation because we can't read."

pped hundreds of books to Project Primer and telephoned

Cronan regularly. "It amazed all of us," she said, "this wealthy, famous man! . . . Gee, I loved *Green Eggs and Ham.*"

Ted's jaw was not healing, and doctors tried to control raging infections with heavy doses of antibiotics. He was urged to inspect a new and larger hyperbaric oxygen chamber that he might be able to endure despite his claustrophobia. At University Medical Center in San Diego, Audrey walked with him into a chamber that could seat eight people. With the door ajar, the doctor explained the benefits of oxygenation of the blood, and described the otherwise inevitable bone death. Hypnosis and sedation were available. Ted seemed calm as the doctor cautiously closed the door and finished his presentation, and Audrey began to think that reason had prevailed. Then he rose, thanked the doctor graciously and strode away. As Audrey caught up, he blurted, "Can you believe he really thinks I'm going to sit in that contraption?" She made one last plea. "All you're offering me is logic," he said plaintively, and she never tried again.

Ted knew his options were diminishing but insisted, "If I can stay out of the hospital I might live forever." He gulped down pain pills and went grimly to work on a story about a boy trying to sell a square blue balloon, an allegory about swindlers that never quite took shape and was abandoned. He gathered his favorite unpublished sketches and images and pinned them to his studio walls. His namesake, Ted Owens, now an art graduate, visited him during these weeks and was astonished when his uncle consulted him as a colleague. "I've got an idea here," Ted said, pointing to one sketch, "and an idea here, but I have no idea in the world how to make them connect." Yet soon these sketches began to evolve into the most powerful graphic work he had done in many years. The only message his books had in common, he had said, was hope, and this was the theme of *Oh, the Places You'll Go!* With almost primordial simplicity, he wrote in the voice of a wise uncle about human frailty, fear and failure.

At the age of eighty-five, Ted still sat in his studio from 10:00 A.M. until 6:00 P.M. He told his nephew, "You have to put in your hours, and finally you make it work." He did just that, eventually completing richly detailed pen-and-ink drawings. "He kept asking me," young Ted recalled, "if I thought the little boy looked the same throughout the book. He worried whether the front view matched the back, or the distant view resembled the close-up." The nephew, trained in the computer age, proposed a foolproof solution: Draw the boy large and reduce him by photocopier to whatever size was needed. Ted nodded gratefully, but when asked later what he had decided to do, he shrugged and said, "Nothing."

There was never any doubt that Ted considered *Oh, the Places You'll Go!* his farewell salute, his last parade, *Mulberry Street* gone worldwide. He inserted deliberate elements of reprise. Smug little Hortons hoisted banners like the pep squad of *Butter Battle* girls. A jumble of skeptical birds marched in opposing ranks on one another's heads, a drawing that had appeared in *The New York Times* with a Dr. Seuss verse called "The Economic Situation Clarified." He called back some of his fanciful castles, mazes, surreal wickets and clanking contraptions that move mountains. As he wrote and rewrote, new Seussian words appeared, like "prickle-ly," "winning-est," and "mind-maker-upper." His description of "a most useless place . . . The Waiting Place . . . for people just waiting . . ." appeared intact in the first draft; he had composed it previously, probably as a song lyric, and set it aside.

> Waiting for the fish to bite
> or waiting for wind to fly a kite
> or waiting around for Friday night
> or waiting, perhaps, for their Uncle Jake
> or a pot to boil, or a Better Break
> or a string of pearls, or a pair of pants
> or a wig with curls, or Another Chance . . .

Once again he was his own toughest editor. In an early draft, *Oh, the Places You'll Go!* ended with the lines "You're off to the races. / So . . . *get on your way!*" By the final draft the lines bore a more sober imperative: "Your mountain is waiting. / So . . . *get on your way!*"

Claudia Prescott typed the entire text on ten pages of white bond paper. Ted had rarely discussed the book-writing process with her, but as this one evolved he took time to explain it in detail. It made her sad, as if "he was schooling me [in] how important color was, for example." He knew it was his last book, she believed, but he never said so.

Everyone at Random House considered Ted too ill by June of 1989 to bring the book to New York for the usual exultant reading, and they expected him to ship it by overnight air. But Ted asked if Cathy Goldsmith might be spared to come out and work with him on the final layouts. She leaped at the opportunity and Audrey urged her to stay in their guest bedroom so she would be near when he had the strength to work, and he could rest at will. She was stunned to find Ted so frail and thin, and yet with his merry eyes and erect posture seeming still so youthful. He worked on the book four or five hours at a time, pausing only to push his glasses up on his forehead and cross the room, hands wedged in his back pockets. "We kept looking at colors until even my eyes hurt," Cathy said. She recognized two of Ted's hoarded illustrations as having been on his studio wall in an *Architectural Digest* photograph published six years earlier: one was of a kind of Turkish mosque suggesting the underside of a herd of elephants, the other an avenue of skyhooks that led to the Waiting Place.

Audrey interrupted the work occasionally to coax Ted out for walks in the garden, where one afternoon he showed Cathy his prized dwarf lime tree, on which grew "the tiniest and most perfect fruit" she'd ever seen.

When they finished the book, he placed his drawings in a twenty- by twenty-four-inch film box and handed it to Cathy. She turned away, tears in her eyes, thinking of their first meeting. "If you don't call me Ted," he had said, "I'm going to call you 'Little You.'" As she boarded the jet for New York, an attendant reached to take the box. "Oh, no, you don't," Cathy said. She planned to buy another ticket if necessary to keep that box at her side.

Within days Cathy received a package from Ted containing a small jewel box. She stared at it, thinking that whatever his gift might be, she should send it back. Then she opened the box and burst out laughing. Inside was a single tiny lime from his tree with a note saying that she had been elected vice president and was entitled to one third of its annual produce, with the other two thirds going to Ted and the Cat in the Hat.

Something was terribly wrong with Audrey. Her chirpy verve was gone, and with it the smile that brightened Ted's day and distracted him from pain. "Audrey," Ted kept saying that summer, "what's the matter? It's me, isn't it? I've been too much trouble, haven't I?" She couldn't answer; it wasn't Ted, but she really didn't know.

"She's mad at me about something," Ted told Janet Schulman. "I can't find out what."

Audrey didn't tell Ted, but she had tried to diagnose her malady. Dismissing the thought of a brain tumor because she felt no dizziness or imbalance, she asked her doctor for antidepressants. She took them and felt worse, often suicidal. Each day was a black tunnel, and it became harder to get up, to jog, to care for Ted, to go out with friends. They were looking at her strangely, and she knew that nothing she said made sense. When she realized she was forgetting the simplest things, she decided she had all the symptoms of Alzheimer's, and set a goal of living on for just two more weeks.

In August the Geisels met close friends for dinner at La Valencia. Audrey was downcast and silent, dabbled with her food and seemed hardly there. Striving to communicate with her, her dinner partner asked if she was depressed. She looked at him gratefully, and Ted listened, amazed, as they talked about the symptoms of depression.

"Why didn't you tell me, Audrey?" he asked.

"I don't know," she said, feeling she should not worry him. "I don't know anything."

Audrey slept a lot that fall and tried new medications. Her daughters conferred and Ted urged more consultations. Finally taking Prozac, she decided she could hang on for four weeks instead of two. Her doctor, warning that it was "more than depression," sent her into a great clanging cylinder for magnetic resonance imaging, and her problem became instantly obvious: a large tumor, probably benign, squeezing the brain into three quarters of its normal space. Audrey was surprised but hopeful, for it was something they could get at and settle one way or another. So was Ted;

when he telephoned Jed Mattes with the diagnosis, the agent sensed his relief.

Audrey went into surgery in January, and within hours was telephoning friends in an animated voice they had not heard for months. "It was my time to be totally euphoric. I had been in such total anguish, and now I was better, just like that!"

The next night Leagrey drove Ted to Scripps Clinic. "He had got himself all dressed up with a silk foulard and carried a feather," Audrey recalled. "I had a football helmet of bandages and he stuck the feather into the helmet and said, 'If you don't deserve a feather in your cap today, you never will.'" Each night he brought her a new feather and on that Easter she found in her favorite eggcup an egg on which he had drawn a perky face with yellow hair, and the egg wore a feather. She kept this Seussian oddment on her desk to remind her of her "miracle."

When *Oh, the Places You'll Go!* appeared early in 1990, there was no hint in the reviews that it might be a publishing phenomenon. The jacket copy was cautious, calling it a book "for upstarts of all ages." The *Booklist* reviewer observed that "writers often tend to get mellow in their later years, but fortunately Dr. Seuss seems just as cantankerous and quirky as ever. . . . Life may be a 'Great Balancing Act,' but through it all 'there's fun to be done.'" The Gannett News Service reviewer described the book as "rangy, wise, and wonderfully witty. . . . This may well be a summing up on his part, his farewell with a flourish." A critic for *The New York Times Book Review* committed that riskiest of Seussian offenses, beginning her review with a parody, "How could he, without our consent, / Give up tickles and giggles, unless it's for Lent?" She concluded: "We'll simply sit here and wait for Dr. Seuss to tell us another wondrously silly tale. . . . We can wait."

But the public didn't wait. The book went promptly on *The New York Times* adult best-seller list and remained there for more than two years, during which it sold about 1.5 million copies. For Ted it became a glorious game. Each midweek Random House would call to report the book's coming ranking in the Sunday *Times Book Review*. "This proves it!" Ted exulted. "I no longer write for children. I write for *people!*" He seemed almost oblivious to the fact that this one book had already brought him royalties of more than $3 million.

He signed a contract with Tri-Star Productions for turning *Oh, the Places You'll Go!* into a full-length film feature, his first since the disastrous *5,000 Fingers* almost forty years earlier, and met repeatedly with its producers, Roland Joffee and Ben Myron. As his waning strength allowed, he sketched new characters and wrote new material. One of his song lyrics dealt with his old theme of loneliness:

> Searching deep in darkened places,
> Reaching into vacant spaces,
> I touch only shadow faces . . .
>> Where are you?
> Empty caves in endless mountains,
> Dusty, dry, deserted fountains . . .
> Pathless, groping, I move hoping
>> Where are you?
> Past songless birds on leafless trees
> Cross waveless oceans, silent seas
> Through fumbling nights that find no day,
> I move and try to find my way . . .

Ted was excited and absorbed, for the film was evolving as an omnibus of many Dr. Seuss books and themes; but it was becoming harder for him to work, and production plans began to stall.

Old friends and colleagues called. The Muppets creator Jim Henson scheduled a lunch at the Tower that spring to discuss a video adaptation of *Oh, the Places You'll Go!* for Ted Turner. But two days before their date, Henson died in New York at the age of fifty-three. The brilliant clown Bill Irwin came to the Tower during his engagement at La Jolla Playhouse and sought Ted's permission to pursue the role of the Cat in the Hat for a proposed Disney special. Ted admired Irwin's talent but had no interest in working with Disney. Ted's stepdaughter Lark, now a sculptor, flew in from Hawaii and he impulsively passed on to her a "fan-shaped brush" that an artist had given him years before. He took time to join the public campaign against drug use, drawing a Dr.

Seuss poster for the *San Diego Tribune* of a boy with a hole in his head ("Dope! You need it like you need a hole in the head"); it was widely reprinted for school use and by the United States Navy for posting at naval bases and on shipboard. He was charmed by an invitation from the Children's Theatre Company of Minneapolis to accompany the group to "the Asian premiere" of his *500 Hats* at the Shanghai Children's Theater. Over the protest of his agent, he had granted the theater royalty-free use of the book, a gift that made him "really happy."

In May friends persuaded Ted and Audrey to come to La Valencia for dinner with his old co-conspirator Art Buchwald. Painfully aware of his worsening jaw condition, Ted repeatedly asked if Buchwald could understand him. It had been months since he had felt able to appear at his favorite restaurant, and being there perked him up. Buchwald slipped across Prospect Street to a bookstore, where he scrawled a sign and hung it in the window: DR. SEUSS IS HAVING DINNER ACROSS THE STREET. Soon chefs, waiters and strangers formed a respectful queue, waiting to approach Ted, one or two at a time, with books for autographing. He signed cheerfully, and every Dr. Seuss book in that store in English, Spanish or French was sold.

In his studio Ted was gathering mementos. He browsed over clippings from *Jack-O-Lantern,* thumbed through files from the Flit campaigns, *Judge* and his wartime service in the Capra unit. He lingered over treasured letters and photographs and a sheaf of "Poems While Shaving" that he had written in New York during the Depression. Early in December he brought out many of these papers as reference sources and began the first in a months-long series of interviews with his biographers. "Can you understand what I'm saying?" he asked time after time. He had always been nervous around tape recorders, and was relieved when a laptop computer became the tool of record. "I've been thinking about a computer," he said, in one of his frequent digressions. "Do you think I could learn?" Audrey, passing through the room, smiled and shook her head at this comment "from a man who didn't know how to fix a toilet by jiggling the handle."

One day, looking back, Ted admitted regrets. "I'm a failure in enough things that I would like to go on and make them better.

I would be a more amenable, lovable person than I am now. I probably would like children better than I do now; individually, I can handle them but in mass . . . they terrify me. I would have studied entirely different things in college. I got through without taking any history." But then his wistfulness vanished and he was laughing again at himself and the world. "Do you know they read my books to patients in mental institutions, hmmm? They say it calms them." On another day he was pensive: "I think my stuff has become useful, not just amusing. That's important to me."

Ted brought out an essay written by novelist Alison Lurie in *The New York Review of Books*. She saluted his "inventive energy" and "singular role in revolutionizing the teaching of reading," but then cited him for sexism. His heroes, she wrote, were always small boys or male animals, and "the most memorable female in his entire oeuvre is the despicable Mayzie, the lazy bird who callously traps Horton into sitting on her egg so that she can fly off to Palm Beach." Ted had not responded to Lurie, but pointed out that most of his characters are animals "and if she can identify their sex, I'll remember her in my will."

The equally venerable Clifton Fadiman, Ted's old admirer, helped to arrange a salute through the Book-of-the-Month Club. It was *Six by Seuss: A Treasury of Dr. Seuss Classics*, the main selection of the club in June 1991 and the first juvenile to garner that spot since *Bambi* in 1928. The book included *Mulberry Street* and *The 500 Hats, Horton Hatches the Egg, Yertle the Turtle, How the Grinch Stole Christmas!* and *The Lorax.* Ted chuckled over a letter seeking permission to photograph him for the cover of the book-club bulletin. "I visited Julia Child last year in Santa Barbara," the photographer wrote, "and . . . I think that I can safely speak for her in saying that it was an enjoyable experience for all of us." What the book club didn't understand, Cathy Goldsmith observed, was that they wanted *Six by Seuss* more than Ted wanted them. Eventually the club accepted an earlier photograph of Dr. Seuss provided by Random House.

In late summer his biographers asked if, after all the messages in his books, something remained unsaid. He cocked his head and said, "Let me think about that." Days later he handed over a sheet of yellow copy paper on which he had written:

Any message or slogan? Whenever things go a bit sour in a job I'm doing, I always tell myself, "You can do better than this."

The best slogan I can think of to leave with the kids of the U.S.A. would be: "We can . . . and we've *got* to . . . do better than this."

Then he drew a line through three words, *the kids of.* After books with pleas against the arms race, prejudice, pollution and greed, and after a lifelong war on illiteracy, he was talking to everyone.

Claudia Prescott, who had worked with Ted for eighteen years, noted the day in early September when he decided he would send no more Cat in the Hat notes, and another day when he declined to autograph any more books. He began giving her instructions that she wrote in longhand in a notepad and labeled "Things to Follow Up On." "Claudia," he said, "you are going to stay on, aren't you?"

Ted had no intention of returning to a hospital. Audrey made his studio sofa into a bed and he lay propped up on pillows as she watched over him. He slept more, rousing himself to look up at her with a quizzical smile and ask, "Am I dead yet?" Audrey took the day shift as nurse and brought in a night nurse. His doctor Ruth Grobstein came by each evening and they talked for hours: "He was in denial," she said. "He really believed in magic." Leagrey, thirty-three years old and living nearby, moved in to help, and with a burst of affection Ted gave her Theophrastus, the ragged brown toy dog that he had kept near him since his childhood in Springfield. "You will take care of the dog, won't you?" he said.

On September 23, as Ted talked to Claudia, he faded in and out of consciousness. "Why don't you rest?" she said. "We can do this later."

"Yes," he replied. "I'm not going to die tomorrow."

Audrey sat beside him throughout the next day, but the magic had run out. At about 10:00 P.M. on September 24, 1991, Theodor Seuss Geisel, a wise and incorrigible child of eighty-seven, died in his sleep, a dozen steps away from the drawing board where he had puzzled out so many books. Clutching the toy dog, Leagrey walked slowly away from him for the last time, down the dark Tower passageway into the living room light, a forlorn silhouette with spiky hair, a surrogate for millions of children and parents clinging to their own memories of the world of Dr. Seuss.

Epilogue

When E. J. Kahn, Jr., did his research for a profile on Theodor Seuss Geisel in *The New Yorker* in 1960, he was haunted by a conversation with a seven-year-old Dr. Seuss reader named Tony. "When Dr. Seuss dies," Tony told Kahn, "that's going to be some awful day."

On that day, as Ted had instructed, his body was cremated; there was no funeral service, nor any grave or marker. His death released a rare torrent of unabashed sentiment in the media. Even journalists who seemed steeled against tenderness or praise found their defenses down when it came to this man. He had not sought celebrity or been widely involved in controversy; he was beloved by three generations of children and parents. Dr. Seuss would live on and there was a eulogistic upwelling, a spontaneous homage to the reclusive man who had created a whole world.

Soon after Audrey reported Ted's death to the editor of the *San Diego Tribune* on the morning of September 25, 1991, commemorative pages were published in his native Springfield and in San Diego. Dr. Seuss became front-page news in hundreds of newspapers across America and in cities abroad, from London to Auckland. In *The New York Times*, the headline stretched halfway across page 1 below the fold: DR. SEUSS, MODERN MOTHER GOOSE, DIES AT 87. A photograph of Ted signing books shared space with his drawing of the Cat in the Hat standing on a ball and balancing a goldfish bowl atop an umbrella handle. The *Times* reported that Ted had "entertained and instructed millions of children and adults around the world." The story continued over half of another page, including excerpts from his books. In an editorial, the *Times* noted that "like all great storytellers, Dr. Seuss begged to be heard. His meter and language were irresistible, especially the Seuss-speak he created when English seemed too skimpy for so rich an imagination." He had died "fortunate in his gifts and in his giving."

Time called Ted "one of the last doctors to make house calls—some 200 million of them in 20 languages, [continuing] beyond Dr. Spock to a unique and hallowed place in the nurseries of the world." The columnist Ellen Goodman deplored the "modern Mother Goose" allusion of *The New York Times* headline, arguing instead that "he was a subversive . . . in the way that people who really speak to children often are. They cut through the treacle, the mush and the fear. They side with the young and dismiss the rest of us for what we are, 'obsolete children.' . . . In Dr. Seuss' reading room, it is still possible to laugh and think at the same time." Columnist Anna Quindlen called him a man who "took words and juggled them, twirled them, bounced them off the page. No matter what the story in his books, the message was clear and unwavering: words are fun. . . . He is remembered for the murder of Dick and Jane, which was a mercy killing of the highest order."

Miles Davis, the jazz trumpeter, died four days after Ted, and Canadian newspaper cartoonist Bruce MacKinnon drew the two men meeting on a heavenly cloud. Both had acquired wings. Davis, holding his trumpet, wore his trademark slouch hat, and Ted his trademark bow tie. "So you're Dr. Seuss," Davis said. Ted replied, "So you're the cat in the hat."

Scores of cartoonists paid homage to a man they knew as one of their own. For Paul Conrad, the tough-minded Pulitzer Prize winner, the Grim Reaper became the Grinch who stole Dr. Seuss. At the *Minneapolis Star Tribune*, Steve Sack drew a cat paraphrasing lines from *One Fish Two Fish*, "From there to here, From here to there, *Sad* things are everywhere." Even comic strips mourned: in *Sibling Revelry*, Man Martin's tiny character Stew bemoaned that "Dr. Seuss is gone forever," but was soon convinced, as he settled down to reread *The Cat in the Hat*, that instead "he's here forever."

The Reverend Jesse Jackson gave a reading of *Green Eggs and Ham* on television's *Saturday Night Live*, and Louis Rukeyser paid tribute during *Wall Street Week*. Senator Dale Bumpers of Arkansas rose on the floor of the United States Senate to eulogize Ted as "a great American original." Clifton Fadiman, whose brief mention of *Mulberry Street* in *The New Yorker* fifty-four years earlier had first recognized Ted as a gifted children's author, called him "the most useful children's writer of our time. He has helped dispel a lot of nonsense that children are taught, and he was the first to show that reading can be fun. . . . His books always maintained their universal cry for fairness, wonder and love."

"He's the big papa," a saddened Maurice Sendak told the *San Diego Tribune*. "*Mulberry Street* was revolutionary work. . . . He wrote great big noisy books with noisy pictures and noisy language. . . . He was a bull in a china closet. . . . He appealed to the animalistic nature of children."

When news of Ted's death reached the Dartmouth campus, students and faculty members began a twenty-four-hour vigil, reading Dr. Seuss books outside College Hall. It was the precursor of an ongoing wave of collegiate tributes, with Dr. Seuss fan clubs receiving administrative sanction on many campuses.

Sales of Dr. Seuss books were undiminished by Ted Geisel's death, and *Oh, the Places You'll Go!* made its annual graduation-month return to the best-seller list of *The New York Times Book Review*. Ongoing interest in his work was indicated by the appearance of critiques and television specials. Late in 1994 Turner Network Television repeatedly aired a ninety-minute special called *In Search of Dr. Seuss*. Negotiations were under way for a theme park in Florida and for completion of the feature-length animation of *Oh, the Places You'll Go!*, on which he had worked in the final year of his life. *Daisy-Head Mayzie*, which he had written as a film animation script, became the basis of a television special, and was published by Random House as a posthumous Dr. Seuss book. His paintings, which had been unheralded in his lifetime, were being gathered in book form.

Ted's contributions to the language were cited in two reference books published in 1992: *The Oxford Companion to the English Language* uses fourteen lines from *Fox in Socks* when discussing "compounds in context"; the sixteenth edition of *Bartlett's Familiar Quotations*, edited by Justin Kaplan, includes references from *Horton Hatches the Egg* and *The Cat in the Hat*.

Following Ted's instructions to Karl ZoBell in changes to his will about a month before his death, Audrey and ZoBell, as co-trustees, established Dr. Seuss Enterprises to oversee the widening world of Dr. Seuss and act as caretaker of the intellectual property. Soon they were in the courts to stop an epidemic of unauthorized usage of the Dr. Seuss name, including bootlegged T-shirts depicting the Cat in the Hat smoking a marijuana joint, sweeping up beer cans and flashing a peace sign.

At the University of California at San Diego in 1993, Audrey dedicated the Geisel Room in the special-collections wing of the library to which she donated his manuscripts and illustrations, dating from 1968 to his death, and some of his correspondence, photographs and awards.

She also completed a renovation of the Tower that Ted had resisted as bothersome in the final years of his life. His early studio in the lookout tower was restored, his main-floor studio was preserved, and his collection of hats was reinstalled in its closet. In an archway leading to the main entrance of the house Audrey embedded the dinosaur footprint that his father had given him in the 1930s, and that he had always kept close. "I like it around," Ted had said, "to remind me that a hundred fifty million years ago guys had problems just as bad as mine."

In the summer of 1994 a mural of the Cat in the Hat appeared above New York City's Forty-second Street in a public art project as "the ringmaster of your imagination . . . saying 42nd Street can be magical." That November a giant Cat balloon joined other storybook characters in Macy's Thanksgiving Day parade.

In his final year Ted's conversation with his biographers had turned gleefully to the Infantograph, his doomed scheme for making a killing at the New York World's Fair in 1939 with a camera that would superimpose photographs of a man and woman to suggest how their child might look. "It was my finest failure," he said. "It should have worked!" In the summer of 1994, three years after Ted's death, Paul G. Allen, co-founder of Microsoft, set up an exhibit of emerging electronic and computer technology to accompany Lollapalooza, an alternative-rock music show that toured thirty-three cities. One software program was "Baby Maker," which enabled a couple to "combine their images digitally to see what their offspring would look like." "Baby Maker" was a hit.

The magical world of the CD-ROM had been only hearsay to Ted in 1991, but he talked of the potential of the computer in teaching reading. In 1994, Living Books, a partnership of Random House and Brøderbund Software, Inc., acquired rights to Dr. Seuss books for production as CD-ROMs. A small book version of each Dr. Seuss title was expected to accompany each CD-ROM. The ability that CD-ROM affords the child viewer in matching word and picture seemed an extension of Ted's pioneering efforts in children's readers to illustrate each key word of text.

Later that year the National Aeronautics and Space Administration, in designing an innovative unmanned craft for exploring deep space, named it the Data Relay Solar Electric Utility Spacecraft. NASA people gave it the acronym of DRSEUS, and, of course, called it Dr. Seuss.

Notes

Prologue

1 Springfield 1900–1915

PAGE

3   Springfield mood: Joseph Carvalho III and Thomas M. Costello, Connecticut Valley Historical Museum (Springfield), a.i.

3   Duryea and Knox automobiles: *Springfield 1636–1986*, edited by Michael F. Konig and Martin Kaufman, 206.

3   62,000 population: Archives, Connecticut Valley Historical Museum

3   world stretched north: Carvalho, a.i.

4   Kalmbach and Geisel: *Progressive Springfield* (1891), 77.

4   75,000 barrels: Ibid.

4   German army: *Springfield Union*, December 5, 1919.

4   There, in 1906: Margaretha Dahmen (Peggy Owens), "The Story of My Mother," June 11, 1943.

4   German, the language: Ibid.

5   two hundred trains: *Springfield (1915) Directory*.

5   downtown quadrangle: In 1905 a grand plan was drawn to develop a cultural core around the Central Library; the George Walter Vincent Smith Museum and the Museum of Natural History, both built in the 1890s, were followed by the Connecticut Valley Historical Museum and Museum of Fine Arts.

6   "Come Back and Guzzle": TSG, a.i.

6   Seuss the baker: Non-Auto. Grandfather Seuss died December 31, 1901, before TSG was born.

6   six feet tall: TSG, a.i.

7   "Apple, mince, lemon": Ibid.

7   More than anyone else: Non-Auto.

7   fate of a cousin: Peggy Dahmen Owens, a.i.

7   "You will never be sorry": TSG, a.i.

7   world title: Ibid. Father's paper target in TSG studio dated March 2, 1902.

7   "My father had": Non-Auto.

8   haunted building: Dahmen, "Story of My Mother."

8   "boiled white shirts": Non-Auto.

9   "sounds of her cough": Dahmen, "Story of My Mother."

9   "my sister's casket": Non-Auto.

9   the Soccer Field: Ibid.

10   "wrong end of a telescope": Rob Wilder, *Parents*, June, 1979. In *American Picturebooks from Noah's Ark to the Beast Within* (New York: Macmillan, 1976), Barbara Bader wrote: "Like [Edward] Lear, with whom he is most often compared, his Nonsense is native to him, the expression of an angle of vision, a cast of mind, different from other people's," 310.

10   Fairfield Street neighbors: Non–Auto.

10   "All these people": Ibid.

10   "No matter what anybody says": Ibid.

11   "I saw Halley's Comet": Ibid.

11   "All that shooting": Ibid.

11   "The great Jehovah": Ibid.

12   "Ted always had a pencil": *Springfield Herald* interview with Theodor Robert Geisel, June 22, 1967.

13   "I'll be back tomorrow": TSG, a.i.

13   father's inventions: Non–Auto.

13   "In 1905, while Albert Einstein": Ibid.

13   Each Christmas Eve: Theodor Geisel Wallace, a.i.

14   *The Hole Book:* TSG, a.i.

14   Johnson's Book Store: the Johnsons also lived on TSG's block on Fairfield Street.

14   "Putnam Hall!": Non–Auto.

14   as many as 50,000 people: archives, Connecticut Valley Historical Museum.

15   "Dragged by two teams": Non–Auto.

15   "1915 San Francisco!": Ibid.

15   "Marnie spent hers": Ibid.

15   GEISEL CALLS MAYOR!: TSG, a.i.

16   "German brewer's kid with the three-legged dog": Ibid.

2 Springfield 1915–1921

PAGE

17   "countless bolognas": Non–Auto.

17   adulthood assumed: Ibid.

17   "You really should try": TSG, a.i.

17   twelve hundred adults: Nancy J. Goff, *Springfield's Ethnic Heritage: The German Community.* 20.

17   Schützenverein, Turnverein: Ibid., 24.

18   "caviar and meringue glace," Non–Auto.

18   "Our fathers did get into some clubs": Ibid.

19   *"Mon chapeau!":* Ibid.

19   "hero, Douglas Fairbanks": Ibid.

19   300,000 barrels: *Springfield Union,* September 4, 1929.

20   "misdeliver a keg": Non–Auto.

20   German Americans stoned: Goff, 27.

20   "liberty cabbage," Ibid.

20   "cream of the physical education": Ibid, 28.

20   Bosch Magneto: Ibid.

21   "pink shirt . . . green flannel bag": Non–Auto.

21   "Our model that day": Ibid.
21   manager of soccer: *The Pnalka* (Yearbook) 1920 ½.
21   "We lost every game": Non-Auto.
21   "Keep the home fires": Ibid.
22   bonds worth $1,000: TSG, a.i.
22   "What's this little boy": Ibid.
22   B average: Ibid.
23   "never amount": Ibid.
23   Helen Hayes: TSG, a.i; theater programs, 1920–21. Connecticut Valley Historical Museum.
23   "no pectoral muscles": Non-Auto.
23   "nobody did much touching": Ibid.
23   Thelma, "whom I loved": Ibid.
23   "I don't know why I kissed Libby": Ibid.
23   Pete the Pessimist: Central High *Recorder*, October 24, 1919.
23   "A Pupil's Nightmare": Ibid., January 21, 1921.
23   T. S. LeSieg: TSG, a.i.
24   minstrel show: Non-Auto.
24   Warren Harding: Ibid.
24   "Smith would say things": Wallace, a.i.
24   Hilaire Belloc: TSG, a.i.
25   "Ted comes of a good family": letter from William C. Hill, February 19, 1925, Dartmouth College archives.

3   Dartmouth 1921–1925

PAGE
26   "If Leon Trotsky": Non-Auto. Hopkins's comments were delivered in a speech to Dartmouth alumni in Chicago, February 1924, and widely covered in the press: Charles E. Widmayer, *Hopkins of Dartmouth* (Hanover, N.H.: University Press of New England, 1977).
26   "Temporarily retired—Brewer": Dartmouth registration, September 20, 1921.
27   disciple of H. L. Mencken: TSG, a.i.
27   "scrap their pencils": *The Dartmouth*, May 26, 1959.
27   Pledge Week came: TSG, a.i.
27   "With my black hair": Ibid.
27   Norman Maclean: Ibid.
28   "The Fatted Calf": *Jack-O-Lantern*, Jan. 1922.
28   he thought briefly: TSG, a.i.
28   asleep in the glare: Ibid.
28   late-night bull: Ibid.
28   "In person Ted could": Radford Tanzer, a.i.
28   "He was a sweet man": Frederick "Pete" Blodgett, a.i.

28   Wilson Library: Robert B. Graham, *The Dartmouth Story* (Hanover, N.H.: Dartmouth Book Store, Inc., 1990), 144.

28   books were piled: Larry Leavitt, a.i.

28   watering trough: Graham, 55.

29   father was looking: TSG, a.i.

29   "as an educational facility": Ibid.

29   red Cadillac taxi: Blodgett, a.i.

29   "red gets more attention": TSG, a.i.

30   "If you will learn": Blodgett, a.i.

30   pinus, acer, quercus: Ibid.

30   "Professor Griggs": Ibid.

30   Blodgett's bears: Ibid.

31   intend to become editor: TSG, a.i.

31   "I am knocking off": TSG letter to Whitney Campbell, July 1926, private papers of Thomas Campbell.

31   "I suppose I should": letter to WC, July 1924.

31   Maclean caught Ted: Norman Maclean interview, *Dartmouth Alumni Magazine*, November 1978.

31   "I wasn't a good brother," TSG, a.i.

32   "in between sips of cocoa": conversation with Edward Connery Lathem, "The Beginnings of Dr. Seuss," *Dartmouth Alumni Magazine*, April 1976.

32   "Nobody . . . thought it was funny": Ibid.

32   "When I went": TSG, a.i.

32   "My friends, there's milk": Non-Auto.

32   "look at any track event": Ibid.

33   "I began to get it": ECL in *Dartmouth Alumni Magazine*.

33   "practically the whole thing": Ibid.

33   "My big desire": TSG, a.i.

33   "Tonight I'd like to chuck": TSG to WC, April 19, 1926.

34   "While Sharp was in town": Ibid., July 1924.

34   turned a $30,000 profit: Ibid.

34   "clever business": Ibid.

34   "a real job": Ibid.

34   "any wisecracks": Ibid.

34   "cream-colored dinner jacket": Alexander Laing, *Dartmouth Alumni Magazine*, October 1939.

35   "not to think like Babbitts": Joe Harrington, *Boston Globe*, January 1961.

35   "This . . . differs from": *Jack-O-Lantern*, September 1925.

35   a dirty joke: TSG interview with EJK, November 21, 1959. NYPL.

35   "three thousand": Ibid.

35   Larry Leavitt scored: Leavitt, a.i.

35   "a football-playing poet", TSG, a.i.

35   "He was not gregarious": Kenneth Montgomery, a.i.
36   "least likely to succeed": Blodgett, a.i.
36   sharing a pint: ECL, *Dartmouth Alumni Magazine*.
36   pact with the upriver bootlegger: Tanzer, a.i.
36   seltzer water: Marian (Mrs. Curtis) Abel, a.i.
36   "for defying the laws": ECL, *Dartmouth Alumni Magazine*.
36   signed his cartoons: Ibid.
37   father, flushed with paternal pride: TSG, a.i.
37   "I have great admiration": letter from W. Benfield Pressey, March
      14, 1925. Dartmouth College archives.
37   "creative or editorial sort": letter from David Lambuth, March 14,
      1925. Dartmouth archives.
37   "English and writing": TSG, a.i.
38   "We'll go you": *Springfield Union*, July 9, 1925.
38   sailed from Boston: *The Dartmouth*, September 17, 1925.

4   Oxford 1925–1926

PAGE
39   lone passenger: TSG, a.i.
40   consider becoming a professor: Ibid.
40   an aging scout: Ibid.
40   studded with jagged glass: Non-Auto.
40   added only two names: Vivian H.H. Green, *The Commonwealth of
      Lincoln College 1427–1977*, (Oxford University Press, 1979), 527.
40   "to overcome those": Ibid., 6.
40   budget was as little: *Hugh Casson's Oxford: A College Companion*,
      (Phaidon Press, Oxford, 1988), 47.
40   John Wesley: Green, *Lincoln College (Oxford*: Thomas-Photos), 9,
      19.
41   "cold, dreary, dripping": Joseph Sagmaster to E. J. Kahn, Jr., De-
      cember 3, 1959. NYPL.
41   "over tea and anchovy toast": Ibid.
41   "appallingly ignorant": EJK, *The New Yorker*, December 17, 1960.
41   Junior Common Room: Green, *Commonwealth*, 576.; bound min-
      utes of JCR, Lincoln College archives.
41   tug-of-war: JCR minutes, May 16, 1926.
41   hot baths were rationed: JCR minutes, January 31, 1926.
41   Ted enthusiastically: TSG, a.i.; minutes of JCR, February 21, 1926.
41   Rhodes scholars: Non-Auto.
41   nor an extrovert: Sir Peter Hutchison, a.i.
41   "other outsiders": Non-Auto.
42   "My big problem": Ibid.
42   Fred Stokvis, Cecil Stapleton: Ibid.

42	"the twin brother": TSG to WC, July 30, 1926. TSG was probably referring to the duke of Devonshire, Sir Victor Christian William Cavendish. Born in 1898, he succeeded his uncle in 1908, as noted in *Burke's Peerage*, 1930.
42	"Papa wore a pith helmet": Ibid.
42	"silks and satins": Ibid.
42	"staged a love affair": Ibid.
42	new Lincoln barge: Green, *Commonwealth*, 581.
42	stiff and taciturn: Ibid., 529.
42	the Munner: Non-Auto.
42	"Sort of elated": Ibid.
42	"Dr. and Mrs. Munro": Ibid.
42	Rector's only question: Ibid.
42	"this extraordinarily clean": Donald Bartlett to EJK, February 3, 1960. NYPL.
43	canon of Zanzibar: *Lincoln College Record*, 1925–26. Lincoln College archives; TSG, a.i.
43	aged scout: Non-Auto.
43	"There is a bit": Ibid.
43	Ted explored: TSG, a.i.
43	"socially irresponsible": Kenneth Clark, *Another Part of the Wood*, (New York: Harper & Row, 1974), 113.
43	"evasion and bluff": Ibid., 103.
44	dreaded slogging: Sagmaster to EJK, Ibid.
44	"a soggy cake": Non-Auto.
44	sconcing: Green, *Commonwealth*, 562; TSG Non-Auto.
44	invitation of Viscountess Astor: in TSG Oxford notebook, Special Collections, UCSD.
44	Jeff: Ibid.
45	An American girl: BPB and TSG, a.i.
45	"horn-rimmed glasses": Percy H. ("Duke") Johnston, a.i.
45	"a certain grace": Ibid.
45	angel Uriel: ECL in *Dartmouth Alumni Magazine*.
45	"You're crazy to be": TSG, a.i.
45	"down in the dumps": Sagmaster to Kahn.
45	"You never saw . . .": Ibid.
46	drawings "of marvelous": Ibid.
46	two-horsepower motorcycle: Non-Auto.
46	"plucked ducks": EJK, *The New Yorker*.
46	"fool's parsley": TSG, a.i.
46	"Duke-ing": TSG to WC, July 30, 1926.
46	"It seems that her father": Ibid.
46	"I played rotten golf": Ibid.
47	"So we became engaged": TSG, a.i.

47	battel books: 1925–26, Lincoln College archives.
47	"Geisel must have been off": Paul Langford, Lincoln College historian, a.i.
47	HPG addresses: 1924–26 archival records of Society of Oxford Home Students, now St. Anne's College, Oxford.
47	A. J. Carlyle: Green, *Commonwealth*, 531.
47	"nephew of the great": ECL in *Dartmouth Alumni Magazine*.
47	"This don, Sir Oliver Onions,": TSG, a.i. Although TSG and HPG used this rollicking Seussian name, the only Onions lecturing at Lincoln in 1925–26 was Charles Talbut Onions, final editor of *The Oxford English Dictionary* (Sir Maurice Shock, rector, Lincoln College, Oxford, a.i.).
48	decisions about his future: TSG to WC, April 19, 1926.
48	staying each night: Bartlett to EJK, February 3, 1960.
48	"dazzling fashion": TSG to WC, April 19, 1926.
48	"a stiff drink" and "explode the bomb": Ibid.
48	"'Mother,' Helen asked": Ibid.
49	"Over cobblestone roads": Ibid.
49	Paris seemed perfect: Ibid.
49	"trying to get some funny": TSG to WC, April 19, 1926.
49	"sophisticated White Russian": Non-Auto.
49	"half our motorbike": TSG to WC, April 19, 1926.
49	final entry: Lincoln College archives, June 10, 1926. (Yet TSG was one of three "notable" Lincoln alumni of the "inter-war" years cited in *The Encyclopaedia of Oxford*, edited by Christopher Hibbert, Macmillan London Ltd., 1988.)
49	Fitzgeralds, Parker, Benchley showed up at Villa America as guests of Gerald and Sara Murphy: Leslie Frewin, *The Late Mrs. Dorothy Parker* (New York: Macmillan, 1986).
49	"Grandfather's money": TSG to WC, July 30, 1926.
49	Queen Victoria, *Bismarck:* Ibid.
49	"go into business": TSG to WC, April 19, 1926.
49	newspaper job abroad: Ibid.
49	"man's limitations": TSG to WC, July 30, 1926.
49	parents and his sister . . . arrived: Ibid.
50	flower-bedecked cow: Dahmen, "Story of My Mother."
50	"Before checking out": Non-Auto.
50	younger brother, Robert: TSG to WC, July 30, 1926.
50	thirty relatives: Ibid.
50	dinner for Seusses: TSG to WC, August 8, 1926.
51	"We gave my cousin": Ibid.
51	world statemen "who have proved": Ibid.
51	Mistinguett . . . Chevalier: Non-Auto.
51	"gorgeous girls": Ibid.

51   "detested tourists": TSG to WC, October 1, 1926.
52   "What he was writing": Non-Auto.
52   "ponderous-minded word-slinger": TSG to WC, October 1, 1926.
52   "What street is this?": Ibid.
52   "a trifle intoxicated": Ibid.
52   "like a chipmunk": Bartlett to EJK, February 3, 1960.
52   "behind a pissoir": TSG to WC, October 1, 1926.
53   "except for a girdle": Ibid.
53   "You must spend more time": Ibid.
53   "darn nice girl": Ibid.
53   "complete study" of modern German drama: Ibid.
54   "He said that nobody": ECL, *Dartmouth Alumni Magazine*.
54   "cattle boat to Corsica": Ibid.
54   "not too hot": TSG to WC, January 6, 1927.
54   "Mrs. Palmer": Ibid.
54   "wasted the mornings": Ibid.
54   "wealthy widows": Ibid.
54   "strutted . . . before the gilded mirrors": Ibid.
54   "Madonna of the Roller Skates": Ibid.
55   "I who came": Ibid.

5   Helen Palmer Geisel 1927–1928

PAGE
56   phone call from the dock: Barbara Palmer Bayler, a.i.
56   Miss Baird's: EJK interview notes, November 1959, NYPL.
56   "Quiet and intelligent": archives, St. Anne's College, Oxford.
56   "I should have done better": HPG to Christine Burrows, August 4, 1926, St. Anne's archives.
57   Sixty theaters: Robert A.M. Stern, Gregory Gilmartin, *New York 1930*, (New York: Rizzoli, 1987), 259.
57   George Howard Palmer: BPB, a.i.
57   Adoniram Judson Palmer. Ibid.
57   "a lopsided smile": Ibid.
57   graduating with honors: Wellesley College transcript.
57   set up his drawing board: TSG, a.i.
58   "the sort you'd like": BPB, a.i.
58   Dartmouth Club: TSG to WC, April 14, 1927.
58   "talented, intense, sympathetic": Ibid.
58   "I have tramped": Ibid.
58   "laugh my god damned head off": Ibid.
58   "P. T. Barnum's White Elephant": Ibid.
59   "what comes up": Ibid.
59   "eminent Europeans": TSG to Alexander Laing, May 1927.

59 "Not having received any": Ibid.

59 "sick and tired of being": Ibid.

59 Algonquin Round Table: Non-Auto. (TSG called Robert Benchley, Dorothy Parker et al. "the greatest wits who ever lived, in their opinion, and, at that time, mine.")

59 *Saturday Evening Post:* Robert Cahn, "The Wonderful World of Dr. Seuss," *Saturday Evening Post,* July 6, 1957.

60 $1,000: ECL in *Dartmouth Alumni Magazine.*

60 moved in with John C. Rose: Ibid.

60 Pirates Den: Lloyd Morris, *Incredible New York* (New York: Random House, 1951), 311.

60 "God, what a place!": ECL manuscript.

60 salary was $75: TSG, a.i.

60 secretly married: BPB, a.i.

61 five o'clock ceremony: Ibid.

61 bristled in the final: Ibid.

61 small champagne supper: TSG to WC, December 4, 1927.

61 Lady Astor impersonation: Ibid.

61 honeymoon at Hotel Traymore: TSG, a.i.

61 "a discordant note": TSG to WC, December 4, 1927.

61 "As far as humor": Non-Auto.

62 *Judge:* papers of TSG, Baker Library, Dartmouth College.

62 "I was saving the name of Geisel": TSG to Bernadette Guiniling, November 19, 1981. Private papers of ASG.

62 "From the sophisticated": TSG to WC, March 25, 1928.

62 "If your stuff": letter from Huntsville, Texas, January 1928, quoted by TSG, a.i.

63 *The New Yorker* one-line gags: TSG, a.i.

63 salaries were cut: ECL, *Dartmouth Alumni Magazine.*

63 "How can you pay income tax": TSG, a.i.

63 When horses died: ECL, Ibid.

63 "Helen and I worked harder": Ibid.

63 "most horribly stewed": TSG to WC. March 25, 1928.

64 "forced conviviality": Ibid.

64 "We'd grab our 65-cent tickets": TSG, a.i.

64 "Perhaps it is bad": TSG to WC, March 25, 1928.

64 Dizzy Club: Ibid.

64 "Only Perkins could play": Ibid.

65 "and 100 berries the picture": Ibid.

65 "Darn it all, another Dragon": *Judge,* January 1928.

65 Grace (Mrs. Lincoln) Cleaves: TSG, a.i.

65 "It wasn't even her regular": Ibid.

65 "Quick, Henry": TSG told EJK this was a parody of Sherlock Holmes's "Quick, Watson, the needle."

65	song was written: Cahn, in *Saturday Evening Post*.
65	bug spray evoked laughter: W. G. Rogers, art columnist, *Springfield Union*, May 11, 1933, wrote: "The funniest advertisements we know . . . are those with the slogan "Quick, Henry, the Flit." Calling Seuss a modernist, Rogers went on: "He exaggerates, he distorts, he contrives figures more fantastic than those of the dadaist or the surrealist—from neither of whom . . . an impassable distance separates him. . . ."
65	too lovable to kill: Cahn, in *Saturday Evening Post*.
66	$12,000 a year from Flit: Wilder, *Parents*, June 1979.

6 New York 1928–1935

PAGE

67	a guide's snapshot: photo album, BPB.
67	The Apthorp: Paul Goldberger, *The City Observed*, New York, (New York: Vintage Books, 1979), 218; *WPA Guide New York City, 1939*.
68	his first poem: TSG Non-Auto.
68	$300 a page: TSG, a.i.
68	Corey Ford: ECL in *Dartmouth Alumni Magazine*.
68	"wealthy, old people": TSG, a.i.
69	find a way to have a small home: Ibid.
69	playing bridge: BPB, a.i.
69	satirized the game: *Judge*, February 11, 1928.
69	"The Tough Coughs": *The Tough Coughs as He Ploughs the Dough, Early Writings and Cartoons by Dr. Seuss*, edited by Richard Marschall (New York: William Morrow, 1987), 57.
69	"Idioms of Iceland": *Life*, July 26, 1929.
70	much of the literary community: Frewin, *Dorothy Parker*.
70	symbols of hope: Morris, *Incredible New York*, 300.
70	"all these people who have nowhere to go": Non-Auto.
70	Democrats: PDO, a.i.
70	accompanied his sister to Reno: Ibid.
71	rattling sound . . . in the attic: Ibid.
71	fell asleep in the midst of a bridge game: Ibid.
71	Christian Science faith: Ibid.
71	neurosurgeon Harvey Cushing: Ibid.
71	*Boners*: ECL in *Dartmouth Alumni Magazine*. *Boners* was published in February; *More Boners* in April. *Boners* ranked fourth on the nonfiction best-seller list for 1931 and, with succeeding volumes, sold "into the hundreds of thousands" (Alice Payne Hackett and James Henry Burke, *80 Years of Best Sellers, 1895–1975* [New York: R. R. Bowker Co., 1977], 111–12).

71   "off-hand . . . we should have said": *American News*, February Books, February 7, 1931, UCLA.

72   "Seuss puts more naive": letter to editor from Samuel F. Schlosser, October 1931. UCLA.

72   "an experiment . . . an ABC book": Non-Auto.

72   Hamburg-Amerika line's motorship *St. Louis*: passenger list, 1931, TSG papers, UCSD.

72   "to clear the air": TSG to Harold Rugg, January 26, 1932, Baker Library, Dartmouth.

72   move to East 96th St.: Ibid. October 5, 1930.

72   "a nutty feud": Thomas Wolfe, *Washington Post*, January 14, 1962.

72   Central Park bench: H. Allen Smith, *The Compleat Practical Joker*, (New York: Garden City Books, 1954), 135.

72   "I brought my maternal grandmother!": TSG, a.i.

73   Surely, Goodness, and Mercy: Non-Auto.

73   murals: Con Troy, *Laugh with Hugh Troy* (Wyomissing, Pa.: Trojan Books, 1983), 78–79. TSG dabbled briefly in murals for private homes and, for the Dartmouth Club, painted the "Rape of the Sabine Woman," now at Dartmouth College.

73   Frank A. Vanderlip family: TSG, Elin Vanderlip, a.i.

73   dime-store pearl: TSG, a.i.

73   "who told the story": Ibid., Cheever-Vanderlip relationship covered in *Home Before Dark*, by his daughter, Susan Cheever (Boston: Houghton Mifflin, 1984).

74   commissions from Standard Oil: Brown, *The Lamp*, Spring 1987.

74   FOIL THE KARBO-NOCKUS!: 1933, TSG papers, UCSD.

74   "We moved": TSG, a.i.

74   dinosaur footprint: Ibid.

74   "Cy had forgotten": Ibid.

74   stubbed their toes: Ibid.

75   "ancient Blarney Stone": Ibid.

75   "The entrance was on 92nd": BPB, a.i.

76   Hugh Troy: Wolfe, *Washington Post*, January 14, 1962.

76   "That night was so lively": Peggy Conklin, a.i.

76   "He was tall": Bob Warren interview, *The Dartmouth*, May 10, 1934. Baker Library, Dartmouth.

76   "I just came back from Peru": Ibid.

77   "headaches and insomnia of anoxemia": TSG, a.i.

77   "polo players": Marian (Mrs. Curtis) Abel, a.i.

78   "shut off from our world": from *Hejji* by Dr. Seuss, April 7, 1935, UCSD.

78   "It was just as well": Mary Stofflet, *Dr. Seuss from Then to Now* (San Diego Museum of Art, 1986).

7 *Mulberry Street* 1936–1938

PAGE

79   thirty nations: bookjacket, *Mulberry Street*, 1937.

79   Ted and Helen boarded *Kungsholm:* TSG, a.i.

79   red postal buses, Ibid.

80   learn yodeling: Ibid.

80   gale-force winds: Ibid.

80   upper-deck lounge: Ibid.

80   "A stupid horse and wagon": TSG papers, UCLA.

80   "Da-da-DA": TSG, a.i.

81   insisted on momentum: Michael J. Bandler, *American Way*, December, 1977.

81   Twenty-seven publishing houses: TSG, a.i. Random House was not among the publishers TSG tried, TSG told EJK, 1959.

81   verse . . . and fantasy: Clifton Fadiman, *Holiday*, April 1959.

81   "What's wrong with kids": TSG, a.i.

82   hailed by Mike McClintock: ECL in *Dartmouth Alumni Magazine.*

82   "a snappier title": Evelyn Shrifte, a.i.

82   "in the dry-cleaning business today": TSG, a.i.

82   taking on new writers: Shrifte, a.i.

83   "He knew what he wanted": Ibid.

83   telegram from Shrifte: August 31, 1937, Vanguard Press papers, CU.

83   15,000 copies: *Publishers Weekly*, April 24, 1943.

83   full-page ad: Ibid., August 28, 1937.

83   magazine did not review it: Ibid., April 24, 1943.

83   citizens queued: *Springfield Union*, October 3, 1937.

83   Fadiman: *The New Yorker*, November 6, 1937.

84   "Highly original": *New York Times*, November 14, 1937.

84   stage fright: *Publishers Weekly*, April 24, 1943.

84   "So completely spontaneous": Moore, *The Atlantic Monthly*, November, 1937.

84   "What an amusing picture book": Potter, July 1938 letter cited by Anne Carroll Moore.

84   "I think it the cleverest": Anne Carroll Moore, *The Art of Beatrix Potter*, (F. Warne and Co., England, 1955).

85   6,000 more copies: Vanguard Press archives, CU.

85   By 1943: Ibid.

85   red turtles, purple elephants: interview with Marnie (Margaretha) Dahmen, *Springfield Union*, November 28, 1937.

85   "like people you know": Ibid.

85   "mind has never grown up": Peter Bunzel, *Life*, April 6, 1959.

85   several hundred hats: Dahmen interview.

86   Seuss Navy: EJK, *The New Yorker*, December 17, 1960. Some said it was a takeoff on the Swiss Navy. Besides Standard Oil, Dr. Seuss creatures were in marketing campaigns for Hankey Bannister Scotch whisky, Narragansett Lager & Ale, Schaefer beer, General Electric and the NBC radio network.

86   "A swarm of phoney Farraguts": *The New York Herald Tribune*, January 22, 1936.

86   "cheaper to give a party": Non-Auto.

86   *Bartholomew Cubbins:* perhaps named after Dartmouth classmate William Cubbins; Kenneth Montgomery, a.i.

87   "I knew nothing about children's books": ECL, unpublished manuscript, Baker Library, Dartmouth.

87   "I decided he was so stuffy": TSG, a.i.

87   housecleaning ritual: Peggy Owens, a.i.

87   number of Cubbins's hats rose: TSG papers, Dartmouth.

87   "the hottest day of July": Ibid.

88   "bit of tomfoolery": *New York Times*, November 13, 1938. Cornelia Meigs, in *A Critical History of Children's Literature* (New York: Macmillan Co. 1953), p. 477, praised TSG for joining in *500 Hats* the "suspense and magic of a highly original fairy tale with irresistible nonsense."

88   "brand-new idea": *Booklist*, November 12, 1939.

88   "the Grimm of our Times": Laing, *Dartmouth Alumni Magazine*, January 1939.

88   "You're wrong as the deuce": *The Dartmouth*, quoted in *New York Times Book Review*, July 23, 1939.

88   "comes as a thrill to a bloke": TSG to Harold Rugg. November 9, 1938, Baker Library, Dartmouth.

89   "the most serious intentions": Cahn, *Saturday Evening Post*, July 6, 1957.

89   speak at a women's college: Ibid.

8   *Horton Hatches the Egg* 1938–1940

PAGE

90   Chrysanthemum-Pearl: Cahn, *Saturday Evening Post*, July 6, 1957.

90   "whip up the most": Ibid.

90   Geisel Christmas cards: scrapbooks of Barbara Cole, La Jolla; PDO.

90   removed her ovaries: Barbara Palmer Bayler, a.i., from conversation with her mother.

91   "it was not": TSG conversation with PDO, 1967–68, in reaction to articles suggesting Dr. Seuss did not like children. PDO, a.i. Most interviews with TSG quoted him as responding to the question "Why no children?" with "You have 'em, I'll amuse 'em!" TSG

did not remember how that started but admitted it was an easy way
out. TSG, a.i.

91 "That week had to be": PDO, a.i.

91 "a stroke of genius": Non-Auto.

91 "unstreeted by the Depression": Ibid.

92 IF YOU MARRIED THAT GAL: Ibid.

92 "It was a hair-raising experience": Ibid.

92 "like William Randolph Hearst": Cahn, *Saturday Evening Post.*

92 Richard Condon: TSG later was a fan of Condon's novels, especially
The Manchurian Candidate (1959) and *Prizzi's Honor* (1982).

92 57th Street studio . . . Grace Moore: TSG, a.i.

92 certificate of dissolution (and other documents on Infantograph
Corporation): ASG private papers.

93 Los Angeles attorney: Law Offices, G. M. Cuthbertson, July 5,
1944. Ibid.

93 Donald Klopfer, whom TSG admired, disliked publicity with
"roughly the same passion with which Cerf courted it.": *Publishers
Weekly*, August 4, 1975.

93 ban on . . . *Ulysses:* The book was seized in 1933 when mailed to
Cerf and Klopfer from Paris; in New York, Judge John Woolsey
gave "one of the historic rulings in obscenity proceedings in the
book's favor": Ibid.

93 Cerf . . . at "21": TSG interview with ECL, 1975.

93 impressed by Cerf: On November 21, 1959, TSG told EJK, "I felt
(Cerf) was a kind of star I wanted my wagon hitched to. You could
tell that Bennett was going somewhere." EJK papers, NYPL.

93 need each other: Beyond that, Cerf told EJK, "simplicity and modesty are in the pattern of genius, and Ted has them." Ibid.

94 *The Seven Lady Godivas:* TSG interview with ECL, 1975.

94 "an outright lie": TSG, a.i.

94 "The country was depressed": ECL manuscript, Dartmouth.

94 "I tried to draw the sexiest-looking women": EJK interview, 1959.

95 royalty statement: Cerf, *At Random* (New York: Random House,
1977), 154.

95 "I quite understand": Cerf to TSG, February 28, 1939.

95 "Helen was an editor": TSG, a.i.

95 "High in the air, crown askew," TSG papers, UCLA.

95 "Even as a baby": Ibid.

96 first-year sales: EJK, *The New Yorker*, December 17, 1960.

96 "A Poem for Mr. Miller": ca. 1939, Butler Library, CU.

96 dazzled Helen's nieces: BPB, a.i.

96 When Ted took a break: TSG, a.i.

97 "I've left a window open": Ibid.

97 "I keep losing": Cahn, *Saturday Evening Post.*

97   "The new book": TSG to Bonino, October 1939, RH files.

97   Saxe Commins had joined Random House in 1933, just as its fall catalog pledged to publish James Joyce's uncensored *Ulysses* as soon as the firm won its court battle to "remove the ridiculous ban" (Dorothy Commins, *What Is an Editor? Saxe Commins at Work* [University of Chicago Press, 1978]), 27.

98   "Who, you?": TSG papers, UCLA.

98   "never stopped stewing": Dorothy Leavitt, a.i.

98   By the time Paris was occupied: TSG, a.i.

98   "I had no great causes": Ibid.

98   her pivotal contribution: Ibid.

98   "it is not the usual": Cerf to Frances Pindyck, April 11, 1940. RH files, CU.

98   advance of $500: Cerf to Pindyck, April 22, 1940, CU.

99   costing $8,000: TSG, a.i.

99   offer of $200: Cerf to Robert Clampett, Schlesinger Productions, Hollywood, October 1940, CU.

99   Ted knew what he wanted: ECL manuscript.

99   *NYT Book Review*, October 13, 1940: Barbara Bader in *American Picturebooks from Noah's Ark to the Beast Within*, p 304, wrote: "My hunch is that, in common with children, he is a natural moralizer; that it comes to him as unselfconsciously (and unambiguously) as rhyming lines from an engine's beat."

99   "I've been sitting": Chrystie to Cerf, September 11, 1940, CU.

100   "steamed up": Cerf to TSG, September 26, 1940. CU.

100   *Pentellic Bilge*: program, Philadelphia Booksellers' Association, November 14, 1940. TSG papers, UCLA. TSG told ECL: "It was not, of course, Bennett's 39th birthday [which had been May 25, 1937], but it was the best and only fun I ever had on any platform."

100   Zinny took Ted's cartoon: EJK, *The New Yorker*.

9   World War II 1941–1946

PAGE

101   "That horse's ass!": ECL manuscript, Dartmouth.

101   "*PM* was against people": TSG, a.i.

101   "You're going to get us": ECL manuscript.

102   "Dear Dr. Seuss:" TSG, a.i.

102   Nye's letter to *PM*: April 28, 1942, TSG papers, UCSD.

102   "And Helen, who never used": ECL manuscript.

102   three—and later, five: EJK interviews, NYPL.

102   the Lindbergh Quarter: *PM*, April 28, 1941. TSG papers, UCSD.

102   "one of our nation's most irritating": TSG Non-Auto.

102   "The Lone Eagle had flown": Ibid.

102	*Mein Early Kampf: PM* cartoons, TSG papers, UCSD.
103	"we were going to have no choice": Non-Auto. TSG added: "N.B. To the younger generation: I'm not talking about Korea, Vietnam, Cambodia. I'm talking about a war that *had* to be fought. If my philosophy irritates yours, please write me in care of Justin Hoogfliet, the boy who stuck his finger in the hole in the dike, Foedersvlied, Holland 09037."
103	He never forgot: TSG, a.i. Crawford, second president of the American Newspaper Guild, had a long career as political writer, war correspondent, and Washington columnist for *Newsweek*; Stone, a role model for generations of liberals and radicals, published *I.F. Stone's Weekly*, an iconoclastic Washington report.
103	"a bunch of young fogeys": Non-Auto.
103	"They were understaffed": ECL manuscript.
103	"It was a short-order business": Ibid. In Non-Auto, TSG said of snap judgments on deadline: "I was intemperate, un-humorous in my attacks . . . and I'd do it again."
103	"Nelson found very few": ECL manuscript.
103	"All the enlightened members": TSG to Shrifte, September 8, 1941. CU.
104	"Velly scary": *PM* cartoons; TSG papers, UCSD.
104	*Newsweek*: "Malice in Wonderland," February 9, 1942.
105	"no sense of the word a vacation": HPG to Shrifte, July 26, 1942, CU.
105	"There isn't a maid": Ibid.
106	"Geisel isn't a Communist": ECL manuscript.
106	"I told the Navy, 'Thanks' ": TSG, a.i.
106	"resembles Beethoven's Fifth": Carnegie Hall program, November 15, 1942, Vanguard Press papers, CU.
106	"Here are the Moviolas": Non-Auto.
107	"tried so earnestly": Paul Horgan, a.i.
107	Capra outfit: names from a.i. with TSG and Lee Katz.
107	"successful pornographer": Non-Auto.
107	Wallace railed against Capra: Wallace, *The Sunday Gentleman*, (New York: Simon & Schuster, 1965) 81.
107	Wonderview Drive: a.i. with neighbor Basil Gammon.
108	"successful but more or less conventional": EJK, *The New Yorker*.
108	"She supported us": Cynthia Lindsay, *Good Housekeeping*, December 1960.
108	intrigued by the Virgin Mary: EJK interview notes, November 1959, NYPL.
108	Geisel life in Hollywood: conversations with NM, 1950s.
109	"our commissary": Lee Katz, a.i.
109	"The first thing you have to do:" Non-Auto.

109   *Private Snafu* series: Chuck Jones, a.i.

110   Anopheles mosquito: Snafu film adapted from army field manual *This is Ann*, written by Leaf, illustrated by TSG. Because it was a military assignment, neither man received credit. TSG papers, UCLA.

110   bicoastal commuter: TSG, a.i.

111   "The Nazi party": script, *Your Job in Germany*, TSG papers, UCLA.

111   "Just be a good soldier": EJK interview notes, NYPL.

111   young army lieutenant named Ronald Reagan: TSG, a.i.

112   Murphy, Boettiger: TSG diary, 1944–45, UCSD.

112   Michelin map: TSG papers, UCSD

112   November 19 for Verdun: TSG diary, UCSD.

112   wore the weapon: EJK papers, NYPL. However, in September 1943 Ted qualified as marksman with M1 rifle with score of 180; Capt. Meredith Willson outscored him with 182. TSG papers, UCSD.

112   Marlene Dietrich: TSG diary, UCSD.

112   "college football scores": Ibid.

113   "two pairs of bare feet": Ibid.

113   "canary-colored Crane bathrooms": Ibid.

113   "elated in a depressed sort of way": TSG papers, UCSD. Among fellow travelers mentioned in TSG wartime diary was Alan Campbell, Dorothy Parker's husband, who infuriated Ms. Parker with the "exhilarated tone" of his wartime letters. Marion Meade, *Dorothy Parker* (New York: Villard Books, 1988), 326.

113   "residents were rummaging": TSG diary, UCSD.

113   "water was cascading down a marble stairway": TSG, a.i.

113   "My film said": Ibid.

113   "Somebody else took the film": Ibid.

113   vehicles stripped of tires: Ibid.

114   "I'll send you to a quiet sector": Ibid.

114   "The thing that probably saved my life:" Ibid.

114   "God, am I glad to see you!": EJK interview, November 19, 1959.

114   "peanut butter and salami": TSG papers, UCSD.

114   "If he had lived": Ibid.

115   As he recalled: EJK, *The New Yorker*.

115   Ted's "extraordinary projection": Horgan, a.i.

116   worked as a tutor: PDO, a.i.

116   "Mother was upset": Ibid.

116   "I'm sure she had agoraphobia": Ibid.

117   "But she'd said": Ibid.

10   Hollywood 1946–1950

PAGE

118   Jerry Wald telephoned: TSG letter to Bill Zavatsky, October 5, 1984. TSG private papers.

118   "the most startling factual film": Parsons quoted in *Hitler Lives?* advertisements, TSG papers, UCSD.

118   $500-a-week: Non-Auto.

118   "Joan Crawford has just lost": Ibid.

118   "jokes for every occasion": TSG to Zavatsky.

119   for not including a girl named Amy: Ibid. *Rebel Without a Cause; the Hypnoanalysis of a Criminal Psychopath*, by Robert Mitchell Lindner (New York: Grune and Stratton, 1944).

119   " 'Her I never screwed' ": TSG to Zavatsky. Actually, on p. 35 of Lindner's book, Harold says of the churchgoing Amy: "I never had any sexual relations with her."

119   "refused to be discovered": Ibid.

119   "due to change in policy": Joseph McBride, *Frank Capra: The Catastrophe of Success* (New York: Simon & Schuster, 1992), 499.

119   Ted blamed MacArthur: TSG to Bill Blakefield, February 11, 1980, TSG papers.

119   Little Guy and the Big Shot: script, May 12, 1947, TSG papers, UCLA.

120   "That wasn't so long ago": Non-Auto.

120   4,500 feet of confiscated: *Hollywood Citizen News*, January 19, 1948.

120   "documentary of fabulous proportions": *Variety*, January 1948.

120   prints disappeared: TSG, a.i.

120   "a decent but forgotten filmmaker": Ted Owens, a.i.

121   Myrna Loy . . . Burgess Meredith: Elin Vanderlip, a.i.

121   "outside in my pajamas": C. Robert Jennings, *Saturday Evening Post*, October 23, 1965.

121   fifteenth-century credenza: Vanderlip, a.i.

121   Deegel trout: PDO, a.i.

121   "exaggerate within a logical sequence": TSG lecture notes from University of Utah, 1949, UCLA.

122   "like a comic book": Ray Freiman to EJK, NYPL.

122   "I shall never cease": Commins's letter quoted in EJK interview notes, NYPL.

122   "I didn't dream it up": *Raleigh* (N.C.) *Times*, January 6, 1951.

122   "cut back on his exclamation points": EJK interview with Bonino, November 2, 1959, NYPL.

123   "Problem was to find": TSG to Bonino, April, 1, 1949, RH.

123   "He is his work": EJK interview notes, 1959, NYPL.

123   extensive lecture notes from Utah: TSG papers, UCLA. TSG be-

lieved in "winnowing out" and told Judith Frutig in *Christian Science Monitor*, May 12, 1978: "For a 60-page book, I'll probably write 500 pages".

11   *The 5,000 Fingers of Dr. T.* 1951–1953

133   "in charge": Ibid., July 1, 1951.

133   "somebody always decides": Ibid., August 26, 1951.

133   "He desperately wanted": Vanderlip, a.i.

133   "Ted . . . simply can't": HPG to BPB, September 20, 1951.

134   "They're really so lovely": Ibid., October 24, 1951.

134   "we have no book": Ibid., November 28, 1951.

134   he was withdrawing from the film: Ibid., January 7, 1952.

134   forty stage carpenters: Ibid., February 14, 1952.

134   Ted's drawings in *The 500 Hats*: Ibid.

134   one hundred and fifty: Ibid., March 13, 1952.

134   "There wasn't enough money": Donald Spoto, *Stanley Kramer, Film Maker* (New York: G. P. Putnam's, 1978), 149. Production costs were $2,750,000, Kramer's most costly Columbia production to date.

134   "especially in one scene": HPG to BPB, March 13, 1952.

134   "This started a chain reaction": TSG, Non-Auto.

135   On May 11: HPG to BPB, May 11, 1952.

135   "Ted simply has to": Ibid.

135   At daybreak: Ibid., June 14, 1952.

135   "At the end": TSG, a.i.

135   "to some foreign land": HPG to BPB, January 14, 1953.

136   Aboard with them: Ibid., March 16, 1953.

136   "some of the most dour": Ibid., March 28, 1953.

136   "the craziest operation": Ibid., April 15, 1953.

137   "Japan's Young Dreams": *Life*, March 29, 1954.

137   "Henry Luce was always anti-Japanese": ECL manuscript, Baker Library, Dartmouth.

137   "We only travel": HPG to BPB, April 28, 1953.

137   *Variety*: June 17, 1953.

137   *New York Times*: June 20, 1953.

137   "It was one": Spoto, *Stanley Kramer*, 149.

138   "As to who was most responsible": Non-Auto.

138   "Japan cured Ted's": HPG to Libby Childs, July 25, 1953. Childs private papers.

138   force in children's literature: TSG expounded on why he preferred writing for children in " . . . But for Grown-Ups Laughing Isn't Any Fun," by Dr. Seuss, *New York Times Book Review*, November 16, 1952.

138   Saxe Commins: Dorothy Commins, *What Is an Editor? Saxe Commins at Work*, 97–98.

138   "He was the kind": TSG, a.i.

138   *Saturday Review*: November 8, 1952.

139   "the clearest, brightest": TSG to Saxe Commins, February 20, 1953, CU.

PAGE

140   "It's been seven years": TSG, a.i.

140   "I want to stay in La Jolla": EJK interview with Phyllis Jackson, 1959.

140   "If I dropped everything": Ibid.

141   "We can live": Chuck Jones, a.i.

142   "This town is inhabited": Raymond Chandler, a.i.

142   "Ed, I've never told": TSG, a.i.

143   "too conservative": Ibid.

143   "still be in [his studio]": PDO, a.i.

143   "There was tenseness": Ibid.

144   "whether [or not] anything happens": ECL manuscript, Dartmouth.

144   "He was forever pausing": PDO, a.i.

144   "It was his hobby and his therapy." Ibid.

144   two extravagances: EJK, *The New Yorker*.

144   David Casey, a.i.

144   anapaestic tetrameter: Arthur Gordon, "The Wonderful Wizard of Soledad Hill," *Woman's Day*, September 1965.

144   "rollicking and easily remembered": Butler, *Children's Literature in Education*, Vol. 20, No. 3, 1989, 175, 181.

144   "a person's a person": in a letter to Dr. Steven Ealy, Armstrong State College, Savannah, Ga., August 7, 1989, TSG linked the theme to the McCarthyism of the 1950s in which he found U.S. citizens "scared of speaking their thoughts aloud."

145   "Horton Hears 'Em!": TSG papers, UCLA.

145   "Seuss onomatopoeic word": Ibid.

145   "On the fifteenth of June": Ibid.

145   canceling plans: HPG to BPB, December 7, 1953.

145   "through black ex-snow": Ibid. January 15, 1954.

146   "Ted will probably be": Ibid.

146   "I know very little": *Excursion* script, TSG papers, UCLA.

146   "It's going to take me": HPG to BPB, March 7, 1954.

146   "Never never": Ibid. December 27, 1953.

147   *Signs of Civilization!*: TSG papers, UCLA.

147   *Whither California?*: TSG private papers.

147   During slaphappy evenings: Elin Vanderlip, a.i.

147   "tasteless and not funny": Ibid.

147   keeping the reason secret: HPG to Bonino, May 1954, RH.

148   John Hersey: *Life*, May 24, 1954.

148   By the next morning: Scripps Metabolic Clinic medical records. (Now at Scripps Clinic and Research Institution, La Jolla.)

148   "Neuronitis acute": Dr. Francis M. Smith, Scripps records.

148   Dr. Ralph Barris: HPG records, Scripps Clinic.
148   moved by ambulance: Ibid, June 2, 1954.
149   chances of survival: TSG to Shrifte, October 10, 1954. CU.
149   Helen could not understand: Ellen Revelle, a.i.
149   endeared himself to nurses: EJK papers, NYPL.
149   Seussian relay of mirrors: Revelle, a.i.
149   began bringing Popsicles: Libby Childs, a.i.
149   "will walk again": TSG to Bonino, July 4, 1954, RH.
149   Peggy spent days: PDO, a.i.
150   "how to dial": TSG to PDO, July 1954.
150   not kept a checkbook: EJK papers, NYPL.
150   "the therapy is just about": TSG to Bonino, August 24, 1954, RH.
150   "R-r-r-r-aaa-bbit!": Chuck Jones, a.i.
150   "Two months ago": TSG to Bonino. August 24, 1954, RH.
150   "Not griping or complaining": Ibid.
151   "wildly original": *NYHT*, August 1954.
151   "a rhymed lesson": *Des Moines Register*, August 1954. *New York Times* called it "probably the most moral tale since the first 'Elsie Dinsmore,' but . . . a lot more fun." September 12, 1954.
151   beach brigade: Revelle, a.i.
151   "From then on," PDO, a.i.
151   "*Woman's Home Companion* . . . Pool": EJK papers, NYPL.
151   "it takes me": HPG to Gladys Palmer, October 16, 1954, BPB papers.
151   "I'm en route": Ibid.
151   "almost entirely recuperated": TSG to Schrifte, October 10, 1954. CU.
151   "everything is going": HPG to Shrifte, October 23, 1954, CU.
152   "A Prayer for a Child": *Collier's*, December 1955.
152   "perhaps in Old Persian": TSG, a.i.
152   "Nobody could possibly": *New York Times*, 1955.
152   "You can't come in!": EJK papers, NYPL.
152   "behind the fun": Dartmouth president John Sloan Dickey, June 12, 1955.
152   "very carefully refrained": TSG, a.i.

13   The Cat in the Hat 1955–1960

PAGE
153   "a leather half-glove": TSG, a.i.
153   Hersey on primers: "Why Do Students Bog Down on First R?" *Life*, May 24, 1954.
154   "Write me a story": TSG, a.i.
154   "play with it": Ibid.

154   Queen Zebra: John G. Fuller, "Trade Winds," *Saturday Review*, December 14, 1957.

154   "There are no adjectives!": TSG, a.i.

154   "being lost with a witch": "How Orlo Got His Book" by Dr. Seuss, *New York Times Book Review*, November 15, 1957.

155   "In verse you can repeat": TSG, a.i.

155   "It took me a year": Ibid.

155   *The Cat in the Hat* ms., UCLA.

155   "probably the most influential": Clifton Fadiman, *Holiday*, April 1959.

156   "harum-scarum masterpiece": E. J. Kahn, Jr., "Children's Friend," *The New Yorker*, December 17, 1960. Barbara Bader in *American Picturebooks from Noah's Ark to the Beast Within*, p. 311, wrote of Dr. Seuss books that "not until *The Cat in the Hat* does chaos take over, and a brash slapbang humor."

156   "the moppets' Milton": *Newsweek*, December 15, 1958.

156   "We were afraid": *New York Herald Tribune*, May 12, 1957.

156   about 12,000 copies a month: RH archives.

156   "Parents understood better": TSG, a.i.

156   "went wild about it": Phyllis Cerf Wagner, a.i. TSG told EJK that PCW and Louise Bonino discussed the idea over dinner at the home of RH executive Bob Haas, attended by the Cerfs, Geisels and Bonino; "a few days later Beginner Books was formed."

156   "Ted and Babar": Leonard Marcus: *Awakened by the Moon* (Boston, Mass.: 1992, Beacon Press).

156   Bennett had impetuously kissed her: Bennett Cerf, a.i.

156   *The Cat in the Hat* was stupendous: PCW, a.i.

157   "usual talkativeness": Scripps Clinic records.

157   "foggy . . . ": TSG to Bonino, April 19, 1957, RH.

157   Robert Cahn, "The Wonderful World of Dr. Seuss," *Saturday Evening Post*, July 6, 1957.

158   "I got hung up": TSG, a.i.

158   second Dr. Seuss blockbuster: HPG to Bonino, May 29, 1957, RH.

158   "Hope you like it": TSG to Bonino, May 26, 1957.

158   "my bride and weary self": Ibid.

158   walk-up sixth floor: Frith to TSG, June 27, 1969, RH.

158   DR. VIOLET VALERIE VOWEL: Nameplate, Frith memorabilia.

159   "bursting into the office": Christopher Cerf, a.i.

159   "most profitable single publishing entity": Bennett Cerf, a.i.

159   "happy genius": PCW, a.i.

159   "a woman who loves combat": Christopher Cerf, a.i.

160   "suit pressed": Random House memo Jim Russell to TSG, September 11, 1957.

161   "Once started": Robert L. Bernstein to Donald Klopfer, February 19, 1958, RH.

161   a four-page account: "The One and Only Dr. Seuss and His Wonderful Autographing Tour," *Publishers Weekly*, December 8, 1958. In Seussian fashion, the Indian was sometimes "Chief Black Feather." EJK papers, 1959, NYPL.

161   "as if I were Santa Claus": TSG, a.i.

162   "truly passionate": Mavis Jukes, a.i.

162   "money came in so fast": PCW, a.i.

162   "we're in the black": HPG to BPB, December 14, 1958.

163   "supposedly finished his new book": Ibid, March 19, 1958.

163   *Yertle*: TSG's final change was to remove a Hitler-like mustache from the power-mad Yertle.

163   "I stack you," TSG to Donald Bartlett, July 17, 1958.

163   "Ted and I don't think": HPG to BPB, March 19, 1958.

163   " . . . there is no question": Donald Klopfer to HPG, October 9, 1958.

164   "Before any illustrator": HPG to PCW, August 1, 1958.

164   generally accurate: PCW memo to Ray Freiman, August 1958.

164   loathed the book: PCW to HPG, August 9, 1958.

164   "does have to be boosted": HPG to Jean Ennis, February 10, 1962. RH.

164   "We have been living": HPG to Robert Palmer, May 17, 1962.

164   "causing a hullabaloo": HPG to Bennett Cerf, September 4, 1959.

165   *Happy Birthday to You!* included Hooded Klopfers, after Donald Klopfer.

165   "One day we drove": HPG to BPB, June 3, 1959.

165   *One Fish Two Fish*: Ted had worked with the idea since scribbling on stationery from the Baucr-Grünwald Hotel on Venice's Grand Canal. UCLA.

165   "Now, if I can just keep Ted": HPG to Bennett Cerf, September 21, 1959. CU.

165   "three grubby bits of crayon": Ray Freiman, a.i.

165   "Every year I think": HPG to BPB, January 7, 1959.

165   Cerf related: Bennett Cerf's Cerfboard, *This Week*, November 27, 1960.

165   "First Ted would say to me": PCW, a.i.

166   "They'd spend three days": Christopher Cerf, a.i.

166   "Please at least eat your turkey!": Ibid.

166   "This reader was essentially": Richard Gladstone, a.i.

167   Random House figures: stock prospectus, October 1, 1959. Beginner Books financial figures: Jerry Harrison, a.i.

167   bored by money: The Geisels lived so simply that friends had little idea of their worth. J. D. "Bim" Thompson, whose children were

14   Green Eggs and Ham 1960–1963

172   "really definitive": TSG, a.i.

172   " . . . the most well brought up": HPG to Jean Ennis, August 26, 1960, RH.

172   "what one has not achieved": HPG to EJK, December 16, 1960. NYPL. HPG added: "It is one thing to be a perfectionist, but it does grow increasingly hard to know just what to be a perfectionist at doing. . . . You have made me realize that the closer [Ted] sticks to books, the more chance he will have to contribute his share to the job of living."

173   "I don't want you even to read": TSG, a.i.

173   "I have to screen": HPG to BPB, undated.

173   "But, oh, it's a struggle!" HPG to Jean Ennis, August 26, 1960.

173   "You've come the wrong week": Robert L. Bernstein a.i.

174   "the 9,373rd version": HPG to BPB, April 10, 1961.

174   "We have given away the piano": HPG to BPB, March 29, 1961.

174   "Grampie was popular:" PDO, a.i.

175   "I hope they won't schedule": HPG to BPB, September 26, 1961.

175   "genteel spinster ladies": Elaine Greene, a.i.

175   "got no place . . . encountered this phenomenon": Ibid.

175   "rejection of Christian names": Dilys Rowe, *The Observer*, London, October 29, 1961.

175   sales in Britain: *Daily Express*, London, June 3, 1965. In a letter on May 9, 1967, from Wm. Collins Sons & Co. Ltd., Julia MacRae wrote TSG, "We have reached the million and a half mark now with Beginner Books."

175   "The English don't so much": Michael Hyde, a.i.

176   "as much or even more": Jerry Harrison, a.i.

176   "sort of the business person": PCW, a.i.

176   "bonepile": UCLA.

177   "as ugly as the city of Las Vegas": HPG to BPB, April 30, 1962.

178   "Be tough": EJK interviews, 1960, NYPL.

178   "best thing that I have ever read": Helen Renthal, *Chicago Tribune* book section, November 11, 1962.

178   "Are they really only six?": "Dr. Seuss Is in Town," Olga Franklin, *Daily Mail*, London, October 13, 1962.

178   *Dr. Seuss's ABC Book* began as doodles on hotel stationery from the Ritz in London and the Tyrol in Innsbruck, Austria.

178   "if Bennett is reading my stuff": TSG, a.i.

179   "Do whatever you have to": Robert L. Bernstein, a.i.

179   "who never came up there": Stan Berenstain, a.i.

179   "Bob Bernstein was not supportive . . . I think the best . . . ": PCW, a.i.

180   "I like them": TSG, a.i.

180   titles more extraordinary: TSG told Judith Frutig in *The Christian*

Science Monitor, May 12, 1978: "Some people say I should throw out the paintings and keep the titles."

180   "a man who isn't happy": "Muse on the Loose Is Dr. Seuss," Art Seidenbaum, Los Angeles Times Calendar, January 5, 1964.

180   "Mrs. Schneelock poured": TSG to Jean Ennis, September 6, 1963; McCall's, November 1964

15 Fox in Socks 1964–1967

PAGE

181   At the Phoenix: The Geisels were in Melbourne, Australia, on May 3, 1964. The report of their visit appeared in the Herald-Sun on May 5.

182   "Ted should be put on the Chamber": HPG to David Hayes of Collins in Sydney, early 1966.

182   "her perfect little pink suit": Anne Marcovecchio Johnson a.i.

182   "progressively more handicapped": Dr. Stanley Willis a.i. She had a mild case of polio as a child, but Dr. Willis is referring to her paralysis in 1954 with Guillain-Barré syndrome.

182   in excess of $200,000: "He makes C-A-T spell big money," Business Week, July 18, 1964.

183   "bundle of nerves": HPG to BPB, March 23, 1964.

183   "everything that we don't want": HPG to BPB, August 11, 1959.

184   Whales Go By: While encouraging adult friends to write for children, TSG made a rare foray into writing for adults in an essay arguing that success isn't everything: "If At First You Don't Succeed—Quit!" The Saturday Evening Post, November 28, 1964.

184   "If we had known then": Lt. (jg) William Staggerson of Navy Helicopter Squadron 1, Ream Field, San Diego, had been the pilot for Geisel and Cerf in 1954.

185   "Do you have a particular specialty?": Audrey Stone Geisel, a.i.

185   "Even when a death": Julie Olfe, a.i.

186   "If the news is bad": HPG to AMJ, August 12, 1965.

186   "It was a love-hate": Jerry Harrison, a.i.

186   "No theater tickets": HPG to AMJ, February 25, 1965.

186   "About two weeks": HPG to David Hayes of Collins in Sydney.

187   "on verse": HPG to BPB undated.

187   his own favorites: Later he called The Lorax his favorite book and TV production. (TSG to Bernadette Guiniling, November 19, 1981.) He said the funniest book he wrote was never published: I Don't Spelk Very Welk. "It goes along for a couple of pages with only a word or two misspelled and then—whoops—a page that reads like Chinese. . . . My publisher insisted that if that book came out no kid would ever learn to spell." TSG, a.i.

187   "The finest line I have": Ibid.

187   "We have made the decision": HPG to Robert L. Bernstein, June 22, 1965.

187   "taking a high dive": Ibid.

187   "this year's figures": On July 19 Helen responded to Bernstein's profit statement by writing, "I'd love to be on hand for the stockholder meeting, which should be a great one."

188   a newspaper friend's book: *Neil Morgan's San Diego* (San Diego: 1963).

188   "toiling busily away": HPG to BPB, March 31, 1966.

188   "paint seems to land": HPG to Billy Collins, August 16, 1966.

188   "paint at least one picture": Ted Owens, a.i.

189   "wanted to make a series": Leslie Raddatz, "Dr. Seuss Climbs Down From His Mountain . . . to Bring the Grinch to Television," *TV Guide*, December 17, 1966.

189   "He was standing there": Chuck Jones, a.i.

190   "The difference is": Ibid.

190   "I had to change": Ibid.

190   "lady Whos don't have": Ibid.

190   "I was an admirer": Maurice Noble, a.i.

191   "[Ted didn't want] a star": Ibid.

191   *Variety*'s report bore an October 4 [1966] dateline from Hollywood.

191   "undisturbed on the printed page": *New York Times*, December 19, 1966. Gould's review was also critical of "the many commercials on behalf of all-service banks."

192   "It's the only way": Chuck Jones, a.i.

192   "equally difficult": Ibid.

192   "part Russian, part Hollywood": HPG to Gladys Palmer, March 16, 1967.

193   "strangely down and jumpy": Helen and Robert L. Bernstein, a.i.

193   "might be trouble": Ibid.

193   "They had so much": Walter Retan, a.i.

193   "a boomerang that won't return": JM, *The San Diego Union*.

193   "if you don't get imagination": "The Logical Insanity of Dr. Seuss," *Time*, August 11, 1967.

194   "Never in three years": Julie Olfe, a.i.

194   "relaxed and refreshed": Libby Childs, a.i.

194   "All seemed well to me": Dr. Robert Tschirgi, a.i.

194   "strangely low": Duke Johnston, a.i.

195   "I didn't know whether to kill myself": Dr. Stanley Willis, a.i.

195   HPG to TSG, undated: Archives, Office of Medical Examiner, County of San Diego.

PAGE

197   "something about Mrs. Geisel": Julie Olfe, a.i.

197   "stood grim-faced": Ibid.

197   Bennett Cerf heard: JM, then a reporter, telephoned Cerf and others prior to writing the obituary in the *San Diego Union* on October 24, 1967. She described HPG as "a fragile-looking woman with the determination of an army general."

198   "her major activities": *New York Times*, October 24, 1967. The *Times* reported that HPG died in her sleep, but cause of death had not been determined.

198   "Somebody named Helen": Peggy Owens, a.i.

198   "shocked into silence": Ibid.

198   "I guess you know": Ibid.

198   "He was in anguish": Ibid.

198   "steadfast confidence . . . gift to him": Julie Olfe, a.i.

198   "When I have a problem": Eileen and Willard P. Vanderlaan, a.i.

198   two close friends: the authors.

199   "There's been a breakthrough": PDO, a.i.

199   "In his head": Julie Olfe, a.i.

200   "Ted always needed someone": Elma Otto, a.i.

200   When Forester arrived: Russell Forester, a.i.

200   "something was lacking . . . but Ted needs me": ASG, a.i.

200   The cardiologist had stood: ASG, a.i.

201   "I've written you kids": TSG to Henri and Donald Bartlett, May 27, 1968.

201   theirs had changed: ASG, a.i.

201   "along came this": Ibid.

201   Ted told a colleague: NM.

202   Frank Kockritz: On July 29, 1968, TSG wrote Julie Olfe: " . . . Frank K. and I are just as insanely occupied as ever before. The temperature is 99 . . . I'm going swimming to prepare my body temperature for the Rodeo tomorrow."

202   "story feeling": TSG to Olfe, July 2, 1968.

202   "using a grapefruit": TSG to Duke Johnston, August 1, 1968.

202   "Audrey came along": Chuck Jones, a.i.

202   "full of broken glass": ASG, a.i.

202   She had planned: Ibid.

203   "I was the kind of mother": Ibid.

203   "the most exciting person": Ibid.

203   "always good at greeting": Ibid.

203   "Save the rolls": Ibid.

203   "with a university degree": Ibid.

204   "so unbelievable, so funny": Ibid.
204   "Helen had become": Anne Marcovecchio Johnson, a.i.
205   "Sometimes he would bounce": ASG, a.i.
205   "I came out with a boffola": TSG, a.i.
205   "at some far distant": ASG, a.i.
206   fees exceeded: TSG to E. James Stephens, March 16, 1969. Stephens, then vice president of Massachusetts Mutual Life Insurance Co. in Springfield, was TSG's stepbrother. His mother, Merle, had married TSG's widower father in 1945.
206   *My Book About Me*: This book elicited challenges to RH about its originality, rare in the career of Dr. Seuss. In an in-house memo, Theon Banos, RH counsel, wrote that a complaint from Cincinnati "may be the first of many letters . . . many energetic teachers and parents have constructed little booklets for their charges . . . to fill in information about himself. . . . *My Book About Me* is a little more than that, and has been executed with originality."
206   "very put out": Michael Frith, a.i.
206   "Dear Carpenter": TSG to Frith, May 2, 1969.
206   "Dear Mike: JEEEEEEZUS!": TSG to Frith, March 10, 1969.
206   "If I do not hear": TSG to Frith, April 30, 1973.
207   "What am I going to do": TSG, a.i.
207   *Portnoy's Complaint*: Carolyn See, "Dr. Seuss and the Naked Ladies," *Esquire*, June 1974.
207   "stunningly handsome": "The man who writes books about fun that is funny," Valerie Davies, *South China Morning Post*, September 16, 1969.
207   "albino rickshaw men": TSG, untitled travel notes, 1969.
207   "To vary the rice diet . . . ": Ibid.
208   "It is absolutely forbidden": Ibid.
209   "we'll do prenatal books": Richard F. Shepard, *New York Times*, October 17, 1968.
209   "Television interviewers": Don Bell, *Chicago Tribune Magazine*, June 7, 1970.
209   "After the party": Ibid.
209   "revolt against coloring books": ECL manuscript.
209   "It's one of the few things": "Seuss on Wry," David Sheff, *Parenting*, February 1987.
210   "a lot of elephants": ECL manuscript. Similar to Chris Dummit, *Dallas Morning News*, June 16, 1983.
210   "He was shortish . . . ": *The Lorax*.
210   "I looked at the drawing": TSG a.i.
211   "It's impossible to tell": "Catching Up with Dr. Seuss," Rob Wilder, *Parents*, June 1979.
211   ahead of its time: In 1969 Robert Cahn of *The Christian Science*

Monitor was the first to win a Pulitzer Prize for national reporting on an environmental topic—the national parks. He later cited *The Lorax* as one of six books, including others by Aldo Leopold, Rachel Carson and Thoreau, that "changed his life." *Gannett Center Journal,* Summer 1990, vi, 161, 179–80.

211   brunch in San Diego: at the home of Deborah Szekely, who founded the Golden Door health spa that Liz Carpenter visited.

211   "I left the room": Liz Carpenter, a.i.

212   "That had always been": Ibid.

212   "If anyone had been": Lyndon Baines Johnson to TSG, June 4, 1971, UCSD.

212   "Really makes me feel": Undated, TSG to Frith. In the following October, TSG wrote the citation awarded at the Kennedy International Awards Ceremony in Washington to Dr. Paul Parkman and Dr. Harry Meyer for their vaccine against rubella or German measles. The citation, read by Kathleen Kennedy, "struck just the right note," the *Washington Post* reported; it concluded, "To both of you we say, God bless/You'll make the world Rubella-less."

17   Audrey Stone Geisel 1971–1974

PAGE

213   "Does this sort": Walter Retan, a.i.

213   recently coaxed away: Ole Risom, who had been Scarry's editor since the 1940s, joined Random House as associate publisher of the juvenile division, and Scarry followed.

213   drawing style: Seuss animals had "little horseshoes" in their eyes from Horton (1940) on. Chuck Jones, a.i.

213   "might never makes": EJK, *The New Yorker,* December 17, 1960.

214   "ready to settle": Selma G. Lanes, *Down the Rabbit Hole* (New York: Atheneum, 1972), 79.

214   "If, as the British": Ibid., 80.

214   "voluminous research to bog": TSG to Lanes, handwritten draft, undated. UCSD.

214   "halfway house": Lanes, ibid., 46–47.

215   traded memories: TSG, a.i.

215   "I think you are taking this job": TSG to Robert Lopshire, March 2, 1961. UCSD. In turn, artists Lopshire, P. D. Eastman and Roy McKie all failed to satisfy TSG with a "drawing book." In 1970 *I Can Draw it Myself* was finally published, with words and illustrations by Dr. Seuss.

215   "That's what you call": Walter Retan, a.i.

215   "That's the worst thing": Stan Berenstain, a.i.

215   "Terrific!" Ibid.

216	more than one hundred: *Parade*, June 13, 1993.
216	"Ted was extremely centered": Stan Berenstain, a.i. In *Ten Apples Up on Top*, Ted scribbled instructions in the margin, telling artist Roy McKie he wanted the angry Mama Bear's expression to be "not mean, but righteously sore."
216	"It isn't a story": TSG to Al Perkins, handwritten memo, undated, UCSD.
216	"It helped": Berenstain, a.i.
216	"This doesn't sound": Retan, a.i.
216	"sort of holding": Ibid.
216	"I was afraid": Ibid.
217	"You're trying to turn off the sun!": Ibid.
217	butterfly bow tie: Michael Frith, a.i.
217	Eighth Peeping Tom: Ibid.
217	"Love Song": Frith TSG memorabilia.
217	"major labor": Frith, a.i.
218	"chewing on a word": Ibid.
218	"Time for a thinking cap!": Ibid.
218	"Name it for Audrey": Ibid.
218	"He couldn't say": ASG, a.i.
219	"Audrey, I'm not eating": TSG, a.i.
219	"more art than words": Joan Knight, a.i.
219	"readers treating him": Ibid.
219	"about the strongest": TSG to Frith, undated.
220	"the center of my life": Roy McKie, a.i.
220	*Marvin K. Mooney*: TSG linked the name to a San Diego Cadillac dealer, Marvin K. Brown.
220	"Random House has gone": Art Buchwald, a.i.
221	"We sure got him": TSG to Buchwald, August 27, 1974. On August 7, 1989 TSG wrote Dr. Steven Ealy of Armstrong State College, Savannah, Ga.: "*Marvin K. Mooney* was not written with Richard Nixon in mind. It was written with 'Irritating-Footdraggers-in-General' in mind."
221	'Son-of-a-bitch': TSG to PDO, May 18, 1972.
221	"especially prepared": TSG to Ted Owens, undated.
221	"a bit confining": Ibid.
221	"loved going in": Ted Owens, a.i.
222	"he would put his head": Ibid.
222	"I was living . . . ": Ibid.
222	"They are so different": ASG, a.i.
222	"the first seven daisies": TSG to PDO, May 1972.
223	"When she stayed": ASG, a.i.
223	"a hard-sell": *Newsweek*, February 21, 1972.
223	softened for television: *The Lorax* first appeared on CBS.

223   "He worked absolutely": Friz Freleng, a.i.

223   "He played the rascal": Michael Hyde, a.i.

224   "Do you know how to say 'Burp' ": Ted Owens, a.i.

225   "I wrote Uug": Claudia Prescott, a.i.

225   "Grammatically speaking": TSG to Walter Retan, February 5, 1973.

225   "two years of abrasive": TSG handwritten and unaddressed memo, undated, ASG private papers.

225   "Ted really should": Walter Retan, a.i.

226   "I haven't ridden": Duke Johnston and ASG, a.i.

18   *I Can Read with My Eyes Shut!* 1975—1980

PAGE

227   "Am I going blind?": ASG, a.i.

227   "as bright as Picasso": TSG, a.i.

227   "like Whistler's mother": Cynthia Gorney, *Washington Post*, May 21, 1979.

228   "with or without": ASG private papers.

228   "magnificently clean": Grace Clark, a.i.

228   "hang up the whites": ASG, a.i.

228   "My eyes": ASG private papers.

228   "Merry Christmas": Ibid.

228   "I don't care": Duke Johnston, a.i.

228   WITH EYE DROPS: ASG private papers.

229   "I thought you were": Duke Johnston, a.i.

229   exhibition catalog: Although no catalog was published, Lathem drew on the interviews in "Words and Pictures Married: The Beginnings of Dr. Seuss, a conversation with Theodor S. Geisel, edited by Edward Connery Lathem" in *Dartmouth Alumni Magazine*, April 1976.

229   "playing together": ECL to authors, December 27, 1993.

229   After Ted fell asleep: ASG, a.i.

230   "I stammered around": TSG to ECL, May 20, 1974.

230   "the Geisel genius": Orton Hicks to TSG, February 27, 1969.

230   "Ted is such a legendary": Frith memo, September 1975, RH.

230   "give us some understanding": Moulton to ECL, September 30, 1975.

230   "nicely rounded short piece": TSG to ECL, June 7, 1976. The Lathem article, excerpted from the transcript, covered the years from Ted's childhood in Springfield through the publication of his first book, *Mulberry Street*.

230   "uncomfortable feeling": Ibid.

231   "Who could possibly": Ibid.

231   "a light-up nose": TSG, a.i.

231   "I am quite content": ECL to TSG, July 28, 1976.
231   "One of these days": Jackson to ECL, August 2, 1976.
231   "cabbages-and-kings": ECL manuscript.
231   "not exactly the master's": Jane Langton, *New York Times Book Review*, November 16, 1975.
231   "[This] is the latest": Alice Ehlert, *Southern Literary Journal*, December 1975.
232   "You're an *author!*": Don Freeman, *San Diego Magazine,* April 1986.
232   "It's easier when I know": Ibid.
232   "Yes," he answered: JM in the *San Diego Union*, December 10, 1976.
233   "It's easier when they wear": Ibid.
233   Al Perkins died on February 10, 1975.
233   "I'll be seein' ": ASG private papers.
234   "My uncle ordered": The Lake Forest verse was delivered on June 4, 1977, and appeared in *The New York Times* June 30.
235   Anne stood beside: Anne M. Johnson, by then vice president of Beginner Books, recalled Ted as "wonderful at these conventions. Hundreds of people were in never-ending lines, and Ted would say, 'I don't want to disappoint anybody's children.' " Johnson, a.i.
235   "As everyone present": Ted wrote this verse for the ABA convention and called it "Small Epic Poem, Size 3½B." It later appeared in *Publishers Weekly*.
236   Revelle College commencement, UCSD: June 1978.
236   "When I get my other": TSG to Johnson, undated 1978, ASG private papers.
236   "to stay alive": TSG to Bernstein, November 3, 1978, Ibid.
236   mispronounced Geisel: the family said "GUY-zel."
236   "In the grubby": ASG private papers.
237   "an autobiography": TSG to Bernstein, November 3, 1978.
237   "broke a log jam": Ibid.
237   "You'll discover": TSG Non-Auto.
237   "I was Born": Ibid.
238   "There are hundreds": Ibid.
238   "Heppelwhite Seuss": Sam Burchell, "*Architectural Digest* Visits Dr. Seuss," December 1978.
239   "Where else": Ibid.
239   "someone I sometimes": TSG autograph, Jeanne Jones papers. Jones later told Hilliard Harper of *Los Angeles Times Magazine* (May 25, 1986): "Ted works very hard and has more discipline than anyone I know. And yet . . . he is . . . the kid on the block I most like to play with."
239   "like a simple Catholic": Jeanne Jones, a.i.

240   "I tend basically": "Why Writers Write," Heidi Schulman in *Los Angeles Times*, May 20, 1979.

240   "It's getting awful": Cynthia Gorney, *Washington Post*, May 21, 1979.

240   "sixty greens": Grace Clark, a.i.

240   "His color sense": Clark quoted by Cynthia Gorney, ibid.

240   "had trouble finding": TSG, a.i.

240   Audrey came home: quoted by Beverly Beyette, *Los Angeles Times*, May 29, 1979.

241   "I ought to give": July 7, 1980. ASG private papers.

241   Cerf had harangued: "Sometimes I think," Cerf had told Don Freeman of the *San Diego Union*, "the main requirement for being a judge on these committees that evaluate children's stories is a pledge that you have not talked to a kid in twenty-seven years."

241   three early books: The Caldecott Honor Books were *McElligot's Pool* (1947), *Bartholomew and the Oobleck* (1949), and *If I Ran the Zoo* (1950).

242   "For the next several": TSG to Ted Owens, 1980.

242   "We ought to blend": NM, *San Diego Tribune*, June 9, 1980.

242   "it made me the toast": ASG, a.i.

242   "It had to be Ted's way": Jerry Harrison, a.i.

242   "He wasn't God": Cathy Goldsmith, a.i.

242   "If you don't call me": Ibid.

242   "Cathy is a fellow sewer worker": TSG, a.i.

19   *The Butter Battle Book* 1981–1984

PAGE

244   "You know what's wrong?": Cathy Goldsmith, a.i.

244   "the children's M. C. Escher": Chuck Jones, a.i.

244   "When Ted picked": Mike Frith, a.i.

245   "sort of psychosis": "A Deuce of a Seuss Inhabits Exhibit", *San Diego Union*, December 10, 1976.

245   "Unless you break": Ed Hutshing, "Paging Dr. Seuss!" *San Diego Union*, March 1, 1986.

245   "Kids exaggerate": "Dr. Seuss: Still a Drawing Card," Michael J. Bandler, *American Way*, 1977.

245   "slightly batty": Karla Kuskin, quoted by Jonathan Cott, *Pipers at the Gates of Dawn* (New York: Random House, 1983).

245   "I'm not waiting": ASG, a.i.

246   "to ease the embarrassment": TSG to Ellis Conklin of United Press International, September 13, 1986.

246   sat for a portrait: Kinstler's portrait was unveiled at the Hopkins Center, Dartmouth, on October 16, 1982. TSG and ASG attended.

246   Mayor Ed Koch incident: *New York Times*, December 9, 1981.

246   "delighted to be caught": *Publishers Weekly*, January 1, 1982.

247   "Meticulosity": Jack Williams, "The Fantasy Worlds of 2 Lions of Kiddy Lit," *San Diego Tribune*, December 9, 1982.

247   "If my characters": Ibid.

247   "Like Gandhi": TSG read his verse on December 13, 1982, and titled it "Hail to Our Chief (And I Don't Mean Ronald Reagan)."

248   "I'm subversive as hell!": TSG to Jonathan Cott in *Pipers at the Gates of Dawn: The Wisdom of Children's Literature.* (New York: Random House, 1983.)

248    $10 Million contract: Herb Cheyette, a.i.

248   "I don't know": Jed Mattes, a.i.

249   "That won't work": Mattes, a.i.

249   "resembled a porcupine": ASG, a.i.

249   "such deadly stupidity": TSG, a.i.

250   "the best book": TSG to Ted Owens, July 6, 1983.

250   "I've always wanted": TSG, a.i.; Frank Stockton's classic puzzler was published one hundred years prior to *BBB*.

250   "I have no idea": Janet Schulman, a.i.

251   "If you were his": Cathy Goldsmith, a.i.

251   "As I dialed New York": ASG, a.i.

251   "a bit too terrifying": RH memo to Schulman, October 3, 1983.

251   "I see what you're": Schulman, a.i.

252   "If there are any hawks": Schulman to Sendak, December 19, 1983, RH.

252   "After all": Ibid.

252   "a problem for him": Dr. Ruth Grobstein, a.i.

253   full-page ad: *New York Times Book Review*, on February 26, 1984.

253   "Thank you, Dr. Seuss": Betty Jean Lifton, *NYTBR*.

253   Buchwald's *BBB* jacket blurb: "We need a Nobel literature prize for people who write children's books. I nominate Dr. Seuss."

253   formal birthday dinner: ASG, a.i.

255   "children are going": Schulman, September 10, 1985.

255   "If there were": Schulman, March 5, 1984

255   "pleased and proud": TSG, a.i.

255   "Right after that": Ibid.

255   "No telephone call was more welcome," he told Jay Johnson of the *San Diego Tribune*. "I was thinking that I was a failure."

255   "It comes right": Maureen Dowd, *New York Times*, April 17, 1984.

255   "usually given to adults": Johnson, *San Diego Tribune*, April 17, 1984.

255   "all hell broke loose": Ibid.

256   "When you get to be": TSG to David Sheff, *Parenting*, February 1987.

256   "Go straight home": Dick Duffy, a.i.
256   "Now seven presidents": TSG, a.i.
256   "But you were right": Ibid.
257      $5 million . . . author's royalties: Jerry Harrison, a.i.
257   "too sophisticated": Claudia Prescott, a.i.
258   "She can work a room": Harrison, a.i.
258   "I thought of her": Mattes, a.i.
258   "I don't want those guys": ASG, a.i.
259   "I hate food": Menu in Jeanne Jones memorabilia.
259   "Why do we have": Dick Duffy, a.i.
259   a fellow artist: former architect Russell Forester.
259   "The facial expression": Jed Mattes, a.i.
259   "When you go": Ibid.
260   "He was very happy": Ibid.

20   *You're Only Old Once!* 1985–1986

PAGE
261   "a series of everything": David W. Dunlap, "Waiting in Fotta-fa-Zee," *New York Times Book Review*, March 23, 1986.
261   "fed up with": TSG to Curtis Abel, February 10, 1984.
262   "other hospitals": Ed Hutshing, *San Diego Union*, March 1, 1986.
262   "I had a pinhead-sized cancer": TSG private papers.
262   "Do you realize": Dr. Ruth Grobstein, a.i.
262   Ted argued: TSG told Dunlap in *NYTBR*: "Putting that animal [Fotta-fa-Zee] in there says, 'This is a Seuss book.'"
263   "a turn-off": Jed Mattes, a.i.
263   Class of 1925: wheelchair pusher, Whelden the wheeler, named for classmate Ford Whelden.
263   early draft: UCSD.
263   "The kids I first wrote": TSG, a.i.
263   "are not funny": Hutshing in *San Diego Union*.
264   "I don't mind autograph parties": Ibid.
264   the waiting lines: Elma Otto, a.i.
264   "I still climb": Dunlap in *New York Times Book Review*.
264   "charming guide": Hilliard Harper in *Los Angeles Times Magazine*, May 25, 1986.
264   "it has forced him": Michael J. Bandler in *Parents*, September 1987.
264   "may even result": Dr. Charles Edwards to TSG, February 13, 1986.
264   "something amiss": Edward Sorel in "The Shape That He's In," *New York Times Book Review*, March 23, 1986.
265   "I hate lawyers": TSG, a.i.
265   book about religion: ASG private papers.

265   "It's time": Steven Brezzo, a.i.

266   "He is ill": San Diego Museum of Art interoffice memo, November 19, 1985.

266   "either Peck's bad boy": Brezzo, a.i.

266   "It seemed overwhelming": Mary Stofflet, a.i.

266   "They'd tried everything": TSG, a.i.

267   "This is simply": Robert Pincus in *San Diego Union*, May 29, 1986.

267   "a pause that if": Brezzo, a.i.

267   "poet laureate": Brezzo introduction, *Dr. Seuss from Then to Now* (San Diego Museum of Art, 1986.)

267   "starved for somebody": Brezzo, a.i.

268   *60 Minutes*: "Oh, by the way," he told Don Freeman in "The Genius of Dr. Seuss," *San Diego Magazine*, May 1986, "I just turned down *60 Minutes*."

268   "Waterloo": Helen Copley, a.i.

268   on to Springfield: May 19–20, 1986. Reporters from New York, Boston and Springfield trailed the Geisels on May 20, and their stories and photographs appeared on May 21.

269   "trusted friend": *Springfield Union*, May 21, 1986.

269   "Behind that wallpaper": Ibid.

270   sixty-foot-long: TSG to Bennett Cerf, March 18, 1958.

270   "I vow, you vow": TSG, a.i.

270   "Of all the reviews": TSG to Gregg Lewis, 1986. ASG private papers.

270   age span of Ted's fans: A young editorial cartoonist, J. D. Crowe, moved from Texas to San Diego on his editor's promise to introduce him to Dr. Seuss. The two men, separated by fifty years, sat together for hours, trading experiences with hate mail and hateful editors, cartoon boards and inks. (*San Diego Tribune*, January 22, 1987.)

270   "The most memorable": Susanna Styron to TSG, October 30, 1988. ASG private papers.

271   "The Cat in the Hat sometimes": TSG to CWD School, March 1985. ASG private papers.

272   "Shannon's Law": Baker in NM column, *San Diego Tribune*, October 3, 1983.

272   Neiman-Marcus party: TSG, a.i.

272   "Nobody's older": *W*, December 1–8, 1986.

272   "Oh, Dr. Seuss": ASG, a.i.

21   Oh, the Places You'll Go! 1987–1991

PAGE

273   "I'm happy I can . . .": Jed Mattes, a.i.

273   "I am Prepared": ASG private papers.

274   "Damn it all": ASG private papers.

274   "Audrey tells me": Herb Klein, a.i.

274   "Look Who Just": *Publishers Weekly*, April 3, 1987.

274   "I've never met": TSG, a.i.

274   Brown commencement: Associated Press, May 26, 1987. TSG's honorary degree from Brown was his eighth and last. The other degrees were from Dartmouth (1956); American International College, Springfield, Mass. (1968); Lake Forest College, Lake Forest, Ill. (1977); Whittier College, Whittier, Calif. (1980); J. F. Kennedy University, Orinda, Calif. (1983); Princeton University (1985); and University of Hartford (1986).

275   Scripps cardiologist: ASG, a.i.

275   "funereal black": TSG to Janet Schulman, September 23, 1988.

275   "a mystery book": Ibid.

275   Spam: Schulman, a.i. Ole Risom, associate publisher of the Random House juvenile division, kept up a correspondence with TSG about Spam for years. "I loved Spam and he loved it," Risom recalled. "He sent me Spam and I sent him my work, 'The Short History of Spam Cooking.'"

276   "I had a gentleman": TSG, a.i.

276   "It remains in my book": Ibid.

276   "Improved conditions": Claudia Melear and Margie Pless to TSG, December 6, 1985, ASG papers.

276   "Unfortunately": TSG to Melear and Pless, January 27, 1986, ASG papers.

276   "I disagree with": TSG to David and Bob Grinch, January 11, 1970, ASG papers.

276   "visualize these poor kids": TSG to Chuck Jones, January 12, 1970, ASG papers.

276   spelled his name Suess: Dr. Fred Suess wrote TSG (March 17, 1986) that "signing your books is my second career."

277   Christopher Sickels, a.i.

277   *I Can Write!* (a Bright & Early book by Theo LeSieg and Roy McKie, 1971): The only book TSG withdrew from the list; it did not meet his standards of clarity and he began doubting its premise for youngest readers. TSG, a.i.

277   "It could tie up": TSG to Jonathan Cott, *Pipers at the Gates of Dawn* (New York: Random House, 1983).

278   book-banning: John M. Glionna, "Timber Town Split to Roots," *Los Angeles Times*, September 18, 1989. In Laytonville, Pop. 900, the controversy caused a run on *The Lorax*: "You can't find the book anywhere within 100 miles. Word is, you have to drive clear up to Eureka just to find a bookstore that hasn't already been cleaned out."

278   "We are insulting": Ibid., October 7, 1989. Columnist Ellen Good-man wrote, "one small woodsy creature has just been saved from the brink of extinction." *Boston Globe*, October 18, 1989.

278   "*The Lorax* doesn't": TSG, a.i.

278   "Teaching a child": Ibid.

279   "It amazed all": Prof. Terry Cronan, a.i.

279   TSG's jaw: He cited his jaw problem and speech difficulty in telling Chuck Jones he could not attend "A Salute to Dr. Seuss," sponsored on November 20, 1989, by the Academy of Motion Picture Arts and Sciences in Los Angeles. After a screening of excerpts from Dr. Seuss films from *Private Snafu* to *The Butter Battle Book*, Friz Freleng and Charles Solomon joined Jones in a discussion of TSG's career.

279   "Can you believe": ASG, a.i.

279   "If I can stay": TSG, who feared hospitals, had used this expression for several years with increasing earnestness. A variant was quoted in *The Washington Post* by Jay Matthews on March 2, 1986.

279   "I've got an idea": Ted Owens, a.i.

280   "Nothing": Ibid.

280   "The Economic Situation Clarified: A prognostic reevaluation by the Dr. Seuss Surveys": *New York Times Magazine*, June 15, 1975.

280   "The Waiting Place," first draft of *Oh, the Places*: UCSD.

281   "he was schooling": Claudia Prescott, a.i.

281   "We kept looking": Cathy Goldsmith, a.i.

282   "Audrey," Ted kept saying: TSG, a.i.

282   "She's mad at me": Janet Schulman, a.i.

282   friends: JM and NM.

283   "It was my time": ASG, a.i.

283   "rangy, wise": Susan Stark, "Super Seuss," *Westchester Newspapers*, February 11, 1990.

283   "How could he": Diane Manuel, *New York Times Book Review*, February 1990.

283   "This proves it": TSG, a.i.

284   "Searching deep": Verse entitled "Where Are You?" ASG papers.

284   The Muppets: Henson was to lunch with TSG on May 18, 1990. He died on May 16.

285   friends: JM and NM.

285   "Can you understand": TSG, a.i.

285   nervous around tape recorders: "I am sorry that I have a phobia about getting taped," he wrote June 12, 1978.

285   "I'm a failure": Ibid.

286   "inventive energy": Alison Lurie, "The Cabinet of Dr. Seuss," *New York Review of Books*, December 20, 1990.

286   In an introduction to *Six by Seuss*, Fadiman called TSG "a perfor-

mer" whose work was a "nonstop, continually varied panorama done in primary words and colors."

Epilogue

INDEX